NICHOLSON

MINI ATLAS
LONDON

Nicholson
An Imprint of HarperCollins*Publishers*

Nicholson Mini Atlas of London

Nicholson
An Imprint of Harper Collins *Publishers*
77-85 Fulham Palace Road, Hammersmith, London W6 8JB

Printed and bound in Singapore.

ISBN 0 7028 3772 5

KM 9462   ANL

The maps in this product are also available for purchase in digital
format, from Bartholomew Data Sales
Tel: +44(0)181 307 4065, Fax: +44 (0)181 307 4813

MINI ATLAS LONDON

CONTENTS

Key to Map Pages 4-5

Key to Map Symbols 6-7

Map Pages 8-42

Central London Maps 43-44

Index to Street Names 45-91

Nicholson

An Imprint of HarperCollins*Publishers*

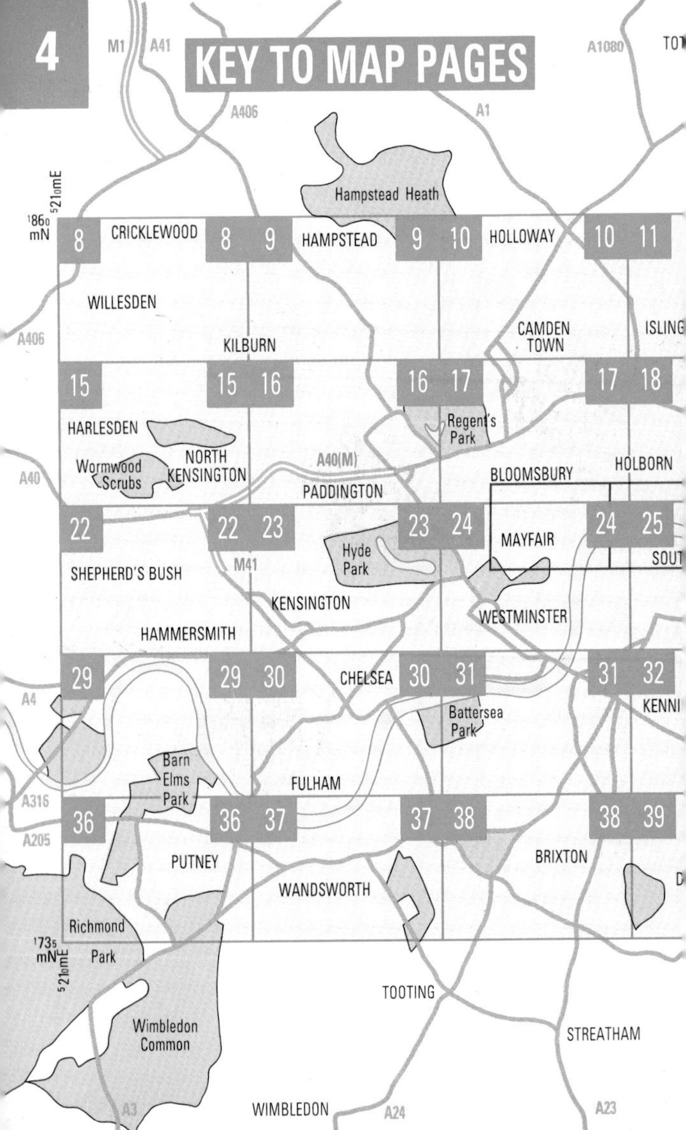

KEY TO MAP PAGES

4

M1 A41 A1080 TO

A406 A1

Hampstead Heath

| 8 | CRICKLEWOOD | 8 | 9 | HAMPSTEAD | 9 | 10 | HOLLOWAY | 10 | 11 |

WILLESDEN

CAMDEN TOWN ISLING

A406

KILBURN

A40

| 15 | | 15 | 16 | | 16 | 17 | | 17 | 18 |

HARLESDEN

Regent's Park

Wormwood Scrubs NORTH KENSINGTON HOLBORN

A40 A40(M) BLOOMSBURY

PADDINGTON

| 22 | | 22 | 23 | | 23 | 24 | MAYFAIR | 24 | 25 |

SHEPHERD'S BUSH M41 Hyde Park SOUT

KENSINGTON

HAMMERSMITH WESTMINSTER

| 29 | | 29 | 30 | CHELSEA | 30 | 31 | | 31 | 32 |

A4 Battersea Park KENNI

Barn Elms Park FULHAM

A316

| 36 | | 36 | 37 | | 37 | 38 | | 38 | 39 |

A205 PUTNEY BRIXTON

WANDSWORTH

Richmond Park

Wimbledon Common

TOOTING

STREATHAM

WIMBLEDON A24 A23

A3

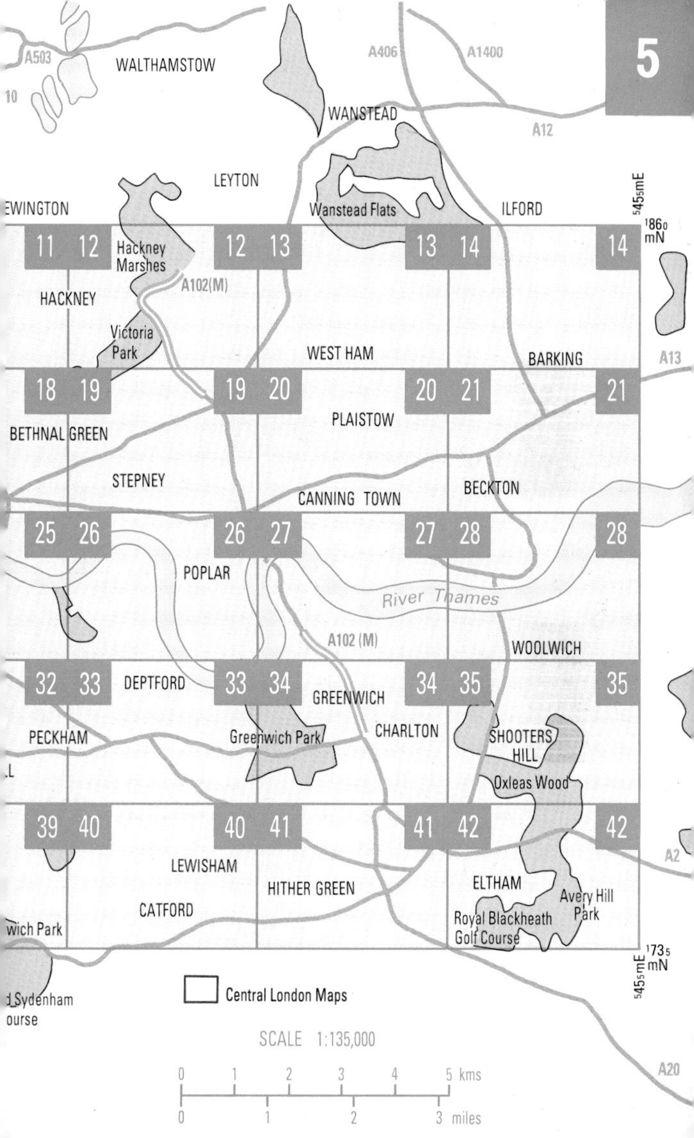

WALTHAMSTOW

WANSTEAD

A503

A406 A1400

A12

10

5

LEYTON

EWINGTON

Wanstead Flats

ILFORD

545mE
186₀
mN

| 11 | 12 | | 12 | 13 | | 13 | 14 | | 14 |

Hackney
Marshes

HACKNEY

A102(M)

Victoria
Park

WEST HAM

BARKING

A13

| 18 | 19 | | 19 | 20 | | 20 | 21 | | 21 |

BETHNAL GREEN

PLAISTOW

STEPNEY

CANNING TOWN

BECKTON

| 25 | 26 | | 26 | 27 | | 27 | 28 | | 28 |

POPLAR

River Thames

A102 (M)

WOOLWICH

| 32 | 33 | | 33 | 34 | | 34 | 35 | | 35 |

DEPTFORD

GREENWICH

Greenwich Park

CHARLTON

SHOOTERS
HILL

Oxleas Wood

PECKHAM

L

| 39 | 40 | | 40 | 41 | | 41 | 42 | | 42 |

LEWISHAM

HITHER GREEN

ELTHAM

Avery Hill
Park

A2

CATFORD

Royal Blackheath
Golf Course

173₅
mN
545mE

wich Park

ı Sydenham
ourse

A20

Central London Maps

SCALE 1:135,000

0 1 2 3 4 5 kms

0 1 2 3 miles

KEY TO MAP SYMBOLS

M41 Motorway	**⇥** Main British Rail Station
Dual **A4** Primary Route	**⊕** Other British Rail Station
Dual **A40** 'A' Road	**⊖** London Underground Station
B504 'B' Road	**⊕** Docklands Light Railway Station
Other Road	**⬤** Bus/Coach Station
Toll	Ⓗ Heliport
Street Market	P Car Park
Restricted Access Road	i Tourist Information Centre
Pedestrian Street	WC Public Toilet
Cycle Path	USA Embassy
Track/Footpath	Pol Police Station
→ One Way Street	Fire Sta Fire Station
_P__V_ Pedestrian/Vehicle Ferry	PO Post Office
Borough Boundary	Lib Library
Postal District Boundary	△ Youth Hostel

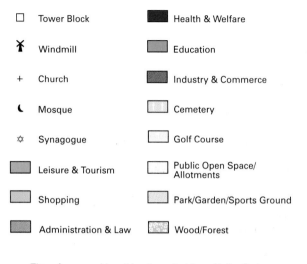

□	Tower Block		Health & Welfare
✠	Windmill		Education
+	Church		Industry & Commerce
☾	Mosque		Cemetery
✡	Synagogue		Golf Course
	Leisure & Tourism		Public Open Space/Allotments
	Shopping		Park/Garden/Sports Ground
	Administration & Law		Wood/Forest

The reference grid on this atlas coincides with the Ordnance Survey National Grid System.

A **3** Grid Reference   **25** Page Continuation Number

Main London Maps

Scale 1:20,000 (3.17 inches to 1 mile)

0	0.25	0.50	0.75	1 kilometre
0		0.25	0.5 mile	

Central London Maps

Scale 1:12,500 (5.1 inches to 1 mile)

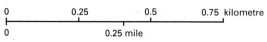

0	0.25	0.5	0.75 kilometre
0		0.25 mile	

NEASDEN
GLADSTONE
PARK
BRENT PARK
Superstore
NEASDEN
College of North West London
DOLLIS HILL
CHURCH END
WILLESDEN
WILLESDEN CEMETERY
WILLESDEN JEWISH CEMETERY
LIBERAL JEWISH CEM
ROUNDWOOD PARK
WILLESDEN GENERAL HOSP
THE MEAN FIDDLER
DUDDEN HILL
LANE
HIGH ROAD
CHURCH ROAD
CRAVEN PK
CRAVEN PARK RD
MANOR PK
NORTH CIRCULAR
NEASDEN LANE
GREAT CENTRAL WAY
CENTRAL WAY
A406
A407
A4088
B4557
B453
FALCON TRD EST
IND EST
CHAPMAN'S PARK IND EST
COBBOLD ESTATE
BUS DEPOT
Power Station
ALLOT
Tennis Courts
Bowling Grn
Amb Sta
Fire Sta
15
NW10
A
B
C
D
1
2
3
4
5

CRICKLEWOOD
NW2
NW6
BRONDESBURY
BRONDESBURY PARK
WILLESDEN GREEN
CRICKLEWOOD BROADWAY
SHOOT UP HILL
CHICHELE ROAD
WALM LANE
WILLESDEN LANE
A407
A5
A4003
A40
CAMDEN
BRENT
BARNET
Warehouse
Superstore
Garage
Pumping Sta
Lib
Sch
Clubho
Tenn Cts
Pav
ANSON HALL
WILLESDEN LIB CEN
Bowling Grn
Tennis Cts
KILBURN
PADDINGTON OLD CEMETERY
QUEEN'S
UNIV COLLEGE GRD
OLIVE ROAD
IVY ROAD
MORA ROAD
ANSON ROAD
MELROSE AVENUE
HASSOP ROAD
PINE ROAD
LARCH ROAD
CEDAR ROAD
ASHFORD ROAD
HOWARD ROAD
OAKLANDS ROAD
HEBER ROAD
BLACKSTONE RD
DAWSON RD
WREN AVE
DICEY AVE
SNEYD RD
TRACEY AVE
HENSON AVE
GARDINER AVE
JAMES AVE
MEREDITH AVE
ASTLEY AVE
RIFFEL ROAD
CHANDOS ROAD
CRANHURST ROAD
GABRIELS ROAD
TEIGNMOUTH ROAD
DARTMOUTH ROAD
EXETER ROAD
FORDWYCH ROAD
SKARDU RD
RONDU RD
MANSTONE RD
MINSTER ROAD
MILL LANE
CHATSWORTH ROAD
BRONDESBURY ROAD
MAPESBURY ROAD
CHRISTCHURCH AVE
CAVENDISH ROAD
WINCHESTER AVE
BRONDESBURY PARK
AYLESTONE AVE
MANOR HOUSE DRIVE
CHUDLEIGH RD
SIDMOUTH ROAD
HANOVER ROAD
MOUNT PLEASANT ROAD
HENLEY RD
TIVERTON ROAD
DUNDONALD RD
OKEHAMPTON ROAD
CREDITON RD
WRENTHAM AVE
SALUSBURY ROAD
KINGSWOOD AVE
WINDERMERE AVE
HOPEFIELD AVE
MONTROSE AVE
VICTORIA RD
WESTBERE ROAD
MENELIK ROAD
ASMARA RD
SOMALI ROAD
WESTCROFT CLOSE
GALSWORTHY RD
HORTON AVE
WATLING GDNS
KILBURN

9
15

A
B
C
D
1
2
3
4
5
8
16
HENDON WAY
A41
FINCHLEY ROAD
UNIVERSITY COLLEGE SPORTS GROUND
BARNET
CAMDEN
HAMPSTEAD CEMETERY
FORTUNE GRN
King's Coll
Hampstead Campus
Open University
Regional Centre
COV RES
GONDAR GARDENS
WEST HAMPSTEAD
SOUTH HAMPSTEAD
WEST HAMPSTEAD (THAMESLINK)
Camden Arts Cen
Fire Sta
Health Cen
Comm Cen
Works
KILBURN
BRONDESBURY
KILBURN GRANGE PARK
KILBURN HIGH ROAD
KILBURN PARK
A5
A4003
B510
B520
B509
NW6
PADDINGTON OLD CEMETERY
Coll of NW Lon
Sports Cen
Clinic
ALEXANDRA EST
ABBEY RD EST
MORTIMER EST
SAATCHI COLLECTION
Regents Plaza Hotel
MILL LANE
WEST END LANE
FORTUNE GREEN ROAD
CANNON HILL
FROGNAL
REDINGTON ROAD
MAYGROVE RD
IVERSON RD
BELSIZE RD
ABBEY RD
PRIORY RD
CANFIELD GDNS
GREENCROFT GDNS
ABERDARE GDNS
BROADHURST GDNS
FAIRHAZEL GDNS
WOODCHURCH RD
CLEVE ROAD
ACOL ROAD
QUEX RD
KINGSGATE RD
MESSINA AVENUE
CHRISTCHURCH AVENUE
WINCHESTER AVE
BRONDESBURY VILLAS
CAMBRIDGE RD
GREVILLE RD
CLIFTON HILL
BOUNDARY RD

9
10
16
D
E
F
G
1
2
3
4
5
HILL
QUEEN MARY'S HOSP
THE PRYORS
HAMPSTEAD PONDS
Parliament Hill
RUNNING TRACK
Pav
Preacher's Hill
HAMPSTEAD
KEATS HO
HAMPSTEAD HEATH
HAMPSTEAD HIGH ST
ROSSLYN HILL
NASSINGTON RD
ALLOT
SAVERNAKE ROAD
CONSTANTINE
MANSFIELD RD B518
FLEET ST
POND ST B518
ROYAL FREE HOSPITAL
Sports Cen
GOSPEL OAK EST
LISMORE CIRCUS
TOWN HALL
Forte Posthouse
Old Town Hall Theatre
Cinema
BELSIZE PARK
HAVERSTOCK
ST. DOMINIC'S PRIORY
FREUD MUSEUM
TAVISTOCK CEN
MAITLAND PARK EST
ST. SILAS ST EST
A502
BELSIZE PARK
Fire Sta
SWISS COTTAGE
Comm Cen
A41
FINCHLEY RD
ADELAIDE B509 ROAD
CHALK FARM
Regents Park Marriott
PRIMROSE HILL
PRIMROSE HILL
COV RES
St. John's Wood Barracks
B525
A5205
PRINCE ALBERT RD
LONDON ZOO
Main Gate
TOWNSHEND EST
CANAL

DARTMOUTH PARK
GOSPEL OAK
NW5
KENTISH TOWN
CAMDEN TOWN
NW1
TUFNELL PARK
PRIMROSE HILL
LISMORE CIRCUS
RUNNING TRACK
Bowling Club
Bowling Grn
Bandstand
Tennis Cts
Lido
Works
Kentish Town City Farm
TOWN & COUNTRY CLUB
Interchange Studios
Drama Cen
Round Ho
Superstore
Camden Lock Mkt
Camden Lock
Youth Cen
Cecil Sharp House
Sports Cen
Royal Mail Depot
Royal Veterinary Coll
Uni of N Lon
Health Cen
Comm Cen
HOSP
Fire Sta
GOSPEL OAK EST
ST. SILAS ST EST
CLARENCE WAY EST
AGAR GROVE EST
CHALK FARM
KENTISH TOWN
CAMDEN ROAD
TUFNELL PARK
CAMDEN TOWN
HIGHGATE ROAD
FORTESS ROAD
JUNCTION ROAD
BRECKNOCK
KENTISH TOWN ROAD
CAMDEN HIGH ST
CAMDEN ROAD
ROYAL COLLEGE ST
ST PANCRAS WAY
CHALK FARM RD
ALBERT ROAD
PARKWAY
DELANCEY ST
MANSFIELD RD
MALDEN RD
PRINCE OF WALES RD
LEIGHTON ROAD
TORRIANO
A400
A5200
A503
A502
A5202
A5205
B518
B517
B509
1
2
3
4
5
A
B
C
D
9
17

HOLLOWAY
LOWER HOLLOWAY
BARNSBURY
ISLINGTON
N7
N1
KING'S CROSS
H.M. PRISON HOLLOWAY
PENTONVILLE PRISON
CALEDONIAN PARK
BARNARD PARK
PARADISE PARK
Freightliners City Farm
CAMLEY NATURAL PARK
London Wildlife Trust
ARSENAL F.C.
ARSENAL
HOLLOWAY ROAD
DRAYTON PARK
CALEDONIAN ROAD
CALEDONIAN ROAD & BARNSBURY
HIGHBURY & ISLINGTON
Uni of North London
City & Islington College
St. George's Theatre
SPORTS GRD
Tennis Courts
Clubhouse
Clock Tower
James Leicester Hall
Swimming Pool
ROYAL MAIL
PANCRAS HOSP & HOSP FOR TROPICAL DISEASES
DEPOT
BR. DEPOT
Gas Works
HARVIST ESTATE
BEMERTON EST
YORK WAY COURT
BUS DES. CEN
HOLLOWAY ROAD
CAMDEN ROAD
SEVEN SISTERS ROAD
HORNSEY ROAD
TOLLINGTON ROAD
PARKHURST RD
CALEDONIAN ROAD
YORK WAY
LIVERPOOL ROAD
UPPER STREET
RICHMOND AVENUE
COPENHAGEN ST
MARKET ROAD
A1
A503
A103
A5203
A5200
B514
B515
D
E
F
G
1
2
3
4
5
11
17

11
A
B
C
D
1
2
3
4
5
10
18
HIGHBURY
N5
HIGHBURY ARSENAL FC
HIGHBURY PARK
HIGHBURY GROVE
HIGHBURY QUADRANT
HIGHBURY NEW PARK
HIGHBURY GRANGE
HIGHBURY CRESCENT
HIGHBURY FIELDS
HIGHBURY & ISLINGTON
HIGHBURY EST
University of North London
ABERDEEN PARK
DRAYTON PARK
CANONBURY
CANONBURY SQUARE
ST PAUL'S ROAD
A1199
A1201
A105
A104
A1200
A1
B104
B102
NEWINGTON GREEN
ESSEX ROAD
NEW NORTH ROAD
BALLS POND ROAD
MILDMAY PARK
DOUGLAS EST
DE BEAUVOIR EST
ROSEMARY GDNS
UPPER STREET
TOWN HALL
THE SUTTON EST
ROYAL MAIL
REGENT'S CANAL
HOXTON
SHOREDITCH PARK
COLVILLE EST
GREEN LANES
STOKE NEWINGTON
CLISSOLD CRESCENT
Swimming Pool
Comm Cen
Health Cen
Swim Pool
Amb Sta
Fire Sta
Sports Cen

11
D
E
F
G
1
2
3
4
5
12
18
SHACKLEWELL
HACKNEY
DALSTON
HAGGERSTON
E8
HACKNEY DOWNS
SPORTS GRD
LONDON FIELDS
HAGGERSTON PARK
CAMBRIDGE HEATH
KINGSLAND HIGH ST
STOKE NEWINGTON ROAD
A10
KINGSLAND ROAD
DALSTON LANE
A104
GRAHAM ROAD
A1207
AMHURST RD
PEMBURY RD
CRICKET. RD
LOWER CLAPTON RD
MARE ST
A107
A106
DALSTON LA
DOWNS PARK RD
DOWNS ROAD
RECTORY RD
MANSE RD
EVERI. RD
AMHURST RD
SYDNER ROAD
FOULDEN RD
FARLEIGH ROAD
SHACKLEWELL RD
SOMERFORD GRO
BEATTY ROAD
NIGHTINGALE EST
KENNINGHALL RD
TIGER WAY
QUEENSDOWN ROAD
CLARENCE ROAD
RICHMOND ROAD
FOREST ROAD
MAPLEDENE ROAD
LAVENDER GROVE
MIDDLETON ROAD
ALBION DRIVE
SHRUBLAND ROAD
REGENTS ROW
WHISTON ROAD
QUEENSBRIDGE ROAD
LANSDOWNE DRIVE
HAGGERSTON ROAD
MALVERN ROAD
RIDLEY ROAD
SANDRINGHAM RD
COLVESTONE CRESCENT
MONTAGUE RD
WILTON WAY
READING LA
BLACKSTONE EST
FIELDS EST
WELL ST
VYNER STREET
WATERLOO EST
BISHOPS B127
Health Centre
Comm Cen
Sch
PO
Lib
Clinic
Tenn Cts
Sports Cen
TOWN HALL
Theatre
MUS.
Fire Sta
Swimming Pool
Gas Works
Hackney Coll
Hospice
HACKNEY CENTRAL
HACKNEY DOWNS
LONDON FLDS
DALSTON KINGSLAND

SOUTH MILLFIELDS
REC GRD
HACKNEY
A
B
C
D
1
2
3
4
5
11
19
CLAPTON PARK
LOWER CLAPTON
HOMERTON HOSPITAL
HOMERTON
MABLEY GREEN
SOUTH HACKNEY
VICTORIA PARK
WELL STREET COMMON
E9
HOMERTON HIGH ST
A102
A106
A107
B113
MORNING LANE
WICK RD
WICK ROAD
CASSLAND ROAD
VICTORIA PARK ROAD
WELL STREET
MARE ST
LOWER CLAPTON RD
CLAPTON RD
URSWICK RD
RUSHMORE RD
CHATSWORTH ROAD
MILLFIELDS ROAD
POWERSCROFT ROAD
GLENARM RD
DUNLACE ROAD
CLIFDEN RD
MEDIAN RD
HOMERTON ROW
HOMERTON GROVE
MARSH HILL
KENWORTHY RD
ORIEL ROAD
HASSETT ROAD
BALLANCE ROAD
HOSPITAL (closed)
HACKNEY CENTRAL
RIVER LEE NAVIGATION
KINGSMEAD WAY
LINDISFARNE WAY
DAUBENEY ROAD
BROOKSBY'S WALK
GLYN ROAD
CHELMER ROAD
TRELAWNEY EST
FRAMPTON PK EST
FRAMPTON PARK ROAD
BRENTHOUSE RD
LODDIGES RD
VALETTE ST
PARAGON RD
KENTON ROAD
HARTLAKE ROAD
GASCOYNE
MEYNELL CRES
GROOMBRIDGE RD
PENSHURST ROAD
LAURISTON RD
GROVE RD
MORPETH ROAD
GORE ROAD
SEWARDSTONE ROAD
BISHOPS B127
WATERLOO EST
DEER PARK
St. Agnes Gate
Gore Gate
Crown Gate East
Crown Gate West
Royal Gate East
Victoria Fountain
Bandstand
Gunmakers Gate
Queens Gate
Three Colt Bri
Skew Bridge
HERTFORD UNION
TOWER HAMLETS
HACKNEY
CAMBRIDGE HEATH
LONDON
Sports Cen
Health Cen
Comm Cen
Amb Sta
Fire Sta
Coll
Sch
Schs
Lib
Clinic
Pav
Tenn Cts
Bowl Grn
PO

12
D
E
F
G
1
2
3
4
5
13
19
A106
RUCKHOLT ROAD
New Spitalfields Market
SHERRIN ROAD
RECREATION GROUND
RIVER LEE or LEA
Pav
Works
Bowl Grn
ETON MANOR SPORTS GRD
Lea Valley Sports Centre
QUARTER MILE LANE
TEMPLE MILL LANE
B112
EASTWAY
EASTWAY CYCLE CIRCUIT
TWEEDALE CT
TAY CT
CLAYS LANE
CLAYS LA CLO
TRAFFORD CLOSE
WALTHAM FOREST
NEWHAM
HIGH ROAD LEYTON
A112
LEYTON
NUTFIELD RD
ETCHING. RD
CRANB. RD
GORDON RD
WESTDOWN ROAD
FRITH ROAD
MILLAIS ROAD
LESLIE
DOWN
STEWART
DRAPERS ROAD
DRAPERS FIELD
REC GRD
CROWNFIELD
COLEGRAVE
CHANDOS
PO
HENRIETTA ST
LEYTON ROAD
MAJOR RD
ALLOT
DUNEDIN
ADELAIDE
ALEXA RD
STA RD
Lib
RUCKHOLT CL
EASTWAY COMMERCIAL CENTRE
WATERDEN ROAD
ALLOTMENTS
LONDON STADIUM HACKNEY
HACKNEY WICK
ARENA FIELD
Cold Stores
INTERNATIONAL FREIGHT TERMINAL
STRATFORD
Depot
Sch
FB
LEABANK SQ
BERKSHIRE RD
ROAD
Works
ALLOT
HACKNEY WICK
CARPENTERS ROAD
WHITEPOST
ROTHBURY ROAD
A115
TREGO RD
DAVEY RD
BOW IND EST
CARPENTERS BUS. PARK
MARSHGATE LANE
WATERWORKS RIVER
STRATFORD
BUS STA
E15
Sports Cen
STATION ST
GREAT EASTERN
EAST CROSS ROUTE
WANSBECK ROAD
ROACH ROAD
WYKE ROAD
SMEED ROAD
BEACHY ROAD
STOUR ROAD
DACE ROAD
BREAM ST
MONIER
RIVER LEE NAVIGATION
Works
MARSHGATE
KNOBS HILL RD
CITY MILL RIVER
WARTON RD
DENNISON PT
KENNAR RD
ROSHER CLO
JUPP ROAD
GIBBINS
DORAN WK
WILMER LEA CLO
Comm Cen
Uni. of E. London
ROWSE CL
BIGGERST RD
ROB. RD
Sch
WICK LANE
Northern Outfall Sewer
RIVER LEE or LEA
CROWO CLO
WICK
ICELAND RD
MAVE RD
AUTUMN ST
DYE HO LA
A102(M)
PUDDING LANE
PUDDING MILL LANE
MILL ROAD
MARSHGATE LANE
RIVER BLAKER RD
BRIDGWATER RD
Works
ROBERTS WAY
LIVINGSTONE RD
Gas Works
ABBEY
Fire Sta
PO
PARNELL
TREDEGAR RD
BLACKWALL
Power Sta
Leisure

CEMETERY
A
B
C
D
1
2
3
4
5
12
20
SOUTH BIRKBECK
HOLLOWAY
BIRCH GRO
Lib
Sports Cen
Sch
LANGTHORNE HOSP
LANGTHORNE RD
CALDERON
FRITH ROAD
MILLAIS ROAD
LESLIE ROAD
NUTFIELD RD
ETCHING. RD
CRANB. RD
DOWNSELL ROAD
STEWART ROAD
DRAPERS ROAD
CROWNFIELD ROAD
CROWNFIELD RD
AMETH RD
ELLINGHAM ROAD
HALL ROAD
BRIERLEY RD
TOR. RD
DRAPERS FIELD REC. GRD
COLEGRAVE
Comm Cen
PO
CHANDOS ROAD
DUNMOW RD
ASHLIN RD
BURGESS RD
GILB. ST
WIN RD
PINE AV
BOND ST
HURD
NEW RD
BRYD
OBHAM A112 RD
LEYTON ROAD
HENRIETTA
MAJOR RD
LEYTON
A112
HIGH ROAD
RANELAGH ROAD
WORSLEY ROAD
STEELE ROAD
BELT. RD
EVE RD
CANN HALL ROAD
RAMSAY ROAD
CANN ROAD
TRUMPINGTON RD
CHICHESTER RD
WRAGBY ROAD
KINGS
JEWISH CEM
WEST HAM CEMETERY
BLENHEIM RD
BORTHWICK RD
ARUNDEL CLO
ARGYLE RD
JANSON ROAD
GURNEY ROAD
BUXTON ROAD
TREVELYAN RD
HEYWORTH RD
BUCK ROAD
CRUIKSHANK RD
IDMISTON ROAD
ST. JAMES ROAD
CORMORANT RD
MAGPIE CLO
TOWER HAMLETS ROAD
WELLINGTON ROAD
ODESSA ROAD
CEMETERY ROAD
HUDDLESTONE RD
PEVENSEY
THORPE ROAD
VANSITTART
FOWLER
DEAN ST
HENNIKER PT
HENNIKER ROAD
MARYLAND STREET
MARYLAND SQUARE
MARYLAND PK
MARYL.
ALBERT SQUARE
ALB. SQ
FOREST
EARLHAM
CLOVA
MEWS
ATHERTON ROAD
ATHERTON MEWS
ROAD
MARYLAND
KEOGH
LOUISE ROAD
CARNARVON ROAD
DORMER CLO
Sports Cen
CEDARS
Uni
TOR. SQ
TOR. RD
GREEN PT
Lib
THE GREEN
WOLFFE
Fire Sta
A118
TOWN
VAUGHAN RD
ELEANOR RD
DYSON ROAD
BOLTON ROAD
WARWICK
ELM RD
KNOX
STORK ROAD
YORK ROAD
REGINALD
HAT FIELD
ASH ROAD
CARR. CLO
CHATSW.
GLO
WAR.
THORO GDNS
COMM. RD
MARYLAND
ST. PAULS
WADDINGTON
WADDINGTON RD
ALMA ST
DORSET PL
THORN GROVE
DAVID
WINDMILL LANE
FRANCIS ST
CAROL CL
STORE
MAL.
ASHTON R.
Depot
STRATFORD
INTERNATIONAL FREIGHT TERMINAL
ANGEL LA
A112 RD
GREAT EASTERN RD
A11
OXF. RD
CRES RD
GROVE
THE GROVE
LEYTONSTONE
MANBEY PK RD
MANBEY GRO
MANBEY ST
WATER
B164
PARK
Sch
Uni of E. London
ROMFORD
COUNTY CT
GROVE GDNS
LITCHFIE.
DEANERY ROAD
STRATFORD
BUS STA
SUB
Shopping Centre
Theatre Royal
SALWAY RD
BROADWAY
OLD TH. CONF. CEN.
STATION ST
FB
E15
Sports
DENNISON PT
KENNAR RD
JUPP ROAD
GIBBINS
DORAN WK
ROSHER CLO
WILMER LEA CLO
Comm Cen
Uni of E. London
JUPP ROAD W.
ROAD
BIGGERST.
Sch
CAM RD
BURFORD ROAD
WHARF RD
CHANNELSEA RD
KERRISON
MKT
Works
Gas Works
ABBEY LANE
BISSON
THREE
ABB. CLO
DELIUS GRO
ROBERTS WAY
LIVINGSTONE RD
GODF ST
MAG CT
Schs
BRYANTS
WIDDIN ST
PITCHFORD ST
PAUL STREET
MARRIOTT RD
ROKEBY
HOTHAM ST
SANDAL ST
ASLA. RD
SKIERS STREET
MORTHAM ST
HUBB
ABBEY
BAKERS ROW
MITRE RD
POND
WEST HAM LA
T.R.A.
MARK ST
VICT. ST
ELLIOT CLO
ALDWORTH RD
FARINGFORD
VERNON ROAD
TENNYSON ROAD
GLENAVON RD
MAIDEN RD
WO. RD
WHI. RD
SHIRL.
VICARAGE LANE
VICARAGE
HAM PARK
Sports Cen
Coll
REC GRD
Tenn Cts
Bowl Grn
HURRY CLO
BYFORD CLO
GOVIER CL
DEVENAY
HARTLAND RD
SKELL RD
ED. TEMME AVE
WEST HAM PARK
Bands
WEST HAM
TA Cen
EVESHAM ROAD
MEESON RD
AMITY RD
MOR RD
PORTWAY
B165
DENSHAM RD
Health Cen
CHURCH
MA. CT
GIFT LA
RICHFORD RD
LIDDINGTON RD
DIRLETON RD
HARBERSON RD
PARK ROAD
WEST
Sch
STRATFORD
NEW PLAISTOW ROAD
A112
PLAISTOW ROAD
A1011 ROAD
STEPHEN'S RD
JOHN ST
GEERE
CAISTOR
REDRIFFE RD
MAUD ROAD
VALETTA GROVE
MAT. GDNS
HARCOURT
HOLBROOK
Coll
PLAISTOW
Works
Comm

13
D
E
F
G
REDBRIDGE
NEWHAM
MANOR PARK
MANOR PARK CEMETERY
Crematorium
E7
CAPEL ROAD
FOREST DRIVE
ALDERSBROOK
WOODFORD ROAD
WOODGRANGE ROAD
WANSTEAD PARK
FOREST GATE
SEBERT ROAD
HAMPTON ROAD
OSBORNE ROAD
CLAREMONT ROAD
WINDSOR ROAD
BALMORAL ROAD
GODWIN ROAD
ROMFORD ROAD
A118
A117
A114
A124
B109
B165
B167
WOODGRANGE PARK
WOODGRANGE PARK CEM
MANOR PARK STATION
HIGH STREET
DURHAM ROAD
CLARENCE ROAD
SHERRARD ROAD
HALLEY ROAD
MONEGA ROAD
STRONE ROAD
SHREWSBURY ROAD
KATHERINE ROAD
GREEN STREET
UPTON LANE
PLASHET CEMETERY
PLASHET PARK
EAST HAM MEML HOSP
Health Cen
Clinic
Lib
Tenn Cts
Bowl Grn
UPTON
UPTON PARK
PLASHET ROAD
BOLEYN ROAD
NEVILLE ROAD
PRIORY PARK
CEARNS HO
BUS GAR
WEST HAM UTD FC
BARKING ROAD
PLAISTOW
STORFORD RD
Comm Cen
Sch
Coll
PO
Mkt
1
2
3
4
5
14
20

14
A
B
C
D
1
2
3
4
5
13
21
Crematorium
MANOR PARK
LITTLE ILFORD
E12
LITTLE ILFORD PARK
BARRINGTON PLAYING FIELDS
WOODGRANGE PARK
WOODGRANGE PARK CEM
PLASHET CEMETERY
PLASHET PARK
EAST HAM MEML HOSP
EAST HAM
BARKING ROAD REC GRD
SPORTS GRD
NEWHAM
PLAYING FIELD
SOUTH WOODFORD TO BARKING RELIEF ROAD
A406
A116
A118
A117
B165
A124
ROMFORD ROAD
FOREST VIEW ROAD
CARLYLE RD
MANOR PARK
ALDERBROOK LA
COLCHESTER AVE
GRANTHAM RD
WALTON RD
WARRIOR SQ
JACK CORNWELL ST
JOHN CORNWALL VC HO
ALFRED PRIOR HO
STEWART RAINBIRD HO
WASHINGTON AV
SEVENTH AVE
EIGHTH AVE
SIXTH AVE
FIFTH AVE
FOURTH AVE
THIRD AVE
SECOND AVE
FIRST AVE
SHERINGHAM AVENUE
DERSINGHAM AVENUE
LAWRENCE AVENUE
PARKHURST ROAD
ALVERS RD
BRANCASTER RD
TREVELYAN AVE
HARCOURT AVENUE
VERNON AV
SCHOOL RD
CHURCH RD
CHURCH ROAD
ST. WINEFRIDE'S AVE
ST. MARY'S APP
LANDSEER AVENUE
GAINSBOROUGH AVENUE
REYNOLDS AVE
LEADER AVE
LEIGHTON AV
DORE AVENUE
MILLAIS AVE
RECTORY RD
ELSENHAM RD
CHESTERFIELD ROAD
BARRINGTON RD
HATHAWAY CRESCENT
HATHAWAY CRES
SHAKESPEARE CRES
SHERIDAN ROAD
ESSEX RD
MORRIS AVE
WARWICK RD
BERKELEY RD
RIXSEN RD
STANLEY RD
COLERIDGE AVE
RUSKIN AVE
GOLDSMITH AVE
ROSEBERY AVENUE
BROWNING ROAD
KENSINGTON AVENUE
GLADSTONE AVENUE
EAST AVE
SIBLEY GROVE
SHELLEY AVE
BYRON AVE
WORDSWORTH AVE
TENNYSON AVE
WOODHOUSE GROVE
HIGH STREET NORTH
SALISBURY RD
BLUEBELL AV
SNOWSHILL RD
NINE ACRES CLO
DEPOT
STEVENAGE ROAD
LEIGH ROAD
ASHFORD RD
NORTHFIELD RD
SPRINGFIELD RD
SHOEBURY RD
BRIDGE RD
SOUTHEND RD
LYDE RD
ALTMORE AVENUE
WATSON AVE
BURGES ROAD
BURGES CT
LATHOM ROAD
CLEMENTS ROAD
CAULFIELD ROAD
CALEDON ROAD
HOLLAND ROAD
SKEFFINGTON ROAD
KEMPTON ROAD
KEPPEL ROAD
STREATFIELD AVE
LATIMER AVE
WALL END
NORFOLK ROAD
BEDFORD ROAD
CALVERTON RD
ST. OLAVES ROAD
MIERS CLO
GROVE
MILTON AVENUE
HEIGHAM ROAD
BENDISH RD
LAWRENCE ROAD
OUTRAM ROAD
HARROW RD
HOLME RD
TEMPLE RD
MALVERN ROAD
STAMFORD ROAD
OAKFIELD ROAD
EVERSLEIGH RD
SPENCER RD
ST. BERNARD'S ROAD
WAKEFIELD ST
ARRAGON ROAD
ABBOTS RD
AINTREE AVE
HARTLEY AVE
CAMPBELL AVE
WINTER AVE
LEIGHTON WAY
THORPE RD
LLOYD RD
BARKING ROAD
LANGDON RD
NELSON ST
SUSSEX ROAD
RANELAGH ROAD
NAPIER RD
WELLINGTON RD
MELBOURNE RD
ST. BARTHOLOMEW'S RD
NAVARRE RD
HENRY RD
BARTLE AVENUE
ERNALD AVENUE
GILLETT AVE
LADYSMITH AVE
KIMBERLEY
MARKET ST
DUKES CT
TOWN HALL
TH annexe
Shopping Cen
Comm Cen
Schs
Sch
PO
Lib
Health Cen
Coll
Pol
Sta
Works
Superstore
Gas holder
Pav
Tenn Cts
Bowl Grn
ZOO
Three Rabbits PH
Earl of Essex PH
SUB
FB

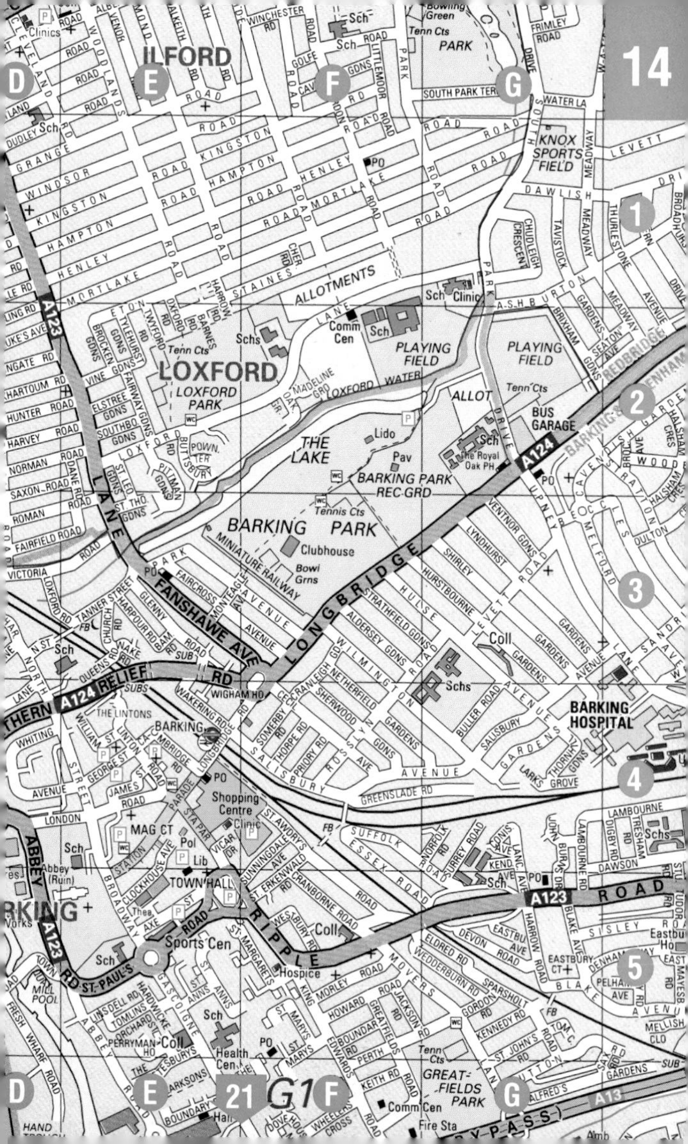

14
ILFORD
LOXFORD
LOXFORD PARK
THE LAKE
BARKING PARK
BARKING PARK REC GRD
KNOX SPORTS FIELD
PLAYING FIELD
ALLOTMENTS
BUS GARAGE
BARKING HOSPITAL
BARKING
Shopping Centre
TOWN HALL
Sports Cen
GREATFIELDS PARK
LONGBRIDGE
FANSHAWE AVE
RIPPLE ROAD
A123
A124
A13
D
E
F
G
1
2
3
4
5
21
G1

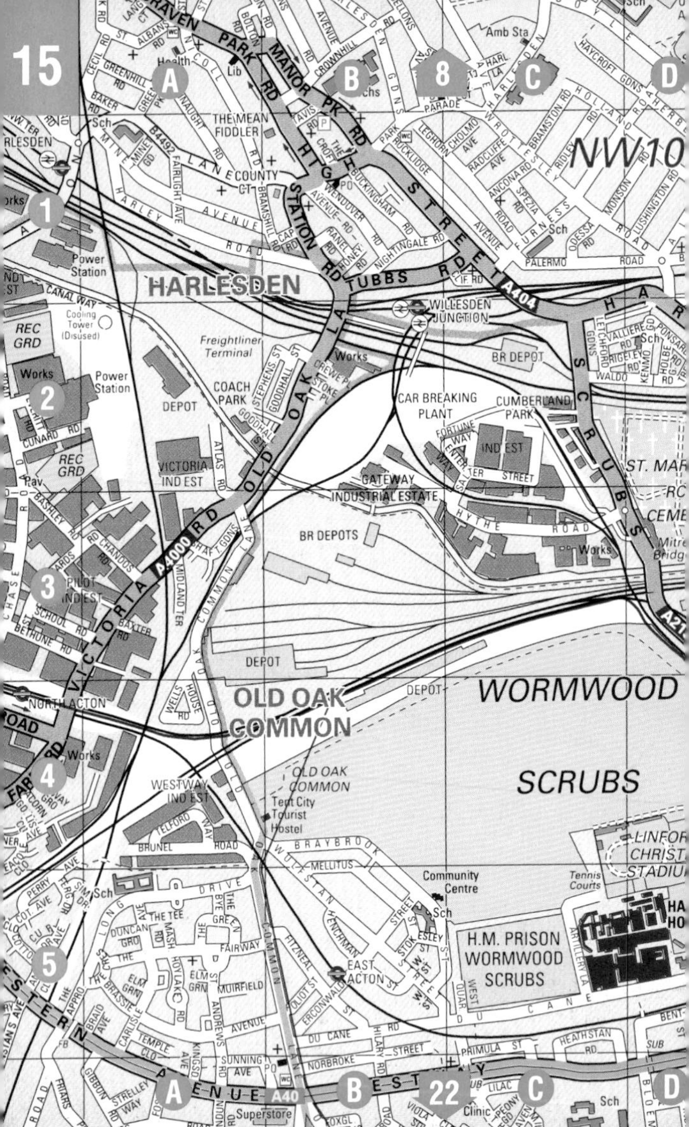

15
A
B
C
D
8
22
1
2
3
4
5
NW10
HARLESDEN
CRAVEN PARK RD
MANOR PK RD
HIGH STREET
STATION RD
TUBBS RD
OLD OAK LA
OLD OAK RD
VICTORIA RD
A4000
A404
A40
SCRUBS LA
THE MEAN FIDDLER
Health
Lib
Amb Sta
Power Station
Cooling Tower (Disused)
REC GRD
Works
CANAL WAY
Freightliner Terminal
COACH PARK
DEPOT
VICTORIA IND EST
WILLESDEN JUNCTION
BR DEPOT
CAR BREAKING PLANT
CUMBERLAND PARK
IND EST
GATEWAY INDUSTRIAL ESTATE
BR DEPOTS
HYTHE ROAD
PILOT IND EST
NORTH ACTON
OLD OAK COMMON
WORMWOOD SCRUBS
WESTWAY IND EST
Tent City Tourist Hostel
Community Centre
H.M. PRISON WORMWOOD SCRUBS
EAST ACTON
DU CANE RD
WESTERN AVENUE
Superstore
Clinic
Sch
ST. MARY'S RC CEMETERY
LINFORD CHRISTIE STADIUM
Tennis Courts

15
D
E
8
F
G
1
2
3
4
5
16
22
KENSAL RISE
QUEEN'S PARK
KENSAL GREEN
KENSAL GREEN CEMETERY
KENSAL TOWN
UNION CANAL (Paddington Branch)
CANAL WAY
Gas Works
Superstore
Canoe Club
LITTLE WORMWOOD SCRUBS REC GRD
W10
ST. CHARLES HOSP
PRINCESS LOUISE HOSPITAL
MONASTERY
City of Westminster College
Sports Cen
NORTH KENSINGTON
NOTTING HILL
PLAYING FIELD
HARROW ROAD
A404
B451
B413
B412
B450
A40(M)
A40
M41
WESTWAY
LADBROKE GROVE
LATIMER ROAD
KENSAL RISE
KENSAL GREEN
BBC Office s
Depot
Sports Cen
Tennis Cts
KENSINGTON & CHELSEA
BRENT
PEABODY EST
SUTTON EST
TRELLICK TOWER
Bowling Grn
Health Cen
Comm Cen
Mortimer Clinic

PADDINGTON OLD CEMETERY
A
B
9
C
D
KILBURN
KILBURN HIGH ROAD
B451
BRONDESBURY RD
KILBURN PARK
Regents Plaza Hotel
MAIDA VALE
QUEEN'S PARK
1
CARLTON VALE
Coll of NW Lon
PADDINGTON RECREATION GROUND
Pavilion
WEST KILBURN
2
Sports Cen
QUEEN'S PARK
15
SHIRLAND RD
B413
W9
MAIDA VALE
Sports Centre
3
HARROW ROAD
MAIDA HILL
TRELLICK TOWER
A404
PADDINGTON COMMUNITY HOSP
Portobello Junct
WESTBOURNE PARK
4
WESTWAY
WESTBOURNE GREEN
ROYAL OAK
PADDINGTON
B412
5
A4027
CHEPSTOW ROAD
WESTBOURNE GROVE
Whiteleys
BAYSWATER
W2
NOTTING HILL
A
B
23
C
D
4206
BAYSWATER

16
PRIMROSE HILL
9
D
E
F
G
ST. JOHN'S WOOD
LORD'S CRICKET GROUND
HOSPITAL OF ST. JOHN & ST. ELIZ
WELLINGTON HOSP
WELLINGTON RD
PRINCE ALBERT ROAD
ST. JOHN'S WOOD ROAD
PARK RD
REGENT'S CANAL
RUNNING TRACK
LONDON ZOO
Tennis Courts
REGENT'S PARK
1
2
3
4
5
17
Winfield House
LONDON CENTRAL MOSQUE
BOATING LAKE
Open Air Theatre
QUEEN MARY'S GARDENS
Bandstand
London Business Sch (Uni of Lon)
Royal College of Obstetricians & Gynaecologists
Hilton International Hotel
MARYLEBONE
Regent's College
Clarence Gate
SHERLOCK HOLMES MUS
MADAME TUSSAUD'S
PLANETARIUM
BAKER ST
GLOUCESTER PL
SAMARITAN & OPHTHALMIC HOSPS
MARYLEBONE RD
EDGWARE ROAD
London Metropole Hotel
Paddington Coll
ST. MARY'S HOSP
PADDINGTON
PRAED ST
SUSSEX GDNS
FITZROY NUFFIELD HOSP
WALLACE COLLECTION
PORTMAN SQUARE
Cumberland Hotel
Mount Royal Hotel
MARBLE ARCH
SEYMOUR ST
Royal Lancaster Hotel
SPEAKER'S
23
A40(M)
A5
A41
A501
A4205
A4209
A5205
A40

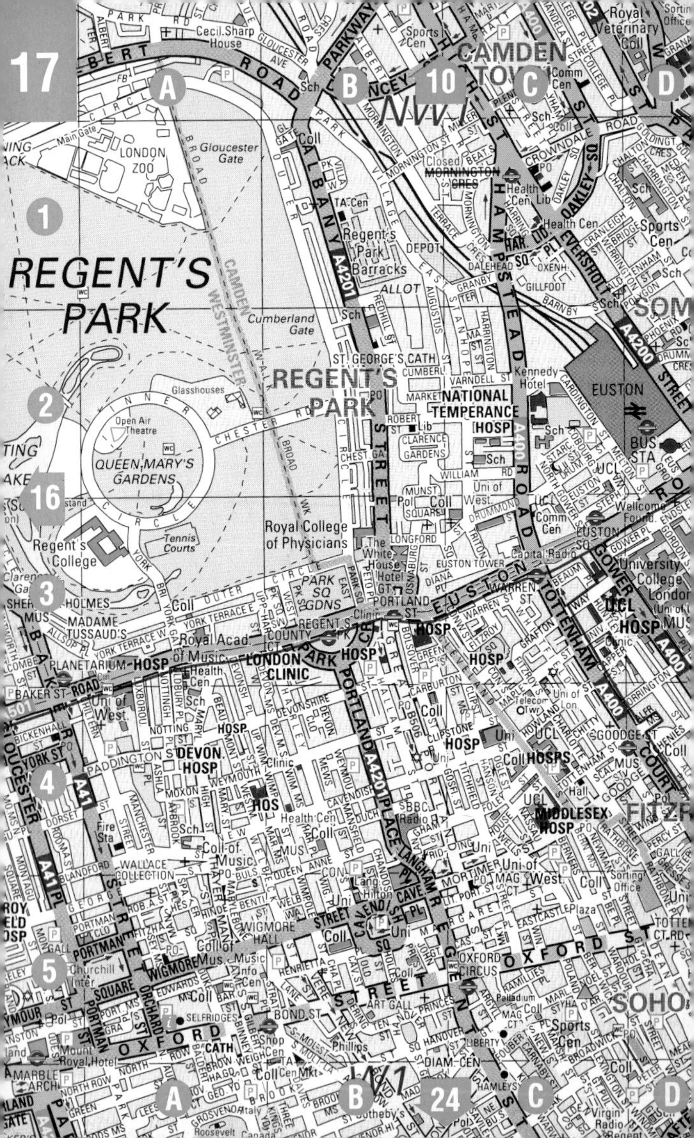
A
B
C
D
1
2
3
4
5
10
16
24
NW1
W1
REGENT'S PARK
LONDON ZOO
Main Gate
Cecil Sharp House
Gloucester Gate
Cumberland Gate
BROAD WALK
CAMDEN
WESTMINSTER
Glasshouses
Open Air Theatre
QUEEN MARY'S GARDENS
INNER CIRCLE
CHESTER RD
OUTER CIRCLE
Tennis Courts
Regent's College
YORK BRI
Royal College of Physicians
REGENT'S PARK
ST. GEORGE'S CATH
CAMDEN TOWN
PARKWAY
ALBANY ST
A4201
Regent's Park Barracks
MORNINGTON CRES
Closed
HAMPSTEAD ROAD
A400
EVERSHOLT ST
A4200
EUSTON
BUS STA
EUSTON ROAD
NATIONAL TEMPERANCE HOSP
CLARENCE GARDENS
MUNSTER SQUARE
Uni of West.
UCL
Kennedy Hotel
Wellcome Found.
Capital Radio
EUSTON TOWER
University College London
GOWER ST
TOTTENHAM COURT RD
The White House Hotel
PORTLAND PL
PARK SQ GDNS
PARK CRES
LONDON CLINIC
MADAME TUSSAUD'S
PLANETARIUM
BAKER ST
MARYLEBONE RD
Royal Acad. of Music
Health Cen
DEVONSHIRE PL
WEYMOUTH ST
NEW CAVENDISH ST
GREAT PORTLAND ST
MIDDLESEX HOSP
FITZROY SQ
CLEVELAND ST
GOODGE ST
BBC Radio
LANGHAM PL
Lang. Hilton
CAVENDISH SQ
WIGMORE ST
WIGMORE HALL
WALLACE COLLECTION
MANCHESTER SQ
GEORGE ST
PORTMAN SQUARE
Churchill Inter.
BAKER ST
A41
GLOUCESTER PL
OXFORD STREET
OXFORD CIRCUS
SELFRIDGES
BOND ST
REGENT ST
MARGARET ST
Palladium
SOHO
Sports Cen
CARNABY ST
HAMLEYS
LIBERTY
HANOVER SQ
Sotheby's
GROSVENOR
Mount Royal Hotel
MARBLE ARCH
PARK LANE
NORTH ROW
Sorting Office
Royal Veterinary Coll
SOMERS TOWN
FITZROVIA

17
10
18
24
D
E
F
G
1
2
3
4
5
ISLINGTON
PENTONVILLE
ST PANCRAS
BLOOMSBURY
HOLBORN
WC1
KING'S CROSS
ST PANCRAS
BRITISH LIB
CAMLEY ST NATURAL PARK
London Wildlife Trust
BARNARD PARK
CALEDONIAN ROAD
COPENHAGEN B514 ST
PENTONVILLE A501 RD
THAMESLINK
KING'S CROSS RD
GRAY'S INN ROAD A5200
FARRINGDON
ROSEBERY AVE
CLERKENWELL ROAD
EASTMAN DENTAL HOSP
Mount Pleasant Post Office
CORAM'S FIELDS
T. CORAM FOUND.
HOSPS
RUSSELL SQ
SOUTHAMPTON ROW
THEOBALD'S ROAD
GRAY'S INN GDNS
HIGH HOLBORN
HOLBORN
A40
BRITISH MUSEUM & BRITISH LIB
NEW OXFORD ST
ST GILES HIGH ST
LINCOLN'S INN FIELDS
ROYAL COURTS OF JUSTICE
KINGSWAY
ALDWYCH
STRAND
FLEET ST
EMBANKMENT
COVENT GDN
ROYAL OPERA HO
Sadler's Wells Theatre
The Angel Centre
Vernon Square Cen
Royal Scot Hotel
Freemasons Hall
City Lit. Inst
Prince Henry's Room
Temple Bar
Silver Vaults
CHANCERY LANE
WESTMINSTER

18
A
B
11
C
D
1
2
17
3
4
5
25
HOXTON
SHOREDITCH PARK
COLVILLE EST
CRANSTON EST
ST. JOHNS EST
PROVOST EST
FINSBURY
KING SQ GDNS
CLERKENWELL
ST. LUKE'S
EC1
EC2
EC4
ANGEL
The Angel Centre
Thames Water Authority
Sadlers Wells Theatre
City Uni
FINSBURY EST
REGENT'S CANAL
CITY ROAD BASIN
WENLOCK BASIN
HACKNEY ISLINGTON
MOORFIELDS EYE HOSP
ST. LUKE'S EST
BURIAL GRD
BUNHILL FLDS
Barracks
Whitbread Brewery
WESLEY'S HO
Charterhouse
St. Bartholomew's Med Coll
FARRINGDON
BARBICAN
BARBICAN ARTS & CONF CEN
EXHIB HALLS
Smithfield Central Mkts
ST. BART'S HOSP
MUSEUM OF LONDON
MOORGATE
The Guildhall
CENT CRIM CT (Old Bailey)
ST. PAUL'S CATH
Chapter Ho
Info. Cen
Coll of Arms
CITY THAMESLINK
Bank of Eng
Stock Exch
Royal Exch
Mansion Ho
BANK
MONUMENT
City of London Coll
Int Finance Cen
BROADGATE
LIVERPOOL
FINSBURY CIRCUS
Guildhall Uni
UPPER ST
ISLINGTON GREEN
A104
A1200
A501
A1
A5201
A201
A40
A1211
A10
B144
B502
B501
B100
B101
CITY ROAD
GOSWELL ROAD
EAST RD
NORTH ROAD
OLD STREET
GREAT EASTERN
ALDERSGATE ST
MOORGATE
LONDON WALL
HOLBORN VIADUCT
NEWGATE ST
CHEAPSIDE
CANNON ST
FARRINGDON ROAD
CHARTERHOUSE ST
NEW BRIDGE ST
QUEEN VICTORIA ST
THREADNEEDLE STREET
CHISWELL STREET
ROPEMAKER ST
SILK ST
FORE ST
WHITECROSS ST
BUNHILL ROW
GOLDEN LANE
CENTRAL ST
IRONMONGER ROW
LEVER ST
PACKINGTON STREET
ESSEX RD
NEW NORTH RD
PITFIELD ST
SHEPHERDESS WALK
WENLOCK ST
MURRAY GROVE
BEVENDEN ST
HABERDASHER ST
GRACECHURCH ST
LOMBARD STREET
KING WILLIAM STREET
CORNHILL
POULTRY
GRESHAM ST
WOOD ST
COLEMAN STREET
BASINGHALL AVE
LUDGATE HILL
FLEET
NEW FETTER LA
SHOE LA
ST. BRIDE
WHITEFRIARS
BLACKFRIARS
THAMES

18
11
D
E
F
G
HAGGERSTON
HAGGERSTON PARK
Hackney City Farm
QUEEN ELIZ. HOSP
BETHNAL GREEN
Gas Works
WATERLOO EST
CAMBRIDGE HEATH
REGENTS ROW
A106
A1208
A1209
A107
A10
A1202
A11
A13
B108
B118
B135
B134
B127
B126
HACKNEY ROAD
KINGSLAND
MARE
CAMBRIDGE HEATH ROAD
BETHNAL GREEN RD
OLD BETHNAL GREEN RD
COLUMBIA ROAD
MILDMAY MISS. HOSP
MUS OF CHILDHOOD
Sports Cen
1
2
E2
19
3
4
5
WEAVERS FLDS
JEWISH BURIAL GRD
Superstore
SHOREDITCH
SHOREDITCH HIGH ST
COMMERCIAL STREET
Old Spitalfields Mkt
Spitalfields Comm Fm
HANBURY
WHITECHAPEL
WHITECHAPEL RD
ROYAL LONDON HOSP TRUST
Toynbee Hall
ALDGATE E. ART GALL
MIDDLESEX STREET
ALDGATE
ALDGATE BUS STA
MINORIES
MANSELL
LEMAN STREET
COMMERCIAL ROAD
TARLING ST EST
SHADWELL
CABLE
TOWER GTWY
25

PARK
12
18
26
A
B
C
D
1
2
3
4
5
St. Agnes Gate
Gore Gate
DEER PARK
Crown Gate West
Gate East
Skew Bridge
GROVE ROAD
Health Centre
WATERLOO EST
Sch
Comm Cen
LONDON CHEST HOSP
SEWARDSTONE ROAD
The Royal Cricketers PH
OLD FORD
ROYAL VICTOR PL
CHISENHALE RD
VIVIAN RD
ZEALAND ROAD
ELLESMERE ROAD
DRIFFIELD ROAD
HEWLETT RD
DALING WAY
ROMAN ROAD
CAMBRIDGE HEATH
BISHOPS B127
BONNER
ST JAMES AV
CRANBROOK EST
MACE ST
Sports Cen
MUS OF CHILDHOOD
Fire Sta
Pol
ALLOT
MEATH GARDENS
REGENT'S CANAL
HAVERF. RD
CORDOVA RD
ANTILL
CHERRYWOOD CLO
LICHFIELD
MORGAN
ABERAVON RD
RHONDDA GRO
COLLTER
SQUARE
E2
BETHNAL GREEN
Lib
BETHNAL GRN GDNS
CORNWALL AVE
BANCROFT RD
GRANTLEY
MILE END
MILE END ROAD
LONDON HOSPITAL (Mile End)
Queen Mary College (Uni of Lon)
Coll
WESTFIELD WAY
BURDETT ROAD
MILE END
MALCOLM RD
WICKFORD ST
A107
CEPHAS ST
CAMBRIDGE HEATH ROAD
STEPNEY GRN
OCEAN EST
Amb Sta
SOLEBAY
HARFORD ST
COMMODORE
REC GRD
ESSIAN ST
Gas Works
Comm Centre
DUCKETT ST
SHANDY
LONDON INDEP HOSP
STEPNEY GREEN
A11
MILE END RD
ADELINA GRO
REDMAN'S
Schs
SMITHY STREET
CLICHY EST
LINDLEY ST
STEPNEY
STEPNEY GREEN
STEPNEY WAY
JAMAICA ST
NEWARK ST
SIDNEY
CLARK ST
MUSBURY ST
JUBILEE
WALTER TER
BROMLEY
BELGRAVE ST
B127
REC GRD
MAROON FLDS EST
LIMEHOUSE
JONSON B140 RD
HALLEY ST
MIDLOTHIAN RD
MILE END STAD
Pav
RHODESWELL
CHUDLEIGH ST
AVIS SQ
LATHAM HO
E1
COMMERCIAL ROAD
Half Moon Theatre
WHITE HORSE RD
YORKSHIRE RD
A13
LIMEHOUSE
LIMEHOUSE BASIN
LIMEHOUSE
TARLING ST EST
DAY HOSP
Health Cen
SHADWELL
MARTHA ST
MARTINEAU EST
Health Cen
Fire Sta
TOWN HALL
Comm Cem
THE HIGHWAY
GLAMIS PLACE
A1203
NARROW
HORSEFERRY
JARDINE RD
Ratcliffe

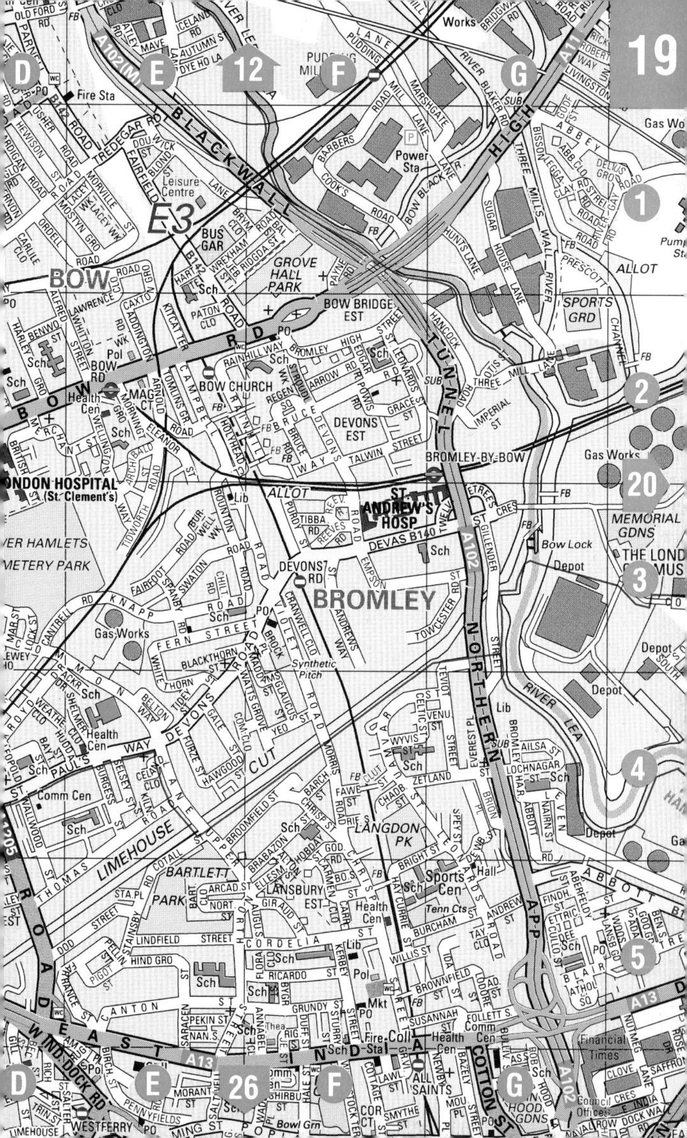

12
20
26
D
E
F
G
1
2
3
4
5
E3
BOW
BROMLEY
BLACKWALL TUNNEL
NORTHERN APP
BOW RD
GROVE HALL PARK
BOW BRIDGE EST
DEVONS EST
LANGDON PK
BARTLETT PARK
LANSBURY EST
LIMEHOUSE CUT
EAST INDIA DOCK RD
RIVER LEA
BOW CHURCH
BROMLEY-BY-BOW
DEVONS RD
ALL SAINTS
WESTFERRY
LONDON HOSPITAL (St. Clement's)
ST. ANDREW'S HOSP
TOWER HAMLETS CEMETERY PARK
MEMORIAL GDNS
Power Sta
Gas Works
Bow Lock
Sports Cen
Leisure Centre
BUS GAR
Fire Sta
Financial Times
Council Offices
ROBIN HOOD GDNS

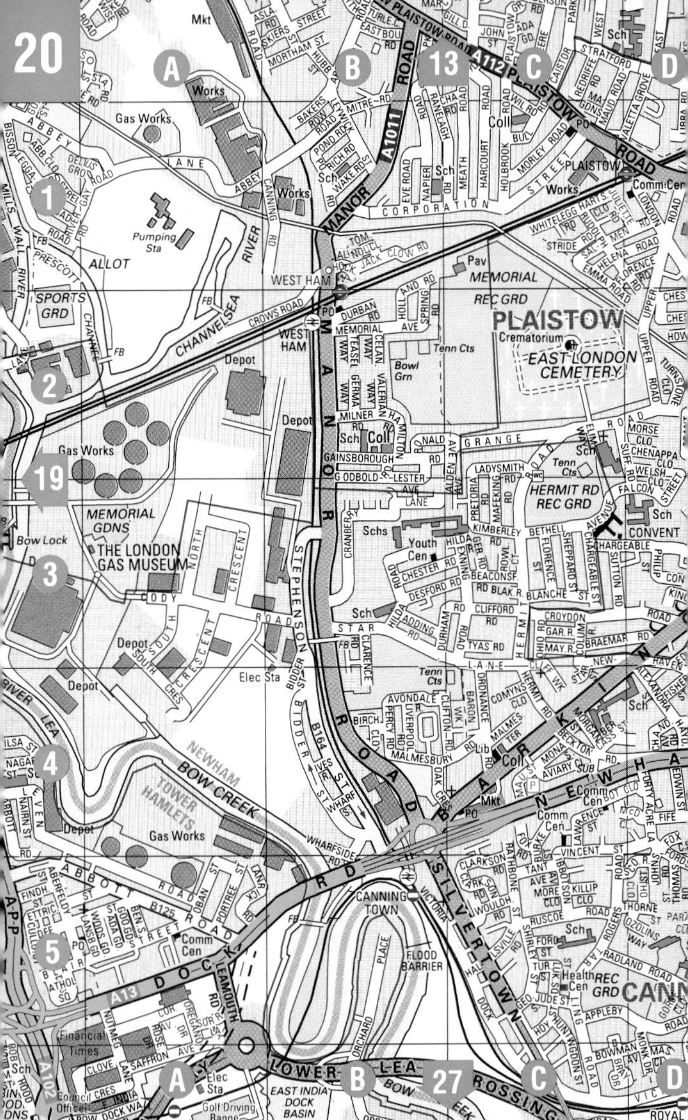

20
A
B
13
C
D
1
2
3
4
5
19
27
Mkt
Works
Gas Works
ABBEY LANE
Pumping Sta
ALLOT
PRESCOTT
SPORTS GRD
CHANNELSEA
CHANNELSEA RIVER
CROWS ROAD
WEST HAM
MANOR ROAD
A1011
NEW PLAISTOW ROAD
A112
PLAISTOW ROAD
CORPORATION
MEMORIAL REC GRD
PLAISTOW
Crematorium
EAST LONDON CEMETERY
Pav
Tenn Cts
Bowl Grn
Depot
Gas Works
MEMORIAL GDNS
Bow Lock
THE LONDON GAS MUSEUM
CODY ROAD
NORTH CRESCENT
SOUTH CRESCENT
STEPHENSON
Depot
Elec Sta
RIVER LEA
NEWHAM
TOWER HAMLETS
BOW CREEK
Gas Works
Depot
ABBOTT ROAD
B125
B164
WHARFSIDE RD
DOCK RD
A13
CANNING TOWN
FLOOD BARRIER
SILVERTOWN
VICTORIA
LEAMOUTH RD
LOWER LEA CROSSING
EAST INDIA DOCK BASIN
Golf Driving Range
Financial Times
Council Offices
A102
ORCHARD PLACE
HERMIT RD REC GRD
GRANGE ROAD
BARKING ROAD
NEWHAM WAY
STAR LANE
REC GRD
CANNING
ROYAL VICTORIA
CONVENT
Sch
Coll
Youth Cen
Comm Cen
Health Cen
Lib
PO

D
E
13
F
G
UPTON PARK
PRIORY PARK
E13
PLAISTOW HOSP
WEST HAM UTD FC
BARKING ROAD
A124
1
BROADGATE
A112
GREENGATE STREET
CENTRAL PARK ROAD
B167
CASTLE PT
JACOBS HO
HALDANE RD
2
PRINCE REGENT LANE
BOUNDARY ROAD
LONSDALE
21
NEWHAM GENERAL HOSPITAL
Comm Cen
Sch
Sports Cen
PLAYING FIELD
3
PLAYING FIELDS
TERENCE MCMILLAN STADIUM
NEWHAM WAY
EAST HAM IND PK
BECKTON DISTRICT PARK NORTH
A13
HOLBORN ROAD
CHADWIN ROAD
TOLLGATE ROAD
4
CANNING TOWN REC GRD
Works
BECKTON
CUSTOM HOUSE
KING GEORGE V PARK
Newham City Farm
5
TOWN
Will Thorne Pav
ROYAL ROAD
ALLOTMENTS
ALLOT
DOCK ROAD
The Flying Angel PH
E
27
F
G
ROYAL ALBERT WAY
CUSTOM HOUSE
PRINCE REGENT
BUS STA
ROYAL ALBERT
Warehouse

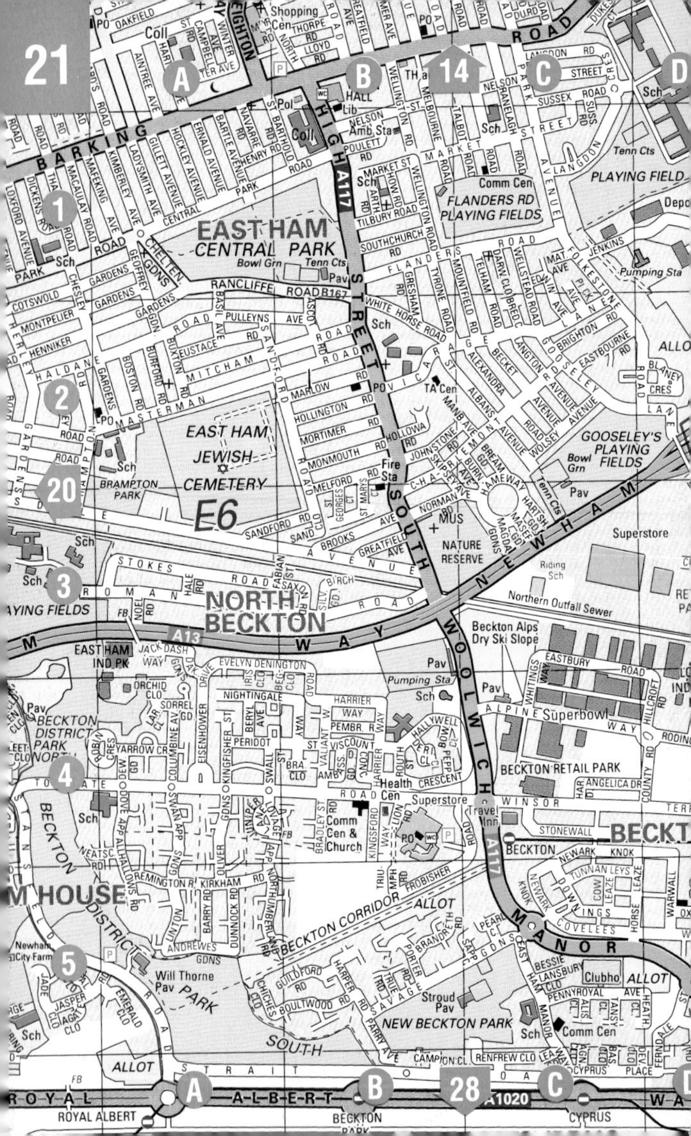

BARKING ROAD
EAST HAM CENTRAL PARK
Bowl Grn
Tenn Cts
Pav
RANCLIFFE ROAD B167
HIGH STREET SOUTH
A117
FLANDERS RD PLAYING FIELDS
Comm Cen
WHITE HORSE ROAD
VICARAGE LANE
GOOSELEY'S PLAYING FIELDS
Pumping Sta
PLAYING FIELD
Depot
EAST HAM JEWISH CEMETERY
E6
BRAMPTON PARK
NATURE RESERVE
MUS
TA Cen
Fire Sta
Superstore
Riding Sch
Northern Outfall Sewer
NEWHAM WAY
A13
NORTH BECKTON
ROMAN ROAD
STOKES ROAD
EAST HAM IND PK
Beckton Alps Dry Ski Slope
EASTBURY ROAD
ALPINE WAY
Superbowl
BECKTON RETAIL PARK
WINSOR TERR
BECKTON DISTRICT PARK NORTH
Health Cen
Comm Cen & Church
Travel Inn
BECKTON
WOOLWICH MANOR WAY
A117
BECKTON CORRIDOR
ALLOT
M HOUSE DISTRICT PARK
Newham City Farm
Will Thorne Pav
NEW BECKTON PARK
Stroud Pav
Clubho
SOUTH STRAIT ROAD
ROYAL ALBERT WAY
A1020
ROYAL ALBERT
BECKTON PARK
CYPRUS
14
20
28
A
B
C
D
1
2
3
4
5

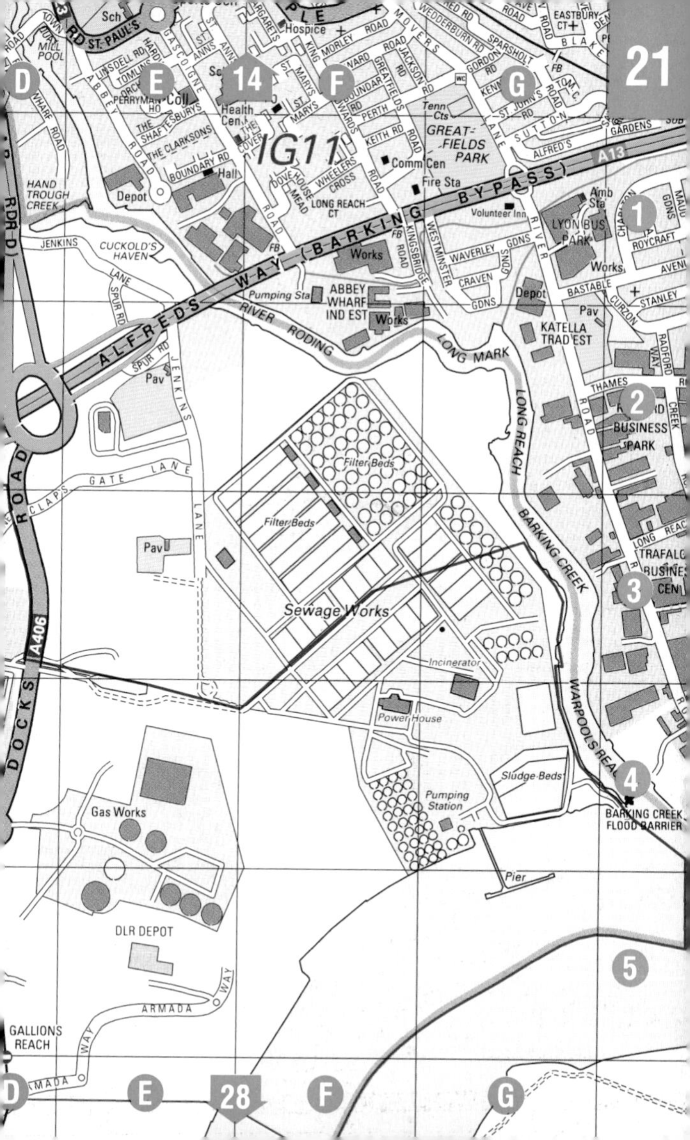

21
14
28
D
E
F
G
1
2
3
4
5
IG11
ALFREDS WAY (BARKING BYPASS)
A13
A406
DOCKS ROAD
RIVER RODING
LONG REACH
BARKING CREEK
WARPOOLS REACH
LONG MARK
Sewage Works
Filter Beds
Incinerator
Power House
Pumping Station
Sludge Beds
Pier
Gas Works
DLR DEPOT
ARMADA WAY
GALLIONS REACH
BARKING CREEK FLOOD BARRIER
CLAPS GATE LANE
JENKINS LANE
HAND TROUGH CREEK
CUCKOLD'S HAVEN
ABBEY WHARF IND EST
KATELLA TRAD EST
LYON BUSINESS PARK
GREATFIELDS PARK
Volunteer Inn
Fire Sta
Comm Cen
Health Cen
Hospice
Depot
Works
Pav
Hall
Coll
Pumping Sta

WORMWOOD SCRUBS
EAST ACTON
A
B
15
C
D
1
2
3
4
5
AVENUE
WESTWAY
A40
Superstore
EAST ACTON
BROMYARD AVE SPORTS GRD
SPORTS GRD
GOVT BLDGS
WORMHOLT PARK
Sports Cen
CLEVERLY ESTATE
W12
ACTON PARK
THE VALE
A4020
UXBRIDGE
ACTON PARK IND EST
ALLIED IND EST
Sewage Works
WENDELL PARK
Tennis Courts
BEDFORD PARK
GOLDHAWK
RAVENSCOURT PARK
ROYAL MASONIC HOSP
QUEEN CHARLOTTE'S HOSP
Amb Sta
STAMFORD BROOK
ACTON GREEN COMN
TURNHAM GREEN
CHISWICK COMN
BUS DEPOT
KING
A315
CHISWICK HIGH
RD
Health Cen
CONVENT
RAVENSCOURT PARK
A
B
29
C
D
W4

NORTH KENSINGTON
NOTTING HILL
SHEPHERD'S BUSH
W11
W14
W6
BBC TV Centre
BBC Office s
WHITE CITY
Daytona Raceway
LATIMER ROAD
WEST CROSS ROUTE
M41
A40(M)
A40
HOLLAND PARK
HOLLAND ROAD
SHEPHERD'S BUSH COMMON
SHEPHERD'S BUSH GRN
GOLDHAWK ROAD
A219
SHEPHERD'S BUSH ROAD
LRT DEPOT
Indoor Tennis Club
KENSINGTON (OLYMPIA)
OLYMPIA
Post Office Savings Bank
A315
A3220
BROOK GREEN
HAMMERSMITH ROAD
Hammersmith & West London College
Novotel
A4
TALGARTH ROAD
BARONS COURT
AVONDALE PARK
HENRY DICKENS COURT
Hammersmith London College
SHEP. BUSH EMPIRE
AFRICA
HAMMERSMITH PARK
ADDISON
15
23
29
D
E
F
G
1
2
3
4
5

16
22
30
A
B
C
D
1
2
3
4
5
W2
W8
SW5
NOTTING HILL
BAYSWATER
KENSINGTON
HOLLAND PARK
HOLLAND HOUSE
Open Air Theatre
ICE HOUSE
YHA
KENSINGTON PALACE
COURT DRESS COLLECTION
Russian Federation
KENSINGTON & CHELSEA
WESTMINSTER
KENS GAR
King's College
COMMONWEALTH INST
LEIGHTON HO MUS
Linley Sambourne Ho
Tennis Cts
LADBROKE SQUARE GARDENS
NOTTING HILL GATE
HOLLAND PARK
BAYSWATER
QUEENSWAY
HIGH ST KEN.
EARLS COURT
SOUTH KENSINGTON
CROMWELL HOSP
Copthorne Tara Hotel
Swallow Int
Forum Hotel
Whiteleys
Black Lion Gate
Orme Sq Gate
Inverness Terrace Gate
Vicarage Gate
GREEK CATHED
CHARLES HO
BURNE JONES HO
NORTH END HOUSE
Mac Owen Thea
OLYMPIA
A40
A4
A315
A4206
A4204
A3220
B450
B415
B411
BAYSWATER RD
NOTTING HILL GATE
HOLLAND PARK AVE
KENSINGTON CHURCH ST
KENSINGTON HIGH ST
KENSINGTON PARK RD
PEMBRIDGE VILLAS
PEMBRIDGE RD
PEMBRIDGE SQUARE
LADBROKE GROVE
WESTBOURNE GROVE
KENSINGTON PALACE GARDENS
CAMPDEN HILL
ADDISON RD
WARWICK GDNS
PEMBROKE RD
EARLS COURT RD
CROMWELL RD
WEST CROMWELL RD
NORTH END RD
BROMPTON RD

D
E
16
F
G
HYDE PARK
THE SERPENTINE
THE LONG WATER
BIRD SANCTUARY
OXFORD STREET where marked is closed to through traffic (except buses & taxis) from 7a.m.-7p.m. Monday - Saturday.
SPEAKER'S CORNER
MARBLE ARCH
Cumberland Hotel
Royal Lancaster Hotel
LANCASTER GATE
Victoria Gate
Marlborough Gate
The Fountains
Lancaster Gate
BUDGE'S WALK
Peter Pan
Physical Energy Statue
SERPENTINE GALLERY
Grosvenor House Hotel
Fountain
Dorchester Hotel
Bandstand
24
Pier
SERPENTINE ROAD
The Lido
Clubhouse
Weir
ROTTEN ROW
CYCLE PATH
Bowling Grn
Tennis Cts
Prince of Wales Gate
Rutland Gate
NEW RIDE
Edinburgh Gate
Albert Gate
Albert Memorial
Alexandra Gate
Coalbrookdale Gate
SOUTH CARRIAGE DRIVE
Barracks
HYDE PARK CORNER
KENSINGTON GORE
KNIGHTSBRIDGE
SW7
ROYAL ALBERT HALL
Roy. Geog. Soc.
Royal College of Music
Imperial College
Queen's Tower
Goethe Institut
VICTORIA & ALBERT MUSEUM
SCIENCE MUS
NAT. HISTORY MUS
EARTH GALLERIES
BADEN-POWELL HO
HARRODS
BROMPTON
SOUTH KENSINGTON
SW3
ROYAL MARSDEN HOSP
ROYAL BROMPTON HOSP
SLOANE SQ
Duke of York's Headquarters
A40
A4202
A4
A3216
A3217
A3218
1
2
3
4
5
D
E
30
F
G

17
A
B
C
D
1
2
3
4
5
23
31
OXFORD CIRCUS
SOHO
W1
MAYFAIR
MARBLE ARCH
PARK LANE
Grosvenor House Hotel
Dorchester Hotel
Hilton Hotel
Metropolitan Hotel
Hotel Inter-Continental
WELLINGTON MUS
HYDE PK COR
HYDE PARK CORNER
Wellington Arch
Albert Gate
Roosevelt Memorial
USA
Canada
Italy
Sotheby's
HAMLEYS
LIBERTY
Palladium
Virgin Radio
Regent Palace Hotel
Trocadero
Eros
PICCADILLY CIRCUS
ROYAL ACAD. OF ARTS
N Ireland Tourist Info Board
Saudi Arabia
Japan
GREEN PARK
Spencer Ho
Bandstand
Lancaster House
St. James's Palace
Clarence Ho
MARLBOROUGH HOUSE
Christie's
ST JAMES'S
ST. JAMES'S PARK
Queen Victoria Memorial
CONSTITUTION HILL
BUCKINGHAM PALACE GARDENS
BUCKINGHAM PALACE
QUEEN'S GALLERY
GUARDS MUS
Wellington Barracks
HOME OFF
CAXTON HALL
THE ROYAL MEWS
WESTMINSTER
WESTMINSTER CATH
Victoria Palace Thea
Apollo Victoria Thea
BUS STA
VICTORIA
SW1
OLD RHS HALL
PLAYING FIELDS
GORDON HOSP
BELGRAVIA
Portugal
Germany
Spain
Belgium
Ireland
KNIGHTSBRIDGE
SLOANE STREET
SLOANE SQ
Duke of York's Headquarters
VICTORIA COACH STA
ECCLESTON ST
BELGRAVE ROAD
VAUXHALL BR RD
PIMLICO
A4
A4201
A4202
A302
A3216
A3217
A3213
B324

17
25
31
D
E
F
G
1
2
3
4
5
STRAND
WC2
SE11
LAMBETH
COVENT GDN
Covent Gdn Mkt
ROYAL OPERA HO
Freemasons Hall
ROYAL COURTS OF JUSTICE
City Lit. Inst
FLEET ST
The Temple
EMBANKMENT
VICTORIA
HQS WELLINGTON
HMS PRESIDENT
TEMPLE
SOMERSET HO
King's Coll
Savoy Hotel
Strand Palace Hotel
LANCASTER PL
WATERLOO BRI
BLACKFRIARS BRI
Oxo Tower
The London Television Centre
National Theatre
QUEEN ELIZABETH HALL
ROYAL FESTIVAL HALL
MOMI
HAYWARD GALLERY
Festival Pier
Cleopatra's Needle
Charing Cross Pier
CHARING CROSS
TRAFALGAR
NAT PORT GALL
NAT GALL
LEICESTER SQ
WILLIAM IV ST
NORTHUMBERLAND AVE
HUNGERFORD BRI
STAMFORD ST
Nautical Sch
Sports Cen
WATERLOO EAST
The Young Vic Theatre
Old Vic Theatre
WATERLOO
WATERLOO INTERNATIONAL
WATERLOO RD
YORK RD
Shell Centre
Old County Hall
PS TATTERSHALL CASTLE
WHITEHALL
ADMIRALTY ARCH
CIVIL SERV
MOD
Horse Guards Parade
Banqueting House
MAFF
CABINET OFF
DOWNING ST
FOREIGN OFFICE
Cenotaph
HM TREASURY
KING CHARLES ST
PARLIAMENT ST
Westminster Pier
WESTMINSTER
WESTMINSTER BRI
A302
A3211
A3036
A301
A201
A3204
B300
Big Ben
HOUSES OF PARLIAMENT
Victoria Tower
Burghers of Calais Mon
ABBEY
Jewel Twr
SANCTUARY
BROAD SANCTUARY
GT COLLEGE ST
MILLBANK
FLORENCE NIGHTINGALE MUS
ST. THOMAS' HOSPITAL
St. Thomas' Medical School
PALACE RD
LAMBETH PALACE GDNS
Lambeth Palace
Lambeth Pier
LAMBETH BRI
LAMBETH RD
SPORTS GRD
WESTMINSTER BRIDGE RD
LAMBETH NORTH
KENNINGTON RD
ST. GEORGE'S CATH
GER. MARY HARMSWORTH PARK
IMPERIAL WAR MUS
BROOK DRIVE
PEABODY SQ
GEORGES CIR
BOROUGH RD
THAMES HOUSE
HORSEFERRY RD
D.O.T.
MILLBANK TOWER
TATE GALLERY
Millbank Barracks
Novotel
LAMBETH WALK
Day Hosp
Health Cen
Nat. Army & Air Force Inst. Depot
WESTMINSTER
LAMBETH

A
B
C
D
18
EC4
ST. PAUL'S
Chapter Ho
ST. PAUL'S CATH
CHEAPSIDE
Mansion Ho
POULTRY
Bank of Eng
Royal Exch
THREADNEEDLE STREET
CORNHILL
City of London Coll
Stock Exch
LOTHBURY
A10
GRACECHURCH ST
CITY THAMESLINK
NEW BRI
LUDGATE
Info. Cen
Coll of Arms
QUEEN VICTORIA
MANSION HO
CANNON ST
Sal Army HQ
UPPER THAMES
London Stone
MONUMENT
The Monument
KING WILLIAM ST
EASTCHEAP
BLACKFRIARS
WHITE LION
TUDOR
Coll
1
Pier
RIVER
Southwark Bridge Steps
Sports Cen
Fire Sta
Swan Lane Pier
Offices
THAM
SOUTHWARK
CITY
BANKSIDE GALL
Shakespeare Globe Thea & Exhib
BANKSIDE
Oxo Tower
Express Newspapers
Power Sta (Disused)
SHAKESPEARE GLOBE MUS
Financial Times
PARK
CLINK
MUS
Glaziers Hall
LONDON BRIDGE HOSP
City Pier
Hay's Galleria
UPPER KING'S REACH TWR
SOUTHWARK
SOUTHWARK BRI
LONDON BRI
CATH
TOOLEY
2
Sports Cen
SUMNER
ST. CHRISTOPHER HOUSE
SOUTHWARK
THRALE
LAVINGTON ST
A3200
ROAD
Mkt
RAILWAY APP
LONDON BRI ST
OP THEA MUS
ST. THOMAS ST
LONDON BRIDGE
GUY'S HOSPITAL
Coll
BRIT LIB
UNION
B300 STREET
24
The Young Vic
Coll
Under Const
NELSON SQ
COPPERFIELD ST
Fire Sta & Mus
A300 BRIDGE
MARSHALSEA RD
Schs
HIGH
A3
NEWCOMEN
MERMAID CT
CORON
CT Lib
SNOWS FIELDS
GUY STREET
TYERS EST
Sch
MITRE RD
The Old Vic
3
A201
A301
ROAD
PEABODY SQ
THE BOROUGH
BOROUGH
A2
PORLOCK ST
LONG LANE
KIPLING EST
LEATHERMARKET
A2198
Leather Mkt
TABARD GDN EST
TABARD GARDENS
Sorting Office
GREAT DOVER STREET
BOROUGH ROAD
SOUTHWARK
BOROUGH
Uni Lib
ST. GEORGES CIR
BRIDGE RD
ST. GEORGES CATH
HOSP
INN. LON CROWN CT
Pol
4
LONDON RD
GEORGES ROAD
GARDEN ROW
NEWINGTON CAUSEWAY
NEWINGTON
TIVERTON STREET
ROCKINGHAM EST
Health Cen
Schs
Coll
Bricklayer's Arms
IMPERIAL WAR MUS
Health Cen
Coronet Centre
A201 NEW KENT ROAD
COUNTY STREET
ELEPHANT & CASTLE
Shop Cen
ELEPHANT & CASTLE
DEACON WAY
SEARLES ROAD
HENSHAW ST
Sports Cen
5
Health Cen
NEWINGTON BUTTS
WALWORTH
HEYGATE ST
BRANDON
SE17
Health Cen
LANE
ROAD
A3204
Lib
Health Cen
Sch
Pol
Nat. Army & Air Force Inst. Depot
KENNINGTON
ALBERTA EST
BROWNING EST
Depot
32
WALWORTH
Health Cen
TAPLOW
COUNTY

ALDGATE
MINORIES
PRESCOT ST
CABLE ST
SHADWELL
ROYAL MINT ST
DOCK ST
THE HIGHWAY
A1203
EAST SMITHFIELD
TOWER HILL
THE TOWER
Tower Pier
London Commodity Exchange
ST. KATHARINE'S DOCK
Ivory Ho
Tower Thistle Hotel
St. Katharine's Pier
Alderman Stairs
PENNINGTON STREET
News International
Tobacco Dock
WAPPING
Sports Cen
Tenn Cts
WAPPING
Wapping Dock Stairs
Wapping Old Stairs
Wapping New Stairs
TOWER BRI
A100
TOWER BRIDGE MUS & EXHIBITIONS
George's Stairs
THE UPPER POOL
LOWER POOL
DESIGN MUSEUM
TEA & COFFEE MUS
Mill Stairs
East Lane Stairs
Cherry Garden Pier
Fountain Stairs
King's Stairs
Princes Stairs
KING'S STAIRS GDNS
BERMONDSEY WALL
JAMAICA ROAD
A200
A2207
ABBEY STREET
BERMONDSEY
BERMONDSEY SPA
SOUTHWARK PARK ROAD
A2206
RAYMOUTH RD
A2208
SOUTHWARK PARK RD
SE16
Lido
TRADING EST
RENNIE EST
MANOR EST
LONGFIELD EST
Superstore
Offices
PATERSON PARK
SOUTH BERMONDSEY
1
2
3
4
5
E
F
G
18
26
32

COMMERCIAL
LIMEHOUSE
SHADWELL
THE HIGHWAY
A1203
CABLE STREET
MARTINEAU EST
WAPPING
Wapping Dock Stairs
New Crane Stairs
Prospect of Whitby PH
KING EDWARD MEML PARK
SHADWELL BASIN
TOWER HAMLETS
SOUTHWARK
ROTHERHITHE TUNNEL
Ratcliffe Cross Stairs
Stone Pier Stairs
The Grapes PH
Lavender Wharf
Sunderland Wharf
HERITAGE MUS
SPORTS GRD
ROTHERHITHE
SALTER ROAD
SURREY WATER
ECOLOGICAL PARK
STAVE HILL
RUSSIA DOCK WOODLAND
BRUNEL ROAD
ALBION EST
CANADA EST
CANADA WATER
Mail Newspapers Printing Wks
CANADA YARD SOUTH
Surrey Quays Shopping Centre
REDRIFF ROAD
GREENLAND DOCK
SOUTH DOCK
NORWAY DOCK
REDRIFF EST
LOWER ROAD
A200
SE16
SOUTHWARK PARK
SURREY QUAYS
HAWKSTONE ROAD
RAYMOUTH RD
A2208
TRADING EST
RENNIE EST
BESTWOOD STREET
CROFTERS COURT
EVELYN STREET
OXESTALLS ROAD
DEPOT
DEPTFORD
PLOUGH WAY
Princes Stairs
Amb Sta
Sports Cen
Lido
GALLERY

19
25
33

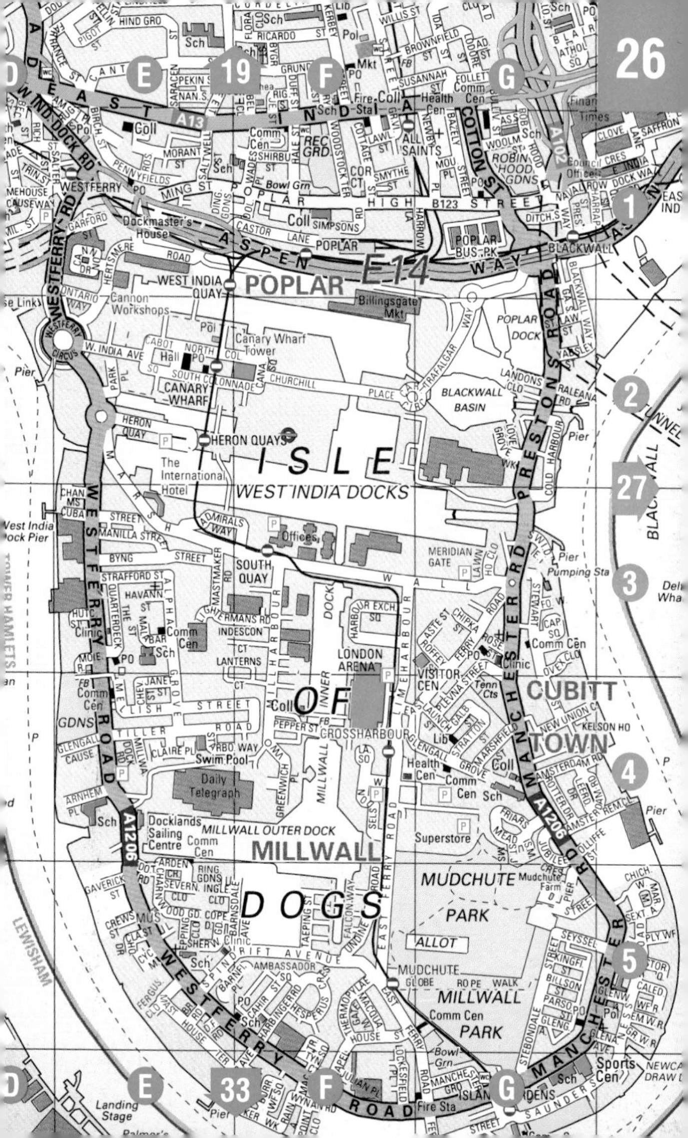
26
19
27
33
D
E
F
G
1
2
3
4
5
EAST INDIA DOCK RD
A13
WESTFERRY RD
WESTFERRY
WESTFERRY CIRCUS
HIND GRO
PIGOT ST
RICARDO ST
PEKIN ST
NAN. S
SARACEN ST
BIRCH ST
MORANT ST
PENNYFIELDS
MING ST
SALTWELL ST
LIMEHOUSE CAUSEWAY
GARFORD ST
Dockmaster's House
HERTSMERE ROAD
WEST INDIA QUAY
POPLAR
E14
ASPEN WAY
CASTOR LANE
POPLAR HIGH B123 STREET
SIMPSONS RD
REC GRD
Bowl Grn
ALL SAINTS
BROWNFIELD ST
SUSANNAH ST
FOLLETT ST
COTTON ST
ROBIN HOOD GDNS
WOOLMORE ST
Finan Times
A102
CLOVE CRES
SAFFRON
Council Offices
E INDIA DOCK WA
NAVAL ROW
BLACKWALL
POPLAR BUS PK
Billingsgate Mkt
Cannon Workshops
ONTARIO WAY
Canary Wharf Tower
CABOT SQ
W. INDIA AVE
NORTH COL.
SOUTH COLONNADE
CANARY WHARF
CHURCHILL PLACE
TRAFALGAR WAY
BLACKWALL BASIN
POPLAR DOCK
PRESTONS ROAD
BLACKWALL WAY
YABSLEY ST
LANDONS CLO
RALEANA RD
HERON QUAY
HERON QUAYS
The International Hotel
ISLE
WEST INDIA DOCKS
COLD HARBOUR
LOVEGROVE WK
Pier
BLACKWALL TUNNEL
West India Dock Pier
CUBA STREET
MANILLA STREET
BYNG STREET
ADMIRALS WAY
Offices
SOUTH QUAY
MASTMAKER RD
MERIDIAN GATE
Pumping Sta
MARSH WALL
STRAFFORD ST
HAVANNAH ST
QUARTERDECK
Clinic
Comm Cen
LIGHTERMANS RD
INDESCON CT
LANTERNS CT
MILLHARBOUR
HARBOUR EXCH. SQ
LONDON ARENA
LIMEHARBOUR
VISITOR CEN
CHIPKA ST
PLEVNA STREET
Tenn Cts
MANCHESTER RD
CUBITT TOWN
NEW UNION CL
KELSON HO
OF
INNER
MILLWALL
CROSSHARBOUR
PEPPER ST
MELLISH STREET
TILLER ROAD
GLENGALL CAUSE
CLAIRE PL
Swim Pool
ARBO. WAY
GLENGALL GROVE
MARSHFIELD ST
AMSTERDAM RD
Health Cen
Daily Telegraph
Superstore
ARNHEM PL
Docklands Sailing Centre
MILLWALL OUTER DOCK
MILLWALL
A1206
EAST FERRY ROAD
MUDCHUTE
Mudchute Farm
PARK
DOGS
ALLOT
GAVERICK ST
CREWS ST
SEVERN
TAEPING ST
FALCON WAY
UNDINE
DRIFT AVENUE
AMBASSADOR SQ
HESPERUS CRES
SPINDRIFT
MUDCHUTE
GLOBE ROPE WALK
MILLWALL PARK
Comm Cen
SEYSSEL
STEBONDALE
PIER STREET
THERMOPYLAE GATE
MACQUARIE
HOUSE ST
LOCKESFIELD
WESTFERRY
HARBINGER RD
CAHIR ST
HOUSE TER
ROAD
Fire Sta
ISLAND GARDENS
SAUNDERS
Sports Cen
Landing Stage
LEWISHAM
TOWER HAMLETS

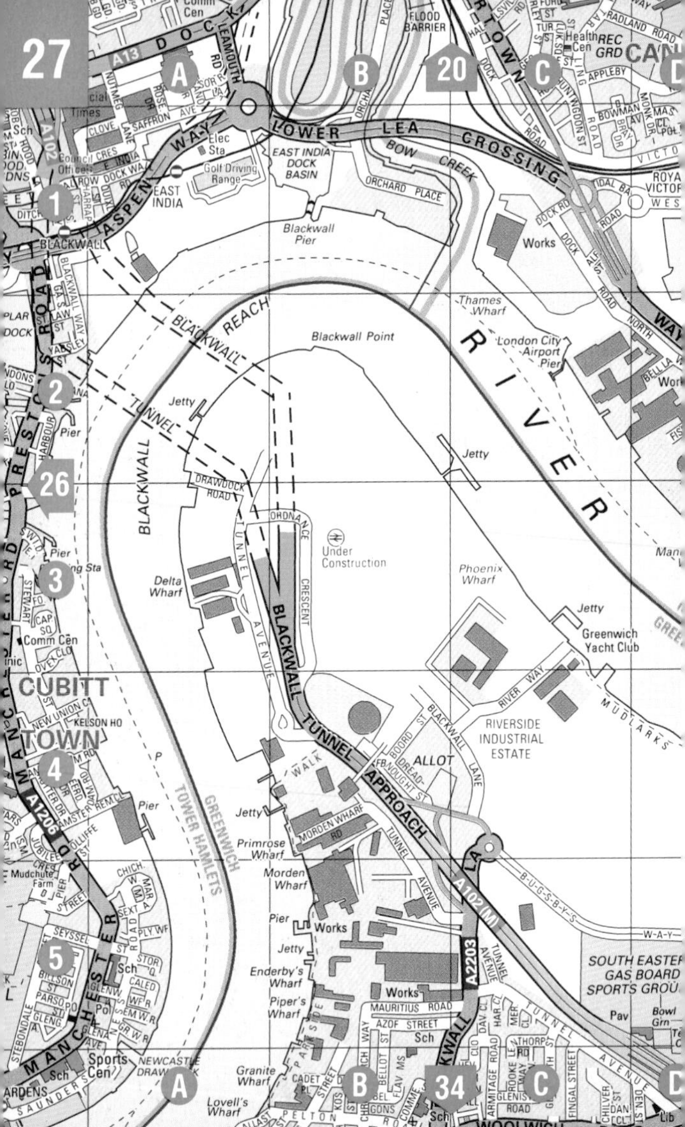

A
B
C
D
1
2
3
4
5
20
26
34
DOCK
A13
LEAMOUTH RD
NUTMEG LANE
ROSE DR
SAFFRON AVE
CLOVE CRES
E. INDIA DOCK WALL RD
ASPEN WAY
Elec Sta
Golf Driving Range
EAST INDIA
BLACKWALL
LOWER LEA CROSSING
EAST INDIA DOCK BASIN
BOW CREEK
ORCHARD PLACE
FLOOD BARRIER
Blackwall Pier
Works
Thames Wharf
RIVER
London City Airport Pier
BLACKWALL REACH
BLACKWALL TUNNEL
Blackwall Point
Jetty
Pier
BLACKWALL
DRAWDOCK ROAD
TUNNEL AVENUE
ORDNANCE CRESCENT
Under Construction
Phoenix Wharf
Greenwich Yacht Club
Delta Wharf
BLACKWALL TUNNEL APPROACH
RIVER WAY
BLACKWALL LANE
RIVERSIDE INDUSTRIAL ESTATE
ALLOT
BOORD ST
DREADNOUGHT ST
MUDLARKS
CUBITT TOWN
KELSON HO
NEW UNION CL
Comm Cen
STEWART
CAP SQ
OVEX CLO
TOWER HAMLETS
GREENWICH
MORDEN WHARF RD
Primrose Wharf
Morden Wharf
Enderby's Wharf
Piper's Wharf
Granite Wharf
Lovell's Wharf
A102(M)
A2203
BUGSBY'S WAY
SOUTH EASTERN GAS BOARD SPORTS GROUND
MAURITIUS ROAD
AZOF STREET
Sch
TUNNEL AVENUE
ARMITAGE ROAD
FINGAL STREET
WOOLWICH ROAD
PELTON
Pav
Bowl Grn
Lib
Mudchute Farm
JUBILEE CRES
SEYSSEL ST
MANCHESTER RD
A1206
PRESTONS ROAD
Sports Cen
NEWCASTLE DRAW DOCK
SAUNDERS
STEBONDALE
RADLAND ROAD
REC GRD
APPLEBY
HUNTINGDON ST
Health Cen
DOCK RD
NORTH WAY

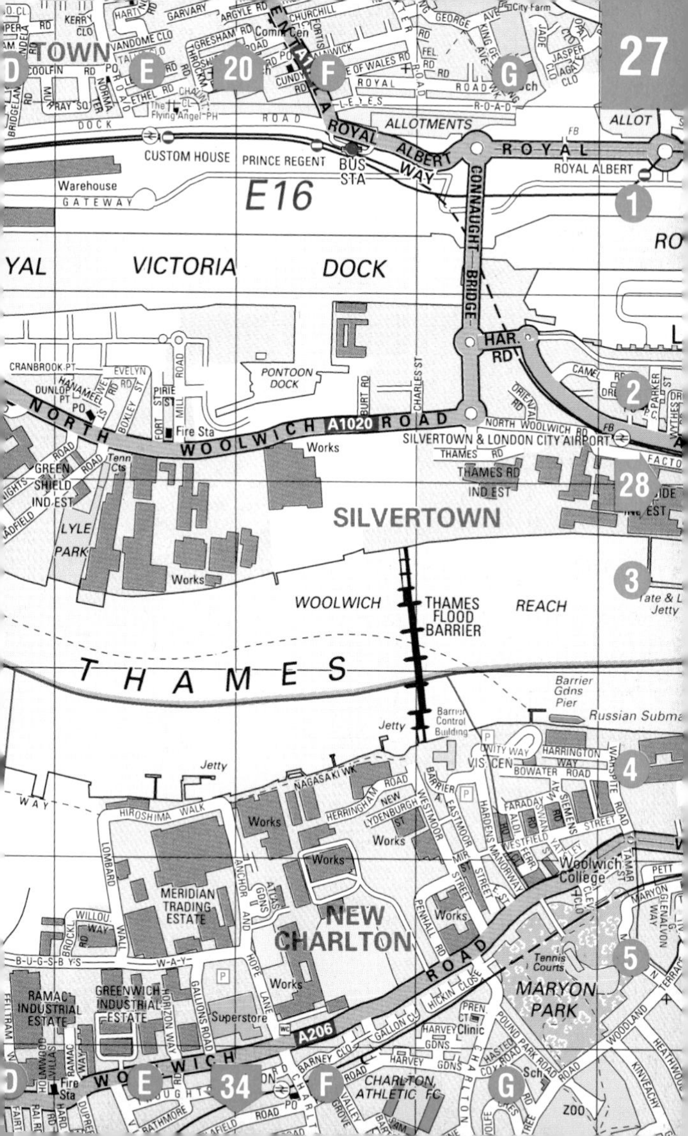

27
TOWN
KERRY CLO
GARVARY RD
ARGYLE RD
CHURCHILL
Comm Cen
GRESHAM RD
VANDOME CLO
COOLFIN RD
MURRAY SQ
ETHEL RD
The Flying Angel PH
DOCK ROAD
CUNDY RD
ROYAL ROAD
LEYES ROAD
GEORGE AVE
City Farm
JADE CLO
JASPER RD
AGATE CLO
ALLOTMENTS
ALLOT
CUSTOM HOUSE
PRINCE REGENT
BUS STA
ROYAL ALBERT WAY
ROYAL
ROYAL ALBERT
Warehouse
GATEWAY
E16
CONNAUGHT BRIDGE
YAL VICTORIA DOCK
RO
HAR. RD
CRANBROOK PT
EVELYN
DUNLOP PT
HANAMEEL ST
PO
BOXLEY ST
PIRIE ST
MILL ROAD
FORT ST
Fire Sta
PONTOON DOCK
BURT RD
CHARLES ST
CAMEL RD
ORIENTAL RD
PARKER ST
WYTHES RD
NORTH WOOLWICH A1020 ROAD
NORTH WOOLWICH RD
SILVERTOWN & LONDON CITY AIRPORT
FB
THAMES RD
THAMES RD IND EST
Works
Tenn Cts
GREEN SHIELD IND EST
LYLE PARK
SILVERTOWN
28
WOOLWICH
THAMES FLOOD BARRIER
REACH
Tate & Lyle Jetty
THAMES
Barrier Gdns Pier
Russian Submarine
Barrier Control Building
Jetty
UNITY WAY
HARRINGTON WAY
VIS. CEN
BOWATER ROAD
WARSPITE ROAD
NAGASAKI WK
HERRINGHAM ROAD
NEW LYDENBURGH ST
BARRIER APP
WESTMOOR
EASTMOOR
HARDENS MANORWAY
FARADAY WAY
SIEMENS RD
SWAN
WESTFIELD ST
YATELEY ST
Woolwich College
TAMAR ST
PETT
MARYON WAY
GLENALVON WAY
HIROSHIMA WALK
LOMBARD WALL
MERIDIAN TRADING ESTATE
ANCHOR AND HOPE LANE
ATLAS GDNS
NEW CHARLTON
MIR STREET
PENHALL RD
Tennis Courts
MARYON PARK
WILLOUGHBY WAY
BUGSBY'S WAY
RAMAC INDUSTRIAL ESTATE
GREENWICH INDUSTRIAL ESTATE
HORIZON WAY
GALLIONS ROAD
Superstore
A206
WOOLWICH ROAD
HICKIN CLOSE
PREN. CT
Clinic
HARVEY GDNS
GALLON CL
BARNEY CLO
POUND PARK ROAD
HASTED ROAD
WOODLAND
HEATHWOOD
KINVEACHY
TERRACE
FELLTRAM WAY
RAMAC WAY
Fire Sta
HOLMWOOD VILLAS
CHARLTON ATHLETIC FC
VALLEY GROVE
Sch
ZOO
D
E
F
G
20
34
1
2
3
4
5

ROYAL ALBERT WAY
A1020
ROYAL ALBERT
BECKTON PARK
CYPRUS
ROYAL ALBERT DOCK
LONDON CITY AIRPORT
KING GEORGE V DOCK
TERMINAL BUILDINGS
Warehouses
ALBERT ROAD
A101
NORTH WOOLWICH
THAMESIDE IND EST
STANDARD IND EST
FACTORY ROAD
PIER RD
A117
ROYAL VICTORIA GDNS
North Woolwich Pier
Woolwich Ferry Pier
WOOLWICH FOOT TUNNEL
Tate & Lyle Jetty
REACH
NEWHAM
GREENWICH
WOOLWICH FREE FERRY
Barrier Gdns Pier
Russian Submarine
SE London Aquatic Cen
South Pontoon
WOOLWICH DOCKYARD IND EST
NEW FERRY APP
WOOLWICH CHURCH STREET
WOOLWICH HIGH ST
JOHN WILSON ST
Woolwich College
WOOLWICH DOCKYARD
MARYON PARK
MULGRAVE POND
ARTILLERY PLACE
Barracks
WELLINGTON
Uni of Greenwich
TOWN HALL
WOOLWICH
HILLREACH B210
GREENHILL
ZOO
21
27
35
A
B
C
D
1
2
3
4
5

21
35
SE28
THAMESMEAD WEST
HM PRISON BELMARSH
BROADWATER GREEN
GALLIONS REACH
PLUMSTEAD ROAD
A206
A2016
WESTERN WAY
PETTMAN CRES
BUS GARAGE
PLUMSTEAD
PLUMSTEAD HIGH
Motor Cross Track
Coll
Pier
Health Cen
Sch
Tenn Cts
Works
Southern Outfall Sewer
NATHAN WAY
HADDEN ROAD
KELLNER WAY
BOUGHTON RD
TOM CRIBB ROAD
BROADWATER
WAREPOINT DRIVE
MERBURY RD
BOAT ST
BATTERY ROAD
TUG RD
GOLDFINCH RD
GOLDFINCH ROAD
WHINCHAT ROAD
NUT HATCH GDN
HARR
WIG PATH
WREN PATH
AVOCET MS
CAMELOT CL
TEMPLE CL
PIER WAY
CARROL PLACE
GOOSANDER WAY
GRIFF MANORWAY
Woolwich Coll of F.E.
JESSUP CLO
MAXEY ROAD
PERROTT ST
POLTHORNE GRO
LENTON ST
BURRAGE GRO
WALKER CLO
WALMER TERRACE
RICHMOND PLACE
INVERMORE
ARTHUR GROVE
DAWSON CLOSE
GLYNDON
VILLAS ROAD
SOUTHPORT ROAD
RISE
STREET
EARL
ELMLEY
CONWAY
COXWELL RD
INGLEDEW RD
LIFFLER ROAD
MIRIAM ROAD
ORISSA RD
GALLOSS ROAD
MINERAL STREET
HECTOR ST
REIDHAVEN RD
GAVIN ST
HEVER
GUNN
PO ST
HARTVILLE
KENTMER RD
WHITE
BARTH
BANNOCKBURN ROAD
MARMADON
BENARES
CERES
NORTH ROAD
HART ROAD
Fire Sta
TEWSON ROAD
Pol
Lib
MUS
Health Cen
Sports Cen
HAWKSM
QUILT ST
SPERANZ ST
Sch
Schs
Comm Cen
PO
SANDBACH PLACE
RAGLAN ROAD
CLAYMILL HOUSE
HUDSON PLACE
BREWERY
MAJENDIE ROAD
BURRAGE
PARRY PL
Mkt
STREET
VIN RD
TROY CT
CLOSE
RUDD
ROAD
ORC RD
ARMADA WAY
GALLIONS REACH
ROAD
ALBERT BASIN
D
E
F
G
1
2
3
4
5

22
36
W4
SW13
CHISWICK
CASTELNAU
BARNES
CHISWICK HIGH RD
KING ST
GREAT WEST RD
HOGARTH LA
BURLINGTON LANE
ALEXANDRA AVE
CHISWICK LA
Hogarth Roundabout
CHISWICK LODGE
CHISWICK HOUSE GROUNDS
CHISWICK HOUSE
HOGARTH'S HOUSE
CORNEY RD CEM
CHISWICK EYOT
CHISWICK WHARF
LEG OF MUTTON NATURE RESERVE
PLAYING FIELD
RIVERSIDE REC GRD
CIVIL SERVICE SPORTS GROUND
FULLERS SPORTS GRD
Riverside Racquet Centre
MEADOW
HOMEFIELD REC GRD
LONSDALE RD
CASTELNAU
ROCKS LANE
CHURCH RD
BARNES HIGH ST
THE TERRACE
BARNES BRIDGE
HIGH STREET
HOUNSLOW
RICHMOND UPON THAMES
A315
A316
A306
A3003
B350
B349
MILL HILL
Swimming Pool
Brewery
Hospice
Temple
Obelisk
Boathouse
Pavilion
Clubhouse
Health Cen
BARNES GREEN
Wharves

HAMMERSMITH
HAMMERSMITH FLYOVER
TALGARTH ROAD
BARONS COURT
HAMMERSMITH CEMETERY
THE QUEEN'S CLUB
CHARING CROSS HOSP
Hammersmith & West London College
Novotel
HAMMERSMITH APOLLO
RIVERSIDE STUDIOS
FRANK BANFIELD PARK
LILLIE ROAD
LILLIE RD REC GRD
DAWES RD
FULHAM CEM
FULHAM
FULHAM PALACE RD
CRAVEN COTTAGE FULHAM FC
BISHOP'S PARK
ALLOTMENTS
Fulham Palace
FULHAM PALACE GDNS
FULHAM HIGH ST
PUTNEY BRIDGE
RIVER
RICHMOND UPON THAMES
HAMMERSMITH & FULHAM
Wharves
Blakes Wharves
Eternit Wharf
Stevenage Wharves
QUEEN ELIZABETH WALK
Pavilions
Boathouse
BARN ELMS SCHOOLS SPORTS CENTRE
PUTNEY
PUTNEY HOSP
LOWER
Bowling Green
Warehouse
Works
A4
A219
A3218
A321
22
30
36
D
E
F
G
1
2
3
4
5

A
B
23
SW5
C
D
CROMWELL
A4
A3220
WEST
ROAD
WEST KENSINGTON
EARLS COURT
EARLS COURT EXHIBITION CENTRE
EARLS COURT GARDENS
EMPRESS STATE BUILDING
Earls Ct Intl Hotel
OLD BROMPTON RD
WEST BROMPTON
BROMPTON CEMETERY
KENSINGTON & CHELSEA
FINBOROUGH ROAD
REDCLIFFE
BROMPTON
COLEHERNE COURT
NORTH END ROAD
1
2
3
4
5
29
Holborn Coll
Swim Pool
NORMAND PARK
A3218
A3219
Comm Cen
Mkt
SAMUEL LEWIS TRUST DWS
STAMFORD BRIDGE CHELSEA FC
Stamford Bridge
FULHAM BROADWAY
FULHAM
FULH. BDY
A304
King's Coll
WALHAM GREEN
EEL BROOK COMMON
Gas Wor
PARSONS GRN
PARSONS GREEN
A308
SW6
WANDSWORTH
BRIDGE
A217
Fulham Info Cen
Fire Sta
Lib
YMCA
Clinic
ARTHUR HENDERSON HO
FULHAM PALACE
FULHAM HIGH ST
NEW KINGS ROAD
HURLINGHAM
HURLINGHAM PARK
SOUTH PARK
SULIVAN COURT
PUTNEY BRIDGE
37
HURLINGHAM COURT
HURLINGHAM CLUB GDNS

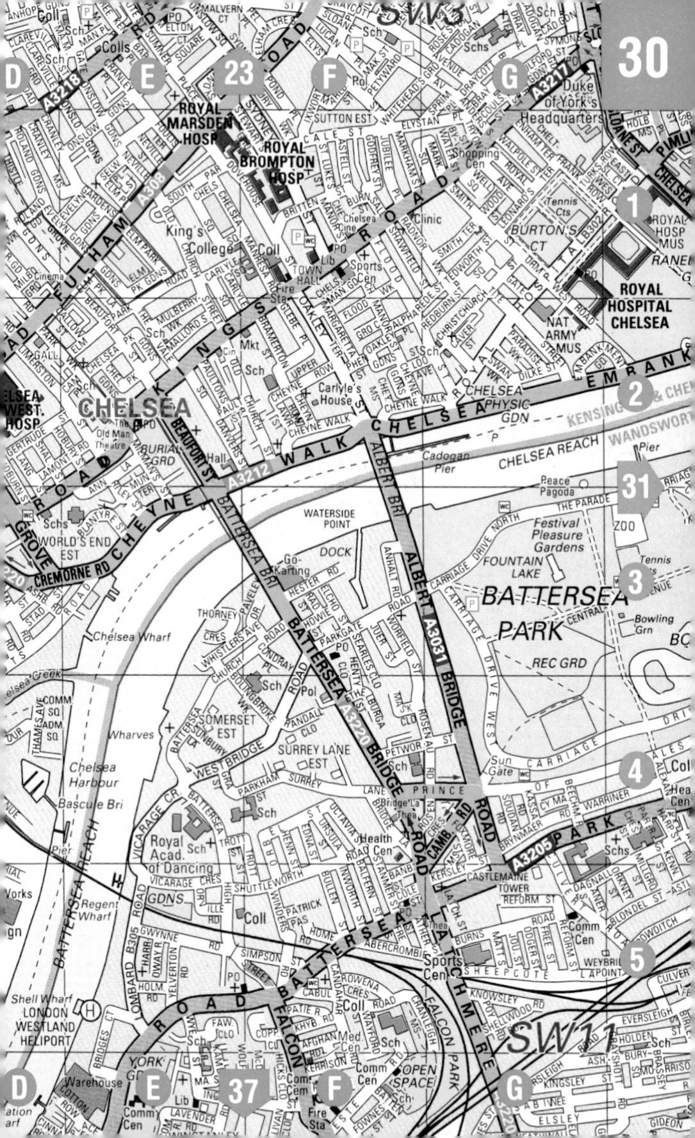

SW3
23
D
E
F
G
A3218
A3217
ROYAL MARSDEN HOSP
ROYAL BROMPTON HOSP
SUTTON EST
CALE ST
Duke of York's Headquarters
Shopping Cen
FULHAM ROAD
A308
KING'S ROAD
King's College
Chelsea Cine
TOWN HALL
Fire Sta
Sports Cen
Clinic
Tennis Cts
BURTON'S CT
ROYAL HOSP MUS
ROYAL HOSPITAL CHELSEA
NAT ARMY MUS
1
2
3
4
5
CHELSEA
Carlyle's House
CHELSEA PHYSIC GDN
CHEYNE WALK
CHELSEA EMBANKMENT
BEAUFORT ST
A3212
CHEYNE WALK
CHELSEA REACH
Cadogan Pier
WORLD'S END EST
CREMORNE RD
Chelsea Wharf
Chelsea Creek
WATERSIDE POINT
DOCK
Go-Karting
BATTERSEA BRI
ALBERT BRI
ALBERT BRIDGE
A3031
Peace Pagoda
31
THE PARADE
ZOO
Festival Pleasure Gardens
FOUNTAIN LAKE
BATTERSEA PARK
REC GRD
CARRIAGE DRIVE NORTH
CARRIAGE DRIVE WEST
Bowling Grn
Sun Gate
THORNEY CRES
SOMERSET EST
SURREY LANE EST
BATTERSEA BRIDGE ROAD
A3220
Chelsea Harbour
Bascule Bri
Wharves
Pier
BATTERSEA REACH
Royal Acad. of Dancing
VICARAGE CRES
PRINCE OF WALES DRIVE
Health Cen
PARK ROAD
A3205
Schs
CASTLEMAINE TOWER
REFORM ST
Comm Cen
Regent Wharf
Coll
BATTERSEA ROAD
LATCHMERE ROAD
FALCON ROAD
FALCON PARK
Sports Cen
SHEEPCOTE
SW11
Shell Wharf
LONDON WESTLAND HELIPORT
Warehouse
Lib
Commy Cen
Med. Cen
Comm Cen
OPEN SPACE
Fire Sta
37

A
B
C
D
24
30
38
1
2
3
4
5
VICTORIA COACH STA
SLOANE SQ
LOWER SLOANE ST
PIMLICO RD
CHELSEA BRIDGE ROAD
Chelsea Barracks
ROYAL HOSP MUS
RANELAGH GARDENS
ROYAL HOSPITAL CHELSEA
NAT ARMY MUS
LISTER HOSP
BELGRAVE ROAD
GORDON HOSP
PIMLICO
CHURCHILL GARDENS
DOLPHIN SQUARE
GROSVENOR ROAD
EMBANKMENT
RIVER THA
KENSINGTON & CHELSEA
WANDSWORTH
CHELSEA REACH
CHELSEA BRI
GROSVENOR BRIDGE
QUEENSTOWN RD
A3216
Battersea Power Station (Disused)
Adrenalin Village
Festival Pleasure Gardens
ZOO
RUNNING TRACK
BOATING LAKE
REC GRD
BATTERSEA PARK
CARRIAGE DRIVE
Battersea Dogs Home
BATTERSEA PARK ROAD
NINE ELMS
New Covent Garden Sorting Office
New Covent Garden Market
LORRY PARK
SW8
PATMORE EST
SAVONA EST
Battersea City Farm
QUEENSTOWN RD (BATTERSEA)
BR DEPOT
BATTERSEA
HEATHBROOK PARK
WANDSWORTH ROAD
SW11

31
24
32
38
D
E
F
G
1
2
3
4
5
SE11
SW9
VAUXHALL
KENNINGTON
SOUTH LAMBETH
TATE GALLERY
MILLBANK TOWER
Millbank Barracks
GOVT OFFS
VAUXHALL BRI
ALBERT EMB
KENNINGTON LANE
HARLEYFORD RD
THE OVAL (SURREY CC GRD)
Oval House Theatre
VAUXHALL PARK
SPRING GDNS
Gas Works
KENNINGTON RD
KENNINGTON PARK
CAMBERWELL
FENTIMAN ROAD
CLAPHAM ROAD
SOUTH LAMBETH RD
WANDSWORTH ROAD
STOCKWELL
STOCKWELL PK EST
STOCKWELL GDNS EST
BRIXTON ROAD
MYATT'S FIELDS SOUTH EST
MOSTYN GDNS
SLADE GDNS
STUDLEY ESTATE
BUS GARAGE
LARKHALL PARK
CLAPHAM RD EST
Nat. Army & Air Force Inst. Depot
Tennis Courts
REC GRD
Lido
MURSELL EST
Warehouse
Activity Cen
A3
A23
A203
A3204
B301

SE17
WALWORTH
KENNINGTON
KENNINGTON PARK
CAMBERWELL
SE5
MYATT'S FIELDS
MYATT'S FIELDS SOUTH EST
THE MAUDSLEY HOSPITAL
KING'S COLLEGE HOSPITAL
DENMARK HILL
LOUGHBOROUGH JUNCTION
CAMBERWELL NEW ROAD
CAMBERWELL ROAD
CAMBERWELL CHURCH ST
COLDHARBOUR LANE
DENMARK HILL
CHAMPION PK
WALWORTH ROAD
KENNINGTON PARK ROAD
BROWNING EST
ELIZ. EST
WYNDHAM EST
ELMINGTON EST
CRAWFORD EST
ALBERTA EST
BRANDON EST
RUST SQUARE
CATHEDRAL
Sports Cen
Sports Centre
Salvation Army College
Nat. Army & Air Force Inst. Depot
Walworth City Farm
Health Cen
Comm Cen
Tenn Cts
Tennis Courts
Depot
A3204
A215
A202
A2217
B214
25
39
31
A
B
C
D
1
2
3
4
5

32
D
E
25
F
G
1
2
3
33
4
5
39
LONGFIELD EST
Offices
LORRY PARK
DUNTON B203
BALACLAVA
THORBURN SQUARE
STRATHN. ST
SIMMS
MANOR EST
TRADING EST
RENNIE EST
ALMOND ROAD
ANCHOR STREET
GALLEYWALL
BUSHWOOD DRIVE
OXLEY CLOSE
PATERSON PARK
ABERCORN WAY
Superstore
ROLLS
B204
ROWCROSS STREET
HUMPHREY ST
Fire Sta
COOPERS ROAD
MAWBEY
MAWBEY EST
MARLBOROUGH GROVE
JAMES ST
STEVENSON CRES
ROSSETTI RD
STUBBS DR
ROTHERHITHE
A2208
ILDERTON
BRAMCOTE
CATLIN STREET
EGAN WAY
SHERW. GDNS
ARGYLE W.
RYDER DRIVE
VERNEY
VARCOE ROAD
GER. CL
RECORD
KENT
A2
MADRON ST
MINA
SHORNCLIFFE RD
NILE TER
TRAFALGAR AVE
B215
COBOURG
GLENGALL
LONCROFT ROAD
WAITE ST
GLEN TER
OSSORY ROAD
MALT ST
OLMAR STREET
LOVEGROVE STREET
Civic Centre
Lib
CANAL GROVE
SANDGATE ST
South Eastern Gas Works
PENARTH ST
HATCHAM
MANOR GROVE
TUSTIN EST
ESS PARK
REC GRD
STREET
SUMNER RD
WAY
GEORGES
BIBURY CLO
EBLEY CLO
DAVEY ST
ALDER CLO
BIANCA RD
LATONA RD
HAYMERLE RD
UNWIN CLO
FRENSHAM STREET
PARK ROAD
FRIARY EST
FRIARY
GREEN HUNDRED RD
ETHNARD
MUS
CRAIG WAY
DEVON ST
DEVONSHIRE GROVE
SYLVAN GROVE
ROAD
LONGHOPE CLO
Sch
Clinic
REDDINS RD
DANIEL GDNS
WILLOWBROOK RD
COLEGROVE ROAD
BIRD
BUSH ROAD
LEDBURY EST
CAROLINE GDNS
DROVER LA
NORTH PECKHAM EST
BLAKES ROAD
NUTT ST
ROSEMARY RD
BOAT WALK
PECKHAM
RADNOR ROAD
LYMPST GARDENS
CARDINE MEWS
ASYLUM
GERVASE ST
Coll
CLIFTON
CULMORE ROAD
CATOR ST
JOWETT STREET
COMMERCIAL
B216
HOLBECK ROW
ELCO.
STUDHOLME ST
SPRING LANE
PENTRIDGE ST
EAST SURREY GRO
CHANDLER WAY
SUMNER EST
BONAR RD
HILL
BULLER CLO
FENHAM ROAD
KINCAID RD
GELDART RD
HOUSE
KINGS GRO
PECKHAM
CAMDEN EST
SCEAUX GDNS
LISFORD STREET
SE15
MONTPELIER ROAD
CARLTON GROVE
HOLLYDENE
Health Centre
SIDMOUTH ROAD
WENTWORTH CRES
CLONEVILLE CLO
GOLDSMITH
MARMONT ROAD
STAFFORDSHIRE ST
MEETING
Pol
PENNETHORNE
QUEENS ROAD PECKHAM
KINGS GROVE
ASTBURY RD
YORK GROVE
DAYTON GRO
ROAD
PECKHAM HIGH ST
QUEENS
S. LON. ART GALL
Fire Sta
PELICAN EST
TALFOURD PL
BUSHEY HILL ROAD
CROFTON
SHENLEY
Sports Cen
BUS STA
The Aylesham Shop Cen
HANOVER PK
CLAYTON RD
CONSORT
COLMORE MS
COSSALL PARK
Schs
BURCHELL RD
LYNDHURST
GRUMMANT ROAD
DENMAN ROAD
LYN. SQ
BELLENDEN ROAD
OPHIR TER
RYE LA
CERISE ROAD
RAUL RD
CICELY RD
MONC. ST
HARDERS RD
COSSALL
GORDON ROAD
NAZARETH GDNS
KIRKWOOD
LUGARD
STANBURY
CAULFIELD RD
FIRBANK RD
HOLLYDALE
DUNDAS RD
ST. MARY'S RD
SHORE ROAD
Mkt
ELM GROVE
HOLLY GROVE
Cinema
PECKHAM RYE
A2215
LYNDHURST GROVE
WARWICK GDNS
LINWOOD CLOSE
BLENHEIM
CHOUMERT
BOURNEMOUTH RD
ALMOND CLO
BLACKPOOL RD
BRAYARDS
PILKI
CON-SORT
HATH. C.
CREWYS RD
WROXTON ROAD
BRABOURN GRO
ANSDELL
CHO. SQ
Comm Cen
WAR. CT
ALPHA GROVE
BIRCH CLO
COPELAND
GODMAN RD
STURDY RD
ELLERY ST
KIMBERLEY
GRIMWADE CLO
EVELINA
A2214
CHADWICK
PARK
CHOUMERT
ROAD
REEDHAM
COSTA ST
LANE
HEATON
WIVEN CLO
MANAOR
CLOSE
RYE
IVANHOE RD
ROAD
STREET
DANBY ST
FENWICK
STERNHALL
PHILIP
MONT. WAY
NUN. GRN
SCY.
Clinic
Lib
MALFORT
AVONDALE RISE
HOWDEN
HOWBURY RD
BARSET

33
A
B
26
C
D
1
2
3
4
5
32
40
ABBEY RD
MILLENDER
W. Health Cen
ST. HELENA ROAD
CROFTERS COURT
SAPPHIRE ROAD
WINDLASS PL
Clinic
Youth Cen
OXESTALLS ROAD
EVELYN
A2208
SOUTH BERMONDSEY
JARROW ROAD
RECULVER ROAD
SKETCHLEY GDNS
DEPOT
Power Station
Sports Cen
THE NEW DEN MILLWALL F.C.
ILDERTON ROAD
ABLETT STREET
ZAMPA ROAD
STOCKHOLM ROAD
DEPTFORD PARK
GRINSTEAD ROAD
INWEN CT
BLACKHORSE ROAD
GOSTERWOOD STREET
Fire Sta
SURREY CANAL ROAD
BRIDGE HOUSE MEADOWS
JUNO WAY
Depot
FOLKESTONE GDNS
South Eastern Gas Works
RECORD ST
PENARTH ST
ROLLINS STREET
SHARRATT
LOVELINCH
HORNSHAY STREET
MANOR GROVE
TUSTIN EST
Sch
HILLBECK CLOSE
PATTERDALE RD
HUNSDON
EDRIC ROAD
MONSON ROAD
ROBERT LOWE CL
BROCKLEHURST
SANFORD STREET
EDWARD ST
FORDHAM PARK
ANGUS ST
ACHILLES ST
Health Cen
BATAVIA RD
A2
NEW CROSS ROAD
Amb Sta
CULMORE ROAD
CLIFTON WAY
SE14
NEW CROSS GATE
Uni of Lon
Lib
BESSON ST
KENDER STREET
HATCHAM PARK RD
HATCHAM GDNS
QUEENS ROAD PECKHAM
A202
Fire Sta
NEW CROSS GATE
BUS GARAGE
Goldsmiths College (Uni. of London)
MUSGROVE ROAD
OMMANEY ROAD
NEW CROSS
ARBUTHNOT RD
ALLOT
Comm Cen
LAUSANNE RD
Coll
BELFORT RD
TELEGRAPH HILL PARK
VESTA ROAD
PEPYS ROAD
EVELINA ROAD
NUNHEAD
B2142 DRAKEFELL ROAD
ST ASAPH ROAD
BROCKLEY
MILLMARK GROVE
MALPAS

MUDCHUTE
MILLWALL PARK
ISLAND GARDENS
WESTFERRY ROAD
MANCHESTER ROAD
SAUNDERS NESS ROAD
TOWER HAMLETS
GREENWICH
GREENWICH REACH
Greenwich Pier
Royal Naval College
Trafalgar Rowing Centre
GIPSY MOTH IV
CUTTY SARK
DEPTFORD
ROYAL NAVAL YARD
SE8
Landing Stage
Palmer's Wharf
Payne's Wharf
Borthwick Wharf
Uni of Greenwich
CREEK ROAD
A200
DEPTFORD CREEK
DEPTFORD CHURCH STREET
A2209
DEPTFORD HIGH STREET
GREENWICH HIGH ROAD
A206
GREENWICH SOUTH ST.
ROYAL HILL
ROMNEY ROAD
BLACKHEATH RD
BLACKHEATH HILL
A2
LEWISHAM ROAD
A211
BROOKMILL ROAD
A2210
RAVENSBOURNE
ST. JOHN'S
Lewisham Coll
A20
LOAMPIT HILL
LOAMPIT VALE
THURSTON RD
LEWISHAM
TA Centre

26
34
40

34
A
B
C
D
1
2
3
4
5
27
33
41
SOUTH EASTERN GAS BOARD SPORTS GROUND
Pav
Jetty
Enderby's Wharf
Piper's Wharf
Works
MAURITIUS
A2203
TUNNEL AVENUE
Sports Cen
NEWCASTLE DRAW DOCK
Granite Wharf
Lovell's Wharf
CADET PL
Sch
HEV.
MINI TOWN HALL
ARMITAGE ROAD
GLENISTER ROAD
GLENFORTH ST
FINGAL STREET
CHILVER ST
WOOLWICH ROAD
Lib
SAUNDERS
TRINITY HOSP
PELTON
BALLAST QU.
LASSELL
HOSKINS
CHRISTCHURCH WAY
BELLOT ST
Comm Cen
PO
GREENWICH DISTRICT HOSP
CALVERT RD
ANNANDALE ROAD
CHEVENING ROAD
EAST GREENWICH PLEASAUNCE
REACH
Trafalgar Rowing Centre
Royal Naval College
GREENWICH FOOT TUNNEL
CRANE
HIGH BRIDGE
Power Sta
The Trident Hall Theatre
TRAFALGAR ROAD
WOODLAND GROVE
EARLSWOOD ST
Health Centre
ANNANDALE RD
TUSKAR
WOODLANDS PK RD
LEMMON RD
DINSDALE RD
HUMBER ROAD
PEACHUM ROAD
A206
ROMNEY ROAD
Sports Cen
MAZE HILL
RESTELL CLOSE
NORFOLK HOUSE
JENNER HOUSE
LISTER HOUSE
VISTA
PARK
QUEEN'S HOUSE
NATIONAL MARITIME MUS
Education Centre
CROSS AVE
VANBRUGH
FOYLE ROAD
WEBB RD
COLERAINE
HARDY
BEACONSFIELD
LYND. CLO
WESTCOMBE
One Tree Hill
Comm Cen
Mkt
GREENWICH SE10
GREENWICH PARK
Greenwich Theatre
LOVERS WK
HIGH RD
Sch
PARK
FERNDALE CT
Circus Gate
THE AVENUE
Clinic
Pol
FLAMSTEED HOUSE (Old Royal Observatory)
BLACKHEATH AVENUE
GREAT CROSS AVE
BOWER AVENUE
VANBRUGH FIELDS
WYCHERLEY CLOSE
COMBE AV
VANBRUGH PARK
PARKSIDE
VANBRUGH
Royal Standard
HEATHWAY
Croom's Hill Gate
The Gardens
THE WILDERNESS DEER PARK
B210
COV RES
Tenn Cts
RANGER'S HOUSE
CHESTERFIELD
GENERAL WOLFE ROAD
CADE ROAD
HYDE VALE
DIAMOND TER
WESTGROVE LA.
CLAYT. MS
Blackheath Gate
CHARLTON WAY
PRINCE CHARLES ROAD
MAZE HILL
VANBRUGH TER
LANGTON WAY
SHOOTER'S HILL
A2
ROAD
Sch
DART HILL
DARTMOUTH GROVE
DARTMOUTH ROW
WHITFIELD RD
LONG POND ROAD
DUKE HUMPHREY ROAD
BLACKHEATH
PRINCE OF WALES RD
B212
ST. GERMANS PLACE
HARE AND BILLET ROAD
TALBOT PL
BLACKHEATH VALE
GOFFERS RD
TA Centre
MONTPELIER ROW
PARAGON PL
SOUTH ROW
THE PARAGON
POND ROAD
ABERDEEN TER
ALL SAINTS DRIVE
ORCHARD DRIVE
Clarendon Hotel
FULTHORP ROAD
MERCIA CLOSE
ELIOT PLACE
GROTE'S PLACE
TRANQUIL VALE
ROYAL PAR
WEMYSS RD
PAGODA GDNS
ELIOT VALE
HEATH LANE
BAIZDON ROAD
CAMDEN ROW
Sch
BLACKHEATH GRO
Lib
PO
PRINCES RISE
LEWISHAM HILL
ST. AUSTELL ROAD
ELIOT HILL
ELIOT PARK
OAKCROFT ROAD
WALERAND ROAD
PARK
ST. JOSEPH'S VALE
HURREN CLOSE
COLLINS ST
BLACKHEATH
BENNETT PARK
CORNER GREEN
GRANVILLE
CRESSINGHAM RD
BELMONT
BLACKHEATH PK
BLACKHEATH

CHARLTON
MARYON PARK
Tennis Courts
27
D
E
F
G
RAMAC INDUSTRIAL ESTATE
GREENWICH INDUS ESTATE
BUGSBY'S WAY
HOPE LANE
Works
GALLIONS ROAD
HORIZON WAY
A206
WOOLWICH ROAD
HICKIN CLOSE
GALLON CL
PREN. CT
Clinic
HARVEY GDNS
BARNEY CLO
CHARLTON RD
HOLMWOOD VILLAS
RAMAC WAY
Fire Sta
TROUGHTON RD
RATHMORE RD
DUPREE RD
HARDEN RD
RAILEY RD
FAIRTHORN RD
GURDON ROAD
Warehouses
DELAFIELD ROAD
SUNDORNE ROAD
PO
FLOYD RD
VALLEY GROVE
CHARLTON ATHLETIC FC
SAM BARTRAM CLO
VALIANT HOUSE
LANSDOWNE MEWS
CHARLTON LANE
HASTED ROAD
PARK ROAD
COXMOUNT RD
Sch
ZOO
KINVEACHY
WOLFE CRES
THORNTREE
MARYON WILSON PARK
McCALL CRES
1
VICTORIA WAY
BERN ASH. DR
FOSS. ROAD
INVERINE ROAD
SWALLOWFIELD ROAD
PRIOLO ROAD
WELLINGTON GDNS
NADINE ST
CHURCH LANE
THE HEIGHTS
LANSDOWNE LANE
ST. PAUL'S CL
Health Cen
BEACHAM CLOSE
GUILD ROAD
ST. ALFEGE ROAD
MACARTHUR TER
CALY. RD
WESTCOMBE PARK
Works
BRAMSHOT AVENUE
WYNDCLIFF ROAD
THE BIRCHES
SANDTOFT RD
TALLIS GROVE
BRAMHOPE LANE
GOLL TER
WELLINGTON MS
ELLISCOMBE RD
CHARLTON
WAR. WK
FLETCHING RD
FAIRFIELD GRO
THE VILLAGE
CHARLTON PARK ROAD
EVERSLEY ROAD
HIGHCOMBE
LITT. KILN DR
LIME COPSE CLO
ELLIS MS
SE7
MULBERRY CLOSE
Pav
2
A102(M)
SIEBERT ROAD
EASTCOMBE AVENUE
HOPEDALE RD
MAYHILL RD
SHERINGTON RD
MASCALLS RD
LEILA PARN.PL
SPRINGFIELD GROVE
Community Centre
CHARLTON PARK
ROAD
HORNFAIR
INVICTA ROAD
Sch
ST. JOSEPH'S CT
B210
CANBERRA ROAD
CHARLTON ROAD
Tennis Cts
FAIRLAWN
MONTCALM ROAD
MERIDIAN RD
INIGO JONES ROAD
35
CRAIG. RD
FURZEFIELD RD
HASSEN RD
COUTH RD
RECTORY FIELD
RECTORY FIELD CRESCENT
THE AVENUE
SHIRLEY HO. DR
MARLBOROUGH
SUTLEJ ROAD
INDUS ROAD
KASHMIR RD
LYVEDEN RD
BANCHORY RD
LIZBAN STREET
SUNF. PL
BOWAT. PL
REYNOLDS PL
NIGERIA ROAD
ST. MAR. C.
GREENBAY ROAD
PRINCE HENRY ROAD
3
SPORTS GROUND
DORN. CL
OLD DOVER ROAD
THE GLADE
CHARLTON DENE
INDUS RD
GRENADA RD
KENYA ROAD
ALLOT
Lido
Bowl Grn
Tennis Cts
PARK
PRIM MS
Lib
Clinic
WAY
SUN LA
A207
SHOOTER'S HILL
ARNOLD HOUSE HOSP
CHI CLO
STANE WAY
TELLSON AVENUE
ABERFORD GDNS
GUNNER
ROAD
ROCHESTER WAY
KIDBROOKE
EASTBROOK ROAD
WOOD. HERVEY
MERRIMAN ROAD
WEYMAN ROAD
FARJEON ROAD
MELTHORPE GDNS
ZANGWILL
THELMA GARDENS
GROVE CT
ROSSE MS
ANNESL. RD
HARRADEN RD
Bowl Grn
Tenn Cts
BEGBIE ROAD
4
WRICKLEMARSH ROAD
KIDBROOKE GARDENS
WESTBROOK ROAD
KIDBROOKE PARK CLOSE
HARGOOD ROAD
HOLBURNE ROAD
CORELLI ROAD
HOLBURNE CLOSE
FAIRFAX GDNS
HOLBURNE GDNS
DURSLEY GDNS
WRICKLE. ROAD
A2213
WHETSTONE
LEWIS RD
Tenn Cts
Sch
FB
RELIEF RD
WOOLACOMBE ROAD
DURSLEY CLO
Morden College
Health Cen
BROOKELSA CLO
DELME CRES
BALCHEN ROAD
KELLAWAY
Tenn Cts
THE PLANTATION
DURSLEY
PLAYING FIELDS
Pav
Clubho
5
SUS. RD
KIDBROOKE PARK ROAD
KIDBROOKE WAY
Tenn Cts
SPORTS GROUNDS
SWEYN PL
PADDO. CLOSE
Tenn Cts
Sch
Depot
41
A2
ROCHESTER WAY
BROAD WALK
SPORTS GROUNDS
Tennis Cts
Tenn Cts
POLEB. RD
HALSBROOK ROAD
HIGHBROOK
LANGBROOK ROAD
SLADEBROOK
SHIREBROOK
SEDGEBROOK ROAD
CROSSBROOK ROAD
KELBROOK RD
FLINTMILL CRES
MA CL
CARNBROOK
BOURNBROOK ROAD
MINI TOWN HALL
Tenn Cts
Superstore

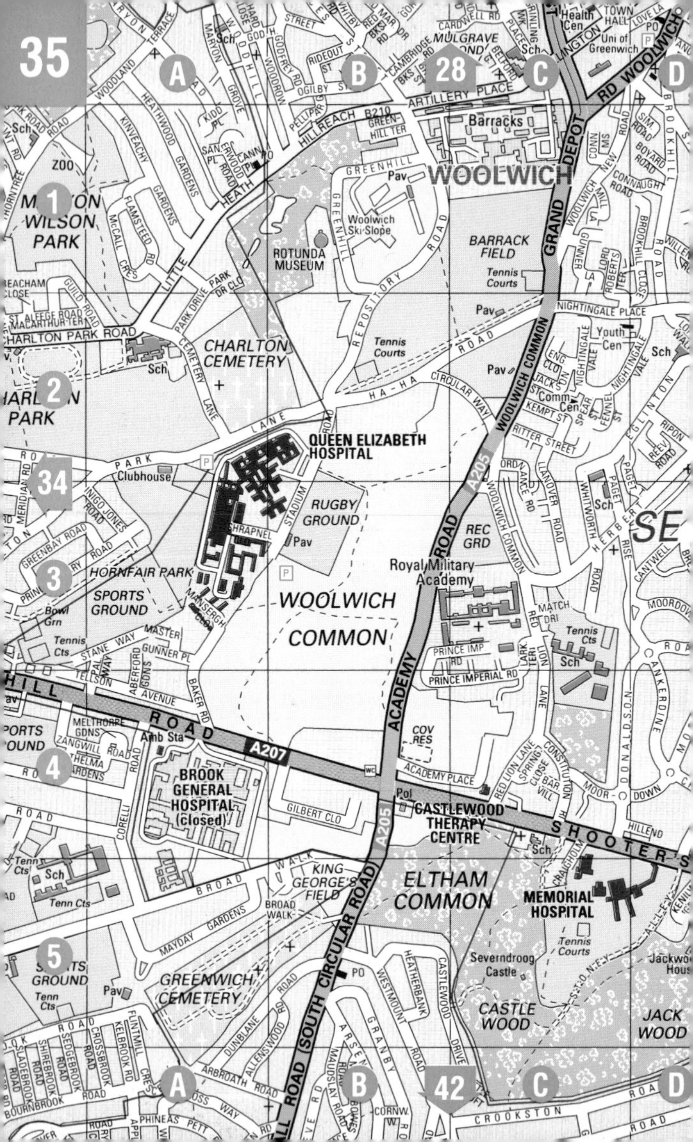

A
B
28
C
D
WOOLWICH
Barracks
ARTILLERY PLACE
MULGRAVE
TOWN HALL
Health Cen
Uni of Greenwich
RD WOOLWICH
GRAND DEPOT
HILLREACH B210
MARYON WILSON PARK
ZOO
ROTUNDA MUSEUM
Woolwich Ski Slope
BARRACK FIELD
Tennis Courts
NIGHTINGALE PLACE
Youth Cen
CHARLTON PARK ROAD
CHARLTON CEMETERY
CEMETERY LANE
REPOSITORY ROAD
HA-HA
CIRCULAR WAY
WOOLWICH COMMON
QUEEN ELIZABETH HOSPITAL
PARK
Clubhouse
34
RUGBY GROUND
STADIUM
SHRAPNEL CLO
Pav
HORNFAIR PARK
SPORTS GROUND
WOOLWICH COMMON
A205
REC GRD
Royal Military Academy
PRINCE IMPERIAL RD
ACADEMY ROAD
HERBERT ROAD
TELLSON AVENUE
BAKER RD
A207
Amb Sta
BROOK GENERAL HOSPITAL (closed)
ACADEMY PLACE
COV RES
CASTLEWOOD THERAPY CENTRE
SHOOTERS HILL ROAD
GILBERT CLO
KING GEORGE'S FIELD
ELTHAM COMMON
MEMORIAL HOSPITAL
BROAD WALK
MAYDAY GARDENS
GREENWICH CEMETERY
SOUTH CIRCULAR ROAD
Severndroog Castle
CASTLE WOOD
JACK WOOD
Tennis Courts
SPORTS GROUND
ARBROATH ROAD
42
CROOKSTON ROAD
1
2
3
4
5

35
28
42
D
E
F
G
1
2
3
4
5
PLUMSTEAD
PLUMSTEAD COMMON
WINN'S COMMON
SHREWSBURY PARK
SHOOTER'S HILL GOLF COURSE
SHOOTER'S HILL
CLOTHWORKERS WOOD
HILL-VIEW CEMETERY
OXLEAS WOOD
EAGLESFIELD REC GRD
SHOULDER OF MUTTON GREEN
PLAYING FIELD
ALLOT
GREENWICH
BEXLEY
A207
A209
SHOOTERS HILL
BELLEGROVE
RAGLAN ROAD
BREWERY
COMMON
PLUMSTEAD COMMON ROAD
OLD MILL ROAD
WINN COMMON ROAD
KINGS HIGHWAY
ST. MARGARET'S GROVE
ST. JOHNS TER
WERNBROOK ST
WAVERLEY CRES
WAVERLEY ROAD
WARWICK TER
VICARAGE PK
VICARAGE RD
MANTHORP RD
DURHAM RISE
BRAMBLEBURY RD
BURWASH RD
HEAVITREE ROAD
GRIFFIN ROAD
ANCONA ROAD
CONGO RD
LEGHORN RD
TUSCAN RD
PIEDMONT ROAD
HEARD
CHESTNUT RISE
PARKDALE ROAD
ROYDENE ROAD
SLADEDALE ROAD
LAKEDALE ROAD
TORMOUNT ROAD
CONWAY ROAD
COXWELL RD
INGLEDEW RD
LIFFLER ROAD
MIRIAM ROAD
ORISSA RD
MINERAL STREET
GALLOSSON ROAD
TEWSON ROAD
HAWKSMOOR CLO
HEATH VILLAS
VICARAGE PARK
COMMON
THE SLADE
RAVINE GROVE
SUTCLIFFE ROAD
FLAXTON ROAD
KIRKHAM
MOUNT CLO
TIMBERCROFT
PEGWELL ST
ALBATROSS ST
LUCKNOW ST
CARDIFF ST
ALABAMA STREET
MELLING STREET
SWINGATE LANE
MALT ST
BASSANT ROAD
GILBOURNE RD
KINGSDALE
IRWIN AVENUE
THORNHILL AVENUE
EASTVIEW AVE
DUNCROFT
LANCASTER ST
RAYMERE GARDENS
LANDSTEAD ROAD
WARLAND ROAD
WELTON ROAD
FLAXTON ROAD
VOCE ROAD
GROVE
HIGH
GARLAND
CLOTHWORKERS ROAD
HATTON CLOSE
DOTHILL RD
MERRYN CLOSE
CHERITON DR
ERINDALE
ERINDALE TER
CHELSWORTH DRIVE
TUAM ROAD
MACOMA ROAD
MACOMA TER
JAGO CLOSE
ENNIS
UPTON RD
ADMASTON RD
OLVE RD
HINSTOCK RD
ROWTON ROAD
WREKIN
NITHDALE ROAD
DALLIN ROAD
GENESTA ROAD
ISLA RD
VAMBERY ROAD
VERNHAM ROAD
KIRK LANE
PLUM LANE
WROTTESLEY ROAD
BARNFIELD RD
BLOOMFIELD ROAD
BLENDON TERRACE
THE OAKS
CAMS ROW
COUPLAND PLACE
CONGLETON GROVE
YOUNG PLACE
CLAYMILL HOUSE
HUDSON PLACE
SANDBACH PLACE
DAWSON CLOSE
ARTHUR GROVE
RICHMOND PLACE
INVERMORE
VILLAS ROAD
ANN ST
ROBERT ST
EARL RISE
ELMLEY STREET
SOUTH ROAD
SOUTHPORT ROAD
MAJENDIE ROAD
DUR. RD
BRINKLOW CRES
ASHRIDGE CRESCENT
MEREWORTH DRIVE
BUSHMOOR CRES
KINLET ROAD
EAGLESFIELD ROAD
FOXCROFT ROAD
CAMDALE RD
RICHMEAD
EDISON GROVE
EDISON ROAD
MILTON RD
KEATS ROAD
DRYDEN
WORDSWORTH RD
BROWNING CLO
SHELLEY DR
TENNYSON CLO
BLAKE CLO
CHAUCER
BURNS CLOSE
BLENHEIM DRIVE
WYCLIFFE CLO
WICKHAM STREET
EXETER
HONITON ROAD
CAMBORNE RD
LYN ROAD
BELLE GROVE CLO
BALTIMORE PLACE
MONTROSE CLOSE
PETERS CLO
MARLIN DR
SANDRINGHAM DR
HILL VIEW DRIVE
ROKESBY CLO
FALCONWOOD AVENUE
SUNDRIDGE AVE
BELMONT AVE
SHERWOOD RD
EASTCOTE ROAD
OXLEAS CLOSE
ASHMORE GR
WOODS LANE
OXLEAS MEADOW
We Anchor In Hope PH
Woodlands Farm
Nursery
Clubhouse
Tennis Courts
Tenn Cts
Bowl Grn
Fire Sta
Comm Cen
Health Cen
Greenwich Young Peoples Theatre
Sch
Schs
PO
Lib
Clinic
Pol
MUS
Sports Cen

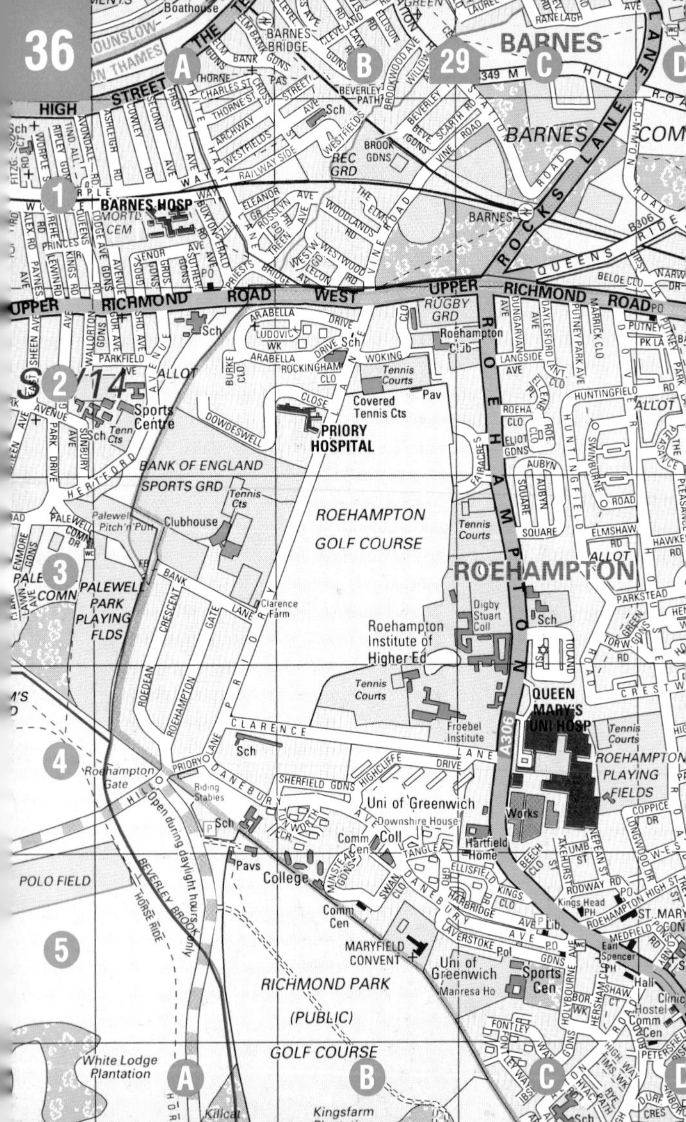

29
BARNES
Boathouse
BARNES BRIDGE
HIGH STREET
BARNES HOSP
MORTL CEM
REC GRD
BROOK GDNS
BARNES COMMON
ROCKS LANE
QUEENS RIDE
UPPER RICHMOND ROAD WEST
UPPER RICHMOND ROAD
RUGBY GRD
Roehampton Club
Tennis Courts
Covered Tennis Cts
Pav
PRIORY HOSPITAL
ALLOT
Sports Centre
BANK OF ENGLAND SPORTS GRD
Clubhouse
Palewell Pitch'n'Putt
PALEWELL PARK PLAYING FLDS
PALEWELL COMN
ROEHAMPTON GOLF COURSE
ROEHAMPTON
ROEHAMPTON LANE
Digby Stuart Coll
Roehampton Institute of Higher Ed
Froebel Institute
QUEEN MARY'S UNI HOSP
ROEHAMPTON PLAYING FIELDS
Works
Clarence Farm
CLARENCE LANE
PRIORY LANE
DANEBURY AVE
Roehampton Gate
Riding Stables
Open during daylight hours only
BEVERLEY BROOK
HORSE RIDE
POLO FIELD
Uni of Greenwich
Downshire House
Comm Cen
Coll
Hartfield Home
College
Pavs
MARYFIELD CONVENT
Uni of Greenwich
Manresa Ho
Sports Cen
RICHMOND PARK (PUBLIC)
GOLF COURSE
White Lodge Plantation
Kingsfarm Plantation
Killcat Corner
Kings Head PH
ROEHAMPTON HIGH ST
Earl Spencer PH
Hall
Clinic
Hostel
A306
B306
B349

36
29
37
D
E
F
G
1
2
3
4
5
PUTNEY
Bowling Green
PUTNEY HO
LOWER
LOWER RICHMOND ROAD
B306
COMMON
HORNE WAY
GDNS
RIVER THAMES
BISHOP'S PARK
ALLOTMENTS
Fulham Palace
FULHAM PALACE GDNS
MUS
Sch
FULHAM HIGH ST
CHURCH GA
PUTNEY BRIDGE
PRIOR BANK GDNS
PUT. BRI APP
PUTNEY BRI
RANELAGH
HURLINGHAM
Centre
SWAN DOCK
Putney Pier
EMBANKMENT
Wharves
FELSHAM RD
EGLISTON MS
EGLISTON RD
ERPINGHAM
HOTHAM
LANDFORD RD
EARLDOM
ROSSDALE
BLACKETT ST
CHARL. RD
REDGRAVE
LACY RD
CLARENDON DRIVE
Sports Cen
Hall
SOUTH CIRCULAR ROAD
A205
Clinic
Shopping Cen
Jubilee Ho
PUTNEY HIGH STREET
PUTNEY A3
MONTSERRAT
WERTER RD
DISRAELI RD
ESMOND ST
ROCK.
BUS GAR
NORROY RD
CHELVERTON
SPENCER WK
QUILL LA
CARDINAL PL
Pol
BURIAL GRD
Thea
YWCA
NURSERY CLO
Lib
PUTNEY
Coll
UPPER RICHMOND ROAD
OXFORD RD
COUNTY CT
EAST PUTNEY
EDWARDS
LUTTRELL
LARPENT
CAMPION RD
COALECROFT RD
HOLROYD
ENMORE RD
TIDESWELL
GWENDOLEN AVE
PUTNEY
ST. JOHN'S AVENUE
HAZLEWELL RD
Health Cen
GWEND. CLO
CAMBALT ROAD
South Thames Coll
CHERRY DR
CARLTON
RAYNERS RD
MERCIER
Schs
SW15
CHARTFIELD AVENUE
WHITNELL WAY
A219
PUTNEY HILL
TINTERN CLO
ENWOOD CLO
KESWICK RD
PENRITH CLO
LAKER PL
BUTTERMERE DR
PORTINSCALE
OAKE CT
WESTLEIGH AVENUE
LYTTON GROVE
RADCLIFFE SQ
LITTLEC. CLO
Clinic
Sch
CORTIS ROAD
TILDESLEY ROAD
PO
Tennis Cts
MANOR FIELDS
HAYWARD GDNS
CARSLAKE RD
INNES GD
PUTNEY HEATH
HEATH RISE
KERSFIELD ROAD
HOLMBUSH
DROMORE RD
RUSHOLME
ROYAL HOSPITAL
Green Man PH
PUTNEY HEATH LA
VAN DYKE CLO
A3 WEST HILL
CROMER VILLAS RD
Whitelands Training College
ROYAL ORCHARD CLO
LINSTEAD WAY
ARNAL CRES
BELL DR
GIRDWOOD ROAD
SKEENA HILL
COMBEMARTIN
HEATH
TELEGRAPH
WILDCROFT
COV RES
Tibbet's Corner
TIBBET'S RIDE
TIBBET'S CORNER
ROSS CT
Telegraph Inn PH
HIGHLANDS
PORTSMOUTH ROAD
BEN CLO
BOWLING GREEN CLO
BEAUFORT CLO
SEATON
KING'S MERE
SIDE
PRINCES WAY
CASTLECOMBE DR
KEEVIL DRIVE
STAPLE CLO
Comm Cen
Sch
WHITLOCK
EDGECOMBE HO
SOUTHMEAD RD
DRIVE
SOUTHFIELDS
MANNINGTREE CLO
WINDLESHAM
INNER
OAK PK GDNS
SAND. CLO

30
36
A
B
C
D
1
2
3
4
5
PUTNEY BRIDGE
HURLINGHAM PARK
HURLINGHAM CLUB GDNS
Hurlingham House
Open Air Pool
Tenn Cts
Pav
HURLINGHAM COURT
RIVERMEAD CT
RANELAGH GDNS
SULIVAN COURT
DAISY LA
SULIVAN
Tennis Cts
Sch
Tennis Courts
PARK
Chelsea College of Art & Design
Works
CARNWATH
DOCK
Trinidad Wharf
Hurlingham Wharf
Fulham Wharf
Superstore
Warehouse
Jetty
THAMES
HAMMERSMITH & FULHAM
WANDSWORTH
WANDSWORTH BRI
WANDSWORTH BRI. END
BUS DEPOT
Solid Waste Transfer Station
Superstore
SMUGGLERS WAY
SWANDON WAY
WANDSWORTH TOWN
LIGHTERMANS WK
POINT PLEASANT
NORTHFIELDS
OSIERS RD
ENTERPRISE WAY
Bell La Creek
WANDSWORTH PARK
Bowling Grn
PUTNEY BRIDGE ROAD
A3209
FAWE PARK ROAD
FB
WANDSWORTH
RICHMOND ROAD
COUNTY CT
OAKHILL RD
EAST PUTNEY
SCHUBERT RD
GALVESTON RD
MEXFIELD RD
DROMFORD RD
SANTOS RD
ERICSSON CLO
ARMOURY WAY
FROGMORE
Brewery
RAM ST
FAIRFIELD ST
MUN. OFF
WANDSWORTH HIGH ST
EAST HILL
WEST HILL
A3
Amb Sta
Fire Sta
Lib
Pol
Coll
Comm Cen
MUS.
BURIAL GRD
Arndale Shopping Centre
Shopping Cen
Clinic
BUCKHOLD ROAD
MERTON ROAD
A218
GARRATT LANE
A217
KING GEORGE'S PARK
Sports Cen
SPORTS GROUND
Whitelands Training College
MELROSE RD
SEYMOUR RD
VIEWFIELD RD
GRANVILLE ROAD
WINCANTON RD
HAMBLEDON RD
GATWICK RD
PULBOROUGH RD
STANDEN ROAD
BRATHWAY RD
CAMBORNE RD
KIMBER ROAD
SMEATON RD
THE BAULK
LONGFIELD ST
Depots
Depot
Comm Cen
Sports Centre
RIVERSIDE BUS CEN
Health Cen
LYDDEN RD
BENDON VALLEY
SOUTHFIELDS
DANE PL
WANDLE WAY
FORSTERS WAY
VANDERBILT RD
ST. JOHNS DR
PIRBRIGHT ROAD
BOWMAN MS
SOUTHFIELDS
MANNINGTREE CLO
EDGECOMBE HO
COMBEMARTIN ROAD
WIMBLEDON PK RD

SW11
London Westland Heliport
Shell Wharf
York Gdns
Warehouse
Comm Cen
Superstore
Winstanley Est
Clinic
Sports Cen
Clapham Junction
Clapham Junction Est
Falcon Park
Open Space
Fire Sta
Shopping Cen
Buses and taxis only
TA Centre
Battersea Arts Centre
Lavender Hill
Lavender Gdns
Battersea Rise
Clapham Common West Side
St. John's Health Care Unit
St. John's Hill
Wands. Common North Side
Spencer Park
St. Mary's Cem
Bolingbroke Hosp
Bolingbroke Grove
Northcote Road
Playing Fields
Wandsworth Common
Fitzhugh Grove Est
Neals Nurseries
H.M. Prison Wandsworth
Heathfield Road
Trinity Road
Windmill Road
Wandsworth Cemetery
Crem
Clubhouse
Bowling Grn
Tenn Cts
Bowl Grn
The Avenue
Balham
A3
A3036
A3205
A3220
A214
B229
B234
30
38
1
2
3
4
5
D
E
F
G

38
31
37
A
B
C
D
1
2
3
4
5
CLAPHAM
CLAPHAM COMMON
SW4
SW12
CLAPHAM PARK
BALHAM
TRINITY HOSPICE
WANDSWORTH ROAD
QUEENSTOWN
CEDARS ROAD
A3216
A3036
LAVENDER HILL
A3
A205
A24
B303
B237
CLAPHAM COMMON NORTH SIDE
LONG ROAD
CLAPHAM COMMON SOUTH SIDE
CLAPHAM COMMON WEST SIDE
THE AVENUE
CAVENDISH ROAD
POYNDERS ROAD
BALHAM HILL
ROAD
ELSPETH
WAKEHURST
WINDMILL DRIVE
MOUNT POND
EAGLE POND
LONG POND
COCK POND
REC GRD
Bandstand
King's College
MACAULAY SQUARE
MACAULAY CT
THE PAVEMENT
CLAPHAM COMMON
CLAPHAM SOUTH
LA RETRAITE CONVENT
OAKLANDS EST
NOTRE DAME EST
Battersea Arts Centre
Go-Karting
HONEYBROOK
NIGHTINGALE LANE
NIGHTINGALE WALK
WEIR EST

38
31
39
D
E
F
G
1
2
3
4
5
STOCKWELL
CLAPHAM RD EST
CLAPHAM NORTH
SOUTH WESTERN HOSP
STOCKWELL PK EST
MYATT'S FIELDS SOUTH EST
MAX ROACH PK
BRIXTON ACADEMY
LOUGHBOROUGH EST
Sports Cen
Brixton College
BRIXTON
COLDHARBOUR LANE
MOORLANDS EST
TOWN HALL
THE FRIDGE
Superstore
ACRE LANE
ELLERSLIE SQ IND EST
Lambeth College
BRIXTON WATER LANE
MORVAL RD
DULWICH ROAD
EFFRA ROAD
Ashby Windmill
H.M. PRISON BRIXTON
SW2
TULSE HILL ESTATE
Bowling Green
Tennis Courts
Lido
BROCKWELL PARK
STREATHAM HILL
CHRISTCHURCH ROAD
STREATHAM PL
BRIXTON HILL
A23
B221
B223

39
MAUDSLEY HOSPITAL
KING'S COLLEGE HOSPITAL
32
Salvation Army College
LOUGHBOROUGH JUNCTION
COLDHARBOUR LANE
RUSKIN PARK
CHAMPION PK
GROVE LANE
DENMARK HILL
MOORLANDS EST
GUINNESS TRUST EST
IND ESTATE
SE24
38
GREENDALE PLAYING FIELDS
PLAYING FIELDS
SUNRAY GDNS
HERNE HILL
HALF MOON LANE
VILLAGE WAY
NORTH DULWICH
DULWICH RD
A2214
A215
A2199
HERNE HILL STADIUM
BROCKWELL PARK
SPORTS GRD
SOUTH BANK UNIVERSITY SPORTS GROUND
BELAIR PARK
CROXTED ROAD
NORWOOD ROAD
MILKWOOD ROAD
BROCKWELL PARK GDNS
PEABODY HILL EST
Dulwich Old Coll
LAMBETH
SOUTHWARK
A
B
C
D
1
2
3
4
5

39
32
40
D
E
F
G
1
2
3
4
5
WARWICK GDNS
LINWOOD
PARK
CLOSE
GROVE
PELH CLO
BLENHEIM GROVE
CHOUMERT
CHO. SQ
Comm Cen
A2215
BOURNEMOUTH RD
ALMOND CLO
BIRCH CLO
BLACKPOOL RD
BRAYARDS
CREWYS RD
Sch
GODMAN RD
COPELAND
PO
CHOUMERT ROAD
SAN. ST
McDERMOTT
WINGFIELD ST
COSTA
ANSTEY ROAD
RELF ROAD
NIGEL RD
STERNHALL
HEATON
ROAD
ELLERY ST
WIVEN CLO
MANATON CLOSE
Lib
MONT. WAY
NUN. GRN
A2214
EVELINA
HOWBURY
BARSET
DANBY STREET
AVONDALE RISE
SOAMES STREET
BELLENDEN ROAD
MAXTED ROAD
HOWDEN STREET
WAGHORN ST
NUTBROOK STREET
RYE PAS
PHILIP WALK
SCYLLA ROAD
Clinic
SCY. RD
NUNHEAD GROVE
IVANHOE RD
MALFORT ROAD
BROMAR
ALBRIGHTON RD
Health Cen
PYTCHLEY ROAD
QUORN ROAD
FB
COPLESTON ROAD
OXENFORD ST
EVER
OGLANDER ROAD
MARSDEN ROAD
MUSCHAMP ROAD
ADYS ROAD
AMOTT RD
KESTON RD
GOWLETT RD
FENWICK ROAD
DEWAR ST
KINSALE ROAD
FEN. GRO
PECKHAM RYE
WHORLTON RD
Coll
NUNHEAD CRES
JAMES ST
NUNHEAD LANE
Comm Cen
BARFORTH RD
CARDEN ROAD
LINDEN GRO
FORESTER RD
TRESCO RD
BELVEDERE MS
ABBOTT MS
LIMES WALK
NUNHEAD
Depot
ONDINE ROAD
HINCKLEY RD
EAST DULWICH ROAD
GOOSE GREEN
NUNHEAD ESTATE
SOLOMAN'S PASS.
WAVENEY AVENUE
SOMERT. RD
TORRIDGE GARDENS
Lib
GROVE VALE
EAST DULWICH
FRANCIS
TALB. ROAD
ELSIE ROAD
DERWENT GRO
MELBOURNE GRO
TINTAGEL CRES
SOLWAY RD
KELMORE GRO
THE GARDENS
OAKHURST GROVE
Sports Cen
PECKHAM RYE COMMON
PECKHAM ROAD
B219
KINGS COLL HOSP DULWICH
DULWICH GROVE
ZENORIA ST
SPURLING RD
CRAWTHEW GROVE
WORLINGHAM RD
CRYSTAL PALACE ROAD
FERRIS RD
TYRRELL ROAD
STRAKER'S ROAD
MATHAM GROVE
FROGLEY RD
NUTFIELD RD
ARCHDALE RD
LACON RD
ASHBOURNE GROVE
NORTH CROSS RD
UPLAND ROAD
Bowling Green
PECKHAM RYE PARK
TROSSACHS RD
TARBERT RD
GLENGARRY
CHESTERFIELD GROVE
BASSANO ST
BLACK. ST
SHAWBURY ROAD
HANSLER ROAD
BAWDALE ROAD
FELLBRIGG
ULVERSCROFT ROAD
DARRELL ROAD
HINDMANS ROAD
HENSLOWE ROAD
Comm Cen
REC GRD
PLAYING FIELDS
HOMESTALL
LYCOTT GRO
PLAYFIELD CRES
Sch
WHATELEY RD
SILVESTER RD
PELLATT ROAD
RODWELL ROAD
HEBER ROAD
JENNINGS ROAD
CYRENA RD
LANDCROFT ROAD
Pol
COLWELL
Health Cen
LORDSHIP LANE
UNDERHILL ROAD
Comm Cen
MUL. CLO
FRIERN ROAD
Sch
PIERMONT GREEN
PIERMONT ROAD
COLYTON
SHELBURY ROAD
DOVEDALE ROAD
SCUTARI
FOREST HILL ROAD
ST AIDAN'S ROAD
DUNSTANS GRO
CORN. TER
RYEDALE
MUNDANIA
THERAPIA ROAD
Tenn Cts
SPORTS GRD
ROAD
BEAUVAL RD
DOVERCOURT RD
EAST DULWICH
GOODRICH ROAD
THOMP RD
MILO RD
A2216
CREBOR ST
ROYAL OAK PL
ROCKELLS PL
BRENCHLEY
WOODWARDE RD
DRUCE RD
DOVERCOURT ROAD
EASTLANDS CRES
LANDELLS ROAD
PLOUGH LANE
BARRY ROAD
Sch
Coll
SE22
HILLCOURT ROAD
CAMBERWELL OLD CEMETERY
WOODVALE
VALE EST
COURT LANE GDNS
EYNELLA ROAD
Lib
ETHEROW ST
NORCROFT GDNS
DUNSTANS ROAD
DONKEY ALLEY
RUDOLPH COURT
LANGTON RISE
PO
CANONBIE
NETHERBY ROAD
SYDMONS CT
Court La Gate
LANE
DAWSON HEIGHTS EST
MOUNT ADON PARK
OVERHILL ROAD
HORSE RIDE
Tennis Courts
Bowling Green
BELVOIR ROAD
UNDERHILL
WOOD
WESTWOOD PARK
TEWKESBURY AVE
RINGMORE RISE
LIPHOOK CRES
COV RES
DULWICH PARK
Clinic
SUNDERLAND COURT
MELFORD ROAD
LORDSHIP LA EST
DRIVE
ROCOMBE CRES
THE HERMITAGE
Tennis Courts
Bowl Grn
SPORTS GROUND
DULWICH COMMON
Tenn Cts
Queen Mary's
BURNFOOT
Bandstand
AMROTH CLO
WESTWOOD
HORNIMAN
Sch

NUNHEAD
WAVERLEY PARK
NUNHEAD CEMETERY
PLAYING FIELDS
COV RES
RYE HILL EST
ALLOTMENTS
FOOTPATH
LEWISHAM
SOUTHWARK
TELEGRAPH HILL PARK
B2142 DRAKEFELL ROAD
ST ASAPH ROAD
EVELINA ROAD
A2214
BROCKLEY
Community Centre
Health Cen
HONOR OAK SPORTS GROUND
Crem
Tennis Courts
Pav
CAMBERWELL NEW CEMETERY
ONE TREE HILL
HONOR OAK
HONOR OAK PARK
AQUARIUS GOLF COURSE
Pumping Station
Clubhouse
PEckHAM RYE PARK
REC GRD
PLAYING FIELDS
CAMBERWELL OLD CEMETERY
GUY'S UMDS ATHLETIC GROUND
BROCKLEY HILL PARK
BLYTHE HILL FIELDS
SE23
GARTHORNE ROAD NATURE RESERVE
Fire Sta
Health Centre
STANSTEAD ROAD
A205
B238
B218
Brockley Jack PH
CROFTON PARK
Lib
Sch
PO
33
39
A
B
C
D
1
2
3
4
5

Lewisham Coll
Breakspears
A20
33
D
E
F
G
LEWISHAM
GRANVILLE
LOAMPIT HILL
LOAMPIT VALE
THURSTON RD
JERRARD ST
HORTON ST
ELSWICK RD
SUNNING RD
ARMOURY RD
LEATH RD
ELVERSON RD
RIVER
SILK MILLS
COLUMBINE WAY
CONINGTON ROAD
WALERAND ROAD
ELIOT PARK
PRINCES RISE
LEWISHAM RD
TACK MEWS
DARLING ROAD
AVON ROAD
DRAKE RD
BEVERLEY COURT
GARSIN MEWS
BREAKSPEARS ROAD
TRESSILLIAN CRES
TRESSILLIAN CRESCENT
HILLY FIELDS CRES
TYRWHITT ROAD
WHITBURN
SANDROCK ROAD
SANDROCK RD
UNDERCLIFF ROAD
OVERCLIFF ROAD
NUDING CLOSE
BROOKBANK ROAD
FOSSIL RD
CLIFFVIEW ROAD
HALESWORTH RD
LADY WELL RD
ALGERNON ROAD
BERTRAND ST
BRANDRAM ST
VIAN ST
ELMIRA STREET
CORNMILL LANE
VINEY ROAD
SHELL RD
ERMINE RD
EMBLETON ROAD
ELLERDALE STREET
VICARS HILL
MARSALA RD
Sch
CRESSINGHAM RD
BOYNE ROAD
LOCKMEAD RD
CATERHAM
BELMONT
LEWIS HIGH ST
LEWIS GRO
Sports Cen
Bowl. Alley
LEE BRIDGE
MARISCHAL RD
LAKE MS
PO
P
LEWISHAM
Lewisham Centre
MOLESWORTH ST
QUAGGY
GILMORE ROAD
CLARENDON RISE
ALBION WAY
MERCHANT GR
BONFIELD ROAD
Lib
LIMES GROVE
CLIPPER WAY
SLAITHWAITE ROAD
MORLEY
COLLEGE CLO
WISTERIA RD
PARK
41
HILLY FIELDS
Bowling Green
Tennis Courts
SE13
Council Depot
CHALSEY ROAD
MONTAGUE AVENUE
ADELAIDE AVENUE
IVY ROAD
LADYWELL CEMETERY
War Memorial
B236
EASTERN ROAD
VEDA ROAD
ALGIERS ROAD
GREATFIELD CLOSE
MERCY TER
CHURCH GROVE
WEARS RD
WHITBURN RD
COURTHILL ROAD
Fire Sta
LONGBRIDGE WAY
GILLIAN ST
LADYWELL ROAD
LADYWELL RD
Comm Cen
CORONATION CT
Sports Cen
A21
HIGH ST
LADYWELL
LEWISHAM HOSPITAL
Pol
LEGGE ST
ROMBOROUGH GDNS
ROMBOROUGH WAY
HITHER GREEN
RYECROFT ROAD
HOLLYHEDGE
3
GROVE
AMYRUTH RD
GORDONBROCK ROAD
ARTHURDON ROAD
FRANCEMARY RD
PHOEBETH ROAD
PEPPERMEAD SQ
MALYONS TER
ELSIEMAUD ROAD
HENRYSON ROAD
HUXBEAR ST
ABBOTSWELL ROAD
LEIGH ROAD
CHUDLEIGH
Water Twr (Dis)
RUSHEY MEAD
FOXBOROUGH GARDENS
DRESSINGTON AVENUE
Ladywell Centre
MALYONS ROAD
Tenn Cts
Sch
Lib
GUYSCLIFF ROAD
CAMPSHILL ROAD
MONUMENT GDNS
War Memorial
LEWISHAM PARK
THORNFORD RD
HARVARD ROAD
KNOWLE CRESCENT
ENNERSDALE
SWITHIN ST
LITTLEWOOD
RADFORD ROAD
FORDYCE RD
LANIER RD
THEODORE ROAD
MOUNTSFIELD COURT
FB
Tenn Cts
Pav
Sports Cen
CATFORD GREYHOUND STADIUM
ALBACORE CRES
BLAGDON ROAD
FELDAY ROAD
Health Centre
MOUNT PLEASANT ROAD
ALDWORTH GROVE
BOXLEY RD
GEORGE LANE
LARA CLOSE
4
The George Inn
MEDUSA ROAD
HAWSTEAD ROAD
DAVENPORT ROAD
ROSENTHAL ROAD
SYCAMORE GRO
Bowling Green
HOSPITAL (closed)
RUSHFORD ROAD
BRIGHTLING ROAD
EWHURST ROAD
LADYWELL FIELDS
BRADGATE
BROOKDALE
SCROOBY ST
PATROL PLACE
WILDFELL ROAD
SE6
FARLEY ROAD
LALEHAM
MOUNTSFIELD PARK REC GRD
STAINTON ROAD
IONA CLOSE
RAVENSBOURNE PARK CRES
Bowl Grn
HOLBEACH ROAD
DOGGETT RD
NELGARDE RD
THOMAS LANE
LEWISHAM TOWN HALL
MERRY WAY
HONLEY ROAD
CUDHAM ST
RINGSTEAD ROAD
MELBOURNE MEWS
CARSWELL ROAD
RUSHEY GREEN
BROWNHILL ROAD
A205 (SOUTH
REDFERN ROAD
5
BOURNVILLE ROAD
WESTDOWN RD
ADENMORE RD
CATFORD BRIDGE
CATFORD ROAD
Lewisham Theatre
PLASSY RD
BOWNESS ROAD
JUTLAND RD
ELMER ROAD
ARNGASK
SPORTSBANK ST
ENGLEHEART
PLAYING FIELDS
CATFORD
Sch
Pav
Clubho
BROMLEY RD
Cannon Cinema
SANGLEY ROAD
SHORNDEAN ST
ST FILLANS ROAD
FORDEL
GLENFARG
CIRCULAR ROAD
PRIVATE BANKS SPORTS GROUND
CANADIAN
CULVERLEY ROAD
Sch
Pav
Comm
SANDHURST

41
A
B
C
D
34
40
1
2
3
4
5
Clarendon Hotel
Sch
ELIOT VALE
ELIOT PLACE
HEATH LANE
PAGODA GDNS
OAKCROFT ROAD
GRANVILLE PK
ST. JOSEPH'S VALE
BAIZDON ROAD
HURREN CLOSE
GROTE'S PLACE
GROTE'S BLDGS
COLLINS
BLACKHEATH
BENNETT PARK
CRESSWELL PARK
BLACKHEATH PK
BLACKHEATH CONCERT HALLS
BLACKHEATH HOSPITAL
LAWN TERRACE
PREN. RD
THE GLEBE
LEE TERRACE
Coll
Schs
CRESSINGHAM RD
BOYNE
CATERHAM RD
BELMONT GROVE
BELMONT B220 HILL
LEE BRIDGE
Bowl. Alley
MARISCHAL RD
SAX. CL.
BLESSINGTON
BISCOE WAY
MERCATOR RD
CLARENDON RISE
GILMORE ROAD
QUAGGY
A20
LEE
ALBION WAY
BONFIELD ROAD
Lib
LIMES
BLAITHWAITE ROAD
BRANDRAM ROAD
CHURCH TERRACE
DACRE PLACE
DACRE PARK
ETON GRO
QUENTIN ROAD
HAYNES CLO
TRIST. SQ.
LOCK CHASE
BOONES RD
PRIORY PARK
PARKGATE
THE PRIORY
MEADOWBANK
MANOR WK
QUAGGY
BLA
ALLOT
SHEARMAN ROAD
FOX
COP. RD
ELMS WK
ARNE WALK
HEATHLEE RD
LEWISHAM
GREENWICH
ROAD B212
BELMONT PARK
KING. PL
DACRE GDNS
Comm Cem
FLUDY ST
BOONE ST
LEE CHURCH ST
CELESTIAL GDNS
GLEN RD
Amb Sta
PO
HIGH ROAD
EAST PARK
MURILLO RD
REM. RD
ABERNETHY RD
LOCHABER RD
OLD ROAD
AISLIBIE ROAD
LENHAM ROAD
Old Tiger's Head PH
MEADOWCOURT RD
Coll
SPORTS G
Tennis Ct
Club
Fire Sta
ELTH
HAMLET CLO
RAVE
WISTERIA ROAD
EASTDOWN PARK
RIVER
WEARDALE RD
Lib
MANOR L.T.
Comm Cen
MANOR HOUSE GARDENS
LAMPMEAD RD
BRIGHTFIELD ROAD
Pol
HEDGLEY ST
COLLEGE PK
DERMODY
HOLLY HILL GDNS
NORTHBROOK RD
CORDWELL RD
MANOR LANE TER
KELLERTON ROAD
CHALCROFT RD
THORNWOOD ROAD
MANOR PARK
LEAHURST ROAD
PASCOE ROAD
Sch
FALMOUTH
WIMBORNE CL.
TAUNTON ROAD
EFFINGHAM
WANTAGE
Health Cen
BURNT ASH ROAD
A2212
LEEGATE
LEYLAND
CARSTON CLOSE
LEYBRIDGE CT
OSBERTON RD
MILL WAY
COURTHILL ROAD
RYECROFT
MONUMENT GDNS
KNOWLES HILL CRESCENT
NIGHTINGALE GROVE
LONG PARK
STAPLEHURST RD
HURST
HANDEN ROAD
MICHELDEVER ROAD
DORVILLE
ALANTHUS CLOSE
SILK CLOSE
HORNFORD
HARVARD ROAD
MERCLO
ENNERSDALE
SMITH ST
FORDYCE RD
LITTLEWOOD
RADFORD ROAD
MOUNTSFIELD COURT
BEACON ROAD
AROMERE
FERNBROOK ROAD
HITHER GREEN
LEE
SOUTHBROOK ROAD
SOUTH MS
UPWOOD
LANIER RD
THEODORE ROAD
SPRINGRICE ROAD
BRIGHTSIDE ROAD
MALRD
ELTHRUDA RD
SPRINGBANK
HITHER GREEN
MANOR LANE
CHILTONIAN IND. ESTATE
LEE
PO
HOSPITAL (closed)
STAINTON ROAD
HITHER GREEN
DUNCRIEVIE RD
WELLMEADOW ROAD
BR DEPOT
HOLME LACEY ROAD
DALLINGER ROAD
WOODYATES
LUCORN CLO
KIMBOLTON CLO
STONEY CLO
BURNT ASH HILL
Bowling Green
MOUNTSFIELD PARK REC GRD
WOODLANDS ST
BLASHFORD STREET
BENIN ST
THE WOODLANDS
TORRIDON ROAD
ARDGOWAN ROAD
MINARD ROAD
BROADFIELD ROAD
WELLMEADOW ROAD
MILBOROUGH CRESCENT
NEWSTEAD ROAD
PARKCROFT ROAD
BIRCH GROVE
WILDWOOD CLO
PITFOLD
MOUNTFIELD CLO
ST. MILDREDS ROAD
BARING
REDRUTH ROAD
ROAD A205 (SOUTH CIRCULAR ROAD)
ARNGASK ROAD
FORDEL ROAD
GLENFARG ROAD
SANDHURST
SHORNDEAN ST
ST. FILLANS ROAD
TORRIDON ROAD
ARDGOWAN ROAD
MINARD ROAD
BROADFIELD ROAD
WELLMEADOW ROAD
VERDANT LANE
FURTHER GREEN ROAD
SOUTH PARK
CUMBERLAND PL
ALLOT
RAYFORD AVENUE
HELDER GROVE
LINCHMERE RD
WAITE DAVIES ROAD
SUMMERFIELD ST
RONVER ROAD
NORTHBROOK PARK
Lib
Sch
PO

41
34
42
D
E
F
G
1
2
3
4
5
KIDBROOKE
ELTHAM
SPORTS GROUND
Tenn Cts
SPORTS GROUNDS
Pav
Depot
Sch
Superstore
Health Cen
Coll
Comm Cen
Lib
MINI TOWN HALL
KIDBROOKE GREEN NATURE RESERVE
ROCHESTER WAY
KIDBROOKE PARK ROAD
A2213
A2
A20
A210
SUTCLIFFE PARK
Sports Cen
Bowl Grn
REC GRD
Clubhouse
WEIGALL ROAD
SPORTS GROUND
Tennis Courts
LYME FARM ROAD
SIDCUP ROAD
ROAD
ELTHAM HILL
WESTHORNE AVENUE
Amb Sta
Yorkshire Grey PH
MIDDLE PARK FIELD
MIDDLE PARK AVENUE
QUEENSCROFT
CIVIL SERVICE SPORTS GROUND
SPORTS GROUNDS
QUAGGY RIVER
Dutch House PH
MOTTINGHAM LANE
ELTHAM PALACE ROAD
ALLOT
OLD ELTHAMIANS SPORTS GROUND
MOORHEAD WAY
GALLUS SQUARE
LEBRUN SQ
EBDON WAY
PINTO WAY
TUDWAY ROAD
ELFORD CLOSE
RYAN CLOSE
ROMERO SQ
CAMBERT WAY
MEADOWSIDE
EDGEWORTH RD
KATHERINE GARDENS
KNOCKHOLT RD
PHILIPPA GARDENS
LEGATT ROAD
FROISSART ROAD
KEYNSHAM ROAD
WINCHCOMB GARDENS
BRENLEY GDNS
KINGSHOLM GDNS
UNIVERSITY OF GREENWICH SPORTS GROUND
COURTLANDS AVE
SUNNYDALE RD
FAIRBY ROAD
SOUTH GDNS
LILIAN BARKER CLO
HORN PARK LANE
SHELDON CLOSE
SCOTSDALE ROAD
STRATHAVEN RD
ABERGELDIE ROAD
CRATHIE ROAD
CEDARHURST DRIVE
RYELANDS CRES
ALWOLD CRESCENT
SIBTHORPE ROAD
SIMNEL ROAD
PASTON CRESCENT
HORSA ROAD
GAVESTONE RD
GAVESTONE CRESCENT
HENGIST ROAD
WOODYATES ROAD
CORONA ROAD
ELWYN GDNS
MELROSE CLOSE
WINN ROAD
CHURCHBURY RD
CAMPFIELD RD
FERNDO RD
GREGORY CRES
GLASBROOK ROAD
CUFF CRES
KINGSGROUND
JOAN CRESCENT
KING JOHN PLAYING FIELDS
Comm Cen
PO
Clinic
Hall

GREENWICH CEMETERY
Severndroog Castle
Tennis Courts
CASTLE WOOD
35
WELL HALL ROAD (SOUTH CIRCULAR)
ARBROATH ROAD
CROOKSTON ROAD
DAIRSIE ROAD
ROCHESTER WAY
DUMBRECK ROAD
SE9
ELIBANK ROAD
EARLSHALL ROAD
GREENVALE ROAD
ELTHAM PARK GDNS
DUNVEGAN ROAD
RELIEF ROAD
Coronet Cinema
KIDBROOKE LANE
AVENUE A205
UNIVERSITY OF GREENWICH SPORTS GROUND
MOAT
WELL HALL PLEASANCE
ELTHAM
41
WAY
BUS STA
GLENLEA
CONV OF MERCY
FROISSART ROAD
TATTERSALL CLOSE
SHERARD ROAD
ST. JOHN'S CEMETERY
ELTHAM HILL
ELTHAM HIGH ST
A208
COURT RD
ORANGERY LANE
TOWN HALL
Sports Cen
QUEENSCROFT REC GROUND
ELTHAM
KINGSGROUND
ALLOT
ELTHAM PALACE
ELTHAM & MOTTINGHAM HOSPITAL
Superstore
FOOTSCRAY ROAD
KING JOHNS WALK
KING JOHN PLAYING FIELDS
ROYAL BLACKHEATH GOLF COURSE
Clubhouse
Coll
SPORTS GRD
MIDDLE PARK AVENUE
JOAN CRESCENT
A20
SANCTUARY
MOTTINGHAM
A B C D
1 2 3 4 5

35
A207
We Anchor In Hope PH
SANDRINGHAM DR
SHOULDER OF MUTTON GREEN
OXLEAS WOOD
OXLEAS MEADOW
FALCONWOOD AVENUE
OXLEAS CLOSE
EASTCOTE ROAD
SUNDRIDGE AVE
BELMONT AVE
SHERWOOD RD
GROVE
ASHMORE
MONTROSE CLOSE
A209
WELLING WAY
DA16
FALCONWOOD
SPORTS GROUND
SHEPHERDLEAS WOOD
ROCHESTER WAY
FALCONWOOD FIELD
ALLOT
Elec Sta
FALCONWOOD
MONTROSE AVENUE
NORTHUMBERLAND AVE
WESTMORELAND AVENUE
CUMBERLAND AVENUE
CORNWALL AVENUE
YORKLAND AVENUE
Schs
A2
ROAD
ELTHAM PARK NORTH
ELTHAM PARK SOUTH
LINGFIELD CRESCENT
BRAYWOOD ROAD
WINCROFTS DRIVE
RIEFIELD ROAD
ELTHAM CEMETERY
Crematorium
EAST
THE SUTHERLAND GREEN
BUCKINGHAM
Comm Cen
Clinic
FALCONWOOD PARADE
PO
CAMBRIDGE AVE
DORSET AVE
HOOK LANE
FB
COLEPITS WOOD ROAD
LANE
ELTHAM WARREN GOLF COURSE
Sch
FAIROAK DRIVE
WOODS
RENNETS WOOD ROAD
RENNETS CLOSE
ORCHARD RISE
BOUNDARY ROAD
RIDGEWAY WEST
B2213
CHESTER ROAD
ORCHARD RISE EAST
GRAVEL PIT LANE
Clubhouse
Environment Study Centre
Tennis Courts
PLAYING FIELD
CROWN WOODS WAY
PACKMORES RD
GORDON RD
BLAIR CLOSE
A210
BLACKFEN ROAD
The Jolly Fenman PH
LEMONWELL DR
ALLOT
Nursery
University of Greenwich
Avery Hill Campus
AVERY HILL
Pavs
AVERY HILL PARK
AVERY HILL ROAD
RESTONS CRESCENT
ANSTRIDGE
ALDERWOOD ROAD
RAINHAM CL
PARISH GATE DR
RIDER CLO
KIRKLANDS CLO
ALEXANDER CLOSE
MONTGOMERY CL
RAEBURN
RONALDSTONE ROAD
QUEENSWOOD ROAD
DA15
HOLBEACH
CLOVERDALE GDNS
PARISH WOOD
Sch
LYDD CT
PERPINS ROAD
WAY LINK
Comm Cen
LINSTEAD
BERWICK CRESCENT
CAITHNESS GDNS
SPORTS GRDS
University of Greenwich Halls of Residence
CAMBRIDGE MISSION SPORTS GROUND
Tenn Cts
RESTONS CRESCENT
RADFIELD WAY
B2214
NORFOLK CRESCENT
ROSEBERY AVENUE
HARBOROUGH AVE
BEVERLEY AVENUE
OAKLANDS
BLAC
CHARLTON ATHLETIC FC TRAIN GROUND
Sports Cen
Bowling Green
Clubhouse
CROYDE CLOSE
HAM RD
SOUTHSPRING
GREENHITHE CLOSE
HAMBLEDON RD
ARLINGTON CLOSE
DAYS LANE
CORBYLANDS ROAD
ANNANDALE
STREAM
SHUTTLE
RIVER SHUTTLE
HALEWAY
OVERMEAD
FOREST WAY
SPORTS GROUNDS
THE FOOTWAY
Pavs
SPORTS GROUND
Clubhouse
MERRILEES ROAD
WOODBINE ROAD
WOODLANDS AVENUE
MILLWALL TRAINING GRD
SPARROWS LANE
ALVERTON GDNS
Works
SIDEWOOD
CAMBRIA CLOSE
D
E
F
G
1
2
3
4
5

MIDDLESEX HOSP
GOODGE ST
MORTIMER ST
BLOOMSBURY
BEDFORD SQUARE
OXFORD ST
OXFORD CIRCUS
TOTTENHAM COURT ROAD
NEW OXFORD ST
ST. GILES HIGH ST
SOHO
SOHO SQUARE
SHAFTESBURY AVE
CHARING CROSS ROAD
REGENT STREET
CONDUIT ST
CARNABY ST
BROADWICK ST
WARDOUR ST
GLASSHOUSE STREET
PICCADILLY CIR
HAYMARKET
TRAFALGAR
NATIONAL GALLERY
PALL MALL
ST. JAMES'S
ST. JAMES'S SQUARE
PICCADILLY
GREEN PARK
MARLBOROUGH HOUSE
Chapel Royal
St. James's Palace
Lancaster House
ROYAL ACAD OF ARTS
MUS OF MANKIND
Birkbeck College
LIBERTY
PALLADIUM
COLL OF MUSIC
Horse Guards Road
ADMIRALTY ARCH
ICA
Duck Island
Bandstand

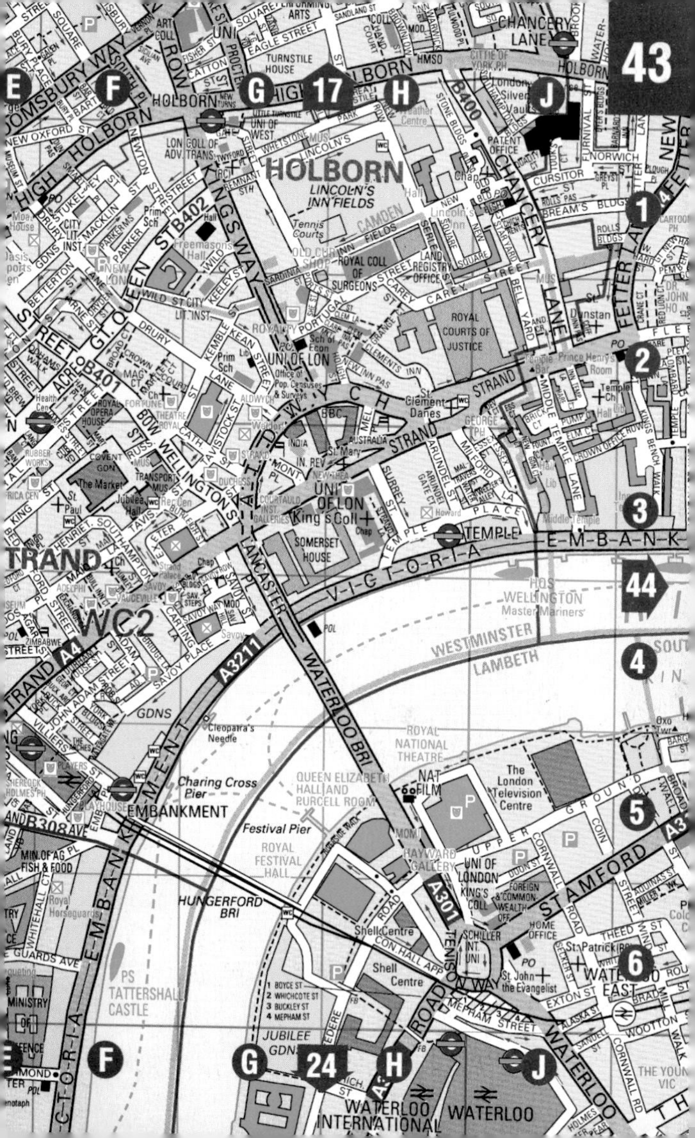

HOLBORN
LINCOLN'S INN FIELDS
CHANCERY LANE
HIGH HOLBORN
BLOOMSBURY WAY
NEW OXFORD ST
KINGSWAY
PERFORMING ARTS
TURNSTILE HOUSE
LONDON Silver Vaults
PATENT OFFICE
CURSITOR ST
BREAM'S BLDGS
FETTER LANE
FLEET ST
ROYAL COLL OF SURGEONS
LAND REGISTRY OFFICE
CAREY STREET
ROYAL COURTS OF JUSTICE
BELL YARD
St. Dunstan
Prince Henry's Room
Temple Bar
MIDDLE TEMPLE LANE
KING'S BENCH WALK
Middle Temple
FREEMASONS Hall
GT. QUEEN ST
DRURY LANE
ROYAL OPERA HOUSE
COVENT GDN
The Market
TRANSPORT MUS
Jubilee Hall
WELLINGTON ST
BOW ST
UNI OF LON
Office of Pop. Censuses & Surveys
ALDWYCH
BBC
INDIA
AUSTRALIA
St. Clement Danes
STRAND
St. Mary
IN. REV
UNI OF LON King's Coll
COURTAULD INST. GALLERIES
SOMERSET HOUSE
ARUNDEL ST
SURREY ST
ESSEX ST
MILFORD LA
TEMPLE PLACE
TEMPLE
VICTORIA EMBANKMENT
HQS WELLINGTON Master Mariners'
WC2
SAVOY PLACE
Savoy
LANCASTER PL
A3211
WATERLOO BRI
A4
ADAM ST
JOHN ADAM STREET
VILLIERS ST
PLAYHOUSE
EMBANKMENT
Cleopatra's Needle
Charing Cross Pier
WESTMINSTER
LAMBETH
ROYAL NATIONAL THEATRE
NAT FILM
The London Television Centre
QUEEN ELIZABETH HALL AND PURCELL ROOM
Festival Pier
ROYAL FESTIVAL HALL
MOMI
HAYWARD GALLERY
UNI OF LONDON KING'S COLL
FOREIGN & COMMONWEALTH OFF
HOME OFFICE
UPPER GROUND
STAMFORD ST
CORNWALL ROAD
COIN ST
A3
A301
HUNGERFORD BRI
MIN. OF AG FISH & FOOD
Royal Horseguards
WHITEHALL CT
HORSE GUARDS AVE
MINISTRY OF DEFENCE
PS TATTERSHALL CASTLE
Shell Centre
CON. HALL APP
TENISON WAY
SCHILLER INT. UNI
St. John the Evangelist
St. Patrick
WATERLOO EAST
MEPHAM STREET
1 BOYCE ST
2 WHICHCOTE ST
3 BUCKLEY ST
4 MEPHAM ST
JUBILEE GDNS
WATERLOO INTERNATIONAL
WATERLOO
WATERLOO RD
THE YOUNG VIC
CORNWALL RD
WOOTTON ST
E F G H J
1 2 3 4 5 6
17
44
24

A
B
18
C
D
E
1
2
3
4
5
6
43
25
HOLBORN
HOLBORN CIRCUS
A40
VIADUCT
B500
FARRINGDON ST
NEW FETTER LANE
A4
FETTER LANE
SHOE LA
ST. ANDREW ST
ST. BRIDE ST
NEWGATE ST
KING EDWARD ST
ALDERSGATE
ST. MARTIN'S LE GRAND
LITTLE BRITAIN
WEST SMITHFIELD
GILTSPUR ST
ST. BARTHOLOMEW'S HOSPITAL
St. Sepulchre
CENTRAL CRIMINAL COURT (Old Bailey)
POSTAL MUS
Cutlers Hall
Goldsmiths' Hall
ST. PAUL'S
St. Vedast
ST. PAUL'S CATHEDRAL
PATERNOSTER SQ
PATERNOSTER ROW
Stationers' Hall
St. Martin
LUDGATE HILL
LUDGATE CIRCUS
CITY THAMESLINK
FLEET STREET
YE OLDE CHESHIRE CHEESE PH
DR. JOHNS HO
CITY LIT INST
St. Dunstan
St. Bride
CRYPT MUSS
NEW BRIDGE ST
WHITEFRIARS ST
BOUVERIE ST
TUDOR STREET
TEMPLE AVENUE
CARMELITE ST
J. CARPENTER ST
TALLIS ST
EC4
Inner Temple
Middle Temple
Temple Ch
CROWN OFFICE ROW
KINGS BENCH WALK
CARTER LANE
ST. PAUL'S CHURCHYARD
CANNON STREET
WATLING
Choir School
QUEEN VICTORIA STREET
Coll of Arms
St. Benet
Swim Pool
SALVATION ARMY INT. HQ
MERMAID THEATRE
BLACKFRIARS
EMBANKMENT
UPPER THAMES ST
HIGH TIMBER ST
City of Lon Sch
Pier
HMS PRESIDENT
RIVER THAMES
Southwark Bridge
SOUTHWARK
KING'S REACH
BLACKFRIARS BRIDGE
A201
H M CUSTOMS & EXCISE
Oxo Twr
UPPER GROUND
KING'S REACH TWR
RIVERSIDE WALK
BANKSIDE GALL
SHAKESPEARE GLOBE THEATRE
BANKSIDE
Power Station (Disused)
Express Newspapers
Under Const
HOPTON ST
HOLLAND STREET
PARK STREET
SHAKESPEARE GLOBE MUS
SUMNER STREET
SUMNER ST
PEABODY TRUST
A3200
STAMFORD STREET
SOUTHWARK STREET
LONDON NAUTICAL SCH
Christ Church
PARIS GARDEN
COLOMBO ST
ST. CHRISTOPHER HOUSE
INLAND REVENUE
PEABODY BLDGS
Colombo Street Sports & Community Centre
MEYMOTT ST
ROUPELL STREET
WATERLOO EAST
HATFIELDS
LAVINGTON STREET
HOME OFFICE
SOUTHWARK
B300
UNION STREET
British Library (India Office & Records)
SOUTHWARK COLLEGE
SCORE ST
THE CUT
WATERLOO
CORNWALL RD
ROAD
ISA. ST
St. Andrew with St. Thomas
SURREY ROW
LOMAN STREET
POCOCK ST
Fire Sta & London Fire Brigade Mus
SOUTHWARK BRIDGE ROAD
BEAR LANE
SUFFOLK ST
GREAT GUILDFORD ST
KEPPEL ROW

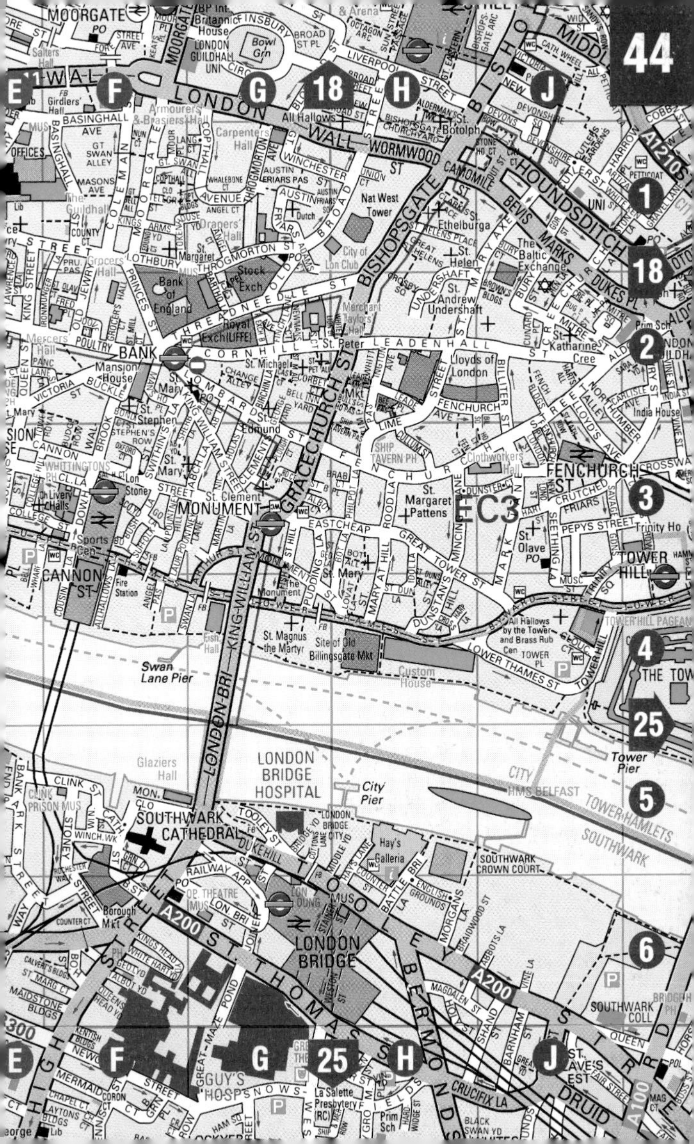
MOORGATE
LONDON WALL
FINSBURY
LONDON GUILDHALL UNI
LIVERPOOL STREET
BISHOPSGATE
HOUNDSDITCH
WORMWOOD ST
CAMOMILE ST
BEVIS MARKS
DUKES PL
The Baltic Exchange
Nat West Tower
City of Lon Club
Stock Exch
Bank of England
Royal Exch(LIFFE)
THREADNEEDLE ST
THROGMORTON ST
LOTHBURY
PRINCES ST
POULTRY
BANK
Mansion House
CORNHILL
LEADENHALL ST
Lloyds of London
FENCHURCH ST
FENCHURCH ST
GRACECHURCH ST
LOMBARD ST
KING WILLIAM STREET
CANNON ST
MONUMENT
EASTCHEAP
GREAT TOWER ST
EC3
TOWER HILL
LOWER THAMES ST
St. Magnus the Martyr
Site of Old Billingsgate Mkt
Custom House
Swan Lane Pier
LONDON BRI
LONDON BRIDGE HOSPITAL
City Pier
HMS BELFAST
Tower Pier
SOUTHWARK CATHEDRAL
Hay's Galleria
SOUTHWARK CROWN COURT
TOOLEY ST
LONDON BRIDGE
ST THOMAS ST
BERMONDSEY
A200
Borough Mkt
GUY'S HOSP
SOUTHWARK COLL
DRUID ST
CRUCIFIX LA
TOWER HAMLETS
SOUTHWARK
E F G H J
18
1 2 3 4 5 6
25

INDEX TO STREETS

General Abbreviations

All	Alley	Dr	Drive	Ind	Industrial	S	South
App	Approach	Dws	Dwellings	Junct	Junction	Sch	School
Arc	Arcade	E	East	La	Lane	Sq	Square
Ave	Avenue	Embk	Embankment	Lo	Lodge	St	Street, Saint
Bdy	Broadway	Est	Estate	Mans	Mansions	Sta	Station
Bldgs	Buildings	Ex	Exchange	Mkt	Market	Ter	Terrace
Bri	Bridge	Fld	Field	Mkts	Markets	Trd	Trading
Cen	Central, Centre	Flds	Fields	Ms	Mews	Twr	Tower
Ch	Church	Fm	Farm	Mt	Mount	Vill	Villas
Chyd	Churchyard	Gdn	Garden	N	North	Vw	View
Circ	Circus	Gdns	Gardens	Par	Parade	W	West
Clo	Close	Gra	Grange	Pas	Passage	WC	Toilet
Comm	Community	Grd	Ground	Pk	Park	Wd	Wood
Cor	Corner	Grds	Grounds	Pl	Place	Wds	Woods
Cotts	Cottages	Grn	Green	Prec	Precinct	Wf	Wharf
Cres	Crescent	Gro	Grove	Pt	Point	Wk	Walk
Ct	Court	Ho	House	Rd	Road	Wks	Works
Ctyd	Courtyard	Hos	Houses	Ri	Rise	Yd	Yard

Abbreviations of Post Towns

Bark.	Barking	Ilf.	Ilford	Sid.	Sidcup	Well.	Welling

NOTES

The figures and letters following a street name indicate the Postal District, page and map square where the name can be four
Street names shown as **bold entries** can be found on the central London pages, 43 and 44.

Abbeville Rd. SW4 38 C4
Abbey Gdns. NW8 16 D1
Abbey Gdns. W6 29 G2
Abbey La. E15 19 G1
Abbey Orchard St. SW1 24 D4
Abbey Rd. E15 20 A1
Abbey Rd. NW6 9 C4
Abbey Rd. NW8 9 C5
Abbey Rd., Bark. 14 D4
Abbey Rd. Est. NW8 9 C5
Abbey St. E13 20 D3
Abbey St. SE1 25 E4
Abbey Wf. Ind. Est., Bark. 21 F1
Abbeyfield Rd. SE16 26 A5
Abbot St. E8 11 E3
Abbots La. SE1 44 J6
Abbot's Pl. NW6 9 C5
Abbot's Rd. E6 13 G5
Abbotsbury Clo. E15 19 G1
Abbotsbury Ms. SE15 40 A1
Abbotsbury Rd. W14 22 G3
Abbotshade Rd. SE16 26 B2
Abbotstone Rd. SW15 36 E1
Abbotswell Rd. SE4 40 D3
Abbotswood Rd. SE22 39 D2
Abbott Rd. E14 19 G5
Abchurch La. EC4 44 G3
Abchurch Yd. EC4 44 F3
Abdale Rd. W12 22 D2
Aberavon Rd. E3 19 C2
Abercorn Clo. NW8 16 D2
Abercorn Pl. NW8 16 D2
Abercorn Way SE1 32 F1
Abercrombie St. SW11 30 F5
Aberdare Gdns. NW6 9 C4
Aberdeen La. N5 11 B2
Aberdeen Pk. N5 11 B2
Aberdeen Pk. Ms. N5 11 B1
Aberdeen Pl. NW8 16 E3
Aberdeen Rd. N5 11 B1
Aberdeen Rd. NW10 8 B2
Aberdeen Ter. SE3 34 A5
Aberdour St. SE1 25 D5
Aberfeldy St. E14 19 G5
Aberford Gdns. SE18 35 A4
Abergeldie Rd. SE12 41 E4
Abernethy Rd. SE13 41 B2
Abersham Rd. E8 11 E2
Abery St. SE18 28 G5
Abingdon Rd. W8 23 B4
Abingdon St. SW1 24 E4
Abingdon Vill. W8 23 B4
Abinger Gro. SE8 33 D2
Abinger Rd. W4 22 A4
Ablett St. SE16 33 A1
Acacia Pl. NW8 16 E1
Acacia Rd. NW8 16 E1
Academy Pl. SE18 35 B4
Academy Rd. SE18 35 B4
Acanthus Dr. SE1 32 F1
Acanthus Rd. SW11 38 A1
Acfold Rd. SW6 30 C4
Achilles Clo. SE1 32 F1
Achilles Rd. NW6 9 B2
Achilles St. SE14 33 C3
Ackmar Rd. SW6 30 B4
Ackroyd Dr. E3 19 D4
Ackroyd Rd. SE23 40 B5
Acland Cres. SE5 39 C2
Acland Rd. NW2 8 D3
Acol Rd. NW6 9 B4
Acorn Wk. SE16 26 C2
Acre La. SW2 38 E2
Acris St. SW18 37 D3
Acton Ms. E8 11 E5
Acton St. WC1 17 F2
Ada Gdns. E14 20 A5
Ada Gdns. E15 13 C5
Ada Pl. E2 11 F5
Ada Rd. SE5 32 D3
Ada St. E8 11 G5
Adair Rd. W10 15 G3
Adam & Eve Ct. W1 43 B1
Adam & Eve Ms. W8 23 B4
Adam St. WC2 43 F4
Adam Wk. SW6 29 E3
Adams Ct. EC2 44 G1
Adams Row W1 24 A1
Adamson Rd. E16 20 D5
Adamson Rd. NW3 9 E4
Adderley St. E14 19 G5
Addington Rd. E3 19 E2
Addington Rd. E16 20 B3
Addington Sq. SE5 32 C2
Addison Ave. W11 22 G2
Addison Bri. Pl. W14 23 A5
Addison Cres. W14 22 G4
Addison Gdns. W14 22 F4
Addison Gro. W4 22 A4
Addison Pl. W11 22 G2
Addison Rd. W14 22 G4
Addle Hill EC4 44 C2
Adelaide Ave. SE4 40 D2
Adelaide Gro. W12 22 C2
Adelaide Rd. NW3 9 E4
Adelaide St. WC2 43 E4
Adelina Gro. E1 19 A4
Adeline Pl. WC1 17 D4
Adelphi Ter. WC2 43 F4
Aden Gro. N16 11 C1
Aden Ter. N16 11 C1
Adeney Clo. W6 29 F2
Adenmore Rd. SE6 40 E5
Adie Rd. W6 22 E4
Adine Rd. E13 20 E3
Adler St. E1 18 F5
Adley St. E5 12 C1
Admaston Rd. SE18 35 E2
Admiral Pl. SE16 26 C2
Admiral Seymour Rd. SE9 42 B2
Admiral Sq. SW10 30 D4
Admiral St. SE8 33 E4
Admirals Way E14 26 E3
Adolphus St. SE8 33 D3
Adpar St. W2 16 E4
Adrian Ms. SW10 30 C2
Adys Rd. SE15 39 E1
Afghan Rd. SW11 30 F5
Agamemnon Rd. NW6 9 A2
Agar Gro. NW1 10 C4
Agar Gro. Est. NW1 10 C4
Agar Pl. NW1 10 C4
Agar St. WC2 43 E4
Agate Clo. E16 20 G5
Agate Rd. W6 22 E4
Agave Rd. NW2 8 E1
Agdon St. EC1 18 A3
Agincourt Rd. NW3 9 G1
Agnes Ave., Ilf. 14 D1
Agnes Clo. E6 2
Agnes Rd. W3 2
Agnes St. E14 1
Agnew Rd. SE23 4
Ailsa St. E14 1
Ainger Rd. NW3
Ainsley St. E2 1
Ainsworth Rd. E9 1
Ainsworth Way NW8
Aintree Ave. E6
Aintree St. SW6 2
Air St. W1 4
Airdrie Clo. N1 1
Airedale Ave. W4 2
Airedale Rd. SW12 3
Aisgill Ave. W14 3
Aislibie Rd. SE12 4
Ajax Rd. NW6
Akehurst St. SW15 3
Akenside Rd. NW3
Akerman Rd. SW9 3
Alabama St. SE18 3
Alan Hocken Way E15 2
Alanthus Clo. SE12
Alaska St. SE1 4
Albacore Cres. SE13 4
Albany, The W1 4
Albany Ctyd. W1 4
Albany Rd. E12 1
Albany Rd. SE5 3
Albany St. NW1 1
Albatross St. SE18 3
Albemarle St. W1 2
Albert Ave. SW8 3
Albert Bri. SW3 3
Albert Bri. SW11 3
Albert Bri. Rd. SW11 3
Albert Ct. SW7 2
Albert Embk. SE1 3
Albert Gdns. E1 1
Albert Pl. W8 2
Albert Rd. E16 2
Albert Rd. NW6 1
Albert Sq. E15 1
Albert Sq. SW8 3
Albert St. NW1 1
Albert Ter. NW1 1
Alberta Est. SE17 3

Name	Page	Grid
...erta St. SE17	32	A1
...ion Ave. SW8	31	D5
...on Dr. E8	11	E4
...on Est. SE16	26	A3
...on Gdns. W6	22	D5
...on Gro. N16	11	D1
...on Hill SE13	33	F5
...on Ms. N1	10	G4
...on Ms. W2	16	F5
...on Pl. EC1	18	A4
...on Pl. W6	22	C5
...on Rd. N16	11	C1
...on Sq. E8	11	E4
...on Ter. E8	11	E4
...on Way SE13	40	G2
...on Yd. E1	18	G4
...ighton Rd. SE22	39	D1
...ury St. SE8	33	E2
...bourne Rd. W12	22	B2
...bridge St. SE17	32	D1
...ebert Ter. SW8	31	E3
...burgh St. SE10	34	D1
...en Ave. E15	20	C3
...enham St. NW1	17	C1
...ensley Rd. W6	22	C5
...er Clo. SE15	32	E2
...erbrook Rd. SW12	38	B4
...erbury Rd. SW13	29	C2
...ermanbury EC2	44	E1
...erney Rd. E1	19	B3
...erney St. SW1	24	B5
...ersey Gdns., Bark. E1		
...ersford Clo. SE4	40	B3
...ersgate St. EC1	18	A4
...ershot Rd. NW6	9	A5
...erton Rd. SE24	39	B1
...erville Rd. SW6	30	A5
...erwood Rd. SE8	42	F4
...erord St. W1	24	A2
...gate EC1	44	E1
...gate High St. EC3	18	E5
...ne St. W12	22	B2
...ington Rd. SE18	27	G4
...ted Rd. NW6	9	B2
...idge Rd. Vill. W11	16	A4
...worth Clo. W9	16	C3
...worth Gro. SE13	40	G4
...worth Rd. E15	13	B4
...wych EC4	43	G3
...ander Ave. NW10	8	D4
...ander Clo., Sid.	42	G4
...ander Pl. SW7	23	F5
...ander Sq. SW3	23	F5
...ander St. W2	16	B5
...andra Ave SW11	31	A4
...andra Cotts. SE14	33	D4
...andra Est. NW8	9	C5
...andra Gdns. W4	29	A3
...andra Pl. NW8	9	D5
...andra Rd. E6	21	C2
...andra Rd. E10	18	E1
...andra Rd. SE16	20	D4
...is St. SE14	33	C3
...is St. E5	12	A1
...rn Rd. SW8	31	D4
...ed Ms. W1	17	D4
...ed Pl. WC1	17	D4
...ed Prior Ho. E12	14	C1
...ed Rd. E15	13	C2
...ed Rd. W2	16	D3
...ed St. E3	19	D2
...ed St. E16	27	C1
...eda St. SW11	31	B4
...ed's Gdns., Bark.	21	G1
...eds Way, Bark.	21	E2
Alfriston Rd. SW11	37	G3
Algernon Rd. NW6	9	B5
Algernon Rd. SE13	40	F1
Algiers Rd. SE13	40	E2
Alice Gilliatt Ct. W14	30	A1
Alice La. E3	12	D5
Alice St. SE1	25	D4
Alie St. E1	18	F5
Alison Clo. E6	21	C5
Aliwal Rd. SW11	37	F2
Alkerden Rd. W4	29	A1
All Saints Dr. SE3	34	B5
All Saints Rd. SW11	16	A5
All Saints St. N1	17	F1
All Souls Ave. NW10	15	A4
Allard Gdns. SW4	38	D3
Allardyce St. SW4	38	F2
Allcroft Rd. NW5	10	A2
Allen Edwards Dr. SW8	31	E4
Allen Rd. E3	19	D1
Allen Rd. N16	11	D1
Allen St. W8	23	B4
Allensbury Pl. NW1	10	G1
Allenswood Rd. SE9	42	A1
Allestree Rd. SW6	29	G3
Allfarthing La. SW18	37	C4
Allgood St. E2	18	F1
Allhallows La. EC4	44	F4
Allhallows Rd. E6	21	A4
Alliance Rd. E13	20	F3
Allied Ind. Est. W3	22	A3
Allingham St. N1	18	B1
Allington Rd. W10	15	G1
Allington St. SW1	24	B4
Allitsen Rd. NW8	16	F1
Allnutt Way SW4	38	D3
Alloa Rd. SE8	33	C1
Alloway Rd. E3	19	C2
Allsop Pl. NW1	16	G3
Alma Gro. SE1	25	E5
Alma Rd. SW18	37	D2
Alma Sq. NW8	16	D2
Alma St. E15	13	A3
Alma St. NW5	10	B3
Alma Ter. SW18	37	F5
Almack Rd. E5	12	A1
Almeida St. N1	11	A4
Almeric Rd. SW11	37	G2
Almond Clo. SE15	32	F5
Almond Rd. SE16	25	G5
Almorah Rd. N1	11	C4
Alnwick Rd. E16	20	F5
Alnwick Rd. SE12	41	E5
Alperton St. W10	15	G3
Alpha Gro. E14	26	E3
Alpha Pl. NW6	16	B1
Alpha Rd. SW3	30	F2
Alpha St. SE14	33	D4
Alpha St. SE15	32	F5
Alpine Rd. SE16	26	A5
Alpine Way E6	21	C4
Alsace Rd. SE17	32	D1
Alscot Rd. SE1	25	E5
Alscot Way SE1	25	E5
Altenburg Gdns. SW11	37	G2
Althea St. SW6	30	C5
Altmore Ave. E6	14	B4
Alton Rd. E14	19	F4
Alvanley Gdns. NW6	9	G3
Alverstone Rd. E12	14	C1
Alverstone Rd. NW2	8	E4
Alverton St. SE8	33	D1
Alvey St. SE17	32	D2
Alvington Cres. E8	11	E2
Alwold Cres. SE12	41	E4
Alwyne Pl. N1	11	B3
Alwyne Rd. N1	11	B3
Alwyne Sq. N1	11	B3
Alwyne Vill. N1	11	A4
Ambassador Gdns. E6	21	B4
Ambassador Sq. E14	26	F5
Ambassador's Ct. SW1	**43**	**B6**
Ambergate St. SE17	32	A1
Amberley Rd. W9	16	B4
Ambleside Rd. NW10	8	B4
Ambrosden Ave. SW1	24	C4
Ambrose St. SE16	25	G5
Amelia St. SE17	32	A1
Amen Cor. EC4	**44**	**C2**
Amen Ct. EC4	**44**	**C1**
America St. SE1	**44**	**D6**
Amerland Rd. SW18	37	A3
Amersham Gro. SE14	33	D3
Amersham Rd. SE14	33	D3
Amersham Vale SE14	33	D3
Amery Gdns. NW10	8	D5
Amethyst Rd. E15	13	A1
Amhurst Pas. E8	11	F2
Amhurst Rd. E8	11	G2
Amhurst Rd. N16	11	F1
Amhurst Ter. E8	11	F1
Amiel St. E1	19	A3
Amies St. SW11	37	G1
Amity Rd. E15	13	C5
Amner Rd. SW11	38	A4
Amor Rd. W6	22	E4
Amott Rd. SE15	39	F1
Amoy Pl. E14	19	E5
Ampton Pl. WC1	17	F2
Ampton St. WC1	17	F2
Amsterdam Rd. E14	26	G4
Amwell St. EC1	17	G2
Amyruth Rd. SE4	40	E3
Ancaster St. SE18	35	G3
Anchor & Hope La. SE7	27	F5
Anchor St. SE16	25	G5
Ancill Clo. W6	29	G2
Ancona Rd. NW10	15	C1
Ancona Rd. SE18	35	F1
Andalus Rd. SW9	38	E1
Anderson Rd. E9	12	B3
Anderson St. SW3	30	G1
Anderton Clo. SE5	39	C1
Andover Pl. NW6	16	C1
Andre St. E8	11	F2
Andrew Borde St. WC2	**43**	**D1**
Andrew St. E14	19	G5
Andrewes Gdns. E6	21	A5
Andrews Crosse WC2	**43**	**J2**
Andrews Pl. SE9	42	D4
Andrew's Rd. E8	11	G5
Anerley St. SW11	30	G5
Angel Ct. EC2	**44**	**G1**
Angel Ct. SW1	**43**	**B6**
Angel La. E15	13	A3
Angel Ms. N1	17	G1
Angel Pas. EC4	**44**	**F4**
Angel Pl. SE1	**44**	**F6**
Angel St. EC1	**44**	**D1**
Angel Wk. W6	29	E1
Angelica Dr. E6	21	C4
Angell Pk. Gdns. SW9	38	G1
Angell Rd. SW9	38	G1
Angerstein La. SE3	34	C3
Angler's La. NW5	10	B3
Anglesea Ave. SE18	28	D5
Anglesea Rd. SE18	28	D5
Anglia Ho. E14	19	B5
Anglo Rd. E3	19	D1
Angrave Ct. E8	11	E5
Angus Rd. E13	20	F2
Angus St. SE14	33	C3
Anhalt Rd. SW11	30	F3
Ankerdine Cres. SE18	35	D4
Anley Rd. W14	22	G4
Ann La. SW10	30	E3
Ann Moss Way SE16	26	A4
Ann St. SE18	35	E1
Anna Clo. E8	11	F5
Annabel Clo. E14	19	F5
Annandale Rd. SE10	34	C1
Annandale Rd. W4	29	A1
Annandale Rd., Sid.	42	G5
Anne St. E13	20	D3
Annesley Rd. SE3	34	E4
Annie Besant Clo. E3	12	D5
Annis Rd. E9	12	C3
Ansdell Rd. SE15	33	A5
Ansdell St. W8	23	C4
Anselm Rd. SW6	30	B2
Ansleigh Pl. W11	22	F1
Anson Rd. N7	10	C1
Anson Rd. NW2	8	D2
Anstey Rd. SE15	39	F1
Anstice Clo. W4	29	A3
Anstridge Rd. SE9	42	F4
Antelope Rd. SE18	28	B4
Antill Rd. E3	19	C2
Antill Ter. E1	19	B5
Anton St. E8	11	F2
Antrim Gro. NW3	9	G3
Antrim Rd. NW3	9	G3
Apothecary St. EC4	**44**	**B2**
Appach Rd. SW2	38	G4
Apple Tree Yd. SW1	**43**	**B5**
Appleby Rd. E8	11	F4
Appleby Rd. E16	20	C5
Appleby St. E2	18	E1
Appleford Rd. W10	15	G3
Applegarth Rd. W14	22	F3
Appleton Rd. SE9	42	A1
Appold St. EC2	18	D4
Approach Rd. E2	19	A1
April St. E8	11	E1
Aquila St. NW8	16	E1
Aquinas St. SE1	**44**	**A6**
Arabella Dr. SW15	36	A2
Arabin Rd. SE4	40	C2
Arbery Rd. E3	19	C2
Arbour Sq. E1	19	B5
Arbroath Rd. SE9	42	A1
Arbuthnot Rd. SE14	33	B5
Arbutus St. E8	11	E5
Arcadia St. E14	19	E5
Arch St. SE1	25	B4
Archangel St. SE16	26	B3
Archbishops Pl. SW2	38	F4
Archdale Rd. SE22	39	E3
Archel Rd. W14	30	A2
Archer St. W1	**43**	**C3**
Archery Clo. W2	16	F5
Archery Rd. SE9	42	B3
Arches, The WC2	**43**	**F5**
Archibald Ms. W1	24	A1
Archibald Rd. N7	10	D1
Archibald St. E3	19	E3
Archway St. SW13	36	A1
Arcola St. E8	11	E2
Ardbeg Rd. SE24	39	C3
Arden Cres. E14	26	E5
Arden Est. N1	18	D1
Ardgowan Rd. SE6	41	B5
Ardilaun Rd. N5	11	B1
Ardleigh Rd. N1	11	D3
Ardmere Rd. SE13	41	A4
Ardwick Rd. NW2	9	B1
Argon Ms. SW6	30	B3
Argyle Pl. W6	22	D5
Argyle Rd. E1	19	B3
Argyle Rd. E15	13	B2
Argyle Rd. E16	20	E5
Argyle Sq. WC1	17	E2
Argyle St. WC1	17	E2
Argyle Way SE16	32	F1
Argyll Rd. W8	23	B3
Argyll St. W1	**43**	**A2**

Arica Rd. SE4 40 C2
Ariel Rd. NW6 9 B3
Ariel Way W12 22 E2
Aristotle Rd. SW4 38 D1
Arklow Rd. SE14 33 D2
Arkwright Rd. NW3 9 D2
Arlesford Rd. SW9 38 E1
Arlingford Rd. SW2 38 G3
Arlington Ave. N1 11 B5
Arlington Clo., Sid. 42 G5
Arlington Lo. SW2 38 F2
Arlington Rd. NW1 10 B5
Arlington Sq. N1 11 B5
Arlington St. SW1 43 A5
Arlington Way EC1 17 G2
Armada St. SE8 33 E2
Armada Way E6 28 E1
Armadale Rd. SW6 30 B3
Armagh Rd. E3 12 D5
Arminger Rd. W12 22 D2
Armitage Rd. SE10 34 C1
Armoury Rd. SE8 33 F5
Armoury Way SW18 37 B3
Armstrong Rd. SW7 23 E4
Armstrong Rd. W3 22 B2
Arnal Cres. SW18 36 G5
Arndale Cen., The SW18 37 C4
Arne St. WC2 43 F2
Arne Wk. SE3 41 C2
Arngask Rd. SE6 41 A5
Arnhem Pl. E14 26 E4
Arnold Circ. E2 18 E2
Arnold Est. SE1 25 E3
Arnold Rd. E3 19 E2
Arnould Ave. SE5 39 C2
Arnside St. SE17 32 B2
Arodene Rd. SW2 38 F4
Arragon Rd. E6 13 G5
Arran Wk. N1 11 B4
Arrow Rd. E3 19 F2
Arsenal Rd. SE9 35 B5
Artesian Rd. W2 16 B5
Arthingworth St. E15 13 B5
Arthur Gro. SE18 28 E5
Arthur Henderson Ho. SW6 30 A5
Arthur Rd. E6 21 B1
Arthur Rd. N7 10 F1
Arthur St. EC4 44 G3
Arthurdon Rd. SE4 40 E3
Artillery La. E1 18 D4
Artillery La. W12 15 C5
Artillery Pl. SE18 28 B5
Artillery Row SW1 24 D4
Artizan St. E1 44 J1
Arundel Clo. E15 13 B1
Arundel Gdns. W11 23 A1
Arundel Great Ct. WC2 43 H3
Arundel Gro. N16 11 D2
Arundel Pl. N1 10 G3
Arundel Sq. N7 10 G3
Arundel St. WC2 43 H3
Arundel Ter. SW13 29 D2
Arvon Rd. N5 10 G2
Ascalon St. SW8 31 C3
Ascham St. NW5 10 C2
Ascot Rd. E6 21 B2
Ash Gro. E8 11 G5
Ash Gro. NW2 8 F1
Ash Rd. E15 13 B2
Ashbourne Gro. SE22 39 E3
Ashbourne Gro. W4 29 A1
Ashbridge St. NW8 16 F3
Ashburn Gdns. SW7 23 D5
Ashburn Pl. SW7 23 D5
Ashburnham Gro. SE10 33 F3
Ashburnham Pl. SE10 33 F3
Ashburnham Retreat SE10 33 F3
Ashburnham Rd. NW10 15 E2
Ashburnham Rd. SW10 30 D3
Ashburton Ave., Ilf. 14 G1
Ashburton Gro. N7 10 G1
Ashburton Rd. E16 20 D5
Ashbury Rd. SW11 37 G1
Ashby Gro. N1 11 B4
Ashby Ms. SE4 33 D5
Ashby Rd. SE4 33 D5
Ashchurch Gro. W12 22 C4
Ashchurch Pk. Vill. W12 22 C4
Ashchurch Ter. W12 22 C4
Ashcombe St. SW6 30 C5
Ashcroft Rd. E3 19 C2
Ashdon Rd. NW10 8 B5
Ashenden Rd. E5 12 C2
Asher Way E1 25 F2
Ashfield Rd. W3 22 B2
Ashfield St. E1 18 G4
Ashford Rd. E6 14 C3
Ashford Rd. NW2 8 F1
Ashington Rd. SW6 30 A5
Ashland Pl. W1 17 A4
Ashleigh Rd. SW14 36 A1
Ashley Cres. SW11 38 A1
Ashley Pl. SW1 24 C4
Ashley Rd. E7 13 F4
Ashlin Rd. E15 13 A1
Ashlone Rd. SW15 36 E1
Ashmead Rd. SE8 33 E5
Ashmere Gro. SW2 38 E2
Ashmill St. NW1 16 F4
Ashmole Pl. SW8 31 F2
Ashmole St. SW8 31 F2
Ashmore Gro., Well. 42 F1
Ashmore Rd. W9 16 A1
Ashness Rd. SW11 37 G3
Ashridge Cres. SE18 35 E3
Ashton Rd. E15 13 A2
Ashton St. E14 26 G1
Ashwin St. E8 11 E3
Ashworth Rd. W9 16 C2
Askew Cres. W12 22 B3
Askew Rd. W12 22 B2
Askham Ct. W12 22 C2
Askham Rd. W12 22 C2
Asland Rd. E15 13 A5
Aslett St. SW18 37 C5
Asmara Rd. NW2 8 G2
Aspen Gdns. W6 29 D1
Aspen Way E14 27 A1
Aspenlea Rd. W6 29 F2
Aspern Gro. NW3 9 F2
Aspinall Rd. SE4 40 B1
Aspinden Rd. SE16 25 G5
Aspley Rd. SW18 37 C3
Assembly Pas. E1 19 A4
Astbury Rd. SE15 33 A4
Aste St. E14 26 G3
Astell St. SW3 30 F1
Astle St. SW11 31 A5
Astley Ave. NW2 8 E2
Aston St. E14 19 C5
Astoria Wk. SW9 38 G1
Astrop Ms. W6 22 E4
Astrop Ter. W6 22 E3
Astwood Ms. SW7 23 C5
Asylum Rd. SE15 32 G3
Atalanta St. SW6 29 F4
Atheldene Rd. SW18 37 D5
Athelstane Gro. E3 19 D1
Athenlay Rd. SE15 40 B3
Atherden Rd. E5 12 A1
Atherfold Rd. SW9 38 E1
Atherstone Ms. SW7 23 D5
Atherton Ms. E7 13 C3
Atherton Rd. E7 13 C3
Atherton Rd. SW13 29 C3
Atherton St. SW11 30 F5
Athlone Rd. SW2 38 F5
Athlone St. NW5 10 A3
Athol Sq. E14 19 G5
Atkins Rd. SW12 38 D5
Atkinson Rd. E16 20 F4
Atlantic Rd. SW9 38 G2
Atlas Gdns. SE7 27 F5
Atlas Ms. N7 10 F3
Atlas Rd. E13 20 D1
Atlas Rd. NW10 15 A2
Atley Rd. E3 12 E5
Atney Rd. SW15 36 G2
Atterbury St. SW1 24 E5
Atwood Rd. W6 22 D5
Aubert Pk. N5 10 G1
Aubert Rd. N5 11 A1
Aubrey Rd. W8 23 A2
Aubrey Wk. W8 23 A2
Aubyn Sq. SW15 36 C2
Auckland Rd. SW11 37 F2
Audley Clo. SW11 38 A1
Audrey St. E2 18 F1
Augurs La. E13 20 E2
Augusta St. E14 19 F5
Augustine Rd. W14 22 F4
Augustus St. NW1 17 B1
Auriga Ms. N16 11 C2
Auriol Rd. W14 22 G5
Austen Ho. NW6 16 B2
Austin Clo. SE23 40 D5
Austin Friars EC2 44 G1
Austin Friars Pas. EC2 44 G1
Austin Friars Sq. EC2 44 G1
Austin Rd. SW11 31 A4
Austin St. E2 18 E2
Austral St. SE11 25 A5
Australia Rd. W12 22 D1
Autumn St. E3 12 E5
Avalon Rd. SW6 30 C4
Ave Maria La. EC4 44 C2
Aveline St. SE11 31 G1
Avening Ter. SW18 37 B4
Avenons Rd. E13 20 D3
Avenue, The NW6 8 F5
Avenue, The SE7 34 F3
Avenue, The SE10 34 A3
Avenue, The SW4 38 A3
Avenue, The SW18 37 F5
Avenue, The W4 22 A4
Avenue Clo. NW8 9 F5
Avenue Gdns. SW14 36 A1
Avenue Rd. E7 13 E1
Avenue Rd. NW3 9 E4
Avenue Rd. NW8 9 E4
Avenue Rd. NW10 15 B1
Averill St. W6 29 F2
Avery Hill Rd. SE9 42 F4
Avery Row W1 24 B1
Aviary Clo. E16 20 C4
Avignon Rd. SE4 40 B1
Avis Sq. E1 19 B5
Avocet Ms. SE28 28 F4
Avon Rd. SE4 40 E1
Avondale Pk. Gdns. W11 22 G1
Avondale Pk. Rd. W11 22 G1
Avondale Ri. SE15 39 E1
Avondale Rd. E16 20 B4
Avondale Sq. SE1 32 F1
Avonley Rd. SE14 33 A3
Avonmore Rd. W14 22 G5
Avonmouth St. SE1 25 B4
Axe St., Bark. 14 E5
Aybrook St. W1 17 A4
Aycliffe Rd. W12 22 B2
Aylesbury Rd. SE17 32
Aylesbury St. EC1 18
Aylesford St. SW1 31
Aylestone Ave. NW6 8
Aylmer Rd. W12 22
Aylward St. E1 19
Aylwyn Est. SE1 25
Aynhoe Rd. W14 22
Ayres Clo. E13 20
Ayres St. SE1 25
Aysgarth Rd. SE21 39
Aytoun Pl. SW9 31
Aytoun Rd. SW9 31
Azenby Rd. SE15 32
Azof St. SE10 27

B

Baalbec Rd. N5 11
Babmaes St. SW1 43
Baches St. N1 18
Back Ch. La. E1 25
Back Hill EC1 17
Bacon Gro. SE1 25
Bacon St. E1 18
Bacon St. E2 18
Bacton NW5 10
Baden Rd., Ilf. 14
Badminton Rd. SW12 38
Badsworth Rd. SE5 32
Bagley's La. SW6 30
Bagshot St. SE17 32
Bainbridge St. WC1 43
Baizdon Rd. SE3 34
Baker Rd. NW10 8
Baker Rd. SE18 35
Baker St. NW1 16
Baker St. W1 16
Bakers Row E15 20
Baker's Row EC1 17
Bakery Clo. SW9 31
Balaam St. E13 20
Balaclava Rd. SE1 25
Balcaskie Rd. SE9 42
Balchen Rd. SE3 34
Balchier Rd. SE22 39
Balcombe St. NW1 16
Balcorne St. E9 12
Balderton St. W1 17
Baldock St. E3 19
Baldwin Cres. SE5 32
Baldwin Ter. N1 18
Baldwin's Gdns. EC1 17
Balfe St. N1 17
Balfern Gro. W4 29
Balfern St. SW11 30
Balfour Pl. SW15 36
Balfour Rd. N5 11
Balfour St. SE17 25
Balham Gro. SW12 38
Balham Hill SW12 38
Balham New Rd. SW12 38
Ballance Rd. E9 12
Ballantine St. SW18 37
Ballast Quay SE10 34
Ballater Rd. SW2 38
Ballina St. SE23 40
Ballingdon Rd. SW11 38
Balliol Rd. W10 15
Ballogie Ave. NW10 8
Balls Pond Rd. N1 11
Balmer Rd. E3 19
Balmes Rd. N1 11
Balmoral Gro. N7 10
Balmoral Ms. W12 22
Balmoral Rd. E7 13
Balmoral Rd. NW2 8
Balmuir Gdns. SW15 36
Balnacraig Ave. NW10 8
Balniel Gate SW1 3

Entry	Pg	Grid
c St. E. EC1	18	B3
c St. W. EC1	18	B3
ernie Gro. SE18	37	A5
borough Gdns. E2	12	
...12		
ford Rd., Bark.	14	E3
bury Ct. W2	43	E3
bury Rd. E9	12	B4
bury St. SW11	30	F5
chory Rd. SE3	34	E2
croft Rd. E1	19	B2
galore St. SW15	36	E1
m St. W6	22	D5
ster Rd. W10	9	G3
k End SE1	44	E5
k La. SW15	36	A3
thurst Rd. SE6	40	D5
kside SE1	44	D4
ton Rd. SW2	38	G2
twell Rd SE13	41	B2
er St. EC1	18	B3
herman Ho. SW8	31	F2
ning St. SE10	34	B1
ckburn Rd. E18	28	G5
stead St. SE15	40	A1
ury St. SE5	32	C3
Ms. W6	22	E4
ers Rd. E15	19	F1
ican, The EC2	18	B4
hard St. SW18	37	C3
chester St. E14	19	F4
lay Clo. SW6	30	B3
lay Rd. E13	20	F3
lay Rd. SW6	30	B3
Rd. W10	22	F1
en St. SE18	35	G3
olph Rd. N7	10	E1
sey Pl. E1	19	A4
sley La. SE10	33	G2
tt St. W10	16	A3
ord St. N1	10	G5
orth Rd. SE15	39	G1
e Ho. Rd. E16	28	D3
e Ho. SE1	44	A5
ing Rd. SE12	41	D5
ing St. N1	11	C5
Pl. W2	23	C1
er Dr. NW1	10	C4
er Ms. SW4	38	B2
er St. SW10	30	D2
ing Rd. E6	21	D2
ing Rd. E13	20	D3
ing Rd. E6	20	B4
ston Gdns. SW5	23	C5
borough St. SE14	33	B3
ry Gdns. W10	15	F3
ry Rd. NW6	9	A3
eycorn Way E14	26	D1
nor Rd. NW6	9	A3
mouth Rd. SW18	37	D4
Elms Pk. SW15	29	E5
abas Rd. E9	12	B2
aby Pl. SW7	23	E5
ard Clo. SE18	28	C4
ard Ms. SW11	37	F2
ard Rd. SW11	37	F2
ard's Inn EC1	43	J1
by St. E15	19	C5
by Way N1	17	C2
es Ave. SW13	29	A5
es Bri. SW13	29	A5
es Bri. W4	29	A5
es Clo. E12	13	G1
es High St. W13	29	A5
es Rd., Ilf.	14	E2
es St. E14	19	C5
es Ter. SE8	33	D1
esbury Ho. SW4	38	D4
Barnet Gro. E2	18	F2
Barney Clo. SE7	34	F1
Barnfield Pl. E14	26	E5
Barnfield Rd. SE18	35	D2
Barnham St. SE1	18	D3
Barnsbury Gro. N7	10	F3
Barnsbury Pk. N1	10	G4
Barnsbury Rd. N1	17	G1
Barnsbury Sq. N1	10	G4
Barnsbury St. N1	10	G4
Barnsbury Ter. N1	10	F4
Barnsdale Ave. E14	26	F5
Barnsdale Rd. W9	16	A3
Barnsley St. E1	18	G3
Barnwell Rd. SW2	38	G3
Barnwood Clo. W9	16	C3
Baron St. N1	17	G1
Baron Wk. E16	20	C4
Barons Clo. W14	29	G1
Barons Keep W14	29	G1
Barons Pl. SE1	24	G3
Baronsmead Rd. SW13	29	C4
Barrett St. W1	17	A5
Barriedale SE14	33	C5
Barrier App. SE7	27	G4
Barrington Rd. E12	14	C3
Barrington Rd SW9	39	A1
Barrington Vill. SE18	35	D1
Barrow Hill Rd NW8	16	F1
Barry Rd. E6	21	A5
Barry Rd. SE22	39	F4
Barset Rd. SE15	40	A1
Barter St. WC1	17	E4
Barth Rd. SE18	28	G5
Bartholomew Clo. EC1	18	B4
Bartholomew Clo. SW18	37	D2
Bartholomew La. EC2	44	G2
Bartholomew Rd. NW5	10	C3
Bartholomew Sq. EC1	18	B3
Bartholomew St. SE1	25	C4
Bartholomew Vill. NW5	10	C3
Bartle Ave. E6	21	A1
Bartle Rd. N11	15	G5
Bartlett Clo. E14	19	E5
Bartlett Ct. EC4	44	A1
Barton Rd. W14	29	G1
Bartram Rd. SE4	40	C2
Barwick Rd. E7	13	E1
Baseing Clo. E6	28	C1
Basil Ave. E6	21	A1
Basil St. SW3	23	G4
Basin S. E16	28	D2
Basing Clo. SE15	32	E4
Basing St. W11	16	A5
Basingdon Way SE5	39	C2
Basinghall Ave. EC2	18	C4
Basinghall St. EC2	44	F1
Basire St. N1	11	B5
Baskerville Rd. SW18	37	F5
Basket Gdns. SE9	42	A3
Basnett Rd. SW11	38	A1
Bassano St. SE22	39	E3
Bassein Pk. Rd. W12	22	A3
Bassett Rd. W10	15	F5
Bassett St. NW5	10	A3
Bassingham Rd. SW18	37	D5
Bastable Ave., Bark.	21	G1
Bastwick St. EC1	18	B3
Basuto Rd. SW6	30	B4
Batavia Rd. SE14	33	C3
Batchelor St. N1	17	G1
Bateman St. W1	43	C2
Bateman's Bldgs. W1	43	C2
Bateman's Row EC2	18	D3
Bath Rd. E7	13	G3
Bath Rd. W4	22	A5
Bath St. EC1	18	B2
Bath Ter. SE1	25	B3
Bathurst Gdns. NW10	15	D1
Bathurst St. W2	23	E1
Bathway SE18	28	C5
Batman Clo. W12	22	D2
Batoum Gdns. W6	22	C2
Batson St. W12	22	C3
Batten St. SW11	37	F1
Battersea Bri. SW3	30	E3
Battersea Bri. SW11	30	E3
Battersea Bri. Rd. SW11	30	E3
Battersea Ch. Rd. SW11	30	E4
Battersea High St. SW11	30	E4
Battersea Pk. SW11	30	G3
Battersea Pk. Rd. SW8	31	B4
Battersea Pk. Rd. SW11	30	F5
Battersea Ri. SW11	37	E3
Battery Rd. SE28	28	G3
Battle Bri. La. SE1	44	H6
Battle Bri. Rd. NW1	17	E1
Battledean Rd. N5	11	A2
Batty St. E1	18	F5
Baulk, The SW18	37	B5
Bavent Rd. SE5	32	B5
Bawdale Rd. SE22	39	E3
Bawtree Rd. SE14	33	C3
Baxendale St. E2	18	F2
Baxter Rd. E16	20	F5
Baxter Rd. N1	11	C3
Baxter Rd. NW10	15	A3
Baxter Rd., Ilf.	14	D2
Bayfield Rd. SE9	41	G2
Bayford Rd. NW10	15	F2
Bayford St. E8	11	G4
Bayham Pl. NW1	10	C5
Bayham St. NW1	10	C5
Bayley St. WC1	17	D4
Baylis Rd. SE1	24	G3
Baynes St. NW1	10	C4
Bayonne Rd. W6	29	G2
Bayswater Rd. W2	23	C1
Baythorne St. E3	19	D4
Baytree Rd. SW2	38	F2
Bazely St. E14	26	G1
Beacham Clo. SE7	34	G1
Beachy Rd. E3	12	E4
Beacon Gate SE14	33	B5
Beacon Hill N7	10	E2
Beacon Rd. SE13	41	A4
Beaconsfield Clo. SE3	33	E2
Beaconsfield Rd. E16	20	C3
Beaconsfield Rd. NW10	8	B3
Beaconsfield Rd. SE3	33	E2
Beaconsfield Rd. SE17	32	D2
Beaconsfield Ter. Rd. W14	22	C3
Beadon Rd. W6	22	E5
Beak St. W1	43	B3
Beale Pl. E3	19	D1
Beale Rd. E3	12	D5
Beanacre Clo. E9	12	D3
Bear All. EC4	44	B1
Bear Gdns. SE1	44	D5
Bear La. SE1	44	C6
Bear St. WC2	43	D3
Bearstead Ri. SE4	40	D3
Beatrice Pl. W8	23	C4
Beatrice Rd. E17	25	F5
Beatson Wk. SE16	26	C2
Beatty Rd. N16	11	D1
Beatty St. NW1	17	C1
Beauchamp Pl. SW3	23	F4
Beauchamp Rd. E7	13	E4
Beauchamp Rd.SW11	37	F2
Beauclerc Rd. W6	22	D4
Beaufort Rd. SW15	36	D5
Beaufort Gdns. SW3	23	F4
Beaufort St. SW3	30	E2
Beaufoy Wk. SE11	24	F5
Beaulieu Clo. SE5	39	C1
Beaumont Ave. W14	30	A1
Beaumont Cres. W14	30	A1
Beaumont Gro. E1	19	B3
Beaumont Rd. E13	20	E2
Beaumont Rd. SW19	36	G5
Beaumont Sq. E1	19	B3
Beaumont St. W1	17	A4
Beaumont Wk. NW3	9	G4
Beauval Rd. SE22	39	E4
Beavor La. W6	22	C5
Bebbington Rd.SE18	28	G5
Beccles Dr., Bark.	14	G3
Beccles St. E14	26	D1
Beck Clo. SE13	33	F4
Beck Rd. E8	11	G5
Becket Ave. E6	21	C2
Becklow Rd. W12	22	B3
Beckton Retail Pk. E6	21	C4
Beckton Rd. E16	20	C4
Beckway St. SE17	25	C5
Beckwith Rd. SE24	39	C4
Bective Rd. E7	13	D1
Bective Rd. SW15	36	G2
Bedale St. SE1	44	F6
Bedford Ave. WC1	17	D4
Bedford Clo. W4	29	A2
Bedford Ct. WC2	43	E4
Bedford Gdns. W8	23	B2
Bedford Ho. SW4	38	E2
Bedford Pl. WC1	17	E4
Bedford Rd. E6	14	C5
Bedford Rd. SW4	38	E1
Bedford Row WC1	17	F4
Bedford Sq. WC1	17	D4
Bedford St. WC2	43	E3
Bedford Way WC1	17	D3
Bedfordbury WC2	43	E4
Bedgebury Rd. SE9	41	G4
Beeby Rd. E16	20	E4
Beech Ave. W3	22	A2
Beech Clo. SW15	36	C5
Beech Ct. SE9	42	A4
Beech St. EC2	18	B4
Beechdale Rd. SW2	38	F4
Beechhill Rd. SE9	42	C3
Beechmore Rd.SW11	30	G4
Beechwood Rd. E8	11	E3
Beecroft Rd. SE4	40	C3
Beehive Clo. E8	11	E4
Beehive Pas. EC3	44	H2
Beehive Pl. SW9	38	G1
Beeston Pl. SW1	24	B4
Beethoven St. W10	15	G2
Begbie Rd. SE3	34	F4
Begonia Clo. E6	21	A4
Beira St. SW12	38	B5
Belfont Wk. N7	10	E1
Belford Gro. SE18	28	C5
Belfort Rd. SE15	33	A5
Belgrade Rd. N16	11	D1
Belgrave Gdns. NW8	9	C5
Belgrave Ms. N. SW1	24	A4
Belgrave Ms. S. SW1	24	A4
Belgrave Ms. W. SW1	24	A4
Belgrave Pl. SW1	24	A4
Belgrave Rd. E13	20	F2
Belgrave Rd. SW1	24	B5
Belgrave Rd. SW13	29	B3
Belgrave Sq. SW1	24	A4

Belgrave St. E1 19 B4
Belgravia Ho. SW4 38 D4
Belgrove St. WC1 17 E2
Belinda Rd. SW9 39 A1
Belitha Vill. N1 10 F4
Bell Dr. SW18 36 G5
Bell Inn Yd. EC3 44 G2
Bell La. E1 18 E4
Bell La. E16 27 D2
Bell St. NW1 16 F4
Bell Water Gate SE18 28 C4
Bell Wf. La. EC4 44 E3
Bell Yd. WC2 43 J2
Bellamy St. SW12 38 B5
Bellefields Rd. SW9 38 F1
Bellegrove Rd., Well. 35 G5
Bellenden Rd. SE15 39 E1
Belleville Rd. SW11 37 F3
Bellevue Pl. E1 19 A3
Bellevue Rd. SW13 29 C5
Bello Clo. SE24 39 A5
Bellot Gdns. SE10 34 B1
Bellot St. SE10 34 B1
Bells All. SW6 30 B5
Bellwood Rd. SE15 40 B2
Belmont Ave., Well. 35 G5
Belmont Clo. SW4 38 C1
Belmont Gro. SE13 41 A1
Belmont Hill SE13 40 G1
Belmont Pk. SE13 41 A2
Belmont Rd. SW4 38 C1
Belmont St. NW1 10 A4
Belmore La. N7 10 D2
Belmore St. SW8 31 D4
Beloe Clo. SW15 36 C1
Belsham St. E9 12 A3
Belsize Ave. NW3 9 E3
Belsize Cres. NW3 9 E2
Belsize Gro. NW3 9 F3
Belsize La. NW3 9 E3
Belsize Pk. NW3 9 E3
Belsize Pk. Gdns. NW3 9 F3
Belsize Rd. NW6 9 C5
Belsize Sq. NW3 9 E3
Belsize Ter. NW3 9 E3
Belson Rd. SE18 28 B5
Belthorn Cres. SW12 38 C5
Belton Rd. E7 13 E4
Belton Rd. E11 13 B1
Belton Rd. NW2 8 C3
Belton Way E3 19 E4
Beltran Rd. SW6 30 C5
Belvedere Ms. SE15 40 A1
Belvedere Rd. SE1 24 F3
Belvoir Rd. SE22 39 F5
Bembridge Clo. NW6 8 G4
Bemerton Est. N1 10 E4
Bemerton St. N1 10 F5
Bemish Rd. SW15 36 F1
Ben Jonson Rd. E1 19 B4
Benbow Rd. W6 22 D4
Benbow St. SE8 33 E2
Bendemeer Rd. SW15 36 F1
Bendish Rd. E6 14 A4
Bendon Valley SW18 37 C5
Benedict Rd. SW9 38 F1
Bengal Rd., Ilf. 14 D1
Bengeworth Rd. SE5 39 B1
Benham Clo. SW11 37 E1
Benhill Rd. SE5 32 C3
Benin St. SE13 41 A5
Benjamin Clo. E8 11 F5
Benjamin St. EC1 18 A4
Benledi St. E14 20 A5
Benn St. E9 12 C3
Bennerley Rd. SW11 37 F3
Bennet's Hill EC4 44 C3
Bennett Gro. SE13 33 F4
Bennett Pk. SE3 41 C1

Bennett Rd. E13 20 F3
Bennett Rd. N16 11 D1
Bennett St. SW1 43 A5
Bennett St. W4 29 A2
Bensbury Clo. SW15 36 E5
Benson Ave. E6 20 F1
Bentham Rd. E9 12 B3
Bentinck St. W1 17 A5
Bentworth Rd. W12 15 D5
Benwell Rd. N7 10 G1
Benwick Clo. SE16 25 G5
Benworth St. E3 19 D2
Berber Rd. SW11 37 G3
Berens Rd. NW10 15 F2
Beresford Rd. N5 11 C2
Beresford Sq. SE18 28 D5
Beresford St. SE18 28 D4
Beresford Ter. N5 11 B2
Berestede Rd. W6 29 B1
Berger Rd. E9 12 B3
Bering Wk. E16 20 G5
Berisford Ms. SW18 37 D4
Berkeley Rd. E12 14 A2
Berkeley Rd. SW13 29 C4
Berkeley Sq. W1 24 B1
Berkeley St. W1 24 B2
Berkley Rd. NW1 9 G4
Berkshire Rd. E9 12 D3
Bermans Way NW10 8 A1
Bermondsey St. SE1 44 H6
Bermondsey Wall E. SE16 25 F3
Bermondsey Wall W. SE16 25 F3
Bernard Ashley Dr. SE7 34 E1
Bernard Cassidy St. E16 20 C4
Bernard St. WC1 17 E3
Bernays Gro. SW9 38 F2
Berners Ms. W1 17 C4
Berners Pl. W1 43 B1
Berners Rd. N1 10 G5
Berners St. W1 17 C4
Berry Clo. NW10 8 A4
Berry St. EC1 18 A3
Berryfield Rd. SE17 32 A1
Berryhill SE9 42 D2
Berryhill Gdns. SE9 42 D2
Berthon St. SE8 33 E3
Bertie Rd. NW10 8 C3
Bertrand St. SE13 40 F1
Berwick Cres., Sid. 42 G4
Berwick Rd. E16 20 E5
Berwick St. W1 43 B1
Beryl Ave. E6 21 A4
Beryl Rd. W6 29 F1
Besant Rd. NW2 8 G1
Bessborough Gdns. SW1 31 D1
Bessborough Pl. SW1 31 D1
Bessborough St. SW1 31 D1
Bessemer Rd. SE5 32 B5
Bessie Lansbury Clo. E6 21 C5
Besson St. SE14 33 A4
Bestwood St. SE8 26 B5
Bethell Ave. E16 20 C3
Bethnal Grn. Rd. E1 18 E3
Bethnal Grn. Rd. E2 18 E3
Bethwin Rd. SE5 32 A3
Betterton St. WC2 43 E2
Bettons Pk. E15 13 B5
Bettridge Rd. SW6 30 A5
Bevan St. N1 11 B5
Bevenden St. N1 18 C2
Beverley Clo. SW13 29 B5
Beverley Ct. SE4 40 D1
Beverley Gdns. SW13 36 B1
Beverley Path SW13 29 B5

Beverley Rd. E6 20 G2
Beverley Rd. SW13 36 B1
Beverley Rd. W4 29 B1
Beverstone Rd. SW2 38 F3
Bevin Clo. SE16 26 C2
Bevington Rd. W10 15 G4
Bevington St. SE16 25 F3
Bevis Marks EC3 44 J1
Bewdley St. N1 10 G4
Bewick St. SW8 31 B5
Bewley St. E1 25 G1
Bexhill Rd. SE4 40 D4
Bexley Rd. SE9 42 D3
Bianca Rd. SE15 32 E2
Bibury Clo. SE15 32 D2
Bickenhall St. W1 16 G4
Bicknell Rd. SE5 39 B1
Bidborough St. WC1 17 E2
Bidder St. E16 20 B4
Biddestone Rd. N7 10 F1
Biddulph Rd. W9 16 C2
Bidwell St. SE15 32 G4
Biggerstaff Rd. E15 12 G5
Bigland St. E1 18 G5
Bignell Rd. SE18 35 D1
Bignold Rd. E7 13 D1
Billing Pl. SW10 30 C3
Billing Rd. SW10 30 C3
Billing St. SW10 30 C3
Billingford Clo. SE4 40 B2
Billington Rd. SE14 33 B3
Billiter Sq. EC3 44 J2
Billiter St. EC3 44 J2
Billson St. E14 26 G5
Bina Gdns. SW5 23 D5
Binden Rd. W12 22 B4
Binfield Rd. SW4 31 E4
Bingfield St. N1 10 E5
Bingham St. N1 11 C3
Bingley Rd. E16 20 F5
Binney St. W1 17 A5
Binns Rd. W4 29 A1
Birch Clo. E16 20 B4
Birch Clo. SE15 32 F5
Birch Gro. SE12 41 C5
Birchdale Rd. E7 13 F2
Birches, The SE7 34 E2
Birchfield St. E14 26 E1
Birchin La. EC3 44 G2
Birchington Rd. NW6 9 B5
Birchlands Ave. SW12 37 G5
Birchmere Row SE3 34 C5
Bird in Bush Rd. SE15 32 F3
Birdbrook Rd. SE3 41 F1
Birdcage Wk. SW1 24 C3
Birdhurst Rd. SW18 37 D2
Birdlip Clo. SE15 32 D2
Birdsfield La. E3 12 D5
Birkbeck Rd. E8 11 E2
Birkenhead St. WC1 17 E2
Birkwood Clo. SW12 38 D5
Birley St. SW11 31 A5
Birse Cres. NW10 8 A1
Biscay Rd. W6 29 F1
Biscoe Way SE13 41 A1
Bishop Kings Rd. W14 22 G5
Bishop St. N1 11 B5
Bishop Way NW10 8 A4
Bishop's Ave. E13 13 E5
Bishop's Ave. SW6 29 F5
Bishops Bri. W2 16 D4
Bishops Bri. Rd. W2 16 C5
Bishop's Ct. EC4 44 B1
Bishop's Ct. WC2 43 J1
Bishop's Pk. Rd. SW6 29 F5
Bishops Rd. SW6 29 G4
Bishops Ter. SE11 24 G5
Bishops Way E2 18 G1

Bishopsgate EC2 44
Bishopsgate Chyd. EC2 44
Bisson Rd. E15 19
Black Friars Ct. EC4 44
Black Friars La. EC4 44
Black Lion La. W6 22
Black Prince Rd. SE1 24
Black Prince Rd. SE11 24
Blackburn Rd. NW6 9
Blackburne's Ms. W1 24
Blackett St. SW15 36
Blackfen Rd., Sid. 42
Blackfriars Bri. EC4 44
Blackfriars Bri. SE1 44
Blackfriars Pas. EC4 44
Blackfriars Rd. SE1 44
Blackheath Ave. SE10 34
Blackheath Gro. SE3 34
Blackheath Hill SE10 33
Blackheath Pk. SE3 41
Blackheath Ri. SE13 33
Blackheath Rd. SE10 33
Blackheath Vale SE3 34
Blackheath Village SE3 34
Blackhorse Rd. SE8 33
Blacklands Ter. SW3 23
Blackpool Rd. SE15 32
Blackstone Est. E8 11
Blackstone Rd. NW2 8
Blackthorn St. E3 19
Blacktree Ms. SW9 38
Blackwall La. SE10 34
Blackwall Pier E14 27
Blackwall Tunnel E14 27
Blackwall Tunnel App. SE10 27
Blackwall Tunnel Northern App. E3 19
Blackwall Tunnel Northern App. E14 19
Blackwall Way E14 26
Blackwater St. SE22 39
Blackwell Clo. E5 12
Blackwood St. SE17 32
Blagdon Rd. SE13 40
Blagrove Rd. W10 15
Blair Clo. N1 11
Blair Clo., Sid. 42
Blair St. E14 19
Blake Ave., Bark. 14
Blake Clo. W10 15
Blake Clo., Well. 35
Blake Gdns. SW6 30
Blake Rd. E16 20
Blaker Rd. E15 12
Blakes Rd. SE15 32
Blanchard Way E8 11
Blanche St. E16 20
Blanchedowne SE5 39
Bland St. SE9 41
Blandfield Rd. SW12 38
Blandford Rd. W4 22
Blandford Sq. NW1 16
Blandford St. W1 16
Blaney Cres. E6 21
Blann Clo. SE9 41
Blantyre St. SW10 30
Blashford NW3 9
Blashford St. SE13 41
Blasker Wk. E14 33
Blendon Ter. SE18 35
Blenheim Cres. W11 22
Blenheim Gdns. NW2 8
Blenheim Gdns. SW2 38
Blenheim Gro. SE15 32
Blenheim Rd. E6 20
Blenheim Rd. E15 13
Blenheim Rd. NW8 16

Street	Map	Grid
heim Rd. W4	22	A4
heim Ter. NW8	16	D1
karne Rd. SW11	37	G4
sington Clo. SE13	41	A1
sington Rd. SE13	41	A2
chley St. N1	18	B1
ett St. SE10	33	G4
field St. W8	23	C4
mfontein Ave. 12	22	D2
mfontein Rd. 12	22	D1
nfield Rd. W9	16	C4
nfield St. EC2	18	C4
nfield Vill. W2	16	C4
del St. SW11	31	A5
din St. E3	19	E1
m Pk. Rd. SW6	30	A3
mfield Rd. SE18	35	D1
mfield Ter. SW1	31	A1
msbury Ho. SW4	38	D4
msbury Sq. WC1	17	E4
msbury St. WC1	17	D4
msbury Way C1	**43**	**E1**
Ct. W1	**43**	**C3**
som St. E1	18	D3
nt St. E14	19	C4
am Gdns. SE9	42	A3
ner Rd. SE5	32	B3
Anchor La. SE16	25	F5
Anchor Yd. E1	25	F1
Ball Yd. SW1	**43**	**A6**
bell Ave. E12	14	A2
bell Way, Ilf.	14	D3
dell St. N7	10	E4
s Rd. SE9	42	C3
on Rd. E5	12	A1
e Clo. SE6	40	D5
e Hill SE6	40	D5
e Hill La. SE6	40	D5
e Rd. W14	22	F4
e St. E2	18	G2
house Wk. SE15	32	E3
in Clo. SW4	38	C1
ng St. E8	11	G5
ey Rd. E8	11	G2
mia Pl. E8	12	A3
au Rd. SW13	29	C3
en St. SE8	33	F5
wn Rd. E6	20	G1
wn Rd. E7	13	D4
wn Rd. N16	11	D2
a Rd. SE16	33	A1
gbroke Gro. W11	37	G4
gbroke Rd. W14	22	F4
gbroke Wk. W11	30	E4
ey St. SW8	31	F3
ver St. W1	17	B3
Ct. EC4	**44**	**A2**
n Cres. SE5	32	A2
n Gdns. NW10	15	F1
n Gdns. SW5	30	C1
n Gdns. Ms. W10	30	C1
n Rd. E15	13	C3
n Rd. NW8	9	C5
n Rd. NW10	8	A5
n St. W1	24	B2
ns, The SW10	30	D1
ns Pl. SW10	30	D1
ay St. SE16	25	G5
re Rd. W11	22	G1
r Rd. SE15	32	F3
hurch Rd. W10	15	G4
Ct. EC4	**44**	**F2**
St. E15	13	B2
way SW8	31	E2
Boneta Rd. SE18	28	B4
Bonfield Rd. SE13	40	G2
Bonham Rd. SW2	38	F3
Bonhill St. EC2	18	C3
Bonner Rd. E2	19	A1
Bonner St. E2	19	A1
Bonneville Gdns. SW4	38	C4
Bonnington Sq. SW8	31	F2
Bonny St. NW1	10	C4
Bonsor St. SE5	32	D3
Book Ms. WC2	**43**	**D2**
Boone St. SE13	41	B2
Boones Rd. SE13	41	B2
Boord St. SE10	27	B4
Boot St. N1	18	D2
Bordon Wk. SW15	36	C5
Boreham Ave. E16	20	D5
Borer's Pas. E1	**44**	**J1**
Borgard Rd. SE18	28	B5
Borland Rd. SE15	40	A2
Borneo St. SW15	36	E1
Borough High St. SE1	25	B3
Borough Rd. SE1	25	A4
Borrodaile Rd. SW18	37	C4
Borthwick Rd. E15	13	B1
Borthwick St. SE8	33	E1
Boscobel Pl. SW1	24	A5
Boscobel St. NW8	16	E3
Boscombe Clo. E5	12	C2
Boscombe Rd. W12	22	C2
Boston Gdns. W4	29	A2
Boston Pl. NW1	16	G3
Boston Rd. E6	21	A2
Boswell St. WC1	17	E4
Bosworth Rd. W10	15	G3
Botha Rd. E13	20	E4
Bothwell Clo. E16	20	C4
Botolph All. EC3	**44**	**H3**
Botolph La. EC3	**44**	**H3**
Boughton Rd. SE28	28	G4
Boulcott St. E1	19	B5
Boultwood Rd. E6	21	B5
Boundary La. E13	20	G2
Boundary La. SE17	32	B2
Boundary Rd. E13	20	F1
Boundary Rd. NW8	9	D5
Boundary Rd., Bark.	14	F5
Boundary Rd., Sid.	42	G3
Boundary St. E2	18	E3
Bourchier St. W1	**43**	**C3**
Bourdon St. W1	24	B1
Bourke Clo. SW4	38	E4
Bournbrook Rd. SE3	41	G1
Bourne Est. EC1	17	G4
Bourne St. SW1	24	A5
Bourne Ter. W2	16	C4
Bournemouth Rd. SE15	32	F5
Bournville Rd. SE6	40	E5
Bousfield Rd. SE14	33	B5
Boutflower Rd. SW11	37	F2
Bouverie Pl. W2	16	E5
Bouverie St. EC4	**44**	**A2**
Boveney Rd. SE23	40	B5
Bovill Rd. SE23	40	B5
Bovingdon Rd. SW6	30	C4
Bow Bri. Est. E3	19	F1
Bow Chyd. EC4	**44**	**E2**
Bow Common La. E3	19	C3
Bow Ind. Est. E15	12	F4
Bow La. EC4	**44**	**E2**
Bow Rd. E3	19	D2
Bow St. E15	13	B2
Bow St. WC2	**43**	**F2**
Bowater Clo. SW2	38	E4
Bowater Pl. SE3	34	E3
Bowater Rd. SE18	27	G4
Bowden St. SE11	31	G1
Bowditch SE8	33	D1
Bowen St. E14	19	F5
Bower Ave. SE10	34	B4
Bower St. E1	19	B5
Bowerdean St. SW6	30	C4
Bowerman Ave. SE14	33	C2
Bowes Rd. W3	22	A1
Bowfell Rd. W6	29	E2
Bowhill Clo. SW9	31	G3
Bowie Clo. SW4	38	D5
Bowl Ct. EC2	18	D3
Bowland Rd. SW4	38	D2
Bowling Grn. Clo. SW15	36	D5
Bowling Grn. La. EC1	17	G3
Bowling Grn. Pl. SE1	25	C3
Bowling Grn. St. SE11	31	G2
Bowman Ave. E16	27	C1
Bowmans Lea SE23	40	A5
Bowness Rd. SE6	40	F5
Bowood Rd. SW11	38	A3
Bowyer Clo. E6	21	B4
Bowyer Pl. SE5	32	B3
Bowyer St. SE5	32	B3
Boxall Rd. SE21	39	D4
Boxley St. E16	27	E2
Boyard Rd. SE18	35	D1
Boyce St. SE1	**43**	**G6**
Boyce Way E13	20	D3
Boyd St. E1	18	F5
Boyfield St. SE1	25	A3
Boyle St. W1	**43**	**A3**
Boyne Rd. SE13	40	G1
Boyne Ter. Ms. W11	23	A2
Boyson Rd. SE17	32	C2
Brabant Ct. EC3	**44**	**H3**
Brabazon St. E14	19	F5
Brabourn Gro. SE15	33	A5
Bracewell Rd. W10	15	E4
Bracken Ave. SW12	38	A4
Bracken Clo. E6	21	B4
Bracken Gdns. SW13	29	C5
Brackenbury Gdns. W6	22	D4
Brackenbury Rd. W6	22	D4
Brackley Rd. W4	29	A1
Brackley Ter. W4	29	A1
Bracklyn St. N1	18	C1
Bracknell Gdns. NW3	9	C1
Bracknell Gate NW3	9	C2
Bracknell Way NW3	9	C1
Brad St. SE1	**44**	**A6**
Bradbourne St. SW6	30	B5
Bradbury St. N16	11	D2
Braddyll St. SE10	34	B1
Bradenham Clo. SE17	32	C2
Bradfield Rd. E16	27	D3
Bradgate Rd. SE6	40	E4
Brading Rd. SW2	38	F5
Bradiston Rd. W9	16	A2
Bradley Stone Rd. E6	21	B4
Bradmead SW8	31	B3
Bradmore Pk. Rd. W6	22	D5
Bradstock Rd. E9	12	B3
Bradwell St. E1	19	B2
Brady St. E1	18	G3
Braemar Rd. E13	20	C3
Braes St. N1	11	A4
Braganza St. SE17	32	A1
Braham St. E1	18	E5
Braid Ave. W3	15	A5
Braidwood St. SE1	**44**	**H6**
Brailsford Rd. SW2	38	G3
Braintree St. E2	19	A3
Bramah Grn. SW9	31	G4
Bramber Rd. W14	30	A2
Bramblebury Rd. SE18	35	E1
Bramcote Gro. SE16	33	A1
Bramcote Rd. SW15	36	D2
Bramerton St. SW3	30	F2
Bramfield Rd. SW11	37	F4
Bramford Rd. SW18	37	D2
Bramham Gdns. SW5	30	C1
Bramhope La. SE7	34	E2
Bramlands Clo. SW11	37	F1
Bramley Rd. W10	22	F1
Brampton Rd. E6	20	G3
Bramshaw Rd. E9	12	B3
Bramshill Rd. NW10	15	A1
Bramshot Ave. SE7	34	D2
Bramston Rd. NW10	15	C1
Bramwell Ms. N1	10	F5
Brancaster Rd. E12	14	B1
Branch Pl. N1	11	C5
Branch Rd. E14	26	C1
Branch St. SE15	32	D3
Brand St. SE10	33	G3
Brandlehow Rd. SW15	37	A2
Brandon Est. SE17	32	A2
Brandon Rd. N7	10	E4
Brandon St. SE17	25	B5
Brandram Rd. SE13	41	B1
Brandreth Rd. E6	21	B5
Brangton Rd. SE11	31	F1
Branksea St. SW6	29	G3
Branksome Rd. SW2	38	E2
Branscombe St. SE13	40	F1
Brantwood Rd. SE24	39	B3
Brassey Rd. NW6	9	A3
Brassey Sq. SW11	38	A1
Brassie Ave. W3	15	A5
Brathway Rd. SW18	37	B5
Bravington Rd. W9	16	A2
Braxfield Rd. SE4	40	C2
Bray NW3	9	F4
Bray Dr. E16	27	C1
Bray Pl. SW3	23	G5
Brayards Rd. SE15	32	G5
Braybrook St. W12	15	B4
Brayburne Ave. SW4	31	C5
Braywood Rd. SE9	42	F2
Bread St. EC4	**44**	**E3**
Breakspears Rd. SE4	40	D1
Bream Gdns. E6	21	C2
Bream St. E3	12	E4
Bream's Bldgs. EC4	**43**	**J1**
Breasley Clo. SW15	36	D2
Brecknock Rd. N7	10	D2
Brecknock Rd. N19	10	C1
Brecknock Rd. Est. N7	10	C1
Brecon Rd. W6	29	G2
Brede Clo. E6	21	C2
Bredon Rd. SE5	39	B1
Breer St. SW6	37	C1
Brenchley Gdns. SE23	40	A4
Brendon Ave. NW10	8	A1
Brendon St. W1	16	F5
Brenley Gdns. SE9	41	G2
Brent Rd. E16	20	D4
Brent Rd. SE18	35	D3
Brenthouse Rd. E9	12	A3
Brenthurst Rd. NW10	8	B3
Brenton St. E14	19	C5
Bressenden Pl. SW1	24	B4
Brett Rd. E8	11	G2
Brewer St. W1	**43**	**B3**
Brewery Rd. N7	10	E4
Brewery Rd. SE18	35	F1
Brewhouse La. E1	25	G2
Brewhouse Rd. SE18	28	B5
Brewhouse St. SW15	36	G
Brewhouse Wk. SE16	26	C
Brewster Gdns. W10	15	E
Brewster Ho. E14	26	D
Briant St. SE14	33	
Briar Rd. NW2	8	1

Briar Wk. SW15 36 D2
Briarwood Rd. SW4 38 D3
Brick Ct. EC4 43 J2
Brick La. E1 18 E3
Brick La. E2 18 E2
Brick St. W1 24 B2
Bride Ct. EC4 44 B2
Bride La. EC4 44 B2
Bride St. N7 10 F3
Bridewain St. SE1 25 E4
Bridewell Pl. EC4 44 B2
Bridge App. NW1 10 A4
Bridge Ave. W6 29 D1
Bridge La. SW11 30 F4
Bridge Meadows SE14 33 B2
Bridge Pk. SW18 37 B3
Bridge Pl. SW1 24 B5
Bridge Rd. E6 14 B4
Bridge Rd. E15 13 A5
Bridge Rd. NW10 8 A3
Bridge St. SW1 24 E3
Bridge Ter. E15 13 A4
Bridge Vw. W6 29 E1
Bridge Yd. SE1 44 G5
Bridgefoot SE1 31 E1
Bridgeland Rd. E16 27 D1
Bridgeman Rd. N1 10 F4
Bridgeman St. NW8 16 F1
Bridgend Rd. SW18 37 D2
Bridges Ct. SW11 37 E1
Bridges Pl. SW6 30 A4
Bridgeway St. NW1 17 C1
Bridgwater Rd. E15 12 G5
Bridle La. W1 43 B3
Bridport Pl. N1 11 C5
Brief St. SE5 32 A4
Brierley Rd. E11 13 A1
Bright St. E14 19 F5
Brightfield Rd. SE12 41 C3
Brightling Rd. SE4 40 D4
Brightlingsea Pl. E14 26 D1
Brighton Rd. E6 21 C2
Brighton Rd. N16 11 D1
Brighton Ter. SW9 38 F2
Brightside Rd. SE13 41 A4
Brill Pl. NW1 17 D1
Brindley St. SE14 33 D4
Brinklow Cres. SE18 35 D3
Brinklow Ho. W2 16 C4
Brinkworth Way E9 12 D3
Brinton Wk. SE1 44 B6
Brion Pl. E14 19 G4
Brisbane St. SE5 32 C3
Briset Rd. SE9 41 G1
Bristol Gdns. W9 16 C3
Bristol Rd. E7 13 F3
Britannia Rd. E14 26 E5
Britannia Rd. SW6 30 C3
Britannia Row N1 11 A5
Britannia St. WC1 17 F2
British Gro. W4 29 B1
British Gro. Pas. W4 29 B1
British St. E3 19 D2
Britten St. SW3 30 F1
Britton St. EC1 18 A3
Brixham Gdns., Ilf. 14 G2
Brixham St. E16 28 B2
Brixton Hill SW2 38 E5
Brixton Oval SW2 38 G2
Brixton Rd. SW9 38 G1
Brixton Sta. Rd. SW9 38 G1
Brixton Water La. SW2 38 G3
Broad Ct. WC2 43 F2
Broad La. EC2 18 D4
Broad Sanctuary SW1 24 D3
Broad Wk. NW1 17 A1
Broad Wk. SE3 34 F5
Broad Wk. W1 24 A2
Broad Wk., The W8 23 D2
Broadbridge Clo. SE3 34 D3
Broadfield La. NW1 10 E4
Broadfield Rd. SE6 41 B5
Broadfields Way NW10 8 B2
Broadgate E13 20 F1
Broadhinton Rd. SW4 38 B1
Broadhurst Gdns. NW6 9 C3
Broadley St. NW8 16 E4
Broadley Ter. NW1 16 F3
Broadwall SE1 44 A5
Broadwater Rd. SE28 28 E4
Broadway E15 13 A4
Broadway SW1 24 D4
Broadway, Bark. 14 E4
Broadway, The E13 20 E1
Broadway Mkt. E8 11 G5
Broadwick St. W1 43 B3
Brock Pl. E3 19 F3
Brock Rd. E13 20 E4
Brockenhurst Gdns., Ilf. 14 E2
Brockham St. SE1 25 B4
Brockill Cres. SE4 40 C2
Brocklebank Rd. SE7 27 E5
Brocklebank Rd. SW18 37 D5
Brocklehurst St. SE14 33 B3
Brockley Footpath SE15 40 A2
Brockley Gdns. SE4 33 D5
Brockley Gro. SE4 40 D3
Brockley Hall Rd. SE4 40 C3
Brockley Ms. SE4 40 C3
Brockley Pk. SE23 40 C5
Brockley Ri. SE23 40 C5
Brockley Rd. SE4 40 D1
Brockley Vw. SE23 40 C5
Brockley Way SE4 40 B3
Brockwell Pk. Gdns. SE24 38 G5
Brockworth Clo. SE15 32 D2
Brodlove La. E1 26 B1
Broken Wf. EC4 44 D3
Brokesley St. E3 19 D2
Bromar Rd. SE5 39 D1
Brome Rd. SE9 42 B1
Bromell's Rd. SW4 38 C2
Bromfelde Rd. SW4 38 D1
Bromfelde Wk. SW4 31 E5
Bromfield St. N1 17 G1
Bromley Hall Rd. E14 19 G4
Bromley High St. E3 19 F2
Bromley St. E1 19 B4
Brompton Pk. Cres. SW6 30 C2
Brompton Pl. SW3 23 F4
Brompton Rd. SW1 23 G3
Brompton Rd. SW3 23 F5
Brompton Rd. SW7 23 F4
Brompton Sq. SW3 23 F4
Bromyard Ave. W3 22 A1
Brondesbury Ct. NW2 8 F3
Brondesbury Pk. NW2 8 E4
Brondesbury Pk. NW6 8 F4
Brondesbury Rd. NW6 16 A1
Brondesbury Vill. NW6 16 A1
Bronsart Rd. SW6 29 G3
Bronte Ho. NW6 16 B2
Bronti Clo. SE17 32 B1
Bronze St. SE8 33 E3
Brook Dr. SE11 24 G4
Brook Gdns. SW13 36 B1
Brook Grn. W6 22 E4
Brook La. SE3 34 E5
Brook St. W1 24 A1
Brook St. W2 23 E1
Brookbank Rd. SE13 40 E1
Brookdale Rd. SE6 40 F4
Brooke St. EC1 17 G4
Brookfield Rd. E9 12 C3
Brookhill Clo. SE18 35 D1
Brookhill Rd. SE18 28 D5
Brooking Rd. E7 13 D2
Brooklands Pk. SE3 41 D1
Brookmill Rd. SE8 33 E4
Brooks Ave. E6 21 B3
Brook's Ms. W1 24 B1
Brooks Rd. E13 13 D5
Brooksbank St. E9 12 A3
Brooksby St. N1 10 G4
Brooksby's Wk. E9 12 B2
Brooksville Ave. NW6 8 G5
Brookville Rd. SW6 30 A3
Brookway SE3 41 D1
Brookwood Ave. SW13 36 B1
Broome Way SE5 32 B3
Broomfield St. E14 19 E4
Broomgrove Rd. SW9 31 F5
Broomhill Rd. SW18 37 B3
Broomhouse La. SW6 30 B5
Broomhouse Rd. SW6 30 B5
Broomsleigh St. NW6 9 A2
Broomwood Rd. SW11 37 G4
Brougham Rd. E8 11 F5
Broughton Dr. SW9 38 G2
Broughton Rd. SW6 30 C5
Broughton St. SW8 31 A5
Brown Hart Gdns. W1 24 A1
Brown St. W1 16 G5
Brownfield St. E14 19 F5
Brownhill Rd. SE6 40 F5
Browning Clo., Well. 35 G4
Browning Est. SE17 32 B1
Browning Rd. E12 14 B3
Browning St. SE17 32 B1
Brownlow Ms. WC1 17 F3
Brownlow Rd. E8 11 E5
Brownlow Rd. NW10 8 A4
Brown's Bldgs. EC3 44 J2
Browns La. NW5 10 B2
Broxash Rd. SW11 38 A4
Broxwood Way NW8 9 F5
Bruce Rd. E3 19 F2
Bruckner St. W10 16 A2
Brune St. E1 18 E4
Brunel Est. W2 16 B4
Brunel Rd. SE16 26 A3
Brunel Rd. W3 15 A4
Brunswick Ct. SE1 25 D3
Brunswick Gdns. W8 23 B2
Brunswick Pk. SE5 32 C4
Brunswick Pl. N1 18 C2
Brunswick Quay SE16 26 B4
Brunswick Sq. WC1 17 E3
Brunswick Vill. SE5 32 D4
Brunton Pl. E14 19 C5
Brushfield St. E1 18 D4
Brussels Rd. SW11 37 E2
Bruton La. W1 24 B1
Bruton Pl. W1 24 B1
Bruton St. W1 24 B1
Bryan Ave. NW10 8 D4
Bryan Rd. SE16 26 D3
Bryanston Pl. W1 16 G4
Bryanston Sq. W1 16 G4
Bryanston St. W1 16 G5
Bryant St. E15 13 A4
Bryantwood Rd. N7 10 G2
Brydges Pl. WC2 43 E4
Brydges Rd. E15 13 A2
Brymay Clo. E3 19 E1
Brynmaer Rd. SW11 30 G4
Bryony Rd. W12 22 C1
Buchan Rd. SE15 40
Buchanan Gdns. NW10 15
Bucharest Rd. SW18 37
Buck St. NW1 10
Buckfast St. E2 18
Buckhold Rd. SW18 37
Buckhurst St. E1 18
Buckingham Arc. WC2 43
Buckingham Ave., Well. 42
Buckingham Gate SW1 24
Buckingham La. SE23 40
Buckingham Palace Rd. SW1 24
Buckingham Rd. E15 13
Buckingham Rd. N1 11
Buckingham Rd. NW10 15
Buckingham St. WC2 43
Buckland Cres. NW3 9
Buckland St. N1 18
Bucklersbury EC4 44
Buckley Rd. NW6 9
Buckley St. SE1 43
Buckmaster Rd. SW11 37
Bucknall St. WC2 43
Bucknell Clo. SW2 38
Buckner Rd. SW2 38
Buckstone Clo. SE23 40
Buckters Rents SE16 26
Buckthorne Rd. SE4 40
Budge Row EC4 44
Budge's Wk. W2 2
Buer Rd. SW6 2
Bugsby's Way SE7 27
Bugsby's Way SE10 27
Bulinga St. SW1 2
Bull Inn Ct. WC2 4
Bull Rd. E15 2
Bull Wf. La. EC4 4
Bullards Pl. E2 1
Bullen St. SW11 3
Buller Clo. SE15 3
Buller Rd., Bark. 1
Bullivant St. E14 1
Bull's Head Pas. EC3 4
Bulmer Pl. W11 2
Bulstrode St. W1 1
Bulwer St. W12 2
Bunhill Row EC1 1
Bunhouse Pl. SW1 3
Bunning Way N7 1
Burbage Clo. SE1 2
Burbage Rd. SE21 3
Burbage Rd. SE24 3
Burcham St. E14 1
Burchell Rd. SE15 3
Burcote Rd. SW18 3
Burder Clo. N1 1
Burdett Rd. E3 1
Burdett Rd. E14 1
Burford Rd. E6 2
Burford Rd. E15 1
Burges Ct. E6 1
Burges Gro. SW13 2
Burges Rd. E6 1
Burgess Hill NW2
Burgess Rd. E15 1
Burgess St. E14 1
Burgh St. N1 1
Burghley Rd. NW5 1
Burghley Twr. W3 2
Burgon St. EC4 4
Burgos Gro. SE10 3
Burgoyne Rd. SW9 3
Burke Clo. SW15 3

ke St. E16 20 C5
land Rd. SW11 37 G3
leigh Pl. SW15 36 F3
leigh St. WC2 43 F3
ley Rd. E16 20 F4
lington Arc. W1 43 A4
lington Clo. W9 16 A3
lington Gdns. W1 43 A4
lington La. W4 29 A3
lington Rd. SW6 29 G5
ma Rd. N16 11 C1
naby St. SW10 30 D3
ne Jones Ho. W14 23 A5
ne St. NW1 16 F4
nels Ave. E6 21 C2
nett Clo. E9 12 A2
ney St. SE10 33 G3
nfoot Ave. SW6 29 G4
nham NW3 9 F4
nham St. E2 19 A2
nley Rd. NW10 8 B2
nley Rd. SW9 31 F5
ns Rd. NW10 8 B5
ns Rd. SW11 30 G5
rnsall St. SW3 30 F1
rnside Clo. SE16 26 B2
nt Ash Hill SE12 41 C4
nt Ash Rd. SE12 41 C3
nthwaite Rd. SW6 30 A3
r Clo. E1 25 F2
rage Gro. SE18 28 E5
rage Pl. SE18 35 D1
rrage Rd. SE18 28 E5
rrard Rd. E16 20 E5
rrard Rd. NW6 9 B2
rrell St. SE1 44 B5
rrells Wf. Sq. E14 33 F1
rrow Rd. SE22 39 D2
rrows Rd. NW10 15 E2
rslem St. E1 18 F5
rstock Rd. SW15 36 G2
rston Rd. SW15 36 F3
rt Rd. E16 27 F2
rton La. SW9 31 G5
rton Rd. NW6 9 A4
rton Rd. SW9 32 A5
rton St. WC1 17 D2
rwash Rd. SE18 35 F1
rwell Wk. E3 19 E3
rwood Pl. W2 16 F5
ry Ct. EC3 44 J1
ry Pl. WC1 17 E4
ry St. EC3 44 J2
ry St. SW1 43 A5
ry Wk. SW3 23 F5
sby Ms. NW5 10 D3
sby Pl. NW5 10 D3
sh Ct. W12 22 F3
sh La. EC4 44 F3
sh Rd. E8 11 G5
sh Rd. SE8 26 B5
shberry Rd. E9 12 C3
shey Hill Rd. SE5 32 D4
shey Rd. E13 20 F1
shmoor Cres. SE18 35 E3
shwood Dr. SE1 25 E5
tcher Row E1 26 B1
tcher Row E14 26 B1
tchers Rd. E16 20 D5
te Gdns. W6 22 F5
te St. SW7 23 E5
tterfly La. SE9 42 D4
ttermere Dr. SW15 36 G3
ttermere Wk. E8 11 E3
tterwick W6 22 E5
ttesland St. N1 18 C2
ttmarsh Clo. SE18 35 D1
ttsbury Rd., Ilf. 14 E2
xted Rd. E8 11 E4
xted Rd. SE22 39 D2
Buxton Rd. E6 21 A2
Buxton Rd. E15 13 B2
Buxton Rd. NW2 8 D3
Buxton Rd. SW14 36 A1
Buxton St. E1 18 E3
Byam St. SW6 30 D5
Bye, The W3 15 A5
Byfeld Gdns. SW13 29 C4
Byfield Clo. SE16 26 C3
Byford Clo. E15 13 B4
Bygrove St. E14 19 F5
Byng Pl. WC1 17 D3
Byng St. E14 26 E3
Byron Ave. E12 14 A3
Byron Clo. E8 11 F5
Byron Ms. NW3 9 F1
Bythorn St. SW9 38 F2
Byward St. EC3 44 J4
Bywater Pl. SE16 26 C2
Bywater St. SW3 30 G1

C

Cabbell St. NW1 16 F4
Cable St. E1 25 F1
Cabot Sq. E14 26 E2
Cabul Rd. SW11 30 F5
Cade Rd. SE10 34 A4
Cader Rd. SW18 37 D4
Cadet Dr. SE1 32 E1
Cadet Pl. SE10 34 B1
Cadiz St. SE17 32 B1
Cadogan Gdns. SW3 23 G5
Cadogan Gate SW1 23 G5
Cadogan La. SW1 24 A4
Cadogan Pl. SW1 23 G4
Cadogan Sq. SW1 23 G4
Cadogan St. SW3 23 G5
Cadogan Ter. E9 12 D3
Caedmon Rd. N7 10 F1
Cahir St. E14 26 F5
Caird St. W10 15 G2
Cairns Rd. SW11 37 F3
Caistor Pk. Rd. E15 13 C5
Caistor Rd. SW12 38 B5
Caithness Rd. W14 22 F4
Calabria Rd. N5 11 A3
Calais St. SE5 32 A4
Calbourne Rd. SW12 37 G5
Caldecot Rd. SE5 32 B5
Calderon Rd. E11 12 G1
Caldervale Rd. SW4 38 D3
Calderwood St. SE18 28 C5
Caldwell St. SW9 31 F3
Cale St. SW3 30 F1
Caledon Rd. E6 14 A5
Caledonia St. N1 17 E1
Caledonian Rd. N1 17 E1
Caledonian Rd. N7 10 F1
Caledonian Wf. Rd. E14 27 A5
Caletock Way SE10 34 C1
Callcott Rd. NW6 9 A4
Callendar Rd. SW7 23 E4
Callow St. SW3 30 E2
Calmington Rd. SE5 32 D1
Calshot St. N1 17 F1
Calthorpe St. WC1 17 F3
Calton Ave. SE21 39 D4
Calvert Ave. E2 18 D2
Calvert Rd. SE10 34 C1
Calverton Rd. E6 14 C5
Calvert's Bldgs. SE1 44 F6
Calvin St. E1 18 E3
Calydon Rd. SE7 34 E1
Calypso Way SE16 26 D5
Cam Rd. E15 13 A5
Cambalt Rd. SW15 36 F3
Cambert Way SE3 41 E2
Camberwell Ch. St. SE5 32 C4
Camberwell Glebe SE5 32 D4
Camberwell Grn. SE5 32 C4
Camberwell Gro. SE5 32 C4
Camberwell New Rd. SE5 31 G2
Camberwell Rd. SE5 32 B2
Camberwell Sta. Rd. SE5 32 B4
Camborne Rd. SW18 37 B5
Cambria Rd. SE5 39 B1
Cambria St. SW6 30 C3
Cambridge Ave. NW6 16 B1
Cambridge Barracks Rd. SE18 28 B5
Cambridge Circ. WC2 43 D2
Cambridge Cres. E2 18 G1
Cambridge Dr. SE12 41 D3
Cambridge Gdns. NW6 16 B1
Cambridge Gdns. W10 15 F5
Cambridge Gro. W6 22 D5
Cambridge Heath Rd. E1 18 G3
Cambridge Heath Rd. E2 19 A3
Cambridge Pl. W8 23 C3
Cambridge Rd. NW6 16 B2
Cambridge Rd. SW11 30 G4
Cambridge Rd. SW13 29 B5
Cambridge Rd., Bark. 14 E4
Cambridge Row SE18 35 D1
Cambridge Sq. W2 16 F5
Cambridge St. SW1 24 B5
Cambus Rd. E16 20 D4
Camden Est. SE15 32 E4
Camden High St. NW1 10 B5
Camden La. N7 10 D3
Camden Ms. NW1 10 C4
Camden Pk. Rd. NW1 10 D3
Camden Pas. N1 11 A5
Camden Rd. N7 10 E1
Camden Rd. NW1 10 C4
Camden Row SE3 34 B5
Camden Sq. NW1 10 D3
Camden St. NW1 10 C4
Camden Wk. N1 11 A5
Camdenhurst St. E14 19 C5
Camel Rd. E16 27 G2
Camellia St. SW8 31 E3
Camelot Clo. SE28 28 F3
Camera Pl. SW10 30 E2
Camilla Rd. SE16 25 G5
Camlet St. E2 18 E3
Camley St. NW1 10 D4
Camomile St. EC3 44 H1
Campana Rd. SW6 30 B4
Campbell Gordon Way NW2 8 D1
Campbell Rd. E3 19 E2
Campbell Rd. E6 14 A5
Campden Gro. W8 23 B3
Campden Hill W8 23 B3
Campden Hill Gdns. W8 23 B2
Campden Hill Rd. W8 23 B2
Campden Hill Sq. W8 23 A2
Campden St. W8 23 B2
Campfield Rd. SE9 41 G5
Campion Clo. E6 28 B1
Campion Rd. SW15 36 E2
Campion Ter. NW2 8 F1
Camplin St. SE14 33 B3
Campshill Rd. SE13 40 G3
Canada Est. SE16 26 A4
Canada Sq. E14 26 F2
Canada St. SE16 26 B3
Canada Way W12 22 D1
Canada Yd. S. SE16 26 B4
Canal App. SE8 33 C1
Canal Clo. E1 19 C3
Canal Clo. W10 15 F3
Canal Gro. SE15 32 F2
Canal Path E2 11 E5
Canal Rd. E3 19 C3
Canal St. SE5 32 C2
Canal Wk. N1 11 C5
Canal Way W10 15 F3
Canary Wf. E14 26 E2
Canberra Rd. SE7 34 F2
Cancell Rd. SW9 31 G4
Candahar Rd. SW11 30 F5
Candy St. E3 12 D5
Canfield Gdns. NW6 9 C4
Canford Rd. SW11 38 A3
Canham Rd. W3 22 A3
Cann Hall Rd. E11 13 B1
Canning Cross SE5 32 D5
Canning Pl. W8 23 D4
Canning Rd. E15 20 B1
Cannon Dr. E14 26 E1
Cannon Hill NW6 9 B2
Cannon Pl. SE7 35 A1
Cannon St. EC4 44 D2
Cannon St. Rd. E1 18 G5
Canon Beck Rd. SE16 26 A3
Canon Row SW1 24 E3
Canon St. N1 11 B5
Canonbie Rd. SE23 40 A5
Canonbury Cres. N1 11 B4
Canonbury Gro. N1 11 B4
Canonbury La. N1 11 A4
Canonbury Pk. N. N1 11 B3
Canonbury Pk. S. N1 11 B3
Canonbury Pl. N1 11 A3
Canonbury Rd. N1 11 A3
Canonbury Sq. N1 11 A4
Canonbury St. N1 11 B4
Canonbury Vill. N1 11 A4
Canrobert St. E2 18 G2
Cantelowes Rd. NW1 10 D3
Canterbury Cres. SW9 38 G1
Canterbury Pl. SE17 25 A5
Canterbury Rd. NW6 16 A1
Canterbury Ter. NW6 16 B1
Canton St. E14 19 E5
Cantrell Rd. E3 19 D3
Cantwell Rd. SE18 35 D3
Canute Gdns. SE16 26 B5
Canvey St. SE1 44 C5
Capel Ct. EC2 44 G2
Capel Pt. E7 13 E1
Capel Rd. E7 13 E1
Capel Rd. E12 13 G1
Capland St. NW8 16 E3
Caple Rd. NW10 15 B1
Capper St. WC1 17 C3
Capstan Rd. SE8 26 D5
Capstan Sq. E14 26 G3
Capstan Way SE16 26 C2
Caradoc Clo. W2 16 B5
Caradoc St. SE10 34 B1
Caraway Clo. E13 20 E4
Carbis Rd. E14 19 D5
Carburton St. W1 17 B4
Carden Rd. SE15 39 G1
Cardiff St. SE18 35 G3
Cardigan Rd. E3 19 D1
Cardigan Rd. SW13 29 C5
Cardigan St. SE11 31 G1
Cardinal Pl. SW15 36 F2
Cardine Ms. SE15 32 G3
Cardington St. NW1 17 C2
Cardozo Rd. N7 10 E2
Cardross St. W6 22 D4
Cardwell Rd. N7 10 E1
Cardwell Rd. SE18 28 B5
Carew St. SE5 32 B5

Carey Gdns. SW8 31 C4
Carey La. EC2 44 D1
Carey St. WC2 43 H2
Carker's La. NW5 10 B2
Carleton Rd. N7 10 D2
Carlile Clo. E3 19 D1
Carlingford Rd. NW3 9 E1
Carlisle Ave. W3 15 A5
Carlisle La. SE1 24 F4
Carlisle Ms. NW8 16 E4
Carlisle Pl. SW1 24 C4
Carlisle Rd. NW6 8 G5
Carlisle St. W1 43 C2
Carlos Pl. W1 24 A1
Carlton Ct. SW9 32 A4
Carlton Dr. SW15 36 F3
Carlton Gdns. SW1 43 C6
Carlton Gro. SE15 32 G4
Carlton Hill NW8 16 C1
Carlton Ho. Ter. SW1 43 C6
Carlton Rd. E12 13 G1
Carlton St. SW1 43 C4
Carlton Twr. Pl. SW1 23 G4
Carlton Vale NW6 16 B1
Carlyle Pl. SW15 36 F2
Carlyle Rd. E12 14 A1
Carlyle Sq. SW3 30 E1
Carmalt Gdns. SW15 36 E2
Carmelite St. EC4 44 A3
Carmen St. E14 19 F5
Carnaby St. W1 43 A2
Carnarvon Rd. E15 13 C3
Carnbrook Rd. SE3 41 G1
Carnecke Gdns. SE9 42 A3
Carnegie St. N1 10 F5
Carnoustie Dr. N1 10 F4
Carnwath Rd. SW6 37 B1
Carol St. NW1 10 C5
Carolina Clo. E15 13 B2
Caroline Gdns. SE15 32 G3
Caroline Pl. SW11 31 A5
Caroline Pl. W2 23 C1
Caroline St. E1 19 B5
Caroline Ter. SW1 24 A5
Carpenters Pl. SW4 38 D2
Carpenters Rd. E15 12 E3
Carr Gro. SE18 28 A5
Carr St. E14 19 C4
Carriage Dr. E. SW11 31 A3
Carriage Dr. N. SW11 30 G3
Carriage Dr. S. SW11 30 G4
Carriage Dr. W. SW11 30 G3
Carrol Clo. NW5 10 B1
Carroll Clo. E15 13 C2
Carron Clo. E14 19 F5
Carronade Pl. SE28 28 E4
Carroun Rd. SW8 31 F3
Carslake Rd. SW15 36 E4
Carson Rd. E16 20 D3
Carston Clo. SE12 41 C3
Carswell Rd. SE6 40 G5
Carter La. EC4 44 C2
Carter Pl. SE17 32 B1
Carter Rd. E13 13 E5
Carter St. SE17 32 B2
Carteret St. SW1 24 D3
Carteret Way SE8 26 C5
Carthew Rd. W6 22 D4
Carthew Vill. W6 22 D4
Carthusian St. EC1 18 B4
Cartier Circle E14 26 F2
Carting La. WC2 43 F4
Cartwright Gdns. WC1 17 E2
Cartwright St. E1 25 E1
Cartwright Way SW13 29 D3
Carver Rd. SE24 39 B4
Cary Rd. E11 13 B1
Casella Rd. SE14 33 B3
Casino Ave. SE24 39 C3
Caspian St. SE5 32 C3
Cassidy Rd. SW6 30 B3
Cassland Rd. E9 12 B4
Casslee Rd. SE6 40 D5
Casson St. E1 18 F4
Castellain Rd. W9 16 C3
Castello Ave. SW15 36 E3
Castelnau SW13 29 C4
Casterbridge NW6 9 C5
Casterbridge Rd. SE3 41 D1
Castile Rd. SE18 28 C5
Castle Baynard St. EC4 44 C3
Castle Ct. EC3 44 G2
Castle La. SW1 24 C4
Castle Pt. E6 20 F1
Castle Rd. NW1 10 B3
Castle St. E6 20 F1
Castle Yd. SE1 44 C5
Castlecombe Dr. SW19 36 F5
Castlehaven Rd. NW1 10 B4
Castlemaine Twr. SW11 30 G5
Castletown Rd. W14 29 G1
Castlewood Dr. SE9 35 B5
Castor La. E14 26 F1
Caterham Rd. SE13 40 G1
Catesby St. SE17 25 C5
Catford Bdy. SE6 40 F5
Catford Rd. SE6 40 E5
Cathay St. SE16 25 G3
Cathcart Rd. SW10 30 C2
Cathcart St. NW5 10 B3
Cathedral Pl. EC4 44 D1
Cathedral St. SE1 44 F5
Catherine Gro. SE10 33 F4
Catherine Pl. SW1 24 C4
Catherine St. WC2 43 G3
Catherine Wheel Yd. SW1 43 A6
Cathles Rd. SW12 38 B4
Cathnor Hill Ct. W12 22 D4
Cathnor Rd. W12 22 D3
Catlin St. SE16 32 F1
Cato Rd. SW4 38 D1
Cator St. SE15 32 E2
Catton St. WC1 17 F4
Caulfield Rd. E6 14 A5
Caulfield Rd. SE15 32 G5
Causeway, The SW18 37 C3
Causton St. SW1 24 D5
Cautley Ave. SW4 38 C3
Cave Rd. E13 20 E1
Cavell St. E1 18 G4
Cavendish Ave. NW8 16 E1
Cavendish Clo. NW8 16 E2
Cavendish Ct. EC3 44 J1
Cavendish Gdns., Bark. 14 G2
Cavendish Pl. W1 17 B5
Cavendish Rd. NW6 8 G4
Cavendish Rd. SW12 38 B4
Cavendish Sq. W1 17 B5
Cavendish St. N1 18 C1
Caversham Rd. NW5 10 C3
Caversham St. SW3 30 G2
Caverswall St. W12 15 E5
Caxton Gro. E3 19 E2
Caxton Rd. W12 22 F2
Caxton St. SW1 24 C4
Cearns Ho. E6 13 G5
Cecil Ave., Bark. 14 F4
Cecil Ct. WC2 43 E4
Cecil Rd. E13 13 D5
Cecil Rd. NW10 8 A5
Cecil Rd., Ilf. 14 D1
Cecilia Rd. E8 11 E2
Cedar Ct. E8 11 E4
Cedar Ct. SE9 42 A4
Cedar Rd. NW2 8 E1
Cedar Way NW1 10 D4
Cedarhurst Dr. SE9 41 F3
Cedarne Rd. SW6 30 C3
Cedars Rd. E15 13 B3
Cedars Rd. SW4 38 B1
Cedars Rd. SW13 29 B5
Celandine Clo. E14 19 E4
Celandine Way E15 20 B2
Celestial Gdns. SE13 41 A2
Celia Rd. N19 10 C1
Celtic St. E14 19 F4
Cemetery La. SE7 35 A2
Cemetery Rd. E7 13 C1
Centaur St. SE1 24 F4
Central Ave. SW11 30 G3
Central Mkts. EC1 18 B4
Central Pk. Rd. E6 20 G1
Central St. EC1 18 B2
Centre St. E2 18 G1
Centurion Clo. N7 10 F4
Cephas Ave. E1 19 A3
Cephas St. E1 19 A3
Cerise Rd. SE15 32 F4
Ceylon Rd. W14 22 F4
Chadbourn St. E14 19 F4
Chadd Grn. E13 13 D5
Chadwell St. EC1 17 G2
Chadwick Rd. NW10 8 B5
Chadwick Rd. SE15 32 E5
Chadwick St. SW1 24 D4
Chadwin Rd. E13 20 E4
Chagford St. NW1 16 G3
Chalcot Cres. NW1 9 G5
Chalcot Gdns. NW3 9 G3
Chalcot Rd. NW1 10 A4
Chalcot Sq. NW1 10 A4
Chalcroft Rd. SE13 41 B3
Chaldon Rd. SW6 29 G3
Chale Rd. SW2 38 E4
Chalk Fm. Rd. NW1 10 A4
Chalk Rd. E13 20 E4
Challoner St. W14 30 A1
Chalsey Rd. SE4 40 D2
Chalton St. NW1 17 C1
Chamber St. E1 25 E1
Chamberlayne Rd. NW10 8 E5
Chambers La. NW10 8 D4
Chambers Rd. N7 10 E1
Chambers St. SE16 25 F3
Chambord St. E2 18 E2
Champion Gro. SE5 39 C1
Champion Hill SE5 39 C1
Champion Hill Est. SE5 39 D1
Champion Pk. SE5 32 C5
Chance St. E1 18 E3
Chance St. E2 18 E3
Chancel St. SE1 44 B6
Chancellors Rd. W6 29 E1
Chancellors St. W6 29 E1
Chancery La. WC2 43 J1
Chandler Ave. E16 20 D4
Chandler Way SE15 32 E3
Chandlers Ms. E14 26 E3
Chandlers Way SW2 38 G5
Chandos Pl. WC2 43 E4
Chandos Rd. E15 13 A2
Chandos Rd. NW2 8 E2
Chandos Rd. NW10 15 A3
Chandos St. W1 17 B4
Change All. EC3 44 G2
Channelsea Rd. E15 13 A5
Chant Sq. E15 13 A4
Chant St. E15 13 A4
Chantrey Rd. SW9 38 F1
Chantry Pt. W9 16 A3
Chantry St. N1 11 A5
Chapel Ho. St. E14 33
Chapel Mkt. N1 17
Chapel Pl. W1 17
Chapel Side W2 23
Chapel St. E15 13
Chapel St. NW1 16
Chapel St. SW1 24
Chaplin Clo. SE1 24
Chaplin Rd. E15 13
Chaplin Rd. NW2 8
Chapman Rd. E9 12
Chapman St. E1 25
Chapmans Pk. Ind. Est. NW10 8
Chapone Pl. W1 43
Chapter Ho. Ct. EC4 44
Chapter Rd. NW2 8
Chapter Rd. SE17 32
Chapter St. SW1 24
Charecroft Way W12 22
Charford Rd. E16 20
Chargeable La. E13 20
Chargeable St. E16 20
Charing Cross WC2 43
Charing Cross Rd. WC2 43
Charlbert St. NW8 16
Charlemont Rd. E6 21
Charles Barry Clo. SW4 38
Charles Dickens Ho. E2 18
Charles Grinling Wk. SE18 28
Charles II St. SW1 43
Charles St. E16 27
Charles St. SW13 29
Charles St. W1 24
Charleston St. SE17 25
Charleville Rd. W14 29
Charlotte Despard Ave. SW11 31
Charlotte Rd. EC2 18
Charlotte Rd. SW13 29
Charlotte St. W1 17
Charlotte Ter. N1 10
Charlton Ch. La. SE7 34
Charlton Dene SE7 34
Charlton Kings Rd. NW5 10
Charlton La. SE7 34
Charlton Pk. La. SE7 34
Charlton Pk. Rd. SE7 34
Charlton Pl. N1 18
Charlton Rd. NW10 8
Charlton Rd. SE3 34
Charlton Rd. SE7 34
Charlton Way SE3 34
Charlwood Pl. SW1 24
Charlwood Rd. SW15 36
Charlwood St. SW1 31
Charnwood Gdns. E14 26
Charrington St. NW1 17
Chart St. N1 18
Charterhouse Sq. EC1 18
Charterhouse St. EC1 17
Charteris Rd. NW6 9
Chartfield Ave. SW15 36
Chase, The E12 13
Chase, The SW4 38
Chaseley St. E14 19
Chatfield Rd. SW11 37
Chatham Pl. E9 12
Chatham Rd. SW11 37
Chatham St. SE17 25
Chatsworth Rd. E15 13
Chatsworth Rd. NW2 8
Chatto Rd. SW11 37
Chaucer Ct. N16 11

ucer Dr. SE1 25 E5
ucer Rd. E7 13 D3
ucer Rd. SE24 38 G3
undrye Clo. SE9 42 A4
untler Clo. E16 20 E5
apside EC2 44 D2
esemans Ter. W14 30 A1
lmer Rd. E9 12 B2
lmsford Clo. W6 29 F2
lmsford Sq. NW10 8 E5
lsea Bri. SW1 31 B2
lsea Bri. SW8 31 B2
lsea Bri. Rd. SW1 31 A1
lsea Embk. SW3 30 F2
lsea Harbour W10 30 E4
lsea Harbour Dr. W10 30 D4
lsea Manor Gdns. SW3 30 F1
lsea Manor St. W3 30 F1
lsea Pk. Gdns. W3 30 E2
lsea Sq. SW3 30 E1
lsham Rd. SW4 38 D1
lsworth Dr. SE18 35 F2
ltenham Gdns. E6 21 A1
ltenham Rd. SE15 40 A2
ltenham Ter. SW3 30 G1
lverton Rd. SW15 36 F2
lwood Wk. SE4 40 C2
nappa Clo. E13 20 D2
ney Rd. NW1 17 E1
nies Pl. NW1 17 D1
nies St. WC1 17 D4
niston Gdns. W8 23 C4
pstow Cres. W11 23 B1
pstow Pl. W2 16 B5
pstow Rd. W2 16 B5
pstow Vill. W11 23 A1
rbury St. N1 18 C1
riton Dr. SE18 35 F3
rry Gdn. St. SE16 25 G3
rrywood Clo. E3 19 C2
rrywood Dr. SW15 36 F3
rtsey Rd., Ilf. 14 F1
ryls Clo. SW6 30 C4
sham Ms. SW1 24 A4
sham Pl. SW1 24 A4
sham St. SW1 24 A4
shire Clo. SE4 33 D5
shire St. E2 18 E3
shunt Rd. E7 13 E3
silton Rd. SW6 30 A4
sley Gdns. E6 20 G1
sney St. SW11 31 A4
sson Rd. W14 30 A2
ster Clo. SW1 24 B3
ster Clo. SW13 36 D1
ster Ct. SE5 32 C3
ster Gate NW1 17 B2
ster Ms. SW1 24 B4
ster Rd. E7 13 G4
ster Rd. E16 20 B3
ster Rd. NW1 17 A2
ster Rd., Sid. 42 G3
ster Row SW1 24 A5
ster Sq. SW1 24 A5
ster St. E2 18 F3
ster St. SW1 24 A4
ster Way SE11 24 G5
sterfield Gdns. W1 24 B2
sterfield Gro. SE22 39 E3
sterfield Hill W1 24 B2
sterfield St. W1 24 B2
sterfield Wk. SE10 34 A4
Chesterfield Way SE15 33 A3
Chesterford Gdns. NW3 9 C1
Chesterford Rd. E12 14 B2
Chesterton Rd. E13 20 D2
Chesterton Rd. W10 15 F4
Chesterton Ter. E13 20 D2
Chestnut Ave. E7 13 E1
Chestnut Gro. SW12 38 A5
Chestnut Ri. SE18 35 G1
Chetwynd Rd. NW5 10 B1
Cheval Pl. SW7 23 F4
Cheval St. E14 26 E4
Chevening Rd. NW6 15 F1
Chevening Rd. SE10 34 C1
Chevron Clo. E16 20 D5
Cheyne Gdns. SW3 30 F2
Cheyne Row SW3 30 F2
Cheyne Wk. SW3 30 F2
Cheyne Wk. SW10 30 E3
Chichele Rd. NW2 8 F2
Chicheley St. SE1 24 F3
Chichester Clo. E6 21 A5
Chichester Clo. SE3 34 F4
Chichester Rents WC2 43 J1
Chichester Rd. NW6 16 B1
Chichester Rd. W2 16 C4
Chichester St. SW1 31 C1
Chichester Way E14 27 A5
Chicksand St. E1 18 E4
Chiddingstone St. SW6 30 B5
Childeric Rd. SE14 33 C3
Childers St. SE8 33 C2
Child's Pl. SW5 23 B5
Child's St. SW5 23 B5
Chiltern St. W1 17 A4
Chilton Gro. SE8 26 B5
Chilton St. E2 18 E3
Chiltonian Ind. Est. SE12 41 C4
Chilver St. SE10 34 C1
Chilworth Ms. W2 16 E5
Chilworth St. W2 16 D5
Ching Ct. WC2 43 E2
Chipka St. E14 26 G3
Chippenham Gdns. NW6 16 B2
Chippenham Ms. W9 16 B3
Chippenham Rd. W9 16 B3
Chipstead St. SW6 30 B4
Chisenhale Rd. E3 19 C1
Chiswell St. EC1 18 C4
Chiswick La. W4 29 A1
Chiswick La. S. W4 29 B1
Chiswick Mall W4 29 B2
Chiswick Mall W6 29 C1
Chiswick Wf. W4 29 B2
Chitty St. W1 17 C4
Chivalry Rd. SW11 37 F3
Chobham Rd. E15 13 A2
Cholmondeley Ave. NW10 15 C1
Choumert Gro. SE15 32 F5
Choumert Rd. SE15 39 E1
Choumert Sq. SE15 32 F5
Chrisp St. E14 19 F4
Christ Ch. Pas. EC1 44 C1
Christchurch Ave. NW6 8 F5
Christchurch St. SW3 30 G2
Christchurch Way SE10 34 B1
Christian Ct. SE16 26 D2
Christian St. E1 18 F5
Christie Rd. E9 12 C3
Christopher Clo. SE16 26 B3
Christopher St. EC2 18 C3
Chryssell Rd. SW9 31 G3
Chubworthy St. SE14 33 C2
Chudleigh Cres., Ilf. 14 G1
Chudleigh Rd. NW6 8 F4
Chudleigh Rd. SE4 40 D3
Chudleigh St. E1 19 B5
Chumleigh St. SE5 32 D2
Church Cres. E9 12 B4
Church Gate SW6 36 G1
Church Gro. SE13 40 F2
Church Hill SE18 28 B4
Church Path NW10 8 A4
Church Pl. SW1 43 B4
Church Rd. E12 14 A2
Church Rd. NW10 8 A4
Church Rd. SW13 29 B5
Church Rd., Bark. 14 E3
Church Row NW3 9 D1
Church St. E15 20 B1
Church St. E16 28 D2
Church St. NW8 16 E4
Church St. W2 16 E4
Church St. W4 29 B2
Church St. Est. NW8 16 E3
Church St. N. E15 13 B5
Church Ter. SE13 41 B1
Church Ter. SW8 31 D5
Church Wk. N16 11 C1
Church Wk. SW13 29 C4
Churchbury Rd. SE9 41 G5
Churchill Gdns. SW1 31 C1
Churchill Gdns. Rd. SW1 31 B1
Churchill Pl. E14 26 F2
Churchill Rd. E16 20 F5
Churchill Rd. NW2 8 D3
Churchill Rd. NW5 10 B1
Churchill Wk. E9 12 A2
Churchmead Rd. NW10 8 C3
Churchway NW1 17 D2
Churston Ave. E13 13 E5
Churton St. SW1 24 C5
Cicada Rd. SW18 37 D4
Cicely Rd. SE15 32 F4
Cinnamon Row SW11 37 D1
Cinnamon St. E1 25 G2
Circular Way SE18 35 B2
Circus Rd. NW8 16 E2
Circus St. SE10 33 G3
Cirencester St. W2 16 C4
City Gdn. Row N1 18 A1
City Rd. EC1 18 A1
Clabon Ms. SW1 23 G4
Clack St. SE16 26 A3
Clacton Rd. E6 20 G2
Claire Pl. E14 26 E4
Clancarty Rd. SW6 30 B5
Clandon St. SE8 33 E5
Clanricarde Gdns. W2 23 B1
Clapham Common N. Side SW4 37 G2
Clapham Common S. Side SW4 38 B4
Clapham Common W. Side SW4 37 G2
Clapham Cres. SW4 38 D2
Clapham High St. SW4 38 D2
Clapham Junct. Est. SW11 37 F2
Clapham Manor St. SW4 38 C1
Clapham Pk. Est. SW4 38 D4
Clapham Pk. Rd. SW4 38 D2
Clapham Rd. SW9 38 E1
Clapham Rd. Est. SW4 38 D1
Clapton Sq. E5 12 A2
Clapton Way E5 11 F1
Clara Pl. SE18 28 C5
Clare Cor. SE9 42 D5
Clare Gdns. E7 13 D1
Clare La. N1 11 B4
Clare Mkt. WC2 43 G2
Clare Rd. NW10 8 C4
Clare Rd. SE14 33 D5
Clare St. E2 18 G1
Claredale St. E2 18 G1
Claremont Clo. E16 28 C2
Claremont Clo. N1 17 G1
Claremont Rd. E7 13 E2
Claremont Rd. W9 16 A1
Claremont Sq. N1 17 G1
Claremont St. E16 28 C2
Claremont St. SE10 33 F2
Clarence Ave. SW4 38 D5
Clarence Cres. SW4 38 D4
Clarence Gdns. NW1 17 B2
Clarence La. SW15 36 A4
Clarence Ms. E5 11 G2
Clarence Ms. SE16 26 B2
Clarence Pl. E5 11 G2
Clarence Rd. E5 11 G1
Clarence Rd. E12 13 G2
Clarence Rd. E16 20 B3
Clarence Rd. NW6 9 A4
Clarence Wk. SW4 31 E5
Clarence Way NW1 10 B4
Clarence Way Est. NW1 10 B4
Clarendon Dr. SW15 36 E1
Clarendon Gdns. W9 16 D3
Clarendon Pl. W2 23 F1
Clarendon Ri. SE13 40 G1
Clarendon Rd. W11 22 G1
Clarendon St. SW1 31 B1
Clareville Gro. SW7 23 D5
Clareville St. SW7 23 D5
Clarges Ms. W1 24 B2
Clarges St. W1 24 B2
Claribel Rd. SW9 32 A5
Clarissa St. E8 11 E5
Clark St. E1 18 G4
Clarks Pl. EC2 44 H1
Clarkson Rd. E16 20 C5
Clarkson St. E2 18 G2
Clarksons, The, Bark. 21 E1
Claude Rd. E13 13 E5
Claude Rd. SE15 32 G5
Claude St. E14 26 E5
Claudia Jones Way SW2 38 E4
Claughton Rd. E13 20 F1
Clavell St. SE10 33 G2
Claverdale Rd. SW2 38 F5
Clavering Ave. SW13 29 D2
Claverton St. SW1 31 C1
Claxton Gro. W6 29 F1
Claybrook Rd. W6 29 F2
Claylands Pl. SW8 31 G3
Claylands Rd. SW8 31 F2
Claymill Ho. SE18 35 E1
Claypole Rd. E15 19 G1
Clays La. E15 12 F2
Clays La. Clo. E15 12 F2
Clayton Ms. SE10 34 A4
Clayton Rd. SE15 32 F4
Clayton St. SE11 31 G2
Cleanthus Rd. SE18 35 D4
Clearwell Dr. W9 16 C3
Cleaver Sq. SE11 31 G1
Cleaver St. SE11 31 G1
Clegg St. E13 20 D1
Clem Attlee Ct. SW6 30 A2
Clematis St. W12 22 C1
Clemence St. E14 19 D4
Clement Ave. SW4 38 D2
Clement Clo. NW6 8 E4
Clements Ave. E16 27 D1

Clement's Inn WC2 43 H2
Clement's Inn Pas. WC2 43 H2
Clements La. EC4 44 G3
Clements Rd. E6 14 A4
Clements Rd. SE16 25 F4
Clephane Rd. N1 11 B3
Clerkenwell Clo. EC1 17 G3
Clerkenwell Grn. EC1 17 G3
Clerkenwell Rd. EC1 17 G3
Clermont Rd. E9 12 A5
Cleve Rd. NW6 9 B4
Cleveland Ave. W4 22 B5
Cleveland Gdns. SW13 29 B5
Cleveland Gdns. W2 16 D5
Cleveland Pl. SW1 43 B5
Cleveland Rd. N1 11 C4
Cleveland Rd. SW13 29 B5
Cleveland Row SW1 43 A6
Cleveland Sq. W2 16 D5
Cleveland St. W1 17 B3
Cleveland Ter. W2 16 D5
Cleveland Way E1 19 A3
Cleveley Clo. SE7 27 G5
Cleverley Est. W12 22 C2
Cleves Rd. E6 13 G5
Clichy Est. E1 19 A4
Clifden Rd. E5 12 A2
Cliff Rd. NW1 10 D3
Cliff Ter. SE8 33 E5
Cliff Vill. NW1 10 D3
Cliff Wk. E16 20 C3
Clifford Dr. SW9 39 A2
Clifford Gdns. NW10 15 E1
Clifford Rd. E16 20 C3
Clifford St. W1 43 A4
Clifford Way NW10 8 B1
Clifford's Inn Pas. EC4 43 J2
Cliffview Rd. SE13 40 E1
Clifton Ave. W12 22 B3
Clifton Cres. SE15 32 G3
Clifton Gdns. W9 16 D3
Clifton Gro. E8 11 F3
Clifton Hill NW8 16 C1
Clifton Pl. W2 16 E5
Clifton Ri. SE14 33 C3
Clifton Rd. E7 13 G3
Clifton Rd. E16 20 B4
Clifton Rd. NW10 15 C1
Clifton Rd. W9 16 D3
Clifton St. EC2 18 D4
Clifton Vill. W9 16 D4
Clifton Way SE15 33 A3
Clink St. SE1 44 F5
Clinton Rd. E3 19 C2
Clinton Rd. E7 13 D1
Clipper Way SE13 40 G2
Clipstone Ms. W1 17 C4
Clipstone St. W1 17 B4
Clissold Cres. N16 11 C1
Clitheroe Rd. SW9 31 E5
Cliveden Pl. SW1 24 A5
Cloak La. EC4 44 F3
Clock Twr. Pl. N7 10 E3
Clockhouse Ave., Bark. 14 E5
Clonbrock Rd. N16 11 D1
Cloncurry St. SW6 29 F5
Clonmel Rd. SW6 30 A3
Cloth Fair EC1 18 A4
Clothier St. E1 44 J1
Clothworkers Rd. SE18 35 F3
Cloudesley Pl. N1 10 G5
Cloudesley Rd. N1 10 G5
Cloudesley Sq. N1 10 G5
Cloudesley St. N1 10 G5
Clova Rd. E7 13 C3
Clove Cres. E14 27 A1
Club Row E1 18 E3
Club Row E2 18 E3
Clunbury St. N1 18 C1
Cluny Ms. SW5 23 B5
Clutton St. E14 19 F4
Clyde St. SE8 33 D2
Clydesdale Rd. W11 16 A5
Clyston St. SW8 31 C5
Coach & Horses Yd. W1 43 A3
Coach Ho. Ms. SE23 40 A4
Coalecroft Rd. SW15 36 E2
Coate St. E2 18 F1
Cobb St. E1 18 E4
Cobbett Rd. SE9 42 A1
Cobbett St. SW8 31 F3
Cobbold Est. NW10 8 B3
Cobbold Rd. NW10 8 B3
Cobbold Rd. W12 22 B3
Cobham Clo. SW11 37 F4
Coborn Rd. E3 19 D2
Coborn St. E3 19 D2
Cobourg Rd. SE5 32 E2
Cobourg St. NW1 17 C2
Cochrane St. NW8 16 E1
Cock La. EC1 18 A4
Cockspur Ct. SW1 43 D5
Cockspur St. SW1 43 D5
Code St. E1 18 E3
Codrington Hill SE23 40 C5
Cody Rd. E16 20 B3
Coin St. SE1 43 J5
Coity Rd. NW5 10 A3
Coke St. E1 18 F5
Colbeck Ms. SW7 23 C5
Cold Blow La. SE14 33 B3
Cold Harbour E14 26 G3
Coldbath St. SE13 33 F4
Coldharbour La. SE5 39 B1
Coldharbour La. SW9 38 G2
Coldstream Gdns. SW18 37 A4
Cole St. SE1 25 B3
Colebeck Ms. N1 11 A3
Colebert Ave. E1 19 A3
Colebrooke Row N1 18 A1
Coleford Rd. SW18 37 D3
Colegrave Rd. E15 13 A2
Colegrove Rd. SE15 32 E2
Coleherne Ct. SW5 30 C1
Coleherne Ms. SW10 30 C1
Coleherne Rd. SW10 30 C1
Colehill La. SW6 29 G4
Coleman Flds. N1 11 B5
Coleman Rd. SE5 32 D3
Coleman St. EC2 44 F1
Colenso Rd. E5 12 A1
Colepits Wd. Rd. SE9 42 F3
Coleraine Rd. SE3 34 C2
Coleridge Ave. E12 14 A3
Coleridge Clo. SW8 31 B5
Colestown St. SW11 30 F5
Colet Gdns. W14 29 F1
Coley St. WC1 17 F3
Colin Rd. NW10 8 C3
Colinette Rd. SW15 36 E2
Coliston Rd. SW18 37 B5
College App. SE10 33 G2
College Cres. NW3 9 E3
College Cross N1 10 G4
College Hill EC4 44 E3
College La. NW5 10 B1
College Pk. Clo. SE13 41 A2
College Pl. NW1 10 C5
College Rd. NW10 15 E1
College Rd. SE21 39 D5
College St. EC4 44 F3
College Ter. E3 19 D2
Collent St. E9 12 A3
Collett Rd. SE16 25 F4
Collier St. N1 17 F1
Collingbourne Rd. W12 22 D2
Collingham Gdns. SW5 23 C5
Collingham Pl. SW5 23 C5
Collingham Rd. SW5 23 C5
Collingwood St. E1 18 G3
Collins Rd. N5 11 B1
Collins St. SE3 34 B5
Colls Rd. SE15 33 A4
Colman Rd. E16 20 F4
Colmore Ms. SE15 32 G4
Colnbrook St. SE1 25 A4
Colne Ho., Bark. 14 D3
Colne Rd. E5 12 C1
Cologne Rd. SW11 37 E2
Colomb St. SE10 34 B1
Colombo St. SE1 44 B6
Colonnade WC1 17 E3
Colston Rd. E7 13 G3
Columbia Rd. E2 18 E2
Columbia Rd. E13 20 C3
Columbine Ave. E6 21 A4
Columbine Way SE13 33 G5
Colvestone Cres. E8 11 E2
Colville Est. N1 11 D5
Colville Gdns. W11 16 A5
Colville Hos. W11 16 A5
Colville Rd. W11 16 A5
Colville Sq. W11 16 A5
Colville Ter. W11 16 A5
Colvin Rd. E6 14 A4
Colwell Rd. SE22 39 E3
Colwith Rd. W6 29 E2
Colyton Rd. SE22 39 G3
Combe Ave. SE3 34 C3
Combe Ms. SE3 34 C3
Combedale Rd. SE10 34 D1
Combemartin Rd. SW18 36 G5
Comber Gro. SE5 32 B3
Combermere Rd. SW9 38 F1
Comeragh Rd. W14 29 G1
Comerford Rd. SE4 40 C2
Comet Clo. E12 13 G1
Comet Pl. SE8 33 E3
Comet St. SE8 33 E3
Commercial Rd. E1 18 F5
Commercial Rd. E14 19 C5
Commercial St. E1 18 E3
Commercial Way SE15 32 E3
Commerell St. SE10 34 B1
Commodore Sq. SW10 30 D4
Commodore St. E1 19 C3
Common Rd. SW13 36 C1
Commondale SW15 36 E1
Commonwealth Ave. W12 22 D1
Community Rd. E15 13 A2
Compayne Gdns. NW6 9 C4
Compton Ave. E6 20 G1
Compton Ave. N1 11 A3
Compton Clo. E3 19 E4
Compton Rd. N1 11 A3
Compton Rd. NW10 15 F2
Compton St. EC1 18 A3
Compton Ter. N1 11 A3
Comus Pl. SE17 25 D5
Comyn Rd. SW11 37 F2
Comyns Clo. E16 20 C4
Concanon Rd. SW2 38 F2
Concert Hall App. SE1 43 H6
Concorde Dr. E6 21 B4
Condell Rd. SW8 31 C4
Conder St. E14 19 C5
Conderton Rd. SE5 39
Condover Cres. SE18 35
Condray Pl. SW11 30
Conduit Ct. WC2 43
Conduit Ms. W2 16
Conduit Pl. W2 16
Conduit Rd. SE18 35
Conduit St. W1 24
Coney Way SW8 31
Congleton Gro. SE18 35
Congo Rd. SE18 35
Congreve Rd. SE9 42
Congreve St. SE17 25
Coniger Rd. SW6 30
Coningham Rd. W12 22
Conington Rd. SE13 33
Coniston Ave., Bark. 14
Coniston Ave., Well. 42
Conistone Way N7 10
Conlan St. W10 15
Conley Rd. NW10 8
Connaught Bri. E16 27
Connaught Pl. W2 23
Connaught Rd. NW10 8
Connaught Rd. SE18 35
Connaught Sq. W2 16
Connaught St. W2 16
Conrad Ho. N16 11
Consort Rd. SE15 32
Constantine Rd. NW3 9
Constitution Hill SW1 24
Constitution Ri. SE18 35
Content St. SE17 25
Conway Rd. SE18 28
Conway St. E13 20
Conway St. W1 17
Conyer St. E3 19
Cook's Rd. E15 19
Cooks Rd. SE17 32
Coolfin Rd. E16 20
Coombe Rd. W4 29
Coombs St. N1 18
Coomer Pl. SW6 30
Cooper Rd. NW10 8
Coopers Clo. E1 19
Coopers La. NW1 17
Coopers Rd. SE1 32
Coopersale Rd. E9 12
Cope Pl. W8 23
Cope St. SE16 26
Copeland Dr. E14 26
Copeland Rd. SE15 32
Copenhagen Pl. E14 19
Copenhagen St. N1 10
Copleston Pas. SE15 32
Copleston Rd. SE15 39
Coppelia Rd. SE3 41
Copperas St. SE8 33
Copperfield Rd. E3 19
Copperfield St. SE1 25
Coppice Dr. SW15 36
Coppock Clo. SW11 30
Copse Clo. SE7 34
Copthall Ave. EC2 44
Copthall Bldgs. EC2 44
Copthall Clo. EC2 44
Copthorne Ave. SW12 38
Coptic St. WC1 17
Coral St. SE1 24
Coram St. WC1 17
Corbet Ct. EC3 44
Corbiere Ho. N1 11
Corbridge Cres. E2 18
Corbylands Rd., Sid. 42
Cordelia Clo. SE24 39
Cordelia St. E14 19
Cordova Rd. E3 19
Cordwell Rd. SE13 41
Corelli Rd. SE3 35

field St. E2 18 G2
ander Ave. E14 20 A5
nne Rd. N19 10 C1
k St. W1 43 A4
k St. Ms. W1 43 A4
mont Rd. SE5 32 A4
morant Rd. E7 13 C2
nelia St. N7 10 F3
ner Grn. SE3 34 D5
ner Ho. St. WC2 43 E5
ney Reach Way W4 29 A3
ney Rd. W4 29 A2
nflower Ter. SE22 39 G4
nhill EC3 44 G2
nmill La. SE13 40 G1
nmow Dr. NW10 8 C1
nwall Ave. E2 19 A2
nwall Ave., Well. 42 G1
nwall Cres. W11 15 G5
nwall Gdns. NW10 8 D3
nwall Gdns. SW7 23 C4
nwall Gro. W4 29 A1
nwall Ms. S. SW7 23 D4
nwall Rd. SE1 43 J5
nwallis Wk. SE9 42 B1
nwood Dr. E1 19 A5
ona Rd. SE12 41 D5
onation Rd. E13 20 F2
onet St. N1 18 D2
poration Row EC1 17 G3
poration St. E15 20 B1
poration St. N7 10 E2
ance Rd. SW2 38 E2
sham St. N1 18 C2
sica St. N5 11 A3
tayne Rd. SW6 30 A5
tis Rd. SW15 36 D4
tis Ter. SW15 36 D4
unna Rd. SW8 31 C4
unna Ter. SW8 31 C4
bycote Ave. SE24 39 B3
mur Clo. W12 22 B4
sall Wk. SE15 32 G4
ser St. SE1 24 G4
ta St. SE15 32 F5
way St. NW1 16 F4
ll St. E14 19 E5
eigh Rd. NW6 9 B4
swold Gdns. E6 20 G2
tage Grn. SE5 32 C3
tage Gro. SW9 38 E1
tage Pl. SW3 23 F4
tage St. E14 26 F1
tesmore Gdns. W8 23 C4
ingham Rd. SW8 31 F3
on Row SW11 37 E1
on St. E14 26 G1
tons La. SE1 44 G5
lgate St. SE4 40 C1
lson St. SW3 30 G1
lter Rd. W6 22 D4
ncillor St. SE5 32 B3
nter Ct. SE1 44 F6
nter St. SE1 44 H6
ntess Rd. NW5 10 C2
nty Gro. SE5 32 B4
nty Rd. E6 21 D4
nty St. SE1 25 B4
pland Pl. SE18 35 E1
rland Gro. SW8 31 D5
rland St. SW8 31 D4
rt La. SE21 39 D4
rt La. Gdns. SE21 39 D5
rt Rd. SE9 42 B4
rt Yd. SE9 42 B4
rtenay St. SE11 31 G1
rtfield Gdns. SW5 23 C5
rtfield Rd. SW7 23 D5
rthill Rd. SE13 40 G2

Courthope Rd. NW3 9 G1
Courtlands Ave. SE12 41 E3
Courtmead Clo. SE24 39 B4
Courtnell St. W2 16 B5
Courtrai Rd. SE23 40 C4
Cousin La. EC4 44 F4
Couthurst Rd. SE3 34 E2
Covelees Wall E6 21 C5
Covent Gdn. WC2 43 F3
Coventry Rd. E1 18 G3
Coventry Rd. E2 18 G3
Coventry St. W1 43 C4
Coverdale Rd. NW2 8 F4
Coverdale Rd. W12 22 D3
Coverdales, The, Bark. 21 F1
Coverley Clo. E1 18 F4
Cow Leaze E6 21 C5
Cowbridge La., Bark. 14 D4
Cowcross St. EC1 18 A4
Cowley Rd. SW9 31 G4
Cowley Rd. SW14 36 A1
Cowley Rd. W3 22 B2
Cowper Ave. E6 14 A4
Cowper Rd. N16 11 D2
Cowper St. EC2 18 C3
Cowthorpe Rd. SW8 31 D4
Coxmount Rd. SE7 34 G1
Coxwell Rd. SE18 35 F1
Crabtree Clo. E2 18 E1
Crabtree La. SW6 29 F3
Craigerne Rd. SE3 34 E3
Craigholm SE18 35 C5
Craignair Rd. SW2 38 G5
Craigs Ct. SW1 43 E5
Craigton Rd. SE9 42 B2
Cramond Clo. W6 29 G2
Crampton St. SE17 25 B5
Cranberry La. E16 20 B3
Cranborne Rd., Bark. 14 F5
Cranbourn All. WC2 43 D3
Cranbourn St. WC2 43 D3
Cranbourne Rd. E15 12 G1
Cranbrook Est. E2 19 B1
Cranbrook Pt. E16 27 D2
Cranbrook Rd. SE8 33 E4
Cranbrook Rd. W4 29 A1
Cranbury Rd. SW6 30 C5
Crane Ct. EC4 44 A2
Crane Gro. N7 10 G3
Crane Mead SE16 26 B5
Crane St. SE10 34 A1
Cranfield Rd. SE4 40 D1
Cranford St. E1 26 B1
Cranhurst Rd. NW2 8 E2
Cranleigh Gdns., Bark. 14 F4
Cranleigh Ms. SW11 30 F5
Cranleigh St. NW1 17 C1
Cranley Gdns. SW7 30 D1
Cranley Ms. SW7 30 D1
Cranley Pl. SW7 23 E5
Cranley Rd. E13 20 E4
Cranmer Ct. SW4 38 D1
Cranmer Rd. E7 13 E1
Cranmer Rd. SW9 31 G3
Cranston Est. N1 18 C1
Cranswick Rd. SE16 32 G1
Cranwell Clo. E3 19 F3
Cranwood St. EC1 18 C2
Cranworth Gdns. SW9 31 G4
Craster Rd. SW2 38 F5
Crathie Rd. SE12 41 E4
Craven Gdns., Bark. 21 G1
Craven Hill W2 23 D1
Craven Hill Gdns. W2 23 D1
Craven Hill Ms. W2 23 D1
Craven Pk. NW10 8 A5
Craven Pk. Ms. NW10 8 A5

Craven Pk. Rd. NW10 8 A5
Craven Pas. WC2 43 E5
Craven Rd. W2 16 D5
Craven St. WC2 43 E5
Craven Ter. W2 23 D1
Crawford Est. SE5 32 B5
Crawford Pl. W1 16 F5
Crawford Rd. SE5 32 B4
Crawford St. W1 16 G4
Crawthew Gro. SE22 39 E2
Crayford Rd. N7 10 D1
Crealock St. SW18 37 C4
Crebor St. SE22 39 F4
Crediton Hill NW6 9 C2
Crediton Rd. NW10 8 F5
Credon Rd. E13 20 F1
Credon Rd. SE16 32 G1
Creechurch La. EC3 44 J2
Creechurch Pl. EC3 44 J2
Creed La. EC4 44 C2
Creek Rd. SE8 33 E2
Creek Rd. SE10 33 F2
Creekside SE8 33 F3
Crefeld Clo. W6 29 F2
Creighton Ave. E6 20 G1
Creighton Rd. NW6 15 F1
Cremer St. E2 18 E1
Cremorne Rd. SW10 30 D3
Crescent, The SW13 29 B5
Crescent, The W3 15 A5
Crescent Gro. SW4 38 C2
Crescent La. SW4 38 C2
Crescent Pl. SW3 23 F5
Crescent Rd. E6 13 F5
Crescent Rd. E13 13 D5
Crescent Rd. SE18 35 D1
Crescent St. N1 10 F4
Crescent Way SE4 40 E1
Cresford Rd. SW6 30 C4
Cresset Rd. E9 12 A3
Cresset St. SW4 38 D1
Cressfield Clo. NW5 10 A2
Cressingham Rd. SE13 40 G1
Cresswell Gdns. SW5 30 D1
Cresswell Pk. SE3 41 C1
Cresswell Pl. SW10 30 D1
Cressy Ct. W6 22 D4
Cressy Pl. E1 19 A4
Cressy Rd. NW3 9 G2
Crestfield St. WC1 17 E2
Crestway SW15 36 C4
Creton St. SE18 28 C4
Crewdson Rd. SW9 31 G3
Crewe Pl. NW10 15 B2
Crews St. E14 26 E5
Crewys Rd. SE15 32 G5
Cricketfield Rd. E5 11 G1
Cricklewood La. NW2 8 F1
Crieff Rd. SW18 37 D4
Crimscott St. SE1 25 D4
Crimsworth Rd. SW8 31 D4
Crinan St. N1 17 E1
Cringle St. SW8 31 C3
Crisp Rd. W6 29 E1
Crispian Clo. NW10 8 A1
Crispin St. E1 18 E4
Cristowe Rd. SW6 30 A5
Croft, The NW10 15 B1
Croft St. SE8 26 C5
Crofters Ct. SE8 26 C5
Crofters Way NW1 10 D5
Crofton Pk. Rd. SE4 40 D4
Crofton Rd. E13 20 E3
Crofton Rd. SE5 32 D4
Croftongate Way SE4 40 C3
Crofts St. E1 25 F1
Croftway NW3 9 B1
Crogsland Rd. NW1 10 A4
Cromer St. WC1 17 E2

Cromer Vill. Rd. SW18 37 A4
Cromford Rd. SW18 37 B3
Crompton St. W2 16 E3
Cromwell Ave. W6 22 D5
Cromwell Cres. SW5 23 B5
Cromwell Gdns. SW7 23 E4
Cromwell Gro. W6 22 E4
Cromwell Ms. SW7 23 E5
Cromwell Pl. SW7 23 E5
Cromwell Rd. E7 13 F4
Cromwell Rd. SW5 23 C5
Cromwell Rd. SW7 23 C5
Cromwell Rd. SW9 32 A4
Crondace Rd. SW6 30 B4
Crondall St. N1 18 C1
Crooke Rd. SE8 33 C1
Crookham Rd. SW6 30 A4
Crookston Rd. SE9 42 C1
Croombs Rd. E16 20 F4
Crooms Hill SE10 33 G3
Crooms Hill Gro. SE10 33 G3
Cropley St. N1 18 C1
Crosby Rd. E7 13 D3
Crosby Row SE1 25 C3
Crosby Sq. EC3 44 H2
Crosby Wk. SW2 38 G5
Cross Ave. SE10 34 A2
Cross La. EC3 44 H4
Cross Rd. SE5 32 D5
Cross St. N1 11 A5
Cross St. SW13 29 A5
Crossbrook Rd. SE3 35 A5
Crossfield Rd. NW3 9 E3
Crossfield St. SE8 33 E3
Crossford St. SW9 31 E5
Crossley St. N7 10 G3
Crossthwaite Ave. SE5 39 C2
Crosswall EC3 25 E1
Crossway N16 11 D2
Croston St. E8 11 F5
Crowder St. E1 25 G1
Crowhurst Clo. SW9 31 G5
Crowland Ter. N1 11 C4
Crown Clo. E3 12 E5
Crown Clo. NW6 9 C3
Crown Ct. EC2 44 E2
Crown Ct. SE12 41 E4
Crown Ct. WC2 43 F2
Crown Ms. W6 22 C5
Crown Office Row EC4 43 J3
Crown Pas. SW1 43 B6
Crown St. SE5 32 B3
Crown Wds. La. SE9 35 E5
Crown Wds. La. SE18 35 D5
Crown Wds. Way SE9 42 F3
Crowndale Rd. NW1 17 C1
Crownfield Rd. E15 13 A1
Crownhill Rd. NW10 8 B5
Crownstone Rd. SW2 38 G3
Crows Rd. E15 20 A2
Crowthorne Rd. W10 15 F5
Croxley Rd. W9 16 A2
Croxted Clo. SE21 39 B5
Croxted Rd. SE21 39 B5
Croxted Rd. SE24 39 B5
Croyde Clo., Sid. 42 F5
Croydon Rd. E13 20 C3
Crozier Ter. E9 12 B2
Crucifix La. SE1 25 D3
Cruden St. N1 11 A5
Cruikshank Rd. E15 13 B1
Cruikshank St. WC1 17 G2
Crutched Friars EC3 44 J3
Crystal Palace Rd. SE22 39 E4
Cuba St. E14 26 E3

Cubitt St. WC1 17 F2
Cubitt Ter. SW4 38 C1
Cubitts Yd. WC2 43 F3
Cudham St. SE6 40 G5
Cudworth St. E1 18 G3
Cuff Cres. SE9 41 G4
Culford Gdns. SW3 23 G5
Culford Gro. N1 11 D3
Culford Rd. N1 11 D4
Cullingworth Rd. NW10 8 C2
Culloden Clo. SE16 32 F1
Culloden St. E14 19 G5
Cullum St. EC3 44 H3
Culmore Rd. SE15 32 G3
Culmstock Rd. SW11 38 A3
Culross St. W1 24 A1
Culvert Pl. SW11 31 A5
Culvert Rd. SW11 30 G4
Cumberland Ave., Well. 42 G1
Cumberland Clo. E8 11 E3
Cumberland Cres. W14 22 G5
Cumberland Gate W1 23 G1
Cumberland Mkt. NW1 17 B2
Cumberland Rd. E12 13 G1
Cumberland Rd. E13 20 E4
Cumberland Rd. SW13 29 B4
Cumberland St. SW1 31 B1
Cumming St. N1 17 F1
Cunard Pl. EC3 44 J2
Cundy Rd. E16 20 F5
Cundy St. SW1 24 A5
Cunningham Pl. NW8 16 E3
Cupar Rd. SW11 31 B4
Cureton St. SW1 24 D5
Curlew St. SE1 25 E3
Curricle St. W3 22 A2
Cursitor St. EC4 43 J1
Curtain Rd. EC2 18 D2
Curtis St. SE1 25 E5
Curtis Way SE1 25 E5
Curve, The W12 22 C1
Curwen Rd. W12 22 C3
Curzon Cres. NW10 8 A4
Curzon St. W1 24 A2
Cut, The SE1 24 G3
Cutcombe Rd. SE5 32 B5
Cuthbert St. W2 16 E3
Cutler St. E1 44 J1
Cutlers Gdns. E1 44 J1
Cyclops Ms. E14 26 E5
Cynthia St. N1 17 F1
Cyprus Pl. E2 19 A1
Cyprus Pl. E6 28 C1
Cyprus St. E2 19 A1
Cyrena Rd. SE22 39 E4
Cyril Mans. SW11 30 G4
Cyrus St. EC1 18 A3
Czar St. SE8 33 E2

D

Dabin Cres. SE10 33 G4
Dacca St. SE8 33 D2
Dace Rd. E3 12 E5
Dacre Gdns. SE13 41 B2
Dacre Pk. SE13 41 B1
Dacre Pl. SE13 41 B1
Dacre Rd. E13 13 E5
Dacre St. SW1 24 D4
Daffodil Gdns., Ilf. 14 D2
Daffodil St. W12 22 B1
Dagmar Gdns. NW10 15 F1
Dagmar Rd. SE5 32 D4
Dagmar Ter. N1 11 A5
Dagnall St. SW11 30 G5
Dagnan Rd. SW12 38 B5
Dahlia Gdns., Ilf. 14 D3
Dairsie Rd. SE9 42 C1
Dairy Ms. SW9 38 E1
Daisy La. SW6 37 B1
Dakota Gdns. E6 21 A3
Dalberg Rd. SW2 38 G3
Dalby Rd. SW18 37 D2
Dalby St. NW5 10 B3
Dale Clo. SE3 41 D1
Dale Rd. SE17 32 A2
Dale St. W4 29 A1
Daleham Gdns. NW3 9 E2
Daleham Ms. NW3 9 E3
Dalehead NW1 17 C1
Daley St. E9 12 B3
Daley Thompson Way SW8 38 B1
Dalgarno Gdns. W10 15 E4
Dalgarno Gdns. Est. W10 15 E3
Dalgarno Way W10 15 E3
Dalgleish St. E14 19 C5
Daling Way E3 19 C1
Dallin Rd. SE18 35 D3
Dalling Rd. W6 22 D5
Dallinger Rd. SE12 41 C4
Dallington St. EC1 18 A3
Dalmeny Ave. N7 10 D1
Dalmeyer Rd. NW10 8 B3
Dalrymple Rd. SE4 40 C2
Dalston La. E8 11 E3
Dalwood St. SE5 32 D4
Dalyell Rd. SW9 38 F1
Dame St. N1 18 B1
Damien St. E1 18 G5
Danbury St. N1 18 A1
Danby St. SE15 39 E1
Dancer Rd. SW6 30 A4
Dando Cres. SE3 41 E1
Dandridge Clo. SE10 34 C1
Dane Rd., Ilf. 14 E2
Danebury Ave. SW15 36 A4
Danecroft Rd. SE24 39 B3
Danehurst St. SW6 29 G4
Danemere St. SW15 36 E1
Danesdale Rd. E9 12 C3
Daneville Rd. SE5 32 C4
Daniel Gdns. SE15 32 E3
Daniels Ms. SE4 40 D2
Daniels Rd. SE15 40 A1
Dansey Pl. W1 43 C3
Dante Rd. SE11 25 A5
Danvers St. SW3 30 E2
Daphne St. SW18 37 D4
D'Arblay St. W1 43 B2
Darfield Rd. SE4 40 D3
Darfield Way W10 15 F5
Darfur St. SW15 36 F1
Darien Rd. SW11 37 E1
Darlan Rd. SW6 30 A3
Darley Rd. SW11 37 G4
Darling Rd. SE4 40 E1
Darling Row E1 18 G3
Darnley Rd. E9 12 A3
Darrell Rd. SE22 39 F3
Darsley Dr. SW8 31 E4
Dart St. W10 15 G2
Dartford St. SE17 32 B2
Dartmouth Clo. W11 16 B5
Dartmouth Gro. SE10 33 G4
Dartmouth Hill SE10 33 G4
Dartmouth Pk. Rd. NW5 10 B1
Dartmouth Pl. W4 29 A2
Dartmouth Rd. NW2 8 F3
Dartmouth Row SE10 33 G4
Dartmouth St. SW1 24 D3
Dartmouth Ter. SE10 34 A4
Darwell Clo. E6 21 C1
Darwin St. SE17 25 C5
Datchelor Pl. SE5 32 C4
Date St. SE17 32 B1
Daubeney Rd. E5 12 C1
Daubeney Twr. SE8 26 D5
Dault Rd. SW18 37 D4
Davenant St. E1 18 F4
Davenport Rd. SE6 40 G4
Daventry St. NW1 16 F4
Davern Clo. SE10 27 C5
Davey Clo. N7 10 F3
Davey Rd. E9 12 E4
Davey St. SE15 32 E2
David St. E15 13 A3
Davidge St. SE1 25 A3
Davidson Gdns. SW8 31 E3
Davies St. W1 24 B1
Davis Rd. W3 22 B2
Davis St. E13 20 E1
Davisville Rd. W12 22 C3
Dawes Rd. SW6 29 G3
Dawes St. SE17 32 C1
Dawlish Dr., Ilf. 14 G1
Dawlish Rd. NW2 8 F3
Dawson Clo. SE18 28 E5
Dawson Heights Est. SE22 39 F5
Dawson Pl. W2 23 B1
Dawson Rd. NW2 8 E2
Dawson St. E2 18 E1
Daylesford Ave. SW15 36 C2
Days La., Sid. 42 G5
Dayton Gro. SE15 33 A4
De Beauvoir Cres. N1 11 D5
De Beauvoir Est. N1 11 C5
De Beauvoir Rd. N1 11 D5
De Beauvoir Sq. N1 11 D4
De Crespigny Pk. SE5 32 C5
De Laune St. SE17 32 A1
De Morgan Rd. SW6 37 C1
De Vere Gdns. W8 23 D3
Deacon Ms. N1 11 C4
Deacon Rd. NW2 8 C2
Deacon Way SE17 25 B5
Deal Porters Way SE16 26 A4
Deal St. E1 18 F4
Dealtry Rd. SW15 36 E2
Dean Bradley St. SW1 24 E4
Dean Farrar St. SW1 24 D4
Dean Rd. NW2 8 E3
Dean Ryle St. SW1 24 E5
Dean Stanley St. SW1 24 E4
Dean St. E7 13 D2
Dean St. W1 43 C1
Deancross St. E1 19 A5
Deanery Rd. E15 13 B3
Deanery St. W1 24 A2
Deans Bldgs. SE17 25 C5
Deans Ct. EC4 44 C2
Dean's Pl. SW1 31 D1
Decima St. SE1 25 D4
Dee St. E14 19 G5
Deeley Rd. SW8 31 D4
Deepdene Gdns. SW2 38 F5
Deepdene Rd. SE5 39 C2
Deerdale Rd. SE24 39 B2
Deerhurst Rd. NW2 8 F3
Dekker Rd. SE21 39 D4
Delafield Rd. SE7 34 E1
Delaford Rd. SE16 32 G1
Delaford St. SW6 29 G3
Delamere Ter. W2 16 C4
Delancey St. NW1 10 B5
Delaware Rd. W9 16 C3
Delawyk Cres. SE24 39 B4
Delhi St. N1 10 E5
Delia St. SW18 37 C5
Delius Gro. E15 19 G1
Dell Clo. E15 13 A5
Dellow St. E1 25 G1
Delme Cres. SE3 34
Deloraine St. SE8 33
Delorme St. W6 29
Delverton Rd. SE17 32
Delvino Rd. SW6 30
Dempster Rd. SW18 37
Denbigh Clo. NW10 8
Denbigh Clo. W11 23
Denbigh Pl. SW1 31
Denbigh Rd. E6 20
Denbigh Rd. W11 23
Denbigh St. SW1 24
Denbigh Ter. W11 23
Dene Clo. SE4 40
Denham St. SE10 34
Denham Way, Bark. 14
Denholme Rd. W9 16
Denman Rd. SE15 32
Denman St. W1 43
Denmark Gro. N1 17
Denmark Hill SE5 32
Denmark Hill Est. SE5 39
Denmark Pl. WC2 43
Denmark Rd. NW6 16
Denmark Rd. SE5 32
Denmark St. E13 20
Denmark St. WC2 43
Denne Ter. E8 11
Dennetts Rd. SE14 33
Denning Clo. NW8 16
Denning Rd. NW3 9
Dennington Pk. Rd. NW6 9
Dennison Pt. E15 12
Denny St. SE11 31
Densham Rd. E15 13
Denton St. SW18 37
Dents Rd. SW11 37
Denyer St. SW3 23
Denzil Rd. NW10 8
Deodar Rd. SW15 36
Deptford Bri. SE8 33
Deptford Bdy. SE8 33
Deptford Ch. St. SE8 33
Deptford Ferry Rd. E14 26
Deptford Grn. SE8 33
Deptford High St. SE8 33
Deptford Strand SE8 26
Deptford Wf. SE8 26
Derby Rd. E7 13
Derby Rd. E9 12
Derbyshire St. E2 18
Dericote St. E8 11
Derifall Clo. E6 21
Dering St. W1 17
Dermody Gdns. SE13 41
Dermody Rd. SE13 41
Derry St. W8 23
Dersingham Ave. E12 14
Derwent Gro. SE22 39
Derwent St. SE10 34
Desenfans Rd. SE21 39
Desford Rd. E16 20
Desmond St. SE14 33
Devalls Clo. E6 28
Devas St. E3 19
Devenay Rd. E15 13
Deverell St. SE1 25
Devereux Ct. WC2 43
Devereux La. SW13 29
Devereux Rd. SW11 37
Devon Rd., Bark. 14
Devon St. SE15 32
Devonia Rd. N1 18
Devonport Rd. W12 22
Devonport St. E1 19
Devons Est. E3 19
Devons Rd. E3 19

nshire Clo. E15 13 B1
nshire Clo. W1 17 B4
nshire Dr. SE10 33 F3
nshire Gro. SE15 32 G2
nshire Ms. S. W1 17 B4
nshire Ms. W. 1 17 A3
nshire Pl. W1 17 A3
nshire Pl. W4 29 A1
nshire Rd. E16 20 E5
nshire Rd. W4 29 A1
nshire St. W1 17 B4
nshire St. W4 29 A1
nshire Ter. W2 16 D5
r St. SE15 39 F1
erry Gdns. E6 21 A4
erry St. E14 19 G4
y Rd. N1 17 G1
urst Rd. W14 22 F4
bury Rd. NW10 8 C2
sford Rd. SE5 32 C4
m Ct. W1 43 C2
ond St. SE15 32 D3
ond Ter. SE10 33 G4
Ho. SW13 29 B4
Pl. NW1 17 B3
n St. N1 11 B5
Ave. NW2 8 E1
ns Est. SE1 25 E3
ns Est. SE16 25 E3
ns Rd. E6 20 G1
ns Sq. SE1 25 B4
ns St. SW8 31 B5
on Rd. SE9 42 A1
Rd. E9 12 B2
St. E2 19 A2
on Rd. SW18 37 D3
St. SW3 30 G2
nd Clo. E7 13 D1
e Gdns. E14 26 E1
y Pl. EC1 18 B2
y Rd. EC1 18 B2
vall Rd. SW18 37 D5
ale Rd. SE3 34 C2
nore Rd. SW12 38 B5
on Rd. E15 13 C5
owe Rd. W6 29 G2
li Rd. E7 13 D3
li Rd. SW15 36 G2
t. E2 18 E2
f La. EC4 44 D3
ery Rd. W6 29 E1
All. SE10 33 F4
ourn St. E14 26 G1
Rd. SE14 33 C4
l Rd. SE9 42 B3
e Ave. NW10 8 D4
n Clo. NW6 9 E4
Hill Ave. SE16 26 B3
Rd. E16 27 C1
St. E1 25 F1
rs Tanner Rd. 26 E5
ead SE1 25 E3
and St. E16 28 C2
y Rd. SE16 25 F4
a's Bldgs. N1 11 D3
t. E14 19 E5
ngton Gro. 7 32 A2
ngton Pl. SE17 32 A2
n St. SE1 24 G3
ennel Hill SE22 39 D1
ennel Hill Est. 22 39 D1
a. NW10 8 A1
ett Rd. SE6 40 E5
ty Rd. E13 20 D3
n St. SE1 44 C6
Rd. SW6 30 A5

Dolland St. SE11 31 F1
Dollis Hill La. NW2 8 B1
Dolman St. SW4 38 F2
Dolphin La. E14 26 F1
Dolphin Sq. SW1 31 C1
Dolphin Sq. W4 29 A3
Dombey St. WC1 17 F4
Domett Clo. SE5 39 C2
Don Phelan Clo. SE5 32 C4
Donald Rd. E13 13 E5
Donaldson Rd. NW6 9 A5
Donaldson Rd. SE18 35 C4
Donegal St. N1 17 F1
Doneraile St. SW6 29 F5
Dongola Rd. E13 20 E2
Donkey All. SE22 39 F5
Donne Pl. SW3 23 F5
Donnington Rd. NW10 8 D4
Doon St. SE1 43 J5
Dora St. E14 19 D5
Doran Gro. SE18 35 G3
Doran Wk. E15 12 G4
Dorchester Ct. SE24 39 B3
Dorchester Dr. SE24 39 B3
Dorchester Gro. W4 29 A1
Dordrecht Rd. W3 22 A2
Dore Ave. E12 14 C2
Doria Rd. SW6 30 A5
Doric Way NW1 17 D2
Doris Rd. E7 13 D4
Dorking Clo. SE8 33 D2
Dorlcote Rd. SW18 37 F5
Dorman Way NW8 9 E5
Dormay St. SW18 37 C3
Dormer Clo. E15 13 C3
Dornberg Clo. SE3 34 D3
Dorncliffe Rd. SW6 29 G5
Dorney NW3 9 F4
Dornfell St. NW6 9 A2
Dorothy Rd. SW11 37 G1
Dorrington St. EC1 17 G4
Dorset Bldgs. EC4 44 B2
Dorset Est. E2 18 E2
Dorset Pl. E15 13 A3
Dorset Ri. EC4 44 B2
Dorset Rd. E7 13 F4
Dorset Rd. SW8 31 E3
Dorset Sq. NW1 16 G3
Dorset St. W1 16 G4
Dorville Cres. W6 22 D4
Dorville Rd. SE12 41 C3
Dothill Rd. SE18 35 F3
Doughty Ms. WC1 17 F3
Doughty St. WC1 17 F3
Douglas Est. N1 11 B3
Douglas Rd. E16 20 D4
Douglas Rd. N1 11 B4
Douglas Rd. NW6 9 A5
Douglas St. SW1 24 D5
Douglas Way SE8 33 D3
Douro Pl. W8 23 C4
Douro St. E3 19 E1
Dove App. E6 21 A4
Dove Ct. EC2 44 F2
Dove Ms. SW5 23 D5
Dove Rd. N1 11 C3
Dove Row E2 11 F5
Dovedale Rd. SE22 39 G3
Dovehouse Mead, Bark. 21 F1
Dovehouse St. SW3 30 E1
Dover Ho. Rd. SW15 36 C2
Dover Pk. Dr. SW15 36 D4
Dover St. W1 24 B1
Dovercourt Rd. SE22 39 D4
Doverfield Rd. SW2 38 E4
Dowdeswell Clo. SW15 36 A2
Dowgate Hill EC4 44 F3
Dowland St. W10 15 G2

Dowlas St. SE5 32 D3
Down Pl. W6 29 D1
Down St. W1 24 B2
Downfield Clo. W9 16 C3
Downham Rd. N1 11 C4
Downing St. SW1 24 E3
Downings E6 21 C5
Downman Rd. SE9 42 A1
Downs Pk. Rd. E5 11 F2
Downs Pk. Rd. E8 11 E2
Downs Rd. E5 11 F1
Downsell Rd. E15 12 G1
Downshire Hill NW3 9 E1
Downside Cres. NW3 9 F2
Downtown Rd. SE16 26 C3
Dowson Clo. SE5 39 C2
Doyle Gdns. NW10 8 C5
D'Oyley St. SW1 24 A5
Draco St. SE17 32 B2
Dragoon Rd. SE8 33 D1
Drake Rd. SE4 40 E1
Drakefell Rd. SE4 40 C1
Drakefell Rd. SE14 33 B5
Drakes Ctyd. NW6 9 A4
Drapers Rd. E15 13 A1
Drawdock Rd. SE10 27 A2
Drawell Clo. SE18 35 G1
Dray Gdns. SW2 38 F3
Draycott Ave. SW3 23 F5
Draycott Pl. SW3 23 G5
Draycott Ter. SW3 23 G5
Drayford Clo. W9 16 A3
Drayson Ms. W8 23 B3
Drayton Gdns. SW10 30 D1
Drayton Pk. N5 10 G2
Drayton Rd. NW10 8 B5
Dreadnought St. SE10 27 B4
Dresden Clo. NW6 9 C3
Dressington Ave. SE4 40 E4
Drew Rd. E16 28 A2
Driffield Rd. E3 19 C1
Dromore Rd. SW15 36 G4
Droop St. W10 15 G3
Drover La. SE15 32 G3
Drovers Pl. SE15 32 G3
Druce Rd. SE21 39 D4
Druid St. SE1 25 D3
Drummond Cres. NW1 17 D2
Drummond Gate SW1 31 D1
Drummond Rd. SE16 25 G4
Drummond St. NW1 17 C3
Drury La. WC2 43 F1
Dryad St. SW15 36 F1
Dryburgh Rd. SW15 36 D1
Dryden Rd., Well. 35 G4
Dryden St. WC2 43 F2
Drysdale St. N1 18 D2
Du Cane Rd. W12 15 B5
Dublin Ave. E8 11 F5
Duchess of Bedford's Wk. W8 23 B3
Duchess St. W1 17 B4
Duchy St. SE1 44 A5
Ducie St. SW4 38 F2
Duck La. W1 43 C2
Duckett St. E1 19 B3
Dudden Hill La. NW10 8 B1
Dudley Rd. NW6 15 G1
Dudley Rd., Ilf. 14 D1
Duff St. E14 19 F5
Dufferin St. EC1 18 B3
Dufour's Pl. W1 43 B2
Duke Hill Rd. SE1 44 B5
Duke Hill St. SE1 44 G5
Duke Humphrey Rd. SE3 34 B4
Duke of Wellington Pl. SW1 24 A3
Duke of York St. SW1 43 B5

Duke St. SW1 43 B5
Duke St. W1 17 A5
Dukes Ct. E6 14 C5
Dukes La. W8 23 C3
Dukes Pl. EC3 44 J2
Dukes Rd. E6 14 C5
Duke's Rd. WC1 17 D2
Dulford St. W11 22 G1
Dulka Rd. SW11 37 G3
Dulwich Rd. SE24 38 G3
Dulwich Village SE21 39 D4
Dumbarton Rd. SW2 38 E4
Dumbreck Rd. SE9 42 B2
Dunbar Rd. E7 13 D3
Dunblane Rd. SE9 35 A5
Dunboyne Rd. NW3 9 G2
Dunbridge St. E2 18 F3
Duncan Gro. W3 15 A5
Duncan Rd. E8 11 G5
Duncan St. N1 18 A1
Duncan Ter. N1 18 A1
Duncannon St. WC2 43 E4
Duncombe Hill SE23 40 C5
Duncrievie Rd. SE13 41 A4
Duncroft SE18 35 G3
Dundalk Rd. SE4 40 C1
Dundas Rd. SE15 33 A5
Dundee Rd. E13 20 E1
Dundee St. E1 25 G2
Dundonald Rd. NW10 8 F5
Dunelm St. E1 19 B5
Dunford Rd. N7 10 F1
Dungarvan Ave. SW15 36 C2
Dunlace Rd. E5 12 A1
Dunloe St. E2 18 E1
Dunlop Pt. E16 27 D2
Dunmore Rd. NW6 8 G5
Dunmow Rd. E15 13 A1
Dunn St. E8 11 E2
Dunnock Rd. E6 21 A5
Dunns Pas. WC1 43 F1
Dunollie Rd. NW5 10 C2
Dunoon Rd. SE23 40 A5
Dunraven Rd. W12 22 C2
Dunsany Rd. W14 22 F4
Dunstans Gro. SE22 39 G4
Dunstans Rd. SE22 39 F5
Dunster Ct. EC3 44 H3
Dunster Gdns. NW6 9 A4
Dunston Rd. E8 11 E5
Dunston Rd. SW11 38 A1
Dunston St. E8 11 E5
Dunton Rd. SE1 25 E5
Dunvegan Rd. SE9 42 B2
Dupree Rd. SE7 34 E1
Durand Gdns. SW9 31 F4
Durant St. E2 18 F2
Durban Rd. E15 20 B2
Durham Ho. St. WC2 43 F4
Durham Ri. SE18 35 E1
Durham Rd. E12 13 G1
Durham Rd. E16 20 B3
Durham Row E1 19 C4
Durham St. SE11 31 F1
Durham Ter. W2 16 C5
Durrell Rd. SW6 30 A4
Durrington Rd. E5 12 C1
Dursley Clo. SE3 34 F5
Dursley Gdns. SE3 34 G4
Dursley Rd. SE3 34 F5
Durward St. E1 18 G4
Dutton St. SE10 33 G4
Dye Ho. La. E3 12 E5
Dyers La. SW15 36 D2
Dylan Rd. SE24 39 A2
Dylways SE5 39 C2
Dymock St. SW6 37 C1
Dyne Rd. NW6 8 G4
Dynham Rd. NW6 9 B4

Dyott St. WC1 43 D1
Dyson Rd. E15 13 C3

E

Eagle Ct. EC1 18 A4
Eagle Pl. SW1 43 B4
Eagle St. WC1 17 F4
Eagle Wf. Rd. N1 18 B1
Eaglesfield Rd. SE18 35 D5
Ealdham Sq. SE9 41 F2
Eamont St. NW8 16 F1
Eardley Cres. SW5 30 B1
Earl Ri. SE18 28 F5
Earl Rd. SE1 32 E1
Earl St. EC2 18 C4
Earldom Rd. SW15 36 E2
Earlham Gro. E7 13 C2
Earlham St. WC2 43 D2
Earls Ct. Gdns. SW5 23 C5
Earls Ct. Rd. SW5 23 B5
Earls Ct. Rd. W8 23 B5
Earls Ct. Sq. SW5 30 C1
Earls Ter. W8 23 A4
Earls Wk. W8 23 B4
Earlsferry Way N1 10 F4
Earlshall Rd. SE9 42 B2
Earlsmead Rd. NW10 15 E2
Earlsthorpe Ms. SW12 38 A4
Earlston Gro. E9 11 G5
Earlswood St. SE10 34 B1
Earnshaw St. WC2 43 D1
Earsby St. W14 22 G5
East Acton La. W3 22 A1
East Arbour St. E1 19 B5
East Ave. E12 14 A4
East Cross Route E3 12 D4
East Dulwich Gro. SE22 39 D3
East Dulwich Rd. SE15 39 F2
East Dulwich Rd. SE22 39 E2
East Ferry Rd. E14 26 F5
East Ham Ind. Est. E6 20 G3
East Ham Manor Way E6 21 C5
East Harding St. EC4 44 A1
East Hill SW18 37 C3
East India Dock Rd. E14 19 E5
East India Dock Wall Rd. E14 27 A1
East La. SE16 25 F3
East Mt. St. E1 18 G4
East Rd. E15 13 D5
East Rd. N1 18 C2
East Rochester Way SE9 42 F2
East Rochester Way, Sid. 42 F2
East Row W10 15 G3
East Smithfield E1 25 E1
East St. SE17 32 B1
East Surrey Gro. SE15 32 E3
East Tenter St. E1 18 E5
Eastbourne Ms. W2 16 D5
Eastbourne Rd. E6 21 C2
Eastbourne Rd. E15 13 B5
Eastbourne Ter. W2 16 D5
Eastbrook Rd. SE3 34 E4
Eastbury Ave., Bark. 14 G5
Eastbury Ct., Bark. 14 G5
Eastbury Gro. W4 29 A1
Eastbury Rd. E6 21 C3
Eastbury Ter. E1 19 B3
Eastcastle St. W1 43 A1
Eastcheap EC3 44 G3
Eastcombe Ave. SE7 34 E2
Eastcote Rd., Well. 35 F5
Eastcote St. SW9 31 F5
Eastdown Pk. SE13 41 A2
Eastern Rd. E13 20 E1
Eastern Rd. SE4 40 E2
Eastlake Rd. SE5 32 B5
Eastlands Cres. SE21 39 E4
Eastmoor St. SE7 27 G4
Eastney St. SE10 34 A1
Eastview Ave. SE18 35 G3
Eastway E9 12 D3
Eastway E10 12 E1
Eaton Clo. SW1 24 A5
Eaton Dr. SW9 39 A2
Eaton Gate SW1 24 A5
Eaton La. SW1 24 B4
Eaton Ms. N. SW1 24 A4
Eaton Ms. S. SW1 24 A5
Eaton Ms. W. SW1 24 A5
Eaton Pl. SW1 24 A4
Eaton Row SW1 24 B4
Eaton Sq. SW1 24 A5
Eaton Ter. SW1 24 A5
Ebbisham Dr. SW8 31 F2
Ebbsfleet Rd. NW2 8 G2
Ebdon Way SE3 41 E1
Ebenezer St. N1 18 C2
Ebley Clo. SE15 32 E2
Ebner St. SW18 37 C3
Ebor St. E1 18 E3
Ebsworth St. SE23 40 B5
Ebury Bri. SW1 31 B1
Ebury Bri. Est. SW1 31 B1
Ebury Bri. Rd. SW1 31 A1
Ebury Ms. SW1 24 B5
Ebury Sq. SW1 24 A5
Ebury St. SW1 24 A5
Eccles Rd. SW11 37 G2
Ecclesbourne Rd. N1 11 B4
Eccleston Bri. SW1 24 B5
Eccleston Ms. SW1 24 A4
Eccleston Pl. SW1 24 B5
Eccleston Sq. SW1 24 B5
Eccleston St. SW1 24 B5
Eckford St. N1 17 G1
Eckstein Rd. SW11 37 F2
Eclipse Rd. E13 20 E4
Edbrooke Rd. W9 16 B3
Eddiscombe Rd. SW6 30 A5
Eddystone Rd. SE4 40 C3
Eden Gro. N7 10 F2
Edenbridge Rd. E9 12 B4
Edenhurst Ave. SW6 37 A1
Edensor Gdns. W4 29 A3
Edensor Rd. W4 29 A3
Edenvale St. SW6 30 C5
Edgar Kail Way SE22 39 D2
Edgar Rd. E3 19 F2
Edgarley Ter. SW6 29 G4
Edge Hill SE18 35 D2
Edgeley Rd. SW4 38 D1
Edgeworth Rd. SE9 41 F2
Edgware Rd. W2 16 E3
Edinburgh Gate SW1 23 G3
Edinburgh Ho. W9 16 C2
Edinburgh Rd. E13 20 E1
Edis St. NW1 10 A5
Edith Gro. SW10 30 D2
Edith Rd. E6 13 G4
Edith Rd. W14 22 G5
Edith Row SW6 30 C4
Edith Ter. SW10 30 D3
Edith Vill. W14 30 A1
Edithna St. SW9 38 E1
Edmeston Clo. E9 12 C3
Edmund St. SE5 32 C3
Edna St. SW11 30 F4
Edric Rd. SE14 33 B3
Edrich Ho. SW4 31 E4
Edward Pl. SE8 33 D2
Edward St. E16 20 D3
Edward St. SE8 33 D2
Edward St. SE14 33 C3
Edward Temme Ave. E15 13 C4
Edwardes Sq. W8 23 A4
Edwards Ms. N1 11 A4
Edwards Ms. W1 17 A5
Edwin Ave. E6 21 C1
Edwin St. E1 19 A3
Edwin St. E16 20 D4
Effie Pl. SW6 30 B3
Effie Rd. SW6 30 B3
Effingham Rd. SE12 41 B3
Effra Par. SW2 38 G3
Effra Rd. SW2 38 G2
Egan Way SE16 32 G1
Egbert St. NW1 10 A5
Egerton Cres. SW3 23 F5
Egerton Dr. SE10 33 F4
Egerton Gdns. NW10 8 E5
Egerton Gdns. SW3 23 F5
Egerton Gdns. Ms. SW3 23 F4
Egerton Pl. SW3 23 F4
Egerton Ter. SW3 23 F4
Egham Rd. E13 20 E4
Eglantine Rd. SW18 37 D3
Eglinton Hill SE18 35 D2
Eglinton Rd. SE18 35 D2
Egliston Ms. SW15 36 E1
Egliston Rd. SW15 36 E1
Egmont St. SE14 33 B3
Eighth Ave. E12 14 B1
Eisenhower Dr. E6 21 A4
Elaine Gro. NW5 10 A2
Elam Clo. SE5 32 A5
Elam St. SE5 32 A5
Eland Rd. SW11 37 G1
Elbe St. SW6 30 D5
Elbury Dr. E16 20 D5
Elcho St. SW11 30 F3
Elcot Ave. SE15 32 F3
Elder St. E1 18 E4
Elderfield Rd. E5 12 B1
Elderflower Way E15 13 B4
Elderslie Rd. SE9 42 C3
Eldon Gro. NW3 9 E2
Eldon Rd. W8 23 C4
Eldon St. EC2 18 C4
Eldred Rd., Bark. 14 G5
Eleanor Clo. SE16 26 B3
Eleanor Gro. SW13 36 A1
Eleanor Rd. E8 11 G3
Eleanor Rd. E15 13 C3
Eleanor St. E3 19 E2
Electric Ave. SW9 38 G2
Electric La. SW9 38 G2
Elephant & Castle SE1 25 A4
Elephant La. SE16 26 A3
Elephant Rd. SE17 25 B5
Elf Row E1 26 A1
Elfindale Rd. SE24 39 B3
Elford Clo. SE3 41 F2
Elfort Rd. N5 10 G1
Elgar St. SE16 26 C3
Elgin Ave. W9 16 B3
Elgin Cres. W11 22 G1
Elgin Est. W9 16 B3
Elia Ms. N1 18 A1
Elia St. N1 18 A1
Elias Pl. SW8 31 G2
Elibank Rd. SE9 42 B2
Elim Est. SE1 25 C4
Elim Way E13 20 C2
Eliot Gdns. SW15 36 C2
Eliot Hill SE13 33 G5
Eliot Ms. NW8 16 D1
Eliot Pk. SE13 33 G5
Eliot Pl. SE3 34 B5
Eliot Vale SE3 34 A5
Elizabeth Ave. N1
Elizabeth Bri. SW1
Elizabeth Est. SE17
Elizabeth Gdns. W3
Elizabeth Ms. NW3
Elizabeth Rd. E6
Elizabeth St. SW1
Elizabeth Ter. SE9
Elkington Rd. E13
Elkstone Rd. W10
Ellaline Rd. W6
Elland Rd. SE15
Ellen St. E1
Ellenborough Pl. SW15
Ellerby St. SW6
Ellerdale Rd. NW3
Ellerdale St. SE13
Ellerslie Gdns. NW10
Ellerslie Rd. W12
Ellerslie Sq. Ind. Est. SW2
Ellerton Rd. SW13
Ellery St. SE15
Ellesmere Rd. E3
Ellesmere Rd. NW10
Ellesmere St. E14
Ellingfort Rd. E8
Ellingham Rd. E15
Ellingham Rd. W12
Ellington St. N7
Elliot Clo. E15
Elliott Rd. SW9
Elliott Rd. W4
Elliott Sq. NW3
Elliotts Row SE11
Ellis Ms. SE7
Ellis St. SW1
Elliscombe Rd. SE7
Ellisfield Dr. SW15
Ellison Rd. SW13
Ellsworth St. E2
Elm Bank Gdns. SW13
Elm Ct. EC4
Elm Grn. W3
Elm Gro. NW2
Elm Gro. SE15
Elm Gro. Rd. SW13
Elm Pk. SW2
Elm Pk. Gdns. SW10
Elm Pk. La. SW3
Elm Pk. Rd. SW3
Elm Pl. SW7
Elm Quay Ct. SW8
Elm Rd. E7
Elm St. WC1
Elm Ter. SE9
Elm Tree Clo. NW8
Elm Tree Rd. NW8
Elm Way NW10
Elmbrook Gdns. SE9
Elmcroft St. E5
Elmdene Rd. SE18
Elmer Rd. SE6
Elmfield Way W9
Elmhurst Rd. E7
Elmhurst St. SW4
Elmington Est. SE5
Elmington Rd. SE5
Elmira St. SE13
Elmley St. SE18
Elmore St. N1
Elms, The SW13
Elms Cres. SW4
Elms Ms. W2
Elms Rd. SW4
Elms Wk. SE3
Elmshaw Rd. SW15
Elmstone Rd. SW6

wood Rd. SE24 39 C3
ıgton Rd. E8 11 F3
ı St. E1 19 C4
dale St. E9 12 A3
enham Rd. E12 14 C2
ıam Rd. W14 22 G3
ıam Ter. W14 22 G3
e Rd. SE22 39 E2
emaud Rd. SE4 40 D3
ey Rd. SW11 37 G1
beth Rd. SW11 37 G2
ed St. SE17 25 C5
ow Clo. SE9 42 C3
ree Gdns., Ilf. 14 E2
vick Rd. SE13 33 F5
vick St. SW6 30 D5
vorthy Ri. NW3 9 F4
worthy Rd. NW3 9 E5
worthy Ter. NW3 9 F4
ynge Rd. SW18 37 E3
am Grn. SE9 41 F3
am Grn. Rd. SE9 41 F2
am High St. SE9 42 B4
am Hill SE9 41 G3
am Palace Rd. SE9 41 F4
am Pk. Gdns. SE9 42 C2
am Rd. SE9 41 F3
am Rd. SE12 41 D3
iron Rd. SW6 30 B4
ruda Rd. SE13 41 A4
sley Rd., Ilf. 14 D1
n Ho. E3 12 D5
n Pl. N16 11 D2
ingham St. SW18 37 D2
aston Ms. SW7 23 D4
aston Pl. SW7 23 D4
erson Rd. SE8 33 F5
erton St. SW1 24 D5
s Rd. NW2 8 E3
in St. E2 18 F2
yn Gdns. SE12 41 D5
stan Pl. SW3 30 F1
stan St. SW3 23 F5
ba St. SE16 25 F3
bankment SW15 29 F5
bankment Gdns. SW3 30 G2
bankment Pl. WC2 43 F5
bleton Rd. SE13 40 F2
den St. SW6 30 C4
erald Clo. E16 21 A5
erald St. WC1 17 F4
erson St. SE1 44 D5
ery Hill St. SW1 24 C4
ily Pl. N7 10 G1
lyn Gdns. W12 22 A3
lyn Rd. W12 22 A3
ma Rd. E13 20 C1
ma St. E2 18 G1
mott Clo. E1 19 C3
peror's Gate SW7 23 C4
pire Wf. Rd. E14 27 A5
press Pl. SW6 30 B1
press St. SE17 32 B2
pson St. E3 19 F3
u Rd. SW8 31 B5
brook St. W10 15 G2
dell St. WC2 43 E1
derby St. SE10 34 B1
dlesham Rd. SW12 38 A5
dsleigh Gdns. WC1 17 D3
dsleigh Pl. WC1 17 D3
dsleigh St. WC1 17 D3
dwell Rd. SE4 33 C5
dymion Rd. SW2 38 F4
field Rd. N1 11 D4
ford St. W1 16 G4
gate St. SE13 40 G2
gineer Clo. SE18 35 C2
Englands La. NW3 9 G3
Englefield Rd. N1 11 C4
Engleheart Rd. SE6 40 F5
Englewood Rd. SW12 38 B4
English Grds. SE1 44 H6
English St. E3 19 D3
Enid St. SE16 25 E4
Enmore Rd. SW15 36 E2
Ennerdale Ho. E3 19 D3
Ennersdale Rd. SE13 41 A3
Ennis Rd. SE18 35 E2
Ennismore Ave. W4 22 B5
Ennismore Gdns. SW7 23 F3
Ennismore Gdns. Ms. SW7 23 F4
Ennismore Ms. SW7 23 F4
Ennismore St. SW7 23 F4
Ensign St. E1 25 F1
Enslin Rd. SE9 42 C5
Enterprise Way NW10 15 C2
Enterprise Way SW18 37 B2
Enterprize Way SE8 26 D5
Epirus Rd. SW6 30 A3
Epping Clo. E14 26 E5
Epple Rd. SW6 30 A4
Epworth St. EC2 18 C3
Erasmus St. SW1 24 D5
Erconwald St. W12 15 B5
Eresby Pl. NW6 9 B4
Eric Clo. E7 13 D1
Eric Rd. E7 13 D1
Eric St. E3 19 D3
Erica St. W12 22 C1
Ericcson Clo. SW18 37 B3
Erindale SE18 35 F2
Erindale Ter. SE18 35 F2
Erlanger Rd. SE14 33 B4
Ermine Rd. SE13 40 F2
Ernald Ave. E6 21 A1
Ernest St. E1 19 B3
Erpingham Rd. SW15 36 E1
Errington Rd. W9 16 A3
Errol St. EC1 18 B3
Erskine Rd. NW3 9 G4
Erwood Rd. SE7 35 A1
Escreet Gro. SE18 28 C5
Esk Rd. E13 20 D3
Esmeralda Rd. SE1 25 F5
Esmond Rd. NW6 9 A5
Esmond St. SW15 36 G2
Esparto St. SW18 37 C5
Essendine Rd. W9 16 B2
Essex Ct. EC4 43 J2
Essex Ct. SW13 29 B5
Essex Pk. Ms. W3 22 A2
Essex Rd. E12 14 A2
Essex Rd. N1 11 A5
Essex Rd. NW10 8 A4
Essex Rd., Bark. 14 F4
Essex St. E7 13 D2
Essex St. WC2 43 J3
Essex Vill. W8 23 B3
Essian St. E1 19 C4
Estcourt Rd. SW6 30 A3
Este Rd. SW11 37 F1
Estelle Rd. NW3 9 G1
Esterbrooke St. SW1 24 D5
Etchingham Rd. E15 12 G1
Eternit Wk. SW6 29 E4
Ethel Rd. E16 20 E5
Ethelburga St. SW11 30 F4
Ethelden Rd. W12 22 D2
Etherow St. SE22 39 F4
Ethnard Rd. SE15 32 G2
Eton Ave. NW3 9 E4
Eton College Rd. NW3 9 G3
Eton Gro. SE13 41 B1
Eton Rd. NW3 9 G4
Eton Rd., Ilf. 14 E2
Eton Vill. NW3 9 G3
Etta St. SE8 33 C2
Ettrick St. E14 19 G5
Eugenia Rd. SE16 26 A5
Europe Rd. SE18 28 B4
Eustace Rd. E6 21 A2
Eustace Rd. SW6 30 B3
Euston Gro. NW1 17 D2
Euston Rd. N1 17 B3
Euston Rd. NW1 17 B3
Euston Sq. NW1 17 D2
Euston St. NW1 17 C2
Evandale Rd. SW9 31 G5
Evangelist Rd. NW5 10 B1
Eve Rd. E11 13 B1
Eve Rd. E15 20 B1
Evelina Rd. SE15 40 A1
Eveline Lowe Est. SE16 25 F4
Evelyn Denington Rd. E6 21 B4
Evelyn Fox Ct. W10 15 E4
Evelyn Gdns. SW7 30 E1
Evelyn Rd. E16 27 E2
Evelyn St. SE8 33 C1
Evelyn Wk. N1 18 C1
Evelyn Yd. W1 43 C1
Evenwood Clo. SW15 36 G3
Everdon Rd. SW13 29 C2
Everest Pl. E14 19 G4
Everest Rd. SE9 42 B3
Everilda St. N1 10 F5
Everington St. W6 29 F2
Eversholt St. NW1 17 C1
Eversleigh Rd. E6 13 G5
Eversleigh Rd. SW11 37 G1
Eversley Rd. SE7 34 E2
Everthorpe Rd. SE15 39 E1
Evesham Rd. E15 13 C4
Evesham St. W11 22 F1
Evesham Wk. SW9 31 G5
Evesham Way SW11 38 A1
Ewald Rd. SW6 30 A5
Ewart Pl. E3 19 D1
Ewart Rd. SE23 40 B5
Ewe Clo. N7 10 E3
Ewen Cres. SW2 38 G5
Ewer St. SE1 44 D6
Ewhurst Rd. SE4 40 D4
Excel Ct. WC2 43 D4
Excelsior Gdns. SE13 33 G5
Exchange Arc. EC2 18 D4
Exchange Ct. WC2 43 F4
Exchange Pl. EC2 18 D4
Exchange Sq. EC2 18 D4
Exeter Rd. E16 20 D4
Exeter Rd. NW2 8 G2
Exeter Rd. SE15 32 E4
Exeter St. WC2 43 F3
Exeter Way SE14 33 D3
Exhibition Clo. W12 22 E1
Exhibition Rd. SW7 23 E3
Exmoor St. W10 15 F4
Exmouth Mkt. EC1 17 G3
Exmouth Pl. E8 11 G4
Exning Rd. E16 20 C3
Exon St. SE17 25 D5
Exton St. SE1 43 J6
Eynella Rd. SE22 39 E5
Eynham Rd. W12 15 E5
Eyot Gdns. W6 29 B1
Eythorne Rd. SW9 31 G4
Ezra St. E2 18 E2

F

Fabian Rd. SW6 30 A3
Fabian St. E6 21 B3
Factory Pl. E14 33 F1
Factory Rd. E16 28 A2
Fairacres SW15 36 C3
Fairbairn Grn. SW9 31 G4
Fairby Rd. SE12 41 E3
Fairclough St. E1 18 F5
Faircross Ave., Bark. 14 E3
Fairdale Gdns. SW15 36 D2
Fairfax Gdns. SE3 34 F4
Fairfax Pl. NW6 9 D4
Fairfax Rd. NW6 9 D4
Fairfax Rd. W4 22 A4
Fairfield Ct. NW10 8 C5
Fairfield Dr. SW18 37 C3
Fairfield Gro. SE7 34 G2
Fairfield Rd. E3 19 E1
Fairfield Rd., Ilf. 14 D3
Fairfield St. SW18 37 C3
Fairfoot Rd. E3 19 E3
Fairhazel Gdns. NW6 9 C3
Fairholme Rd. W14 29 G1
Fairland Rd. E15 13 C3
Fairlawn SE7 34 F2
Fairlie Gdns. SE23 40 A5
Fairlight Ave. NW10 15 A1
Fairmount Rd. SW2 38 F4
Fairoak Dr. SE9 42 F3
Fairthorn Rd. SE7 34 D1
Fairview Pl. SW2 38 F5
Fairway, The W3 15 A5
Fairway Gdns., Ilf. 14 E2
Fakruddin St. E1 18 F3
Falcon Clo. SE1 44 C5
Falcon Gro. SW11 37 F1
Falcon La. SW11 37 F1
Falcon Rd. SW11 30 F5
Falcon St. E13 20 C3
Falcon Ter. SW11 37 F1
Falcon Trd. Est. NW10 8 A1
Falcon Way E14 26 F5
Falconberg Ct. W1 43 D1
Falconberg Ms. W1 43 C1
Falconwood Ave., Well. 35 F5
Falconwood Par., Well. 42 G2
Falkirk Ho. W9 16 C2
Falkirk St. N1 18 D1
Falkland Rd. NW5 10 C2
Falmouth Clo. SE12 41 C3
Falmouth Rd. SE1 25 B4
Falmouth St. E15 13 A2
Fann St. EC1 18 B3
Fann St. EC2 18 B3
Fanshaw St. N1 18 D2
Fanshawe Ave., Bark. 14 E3
Fanthorpe St. SW15 36 E1
Faraday Rd. E15 13 C3
Faraday Rd. W10 15 G4
Faraday Way SE18 27 G4
Fareham St. W1 43 C1
Faringford Rd. E15 13 B4
Farjeon Rd. SE3 34 G4
Farleigh Rd. N16 11 E1
Farley Rd. SE6 40 G5
Farlow Rd. SW15 36 E1
Farlton Rd. SW18 37 C5
Farm La. SW6 30 B2
Farm St. W1 24 B1
Farmdale Rd. SE10 34 D1
Farmers Rd. SE5 32 A3
Farnaby Rd. SE9 41 F2
Farncombe St. SE16 25 F3
Farnham Pl. SE1 44 C6
Farnham Royal SE11 31 F1
Faroe Rd. W14 22 F4
Farrance St. E14 19 E5
Farrier St. NW1 10 B4
Farrier Wk. SW10 30 D2
Farringdon La. EC1 17 G3
Farringdon Rd. EC1 17 G3
Farringdon St. EC4 44 B1
Farrins Rents SE16 26 C2

Farrow La. SE14 33 A3
Fashion St. E1 18 E4
Fassett Rd. E8 11 F3
Fassett Sq. E8 11 F3
Faulkner St. SE14 33 A4
Favart Rd. SW6 30 B4
Faversham Rd. SE6 40 D5
Fawcett Clo. SW11 30 E5
Fawcett Rd. NW10 8 B4
Fawcett St. SW10 30 C2
Fawe Pk. Rd. SW15 37 A2
Fawe St. E14 19 F4
Fawley Rd. NW6 9 C2
Fawn Rd. E13 20 F1
Fawnbrake Ave. SE24 39 A3
Fearon St. SE10 34 D1
Feathers Pl. SE10 34 A2
Featherstone St. EC1 18 C3
Featley Rd. SW9 39 A1
Felday Rd. SE13 40 F4
Felden St. SW6 30 A4
Felgate Ms. W6 22 D5
Felixstowe Rd. NW10 15 D2
Fellbrigg Rd. SE22 39 E3
Fellows Rd. NW3 9 E4
Felltram Way SE7 27 D5
Felsberg Rd. SW2 38 E4
Felsham Rd. SW15 36 F1
Felstead St. E9 12 D3
Felsted Rd. E16 20 G5
Felton St. N1 11 C5
Fen Ct. EC3 44 H3
Fenchurch Ave. EC3 44 H2
Fenchurch Bldgs. EC3 44 J2
Fenchurch Pl. EC3 44 J3
Fenchurch St. EC3 44 H3
Fendall St. SE1 25 D4
Fenelon Pl. W14 23 A5
Fenham Rd. SE15 32 F3
Fenn St. E9 12 A2
Fennel St. SE18 35 C2
Fentiman Rd. SW8 31 E2
Fenton Clo. SW9 31 F5
Fentons Ave. E13 20 E1
Fenwick Gro. SE15 39 F1
Fenwick Pl. SW9 38 E1
Fenwick Rd. SE15 39 F1
Ferdinand St. NW1 10 A4
Ferguson Clo. E14 26 E5
Fermoy Rd. W9 16 A3
Fern St. E3 19 E3
Fernbrook Rd. SE13 41 B4
Ferncliff Rd. E8 11 F2
Ferndale Ct. SE3 34 C3
Ferndale Rd. E7 13 E4
Ferndale Rd. SW4 38 F2
Ferndale Rd. SW9 38 E2
Ferndale St. E6 28 D1
Ferndene Rd. SE24 39 B2
Ferndown Rd. SE9 41 G5
Fernhead Rd. W9 16 A2
Fernhill St. E16 28 B2
Fernholme Rd. SE15 40 B3
Fernhurst Rd. SW6 29 G4
Ferns Rd. E15 13 C3
Fernshaw Rd. SW10 30 D2
Ferntower Rd. N5 11 C2
Ferranti Clo. SE18 27 G4
Ferrier St. SW18 37 C2
Ferris Rd. SE22 39 F2
Ferry La. SW13 29 B2
Ferry Rd. SW13 29 C3
Ferry St. E14 33 G1
Festing Rd. SW15 36 F1
Fetter La. EC4 44 A2
Ffinch St. SE8 33 E3
Field Rd. E7 13 D1
Field Rd. W6 29 G1
Field St. WC1 17 F2
Fieldgate St. E1 18 F4
Fielding Ho. NW6 16 B2
Fielding Rd. W14 22 F4
Fielding St. SE17 32 B2
Fields Est. E8 11 F4
Fieldway Cres. N5 10 G2
Fife Rd. E16 20 D4
Fifth Ave. E12 14 B1
Fifth Ave. W10 15 G2
Filmer Rd. SW6 29 G4
Finborough Rd. SW10 30 C1
Finch La. EC3 44 G2
Finchley Pl. NW8 16 E1
Finchley Rd. NW3 9 C2
Finchley Rd. NW8 9 E4
Finck St. SE1 24 F3
Finden Rd. E7 13 E2
Findhorn St. E14 19 G5
Findon Rd. W12 22 C3
Fingal St. SE10 34 C1
Finland Quay SE16 26 C4
Finland Rd. SE4 40 C1
Finland St. SE16 26 C4
Finlay St. SW6 29 F4
Finnis St. E2 18 G2
Finsbury Circ. EC2 18 C4
Finsbury Est. EC1 17 G2
Finsbury Mkt. EC2 18 D3
Finsbury Pavement EC2 18 C4
Finsbury Sq. EC2 18 C4
Finsbury St. EC2 18 C4
Finsen Rd. SE5 39 B1
Finstock Rd. W10 15 F5
Fir Trees Clo. SE16 26 C2
Firbank Clo. E16 20 G4
Firbank Rd. SE15 32 G5
Firs Clo. SE23 40 B5
First Ave. E12 14 A1
First Ave. E13 20 D2
First Ave. SW14 36 A1
First Ave. W3 22 B2
First Ave. W10 16 A3
First St. SW3 23 F5
Firth Gdns. SW6 29 G4
Fish St. Hill EC3 44 G4
Fisher St. E16 20 D4
Fisher St. WC1 17 F4
Fishermans Dr. SE16 26 B3
Fisherton St. NW8 16 E3
Fisherton St. Est. NW8 16 E3
Fisons Rd. E16 27 D2
Fitzalan St. SE11 24 F5
Fitzgeorge Ave. W14 22 G5
Fitzgerald Ave. SW14 36 A1
Fitzhardinge St. W1 17 A5
Fitzhugh Gro. SW18 37 E4
Fitzhugh Gro. Est. SW18 37 E4
Fitzjames Ave. W14 22 G5
Fitzjohn's Ave. NW3 9 E2
Fitzmaurice Pl. W1 24 B2
Fitzneal St. W12 15 B5
Fitzroy Rd. NW1 10 A5
Fitzroy Sq. W1 17 C3
Fitzroy St. W1 17 C3
Fitzwilliam Rd. SW4 38 C1
Fiveways Rd. SW9 31 G5
Flamborough St. E14 19 C5
Flamsteed Rd. SE7 35 A1
Flanchford Rd. W12 22 B4
Flanders Rd. E6 21 B1
Flanders Rd. W4 22 A5
Flanders Way E9 12 B3
Flask Wk. NW3 9 D1
Flavell Ms. SE10 34 B1
Flaxman Ct. W1 43 C2
Flaxman Rd. SE5 39 A1
Flaxman Ter. WC1 17 D2
Flaxton Rd. SE18 35 F3
Fleet Rd. NW3 9 F2
Fleet St. EC4 44 A2
Fleetwood Clo. E16 20 G4
Fleetwood Rd. NW10 8 C2
Fleming Rd. SE17 32 A2
Fletcher St. E1 25 F1
Fletching Rd. SE7 34 F2
Fleur de Lis St. E1 18 D3
Flint St. SE17 25 C5
Flintmill Cres. SE3 35 A5
Flinton St. SE17 32 D1
Flitcroft St. WC2 43 D2
Flodden Rd. SE5 32 B4
Flood St. SW3 30 F1
Flood Wk. SW3 30 F2
Flora Clo. E14 19 F5
Floral St. WC2 43 E3
Florence Rd. E6 13 F5
Florence Rd. E13 20 C1
Florence Rd. SE14 33 D4
Florence St. E16 20 C3
Florence St. N1 11 A4
Florence Ter. SE14 33 D4
Florian Rd. SW15 36 G2
Florida St. E2 18 F2
Floss St. SW15 29 E5
Flower Wk., The SW7 23 D3
Floyd Rd. SE7 34 F1
Fludyer St. SE13 41 B2
Foley St. W1 17 C4
Folgate St. E1 18 D4
Foliot St. W12 15 B5
Folkestone Rd. E6 21 C1
Follett St. E14 19 G5
Folly Wall E14 26 G3
Fontarabia Rd. SW11 38 A2
Fontley Way SW15 36 C5
Footscray Rd. SE9 42 C4
Footway, The SE9 42 E5
Ford Rd. E3 12 C5
Ford Sq. E1 18 G4
Ford St. E16 20 C5
Fordham St. E1 18 F5
Fordingley Rd. W9 16 A2
Fords Pk. Rd. E16 20 D5
Fordwych Rd. NW2 8 G1
Fordyce Rd. SE13 40 G4
Fore St. EC2 18 B4
Foreshore SE8 26 D5
Forest Gro. E8 11 E3
Forest Hill Rd. SE22 39 G3
Forest Hill Rd. SE23 40 A4
Forest La. E7 13 D2
Forest La. E15 13 B3
Forest Rd. E7 13 D1
Forest Rd. E8 11 E3
Forest St. E7 13 D2
Forest Vw. Rd. E12 14 A1
Forest Way, Sid. 42 F5
Forester Rd. SE15 39 G2
Forfar Rd. SW11 31 A4
Formosa St. W9 16 C3
Forset St. W1 16 F5
Forster Rd. SW2 38 E5
Forsyth Gdns. SE17 32 A2
Forsythia Clo., Ilf. 14 D2
Fort Rd. SE1 25 E5
Fort St. E1 18 D4
Fort St. E16 27 E2
Fortess Rd. NW5 10 B2
Forthbridge Rd. SW11 38 A2
Fortis Clo. E16 20 F5
Fortune Gate Rd. NW10 8 A5
Fortune Grn. Rd. NW6 9 B1
Fortune St. EC1 18 B3
Fortune Way NW10 15 C2
Forty Acre La. E16 20 D4
Foskett Rd. SW6 30 A5
Fossdene Rd. SE7 34 E1
Fossil Rd. SE13 40
Foster La. EC2 44
Foster Rd. E13 20
Foster Rd. W3 22
Fothergill Clo. E13 20
Foubert's Pl. W1 43
Foulden Rd. N16 11
Foulis Ter. SW7 30
Founders Ct. EC2 44
Foundry Clo. SE16 26
Fount St. SW8 31
Fountain Ct. EC4 43
Fountain Pl. SW9 31
Fournier St. E1 18
Fourth Ave. E12 14
Fourth Ave. W10 15
Fowler Clo. SW11 37
Fowler Rd. E7 13
Fownes St. SW11 37
Fox Clo. E1 19
Fox Clo. E16 20
Fox Rd. E16 20
Foxberry Rd. SE4 40
Foxborough Gdns. SE4 40
Foxcroft Rd. SE18 35
Foxes Dale SE3 41
Foxglove St. W12 22
Foxhole Rd. SE9 42
Foxley Rd. SW9 31
Foxmore St. SW11 30
Foxwell St. SE4 40
Foxwood Rd. SE3 41
Foyle Rd. SE3 34
Framfield Rd. N5 11
Frampton Pk. Est. E9 12
Frampton Pk. Rd. E9 12
Frampton St. NW8 16
Francemary Rd. SE4 40
Frances St. SE18 28
Francis Chichester Way SW11 31
Francis St. E15 13
Francis St. SW1 24
Franconia Rd. SW4 38
Frank St. E13 20
Frankfurt Rd. SE24 39
Frankham St. SE8 33
Frankland Clo. SE16 26
Frankland Rd. SW7 23
Franklin Clo. SE13 33
Franklin's Row SW3 30
Franklyn Rd. NW10 8
Fraser St. W4 29
Frazier St. SE1 24
Frean St. SE16 25
Frederick Clo. W2 23
Frederick Cres. SW9 32
Frederick Pl. SE18 35
Frederick St. WC1 17
Frederick's Pl. EC2 44
Freedom St. SW11 30
Freegrove Rd. N7 10
Freemasons Rd. E16 20
Freke Rd. SW11 38
Fremantle St. SE17 32
Fremont St. E9 12
Frendsbury Rd. SE4 40
Frensham St. SE15 32
Frere St. SW11 30
Fresh Wf. Rd., Bark. 14
Freshfield Ave. E8 11
Freston Rd. W10 22
Freston Rd. W11 22
Friar St. EC4 44
Friars Mead E14 26
Friars Ms. SE9 42
Friars Rd. E6 13
Friary Ct. SW1 43
Friary Est. SE15 32

ıry Rd. SE15 32 F3
lay St. EC4 44 D2
end St. EC1 18 A2
endly St. SE8 33 E5
ern Rd. SE22 39 F5
nley Way E1 19 B3
ton Rd. E6 20 G2
ton St. SW6 30 C5
h Rd. E11 12 G1
h St. W1 43 C2
nville Gdns. W12 22 E2
bisher Rd. E6 21 B5
bisher St. SE10 34 B2
gley Rd. SE22 39 E2
gmore SW18 37 B3
gnal NW3 9 D2
gnal Clo. NW3 9 D2
gnal Ct. NW3 9 D3
gnal Gdns. NW3 9 D1
gnal La. NW3 9 C2
gnal Way NW3 9 D1
ssart Rd. SE9 41 G3
me St. N1 18 B1
ude St. SW8 31 B5
Rd. E6 13 G4
Rd. NW10 8 B5
ham Bdy. SW6 30 B3
ham High St. SW6 29 G5
ham Palace Rd. SW6 29 F2
ham Palace Rd. W6 29 E1
ham Pk. Gdns. SW6 30 A5
ham Pk. Rd. SW6 30 A5
ham Rd. SW3 30 E1
ham Rd. SW6 29 G5
ham Rd. SW10 30 E1
erton Rd. SW18 37 D3
mead St. SW6 30 C4
mer Rd. E16 20 G4
horp Rd. SE3 34 C5
ber St. W6 22 D4
ey Rd. SE15 32 F3
ong Rd. N7 10 G3
mage St. SW18 37 C5
ness Rd. NW10 15 C1
ness Rd. SW6 30 C5
nival St. EC4 43 J1
ow La. E9 12 A2
her Grn. Rd. SE6 41 B5
e St. E3 19 E4
efield Rd. SE3 34 E3
eld Ct. E7 13 D3
eld Rd. SW9 38 G1
es St. SW1 24 D5

G

les Clo. SE5 32 D4
riel St. SE23 40 B5
rielle Ct. NW3 9 E3
Clo. E13 20 E2
nsborough Ave. E12 14 C2
nsborough Rd. E15 20 B2
nsborough Rd. W4 22 B5
nsford St. SE1 25 E3
loch Rd. SE5 32 D5
sford St. NW5 10 C3
ta Rd. SW13 29 C3
braith St. E14 26 G4
e St. E3 19 E4
ena Rd. W6 22 D5
es Gdns. E2 18 G2
esbury Rd. SW18 37 D4
eywall Rd. SE16 25 G5
ia Rd. N5 11 A2
ions Rd. E16 28 D1
ions Rd. SE7 27 E5
on Clo. SE7 27 F5
Gallosson Rd. SE18 28 G5
Galloway Rd. W12 22 C2
Gallus Sq. SE3 41 E1
Galsworthy Rd. NW2 8 G1
Galton St. W10 15 G2
Galveston Rd. SW15 37 A3
Galway St. EC1 18 B2
Gambetta St. SW8 31 B5
Gambia St. SE1 44 C6
Gamlen Rd. SW15 36 F2
Ganton St. W1 43 A3
Garden Clo. SW15 36 D5
Garden Ct. EC4 43 J3
Garden Rd. NW8 16 D2
Garden Row SE1 25 A4
Garden St. E1 19 B4
Gardens, The SE22 39 F2
Gardiner Ave. NW2 8 E2
Gardner Rd. E13 20 E3
Gardners La. EC4 44 D3
Garfield Rd. E13 20 C3
Garfield Rd. SW11 38 A1
Garford St. E14 26 E1
Garibaldi St. SE18 28 G5
Garland Rd. SE18 35 F3
Garlick Hill EC4 44 E3
Garlinge Rd. NW2 9 A3
Garnet Rd. NW10 8 A3
Garnet St. E1 26 A1
Garnett Clo. SE9 42 B1
Garnett Rd. NW3 9 G2
Garratt La. SW18 37 C3
Garrick Clo. SW18 37 D2
Garrick St. WC2 43 E3
Garsington Ms. SE4 40 D1
Garthorne Rd. SE23 40 B5
Garton Pl. SW18 37 D4
Gartons Way SW11 37 D1
Garvary Rd. E16 20 E5
Garway Rd. W2 16 C5
Gascoigne Pl. E2 18 E2
Gascoigne Rd., Bark. 14 E5
Gascony Ave. NW6 9 B4
Gascoyne Rd. E9 12 B4
Gaselee St. E14 26 G1
Gaskarth Rd. SW12 38 B4
Gaskell St. SW4 31 E5
Gaskin St. N1 11 A5
Gastein Rd. W6 29 F2
Gataker St. SE16 25 G4
Gate Ms. SW7 23 F3
Gate St. WC2 43 G1
Gateforth St. NW8 16 F3
Gateley Rd. SW9 38 F1
Gateway SE17 32 B2
Gateway Ind. Est. NW10 15 B2
Gatliff Rd. SW1 31 B1
Gatwick Rd. SW18 37 A5
Gauden Clo. SW4 38 D1
Gauden Rd. SW4 31 D5
Gaunt St. SE1 25 B4
Gautrey Rd. SE15 33 A5
Gaverick St. E14 26 E5
Gavestone Cres. SE12 41 E5
Gavestone Rd. SE12 41 E5
Gavin St. SE18 28 G5
Gawber St. E2 19 A2
Gay Clo. NW2 8 D2
Gay Rd. E15 20 A1
Gaydon Ho. W2 16 C4
Gayfere St. SW1 24 E4
Gayford Rd. W12 22 B3
Gayhurst Rd. E8 11 F4
Gayton Cres. NW3 9 E1
Gayton Rd. NW3 9 E1
Gayville Rd. SW11 37 G4
Geary Rd. NW10 8 C2
Geary St. N7 10 F2
Gedling Pl. SE1 25 E4
Gee St. EC1 18 B3
Geere Rd. E15 13 C5
Geffrye St. E2 18 E1
Geldart Rd. SE15 32 G3
Gellatly Rd. SE14 33 A5
General Gordon Pl. SE18 28 D5
General Wolfe Rd. SE10 34 A4
Genesta Rd. SE18 35 D2
Geneva Dr. SW9 38 G2
Genoa Ave. SW15 36 E3
Geoffrey Clo. SE5 32 B5
Geoffrey Gdns. E6 21 A1
Geoffrey Rd. SE4 40 D1
George Beard Rd. SE8 26 D5
George Ct. WC2 43 F4
George Inn Yd. SE1 44 F6
George La. SE13 40 G4
George Row SE16 25 F3
George St. E16 20 C5
George St. W1 16 G5
George St., Bark. 14 E4
George Yd. EC3 44 G2
George Yd. W1 24 A1
George's Rd. N7 10 F2
Georgiana St. NW1 10 C5
Gerald Rd. E16 20 C3
Gerald Rd. SW1 24 A5
Geraldine Rd. SW18 37 D3
Geraldine St. SE11 25 A4
Gerard Rd. SW13 29 B4
Gerards Clo. SE16 33 A1
Germander Way E15 20 B2
Gernon Rd. E3 19 C1
Gerrard Pl. W1 43 D3
Gerrard Rd. N1 18 A1
Gerrard St. W1 43 D3
Gerridge St. SE1 24 G4
Gertrude St. SW10 30 D2
Gervase St. SE15 32 G3
Ghent Way E8 11 E3
Giant Arches Rd. SE24 39 B5
Gibbins Rd. E15 12 G4
Gibbon Rd. SE15 33 A5
Gibbon Rd. W3 22 A1
Gibbons Rd. NW10 8 A3
Gibbs Grn. W14 30 A1
Gibraltar Wk. E2 18 E2
Gibson Rd. SE11 24 F5
Gibson Sq. N1 10 G5
Gibson St. SE10 34 B1
Gideon Rd. SW11 38 A1
Giffin St. SE8 33 E3
Gifford St. N1 10 E4
Gift La. E15 13 C5
Gilbert Clo. SE18 35 B4
Gilbert Rd. SE11 24 G5
Gilbert St. E15 13 B1
Gilbert St. W1 17 A5
Gilden Cres. NW5 10 A2
Gilkes Cres. SE21 39 D4
Gilkes Pl. SE21 39 D4
Gill Ave. E16 20 D5
Gill St. E14 26 D1
Gillender St. E3 19 G3
Gillender St. E14 19 G3
Gillett Ave. E6 21 A1
Gillett St. N16 11 D2
Gillfoot NW1 17 C1
Gillian St. SE13 40 F3
Gillies St. NW5 10 A2
Gilling Ct. NW3 9 F3
Gillingham St. SW1 24 C5
Gillman Dr. E15 13 C5
Gilmore Rd. SE13 41 A2
Gilpin Rd. E5 12 C1
Gilstead Rd. SW6 30 C5
Gilston Rd. SW10 30 D1
Giltspur St. EC1 44 C1
Gipsy La. SW15 36 C1
Giraud St. E14 19 F5
Girdlers Rd. W14 22 F5
Girdwood Rd. SW18 36 G5
Gironde Rd. SW6 30 A3
Gladding Rd. E12 13 G1
Glade, The SE7 34 F3
Gladiator St. SE23 40 C5
Gladstone Ave. E12 14 A4
Gladstone Pk. Gdns. NW2 8 D1
Gladstone St. SE1 25 A4
Gladstone Ter. SW8 31 B4
Gladwyn Rd. SW15 36 F1
Gladys Rd. NW6 9 B4
Glamis Pl. E1 26 A1
Glamis Rd. E1 26 A1
Glanville Rd. SW2 38 E3
Glasbrook Rd. SE9 41 G5
Glasgow Ho. W9 16 C1
Glasgow Rd. E13 20 E1
Glasgow Ter. SW1 31 C1
Glass Yd. SE18 28 C4
Glasshill St. SE1 25 A3
Glasshouse All. EC4 44 A2
Glasshouse Flds. E1 26 B1
Glasshouse St. W1 43 B4
Glasshouse Wk. SE11 31 E1
Glastonbury St. NW6 9 A2
Glaucus St. E3 19 F4
Glazbury Rd. W14 22 G5
Glebe, The SE3 41 B1
Glebe Pl. SW3 30 F2
Glebe Rd. NW10 8 B3
Glebe Rd. SW13 29 C5
Glebe St. W4 29 A1
Gledhow Gdns. SW5 23 D5
Gledstanes Rd. W14 29 G1
Glegg Pl. SW15 36 F2
Glen Rd. E13 20 F3
Glenaffric Ave. E14 27 A5
Glenalvon Way SE18 28 A5
Glenarm Rd. E5 12 A2
Glenavon Rd. E15 13 B4
Glenbrook Rd. NW6 9 B2
Glencairne Clo. E16 20 G4
Glendall St. SW9 38 F2
Glendarvon St. SW15 36 F1
Glendower Pl. SW7 23 E5
Glendun Rd. W3 22 A1
Glenelg Rd. SW2 38 E3
Glenesk Rd. SE9 42 C1
Glenfinlas Way SE5 32 A3
Glenforth St. SE10 34 C1
Glengall Causeway E14 26 E4
Glengall Gro. E14 26 G4
Glengall Rd. NW6 9 A5
Glengall Rd. SE15 32 E1
Glengall Ter. SE15 32 E2
Glengarnock Ave. E14 26 G5
Glengarry Rd. SE22 39 D3
Glenhouse Rd. SE9 42 C3
Glenhurst Ave. NW5 10 A1
Glenilla Rd. NW3 9 F3
Glenister Rd. SE10 34 C1
Glenister St. E16 28 C2
Glenlea Rd. SE9 42 C3
Glenloch Rd. NW3 9 F3
Glenluce Rd. SE3 34 D2
Glenlyon Rd. SE9 42 C3
Glenmore Rd. NW3 9 F3
Glenny Rd., Bark. 14 E3
Glenparke Rd. E7 13 E3
Glenrosa St. SW6 30 D5
Glenroy St. W12 15 E5
Glensdale Rd. SE4 40 D1
Glenshiel Rd. SE9 42 C3
Glentham Rd. SW13 29 C2

Glenthorne Rd. W6 22 D5
Glenton Rd. SE13 41 B2
Glentworth St. NW1 16 G3
Glenure Rd. SE9 42 C3
Glenville Gro. SE8 33 D3
Glenville Ms. SW18 37 C5
Glenworth Ave. E14 27 A5
Gliddon Rd. W14 22 G5
Globe Pond Rd. SE16 26 C2
Globe Rd. E1 19 B3
Globe Rd. E2 19 A2
Globe Rd. E15 13 C2
Globe St. SE1 25 C3
Gloucester Ave. NW1 10 A4
Gloucester Circ. SE10 33 G3
Gloucester Ct. EC3 44 J4
Gloucester Cres. NW1 10 B5
Gloucester Gate NW1 17 B1
Gloucester Gro. Est. SE15 32 D2
Gloucester Ho. NW6 16 B1
Gloucester Ms. W2 16 D5
Gloucester Pl. NW1 16 G3
Gloucester Pl. W1 16 G4
Gloucester Rd. SW7 23 D4
Gloucester Sq. W2 16 E5
Gloucester St. SW1 31 C1
Gloucester Ter. W2 16 C5
Gloucester Wk. W8 23 B3
Gloucester Way EC1 17 G2
Glycena Rd. SW11 37 G1
Glyn Rd. E5 12 B1
Glynde St. SE4 40 D4
Glyndon Rd. SE18 28 E5
Glynfield Rd. NW10 8 A4
Godalming Rd. E14 19 F4
Godbold Rd. E15 20 B2
Godfrey Hill SE18 28 A5
Godfrey Rd. SE18 28 B5
Godfrey St. E15 19 G1
Godfrey St. SW3 30 F1
Goding St. SE11 31 E1
Godliman St. EC4 44 D2
Godman Rd. SE15 32 G5
Godolphin Rd. W12 22 D2
Godwin Rd. E7 13 E1
Goffers Rd. SE3 34 B5
Golborne Rd. W10 15 G4
Golden La. EC1 18 B3
Golden Sq. W1 43 B3
Goldfinch Rd. SE28 28 F4
Goldhawk Rd. W6 22 B5
Goldhawk Rd. W12 22 C4
Goldhurst Ter. NW6 9 C4
Golding St. E1 18 F5
Goldington Cres. NW1 17 D1
Goldington Cres. Gdns. NW1 17 D1
Goldington St. NW1 17 D1
Goldman Clo. E2 18 F3
Goldney Rd. W9 16 B3
Goldsborough Rd. SW8 31 D4
Goldsmith Ave. E12 14 A3
Goldsmith Rd. SE15 32 F4
Goldsmith St. EC2 44 E1
Goldsmith's Row E2 18 F1
Goldsmith's Sq. E2 18 F1
Goldsworthy Gdns. SE16 26 A5
Goldwin Clo. SE14 33 A4
Goldwing Clo. E16 20 D5
Gollogly Ter. SE7 34 F1
Gomm Rd. SE16 26 A4
Gondar Gdns. NW6 9 A2
Gonson Pl. SE8 33 E2
Gonson St. SE8 33 F2
Goodge St. W1 17 C4
Goodhall St. NW10 15 A2
Goodhart Pl. E14 26 C1
Goodinge Clo. N7 10 E3
Goodman's Stile E1 18 F5
Goodmans Yd. E1 25 E1
Goodrich Rd. SE22 39 E4
Goods Way NW1 17 E1
Goodson Rd. NW10 8 A4
Goodway Gdns. E14 20 A5
Goodwin Clo. SE16 25 F4
Goodwin Rd. W12 22 C3
Goodwins Ct. WC2 43 E3
Goodwood Rd. SE14 33 C3
Goosander Way SE28 28 F4
Gooseley La. E6 21 C2
Gophir La. EC4 44 F3
Gopsall St. N1 11 C5
Gordon Ave. SW14 36 A2
Gordon Ct. W12 15 D5
Gordon Gro. SE5 32 A5
Gordon Ho. Rd. NW5 10 A1
Gordon Pl. W8 23 B3
Gordon Rd. E15 12 G1
Gordon Rd. SE15 32 G5
Gordon Rd., Bark. 14 G5
Gordon Rd., Sid. 42 G3
Gordon Sq. WC1 17 D3
Gordon St. WC1 17 D3
Gordonbrock Rd. SE4 40 E3
Gore Rd. E9 12 A5
Gore St. SW7 23 D4
Gorefield Pl. NW6 16 B1
Goring St. EC3 44 J1
Gorleston St. W14 22 G5
Gorman Rd. SE18 28 B5
Gorse Clo. E16 20 D5
Gorst Rd. SW11 37 G4
Gorsuch St. E2 18 E2
Gosfield St. W1 17 C4
Goslett Yd. WC2 43 D2
Gosling Way SW9 31 G4
Gospel Oak Est. NW5 9 G2
Gosset St. E2 18 E2
Gosterwood St. SE8 33 C2
Goswell Rd. EC1 18 A1
Gough Rd. E15 13 C1
Gough Sq. EC4 44 A1
Gough St. WC1 17 F3
Goulston St. E1 18 E5
Goulton Rd. E5 11 G1
Gourock Rd. SE9 42 C3
Govier Clo. E15 13 B4
Gowan Ave. SW6 29 G4
Gowan Rd. NW10 8 D3
Gower Clo. SW4 38 C4
Gower Ms. WC1 17 D4
Gower Pl. WC1 17 C3
Gower Rd. E7 13 D3
Gower St. WC1 17 C3
Gower's Wk. E1 18 F5
Gowlett Rd. SE15 39 F1
Gowrie Rd. SW11 38 A1
Grace St. E3 19 F2
Gracechurch St. EC3 44 G3
Graces Ms. SE5 32 C5
Graces Rd. SE5 32 D5
Grafton Cres. NW1 10 B3
Grafton Pl. NW1 17 D2
Grafton Rd. NW5 10 A2
Grafton Sq. SW4 38 C1
Grafton St. W1 24 B1
Grafton Ter. NW5 9 G2
Grafton Way W1 17 C3
Grafton Way WC1 17 C3
Graham Rd. E8 11 F3
Graham Rd. E13 20 D2
Graham St. N1 18 A1
Graham Ter. SW1 24 A5
Granard Ave. SW15 36 D3
Granard Rd. SW12 37 G5
Granary Rd. E1 18 G3
Granary St. NW1 10 D5
Granby Rd. SE9 35 B5
Granby St. E2 18 E3
Granby Ter. NW1 17 C1
Grand Depot Rd. SE18 35 C1
Grand Union Cres. E8 11 F5
Grand Union Wk. NW1 10 B4
Grandison Rd. SW11 37 G3
Granfield St. SW11 30 E4
Grange, The SE1 25 E4
Grange Ct. WC2 43 H2
Grange Gro. N1 11 B3
Grange Pl. NW6 9 B4
Grange Rd. E13 20 C2
Grange Rd. NW10 8 D3
Grange Rd. SE1 25 D4
Grange Rd. SW13 29 C4
Grange Rd., Ilf. 14 D1
Grange Wk. SE1 25 D4
Grange Yd. SE1 25 E4
Grangehill Rd. SE9 42 B2
Grangewood St. E6 13 G5
Gransden Ave. E8 11 G4
Grant Rd. SW11 37 E2
Grant St. E13 20 D2
Grantbridge St. N1 18 A1
Grantham Rd. E12 14 C1
Grantham Rd. SW9 38 E1
Grantham Rd. W4 29 A3
Grantley St. E1 19 B2
Grantully Rd. W9 16 C2
Granville Ct. N1 11 C5
Granville Gro. SE13 40 G1
Granville Pk. SE13 40 G1
Granville Pl. W1 17 A5
Granville Rd. NW6 16 B1
Granville Rd. SW18 37 A5
Granville Sq. WC1 17 F2
Granville St. WC1 17 F2
Grape St. WC2 43 E1
Grasmere Rd. E13 20 D1
Gratton Rd. W14 22 G4
Gravel Pit La. SE9 42 E3
Gravesend Rd. W12 22 C1
Gray's Inn WC1 17 F4
Gray's Inn Rd. WC1 17 E2
Grayshott Rd. SW11 31 A5
Great Bell All. EC2 44 F1
Great Castle St. W1 17 B5
Great Cen. St. NW1 16 G4
Great Chapel St. W1 43 C1
Great Ch. La. W6 29 F1
Great College St. SW1 24 E4
Great Cross Ave. SE10 34 B3
Great Cumberland Pl. W1 16 G5
Great Dover St. SE1 25 C3
Great Eastern Rd. E15 13 A4
Great Eastern St. EC2 18 D2
Great George St. SW1 24 D3
Great Guildford St. SE1 44 D5
Great James St. WC1 17 F4
Great Marlborough St. W1 43 A2
Great Maze Pond SE1 25 C2
Great New St. EC4 44 A1
Great Newport St. WC2 43 D3
Great Ormond St. WC1 17 E4
Great Percy St. WC1 17 F2
Great Peter St. SW1 24 D4
Great Portland St. W1 17 B3
Great Pulteney St. W1 43 B3
Great Queen St. WC2 43
Great Russell St. WC1 43
Great St. Helens EC3 44
Great St. Thomas Apostle EC4 44
Great Scotland Yd. SW1 43
Great Smith St. SW1 24
Great Spilmans SE22 39
Great Suffolk St. SE1 44
Great Sutton St. EC1 18
Great Swan All. EC2 44
Great Titchfield St. W1 17
Great Twr. St. EC3 44
Great Trinity La. EC4 44
Great W. Rd. W6 29
Great Western Rd. W9 16
Great Western Rd. W11 16
Great Winchester St. EC2 44
Great Windmill St. W1 43
Greatfield Ave. E6 21
Greatfield Clo. SE4 40
Greatfields Rd., Bark. 14
Greatorex St. E1 18
Greek Ct. W1 43
Greek St. W1 43
Greek Yd. WC2 43
Green, The E15 13
Green, The W3 15
Green, The, Well. 42
Green Arbour Ct. EC1 44
Green Bank E1 25
Green Dale SE22 39
Green Dragon Ct. SE1 44
Green Hill Ter. SE18 35
Green Hundred Rd. SE15 32
Green Pt. E15 13
Green Shield Ind. Est. E16 27
Green St. E7 13
Green St. E13 13
Green St. W1 23
Green Way SE9 41
Greenacres SE9 42
Greenaway Gdns. NW3 9
Greenbay Rd. SE7 34
Greenberry St. NW8 16
Greencoat Pl. SW1 24
Greencroft Gdns. NW6 9
Greenend Rd. W4 22
Greenfell St. SE10 27
Greenfield Rd. E1 18
Greengate St. E13 20
Greenham Clo. SE1 24
Greenhill SE18 35
Greenhill Gro. E12 14
Greenhill Pk. NW10 8
Greenhill Rd. NW10 8
Greenhithe Clo., Sid. 42
Greenholm Rd. SE9 42
Greenland Quay SE16 26
Greenland Rd. NW1 10
Greenlaw St. SE18 28
Greenman St. N1 11
Green's Ct. W1 43
Green's End SE18 28
Greenside Rd. W12 22
Greenslade Rd., Bark. 14
Greenstead Gdns. SW15 36
Greenvale Rd. SE9 42

enwell St. W1 17 B3
enwich Ch. St. 33 G2
E10
enwich High Rd. 33 F4
E10
enwich Ind. Est. 27 E5
E7
enwich Mkt. SE10 33 G2
enwich Pk. SE10 34 A3
enwich Pk. St. 34 A1
E10
enwich S. St. 33 F4
E10
enwich Vw. Pl. 26 F4
14
enwood Rd. E8 11 F3
et St. SE1 44 A6
gor Ms. SE3 34 D3
gory Cres. SE9 41 G5
gory Pl. W8 23 C3
nada Rd. SE7 34 F3
nade St. E14 26 D1
nadier St. E16 28 C2
ndon St. NW8 16 F3
nfell Rd. W11 22 F1
nfell Twr. W11 22 F1
nville Ms. SW7 23 D5
nville Pl. SW7 23 D4
nville St. WC1 17 E3
sham Rd. E6 21 B1
sham Rd. E16 20 E5
sham Rd. SW9 38 G1
sham St. EC2 44 E1
sse St. W1 43 C1
ssenhall Rd. 37 A4
W18
swell St. SW6 29 F4
ville Hall NW6 16 C1
ville Pl. NW6 16 C1
ville Rd. NW6 16 C1
ville St. EC1 17 G4
y Eagle St. E1 18 E4
ycoat Pl. SW1 24 D4
ycoat St. SW1 24 D4
yfriars Pas. EC1 44 C1
yhound Rd. NW10 15 D2
yhound Rd. W6 29 F2
yhound Rd. W14 29 G2
ystead Rd. SE23 40 A5
ystoke Pl. EC4 43 J1
erson Rd. SE23 40 B5
fin Clo. NW10 8 D2
ffin Manorway 28 F4
SE28
ffin Rd. SE18 35 F1
mston Rd. SW6 30 A5
mwade Clo. SE15 40 A1
nling Pl. SE8 33 E2
nstead Rd. SE8 33 C1
tleton Rd. W9 16 B3
cer's Hall Ct. EC2 44 F2
om Cres. SW18 37 E5
om Pl. SW1 24 A4
ombridge Rd. E9 12 B4
sse Way SW15 36 D4
svenor Ave. N5 11 B2
svenor Ave. 36 A1
SW14
svenor Cres. SW1 24 A3
svenor Cres. Ms. 24 A3
SW1
svenor Est. SW1 24 D5
svenor Gdns. E6 20 G2
svenor Gdns. 8 E2
NW2
svenor Gdns. 24 B4
SW1
svenor Gdns. 36 A1
SW14
svenor Hill W1 24 B1

Grosvenor Pk. SE5 32 B3
Grosvenor Pl. SW1 24 A3
Grosvenor Rd. E6 13 G5
Grosvenor Rd. E7 13 E3
Grosvenor Rd. SW1 31 B2
Grosvenor Sq. W1 24 A1
Grosvenor St. W1 24 B1
Grosvenor Ter. SE5 32 B2
Grosvenor Wf. Rd. 27 A5
E14
Grote's Bldgs. SE3 34 B5
Grote's Pl. SE3 34 B5
Grove, The E15 13 B3
Grove Cotts. SW3 30 F2
Grove Ct. SE3 34 D4
Grove Cres. SE5 32 D5
Grove Cres. Rd. E15 13 A3
Grove End Rd. NW8 16 E1
Grove Gdns. E15 13 B3
Grove Hill Rd. SE5 39 D1
Grove La. SE5 32 D5
Grove Mkt. Pl. SE9 42 B4
Grove Ms. W6 22 E4
Grove Pk. SE5 32 D5
Grove Rd. E3 12 B5
Grove Rd. NW2 8 E3
Grove Rd. SW13 29 B5
Grove St. SE8 26 D5
Grove Vale SE22 39 D2
Grove Vill. E14 26 F1
Groveland Ct. EC4 44 E2
Grovelands Clo. SE5 32 D5
Groveway SW9 31 F4
Grummant Rd. SE15 32 E4
Grundy St. E14 19 F5
Gubyon Ave. SE24 39 A3
Guernsey Gro. SE24 39 B5
Guibal Rd. SE12 41 E5
Guild Rd. SE7 34 G1
Guildford Gro. SE10 33 F4
Guildford Rd. E6 21 B5
Guildford Rd. SW8 31 E4
Guildhall Bldgs. EC2 44 F1
Guildhouse St. SW1 24 C5
Guilford Pl. WC1 17 F3
Guilford St. WC1 17 E3
Guilsborough Clo. 8 A4
NW10
Guinness Bldgs. SE1 25 D5
Guinness Clo. E9 12 C4
Guinness Trust 32 A1
Bldgs. SE11
Guinness Trust Est. 39 A2
SW9
Guion Rd. SW6 30 A5
Gulliver St. SE16 26 D4
Gun St. E1 18 E4
Gunmakers La. E3 12 C5
Gunner La. SE18 35 C1
Gunning St. SE18 28 G5
Gunpowder Sq. EC4 44 A1
Gunstor Rd. N16 11 D1
Gunter Gro. SW10 30 D2
Gunterstone Rd. W14 22 G5
Gunthorpe St. E1 18 E4
Gunwhale Clo. SE16 26 B2
Gurdon Rd. SE7 34 D1
Gurney Clo., Bark. 14 D3
Gurney Rd. E15 13 B2
Gutter La. EC2 44 E1
Guy St. SE1 25 C3
Guyscliff Rd. SE13 40 G3
Gwendolen Ave. 36 F2
SW15
Gwendolen Clo. 36 F3
SW15
Gwendoline Ave. E13 13 E5
Gwendwr Rd. W14 29 G1
Gwyn Clo. SW6 30 D3
Gwynne Clo. W4 29 B2

Gwynne Rd. SW11 30 E5
Gylcote Clo. SE5 39 C2

H

Ha-Ha Rd. SE18 35 B2
Haarlem Rd. W14 22 F4
Haberdasher St. N1 18 C2
Hackford Rd. SW9 31 F4
Hackney Rd. E2 18 E2
Hadden Rd. SE28 28 G4
Haddo St. SE10 33 G2
Haddonfield SE8 26 B5
Hadleigh St. E2 19 A2
Hadley St. NW1 10 B3
Hadrian St. SE10 34 B1
Hadyn Pk. Rd. W12 22 C3
Hafer Rd. SW11 37 G2
Haggerston Rd. E8 11 E4
Haig Rd. E. E13 20 F2
Haig Rd. W. E13 20 F2
Haimo Rd. SE9 41 G3
Hainford Clo. SE4 40 B2
Hainton Clo. E1 18 G5
Halcomb St. N1 11 D5
Haldane Rd. E6 20 G2
Haldane Rd. SW6 30 A3
Haldon Rd. SW18 37 A3
Hale Rd. E6 21 A3
Hale St. E14 26 F1
Halesworth Rd. SE13 40 F1
Half Moon Cres. N1 17 F1
Half Moon La. SE24 39 B4
Half Moon St. W1 24 B2
Halford Rd. SW6 30 B2
Halfway St., Sid. 42 F5
Halkin Pl. SW1 24 A4
Halkin St. SW1 24 A3
Hall, The SE3 41 D1
Hall Pl. W2 16 E3
Hall Rd. E6 14 B5
Hall Rd. E15 13 A1
Hall Rd. NW8 16 D2
Hall St. EC1 18 A2
Hallam Rd. SW13 36 D1
Hallam St. W1 17 B4
Halley Gdns. SE13 41 A2
Halley Rd. E7 13 F3
Halley Rd. E12 13 G3
Halley St. E14 19 C4
Halliford St. N1 11 B4
Halliwell Rd. SW2 38 F4
Hallsville Rd. E16 20 C5
Hallywell Cres. E6 21 B4
Halons Rd. SE9 42 C5
Halsbrook Rd. SE3 41 F1
Halsbury Rd. W12 22 C2
Halsey St. SW3 23 G5
Halsmere Rd. SE5 32 A4
Halston Clo. SW11 37 G4
Halstow Rd. NW10 15 F2
Halstow Rd. SE10 34 D1
Halton Rd. N1 11 A4
Ham Pk. Rd. E7 13 D4
Ham Pk. Rd. E15 13 C4
Ham Yd. W1 43 C3
Hambalt Rd. SW4 38 C3
Hamble St. SW6 37 C1
Hambledon Rd. SW18 37 A5
Hambledown Rd., 42 F5
Sid.
Hambridge Way SW2 38 G5
Hameway E6 21 C3
Hamfrith Rd. E15 13 C3
Hamilton Clo. NW8 16 E2
Hamilton Gdns. NW8 16 D2
Hamilton Pk. N5 11 A1
Hamilton Pk. W. N5 11 A1
Hamilton Pl. W1 24 A2
Hamilton Rd. E15 20 B2
Hamilton Rd. NW10 8 C2

Hamilton Rd. W4 22 A3
Hamilton Rd., Ilf. 14 D1
Hamilton Ter. NW8 16 C1
Hamlea Clo. SE12 41 D3
Hamlet, The SE5 39 C1
Hamlet Gdns. W6 22 C5
Hamlets Way E3 19 D3
Hammersmith Bri. 29 D1
SW13
Hammersmith Bri. 29 E1
Rd. W6
Hammersmith Bdy. 22 E5
W6
Hammersmith 29 E1
Flyover W6
Hammersmith Gro. 22 E3
W6
Hammersmith Rd. W6 22 F5
Hammersmith Rd. 22 F5
W14
Hammersmith Ter. 29 C1
W6
Hammond St. NW5 10 C3
Hampson Way SW8 31 F4
Hampstead Grn. NW3 9 F2
Hampstead High St. 9 D1
NW3
Hampstead Hill 9 E1
Gdns. NW3
Hampstead Rd. NW1 17 C1
Hampton Clo. NW6 16 B2
Hampton Rd. E7 13 E2
Hampton Rd., Ilf. 14 D1
Hampton St. SE1 25 B5
Hampton St. SE17 25 A5
Hanameel St. E16 27 E2
Hanbury St. E1 18 E4
Hancock Rd. E3 19 G2
Handel St. WC1 17 E3
Handen Rd. SE12 41 B3
Handforth Rd. SW9 31 G3
Handley Rd. E9 12 A5
Hankey Pl. SE1 25 C3
Hannell Rd. SW6 29 G3
Hannibal Rd. E1 19 A4
Hannington Rd. SW4 38 B1
Hanover Gdns. SE11 31 G2
Hanover Gate NW1 16 F2
Hanover Pk. SE15 32 F4
Hanover Pl. WC2 43 F2
Hanover Rd. NW10 8 E4
Hanover Sq. W1 17 B5
Hanover St. W1 17 B5
Hanover Ter. NW1 16 F2
Hans Cres. SW1 23 G4
Hans Pl. SW1 23 G4
Hans Rd. SW3 23 G4
Hansler Rd. SE22 39 E3
Hanson Clo. SW12 38 B5
Hanson St. W1 17 C4
Hanway Pl. W1 43 C1
Hanway St. W1 43 C1
Harben Rd. NW6 9 D4
Harberson Rd. E15 13 C5
Harbet Rd. W2 16 E4
Harbinger Rd. E14 26 F5
Harbledown Rd. SW6 30 B4
Harbord St. SW6 29 F4
Harborough Ave., 42 G5
Sid.
Harbour Ave. SW10 30 D4
Harbour Ex. Sq. E14 26 F3
Harbour Rd. SE5 39 B1
Harbridge Ave. SW15 36 B5
Harbut Rd. SW11 37 E2
Harcourt Ave. E12 14 B1
Harcourt Rd. E15 20 C1
Harcourt Rd. SE4 40 C2
Harcourt St. W1 16 F4
Harcourt Ter. SW10 30 C1

Hardens Manorway SE7 27 G4
Harders Rd. SE15 32 G5
Hardinge Rd. NW10 8 D5
Hardinge St. E1 19 A5
Hardman Rd. SE7 34 E1
Hardwick St. EC1 17 G2
Hardwicke St., Bark. 14 E5
Hardy Rd. SE3 34 C2
Hare & Billet Rd. SE3 34 A4
Hare Ct. EC4 43 J2
Hare Pl. EC4 44 A2
Hare Row E2 18 G1
Hare St. SE18 28 C4
Hare Wk. N1 18 D1
Harebell Dr. E6 21 C4
Harecourt Rd. N1 11 B3
Haredale Rd. SE24 39 B2
Haredon Clo. SE23 40 A5
Harefield Ms. SE4 40 D1
Harefield Rd. SE4 40 D1
Harewood Ave. NW1 16 F3
Harfield Gdns. SE5 39 D1
Harford St. E1 19 C3
Hargood Rd. SE3 34 F4
Hargwyne St. SW9 38 F1
Harlescott Rd. SE15 40 B2
Harlesden Gdns. NW10 8 B5
Harlesden La. NW10 8 C5
Harlesden Rd. NW10 8 C5
Harley Gdns. SW10 30 D1
Harley Gro. E3 19 D2
Harley Pl. W1 17 B4
Harley Rd. NW3 9 E4
Harley Rd. NW10 15 A1
Harley St. W1 17 B4
Harleyford Rd. SE11 31 F2
Harleyford St. SE11 31 G2
Harmood St. NW1 10 B3
Harmsworth St. SE17 32 A1
Harold Est. SE1 25 D4
Harold Rd. E13 13 E5
Harp All. EC4 44 B1
Harp La. EC3 44 H4
Harper Rd. E6 21 B5
Harper Rd. SE1 25 B4
Harpley Sq. E1 19 A2
Harpour Rd., Bark. 14 E3
Harpsden St. SW11 31 A4
Harpur St. WC1 17 F4
Harraden Rd. SE3 34 F4
Harrap St. E14 26 G1
Harrier Ms. SE28 28 F4
Harrier Way E6 21 B4
Harriet Clo. E8 11 F5
Harriet Wk. SW1 23 G3
Harrington Gdns. SW7 23 D5
Harrington Rd. SW7 23 E5
Harrington Sq. NW1 17 C1
Harrington St. NW1 17 C2
Harrington Way SE18 27 G4
Harriott Clo. SE10 27 C5
Harris St. SE5 32 C3
Harrison St. WC1 17 E2
Harrow La. E14 26 G1
Harrow Pl. E1 18 D5
Harrow Rd. E6 14 A5
Harrow Rd. NW10 15 D2
Harrow Rd. W2 15 F2
Harrow Rd. W9 15 F2
Harrow Rd. W10 15 F2
Harrow Rd., Bark. 14 G5
Harrow Rd., Ilf. 14 E1
Harroway Rd. SW11 30 E5
Harrowby St. W1 16 F5
Harrowgate Rd. E9 12 C3
Hart St. EC3 44 J3
Hartfield Ter. E3 19 E1
Hartham Clo. N7 10 E2
Hartham Rd. N7 10 E2
Hartington Rd. E16 20 E5
Hartington Rd. SW8 31 E4
Hartismere Rd. SW6 30 A3
Hartlake Rd. E9 12 B3
Hartland Rd. E15 13 C4
Hartland Rd. NW1 10 B4
Hartland Rd. NW6 16 A1
Hartley Ave. E6 14 A5
Hartley St. E2 19 A2
Hartmann Rd. E16 27 G2
Harton St. SE8 33 E4
Harts La. SE14 33 C3
Harts La., Bark. 14 D3
Hartshorn All. EC3 44 J2
Hartshorn Gdns. E6 21 C3
Hartswood Rd. W12 22 B3
Hartsworth Clo. E13 20 C1
Hartville Rd. SE18 28 G5
Harvard Rd. SE13 40 G3
Harvey Gdns. SE7 34 F1
Harvey Rd. SE5 32 C4
Harvey Rd., Ilf. 14 D2
Harvey St. N1 11 C5
Harvist Est. N7 10 G1
Harvist Rd. NW6 15 F1
Harwich La. EC2 18 D4
Harwood Rd. SW6 30 B3
Harwood Ter. SW6 30 C4
Hascombe Ter. SE5 32 C5
Haselrigge Rd. SW4 38 D2
Hasker St. SW3 23 F5
Haslam Clo. N1 10 G4
Hassendean Rd. SE3 34 E2
Hassett Rd. E9 12 B3
Hassop Rd. NW2 8 F1
Hasted Rd. SE7 34 G1
Hastings Clo. SE15 32 F3
Hastings St. WC1 17 E2
Hatcham Pk. Rd. SE14 33 B4
Hatcham Rd. SE15 33 A2
Hatcliffe Clo. SE3 41 C1
Hatfield Rd. E15 13 B2
Hatfields SE1 44 A5
Hathaway Cres. E12 14 B3
Hatherley Gdns. E6 20 G1
Hatherley Gro. W2 16 C5
Hathorne Clo. SE15 32 G5
Hatton Clo. SE18 35 F3
Hatton Gdn. EC1 17 G3
Hatton Pl. EC1 17 G3
Hatton Wall EC1 17 G4
Havannah St. E14 26 E3
Havelock St. N1 10 E5
Havelock Ter. SW8 31 B3
Haverfield Rd. E3 19 C2
Haverstock Hill NW3 9 G3
Haverstock Rd. NW5 10 A2
Haverstock St. N1 18 A1
Havil St. SE5 32 D3
Hawarden Gro. SE24 39 B5
Hawes St. N1 11 A4
Hawgood St. E3 19 E4
Hawkesbury Rd. SW15 36 D3
Hawkshead Rd. NW10 8 B4
Hawkshead Rd. W4 22 A3
Hawkslade Rd. SE15 40 B3
Hawksmoor Clo. SE18 35 G1
Hawksmoor St. W6 29 F2
Hawkstone Rd. SE16 26 A5
Hawley Cres. NW1 10 B4
Hawley Rd. NW1 10 B4
Hawley St. NW1 10 B4
Hawstead Rd. SE6 40 F4
Hawthorn Rd. NW10 8 C4
Hawthorne Clo. N1 11 D3
Hawtrey Rd. NW3 9 F4
Hay Clo. E15 13 B4
Hay Currie St. E14 19 F5
Hay Hill W1 24 B1
Hay St. E2 11 F5
Haycroft Gdns. NW10 8 C5
Haycroft Rd. SW2 38 E3
Hayday Rd. E16 20 D4
Hayles St. SE11 25 A5
Haymarket SW1 43 C4
Haymarket Arc. SW1 43 C4
Haymerle Rd. SE15 32 F2
Haynes Clo. SE3 41 B1
Hay's La. SE1 44 H6
Hay's Ms. W1 24 B2
Hayter Rd. SW2 38 E3
Hayward Gdns. SW15 36 E4
Hazel Rd. NW10 15 D2
Hazelbourne Rd. SW12 38 B4
Hazeldon Rd. SE4 40 C3
Hazelmere Rd. NW6 9 A5
Hazlebury Rd. SW6 30 C5
Hazlewell Rd. SW15 36 D3
Hazlewood Cres. W10 15 G3
Hazlitt Rd. W14 22 G4
Head St. E1 19 B5
Headfort Pl. SW1 24 A3
Headlam Rd. SW4 38 D4
Headlam St. E1 18 G3
Heald St. SE14 33 D4
Healey St. NW1 10 B3
Hearn St. EC2 18 D3
Heath Dr. NW3 9 C1
Heath Hurst Rd. NW3 9 F1
Heath La. SE3 34 A5
Heath Ri. SW15 36 F4
Heath Rd. SW8 31 B5
Heath Side NW3 9 E1
Heathcote St. WC1 17 F3
Heather Clo. E6 21 D5
Heather Clo. SW8 38 B1
Heatherbank SE9 35 B5
Heathfield Clo. E16 20 G4
Heathfield Pk. NW2 8 E3
Heathfield Rd. SW18 37 D4
Heathfield Sq. SW18 37 E5
Heathfield Ter. SE18 35 G2
Heathlee Rd. SE3 41 C2
Heathmans Rd. SW6 30 A4
Heathstan Rd. W12 15 C5
Heathview Gdns. SW15 36 E5
Heathwall St. SW11 37 G1
Heathway SE3 34 D3
Heathwood Gdns. SE7 28 A5
Heaton Rd. SE15 39 F1
Heavitree Clo. SE18 35 F1
Heavitree Rd. SE18 35 F1
Heber Rd. NW2 8 F2
Heber Rd. SE22 39 E4
Hebron Rd. W6 22 D4
Hector St. SE18 28 G5
Heddington Gro. N7 10 F2
Heddon St. W1 43 A3
Hedgers Gro. E9 12 C3
Hedgley St. SE12 41 C3
Heigham Rd. E6 14 A4
Heights, The SE7 34 F1
Heiron St. SE17 32 A2
Helby Rd. SW4 38 D4
Helder Gro. SE12 41 C5
Helena Rd. E13 20 C1
Helena Rd. NW10 8 D2
Helix Rd. SW2 38 F4
Helmet Row EC1 18 B3
Helmsley Pl. E8 11 G4
Hemans St. SW8 31 D3
Hemberton Rd. SW9 38 E1
Hemingford Rd. N1 10 F5
Hemlock Rd. W12 22 B1
Hemming St. E1 18 F3
Hemstal Rd. NW6 9
Hemsworth St. N1 18
Henchman St. W12 15
Henderson Rd. E7 13
Henderson Rd. SW18 37
Hendrick Ave. SW12 37
Heneage La. EC3 44
Heneage St. E1 18
Hengist Rd. SE12 41
Hengrave Rd. SE23 40
Henley Dr. SE1 25
Henley Rd. E16 28
Henley Rd. NW10 8
Henley Rd., Ilf. 14
Henley St. SW11 31
Henniker Gdns. E6 20
Henniker Pt. E15 13
Henniker Rd. E15 13
Henning St. SW11 30
Henrietta Pl. W1 17
Henrietta St. E15 12
Henrietta St. WC2 43
Henriques St. E1 18
Henry Dickens Ct. W11 22
Henry Jackson Rd. SW15 36
Henry Rd. E6 21
Henryson Rd. SE4 40
Henshall St. N1 11
Henshaw St. SE17 25
Henslowe Rd. SE22 39
Henson Ave. NW2 8
Henstridge Pl. NW8 16
Henty Clo. SW11 30
Henty Wk. SW15 36
Henwick Rd. SE9 41
Hepscott Rd. E9 12
Herbal Hill EC1 17
Herbert Gdns. NW10 8
Herbert Rd. E12 14
Herbert Rd. SE18 35
Herbert St. E13 20
Herbert St. NW5 10
Herbrand St. WC1 17
Hercules Rd. SE1 24
Hereford Ho. NW6 16
Hereford Pl. SE14 33
Hereford Rd. W2 16
Hereford Sq. SW7 23
Hereford St. E2 18
Hermit Rd. E16 20
Hermit St. EC1 18
Hermitage, The SW13 29
Hermitage Row E8 11
Hermitage Wall E1 25
Herndon Rd. SW18 37
Herne Hill SE24 39
Herne Hill Rd. SE24 39
Herne Pl. SE24 39
Heron Clo. NW10 8
Heron Pl. SE16 26
Heron Quay E14 26
Heron Rd. SE24 39
Herrick St. SW1 24
Herries St. W10 15
Herringham Rd. SE7 27
Hersant Clo. NW10 8
Herschell Rd. SE23 40
Hersham Clo. SW15 36
Hertford Rd. N1 11
Hertford Rd., Bark. 14
Hertford St. W1 24
Hertsmere Rd. E14 26
Hervey Rd. SE3 34
Hesketh Pl. W11 22
Hesper Ms. SW5 30
Hesperus Cres. E14 26
Hessel St. E1 18

ster Rd. SW11	30	F3
stercombe Ave.	29	G5
SW6		
ston St. SE14	33	E4
herington Rd.	38	E2
SW4		
tley Rd. W12	22	D2
velius Clo. SE10	34	C1
verham Rd. SE18	28	G5
wer St. W10	15	F4
wison St. E3	19	D1
wlett Rd. E3	19	C1
yford Ave. SW8	31	E3
ygate St. SE17	25	B5
yworth Rd. E15	11	G1
yworth Rd. E15	13	C1
hisson Rd. SE15	40	A3
kin Clo. SE7	27	G5
kling Rd., Ilf.	14	D2
kman Clo. E16	20	G4
kmore Wk. SW4	38	C1
ks Clo. SW11	37	F1
ks St. SE8	33	C1
e Pl. SW1	24	D5
h Gro. SE18	35	F3
h Holborn WC1	**43**	**E1**
h Rd. (Willesden)	8	B3
NW10		
h Rd. Leyton E15	12	G1
h Rd.	13	B1
Leytonstone E11		
h St.	13	B1
Leytonstone E15		
h St. E13	20	D1
h St. E15	19	G1
h St. (Harlesden)	15	B1
NW10		
h St. SW6	36	G1
h St. N. E6	14	A4
h St. N. E6	14	B4
h St. S. E6	21	B1
h Timber St. EC4	**44**	**D3**
hbridge SE10	34	A1
hbridge Rd., Bark.	14	D5
hbrook Rd. SE3	41	G1
hbury Cor. N5	11	A2
hbury Cres. N5	11	A2
hbury Gra. N5	11	B1
hbury Gro. N5	11	A3
hbury New Pk. N5	11	B2
hbury Pk. N5	11	A1
hbury Pl. N1	11	A3
hbury Sta. Rd. N1	10	G3
hbury Ter. N5	11	A2
hbury Ter. Ms. N5	11	A2
hcliffe Dr. SW15	36	E5
hcombe SE7	34	E2
hdown Rd. SW15	36	D4
hgate Rd. NW5	10	B1
hlands Heath	36	E5
SW15		
hlever Rd. W10	15	E4
hmere Rd. SE3	34	B3
hshore Rd. SE15	32	E5
hway, The E1	25	F1
hway, The E14	26	B1
ary Clo. SW6	30	C3
ary Rd. W12	15	B5
da Rd. E6	13	G4
da Rd. E6	20	B3
da Ter. SW9	31	G5
dyard Rd. SW6	30	B2
ey Rd. NW10	15	E2
grove Rd. NW6	9	D4
Fm. Rd. W10	15	E4
Rd. NW8	16	D1
St. W1	24	A1
Vw. Dr., Well.	35	G5

Hillbeck Clo. SE15	33	A3
Hillcourt Rd. SE22	39	G4
Hillcroft Rd. E6	21	D4
Hilldrop Cres. N7	10	D2
Hilldrop Est. N7	10	D2
Hilldrop La. N7	10	D2
Hilldrop Rd. N7	10	D2
Hillend SE18	35	D4
Hillersdon Ave. SW13	29	C1
Hillfield Clo. NW3	9	F2
Hillfield Rd. NW6	9	A2
Hillgate Pl. SW12	38	B5
Hillgate Pl. W8	23	B2
Hillgate St. W8	23	B2
Hillier Rd. SW11	37	G4
Hillingdon St. SE5	32	A2
Hillingdon St. SE17	32	A2
Hillman Dr. W10	15	E3
Hillman St. E8	11	G3
Hillmarton Rd. N7	10	E2
Hillmead Dr. SW9	39	A2
Hillreach SE18	35	B1
Hills Pl. W1	**43**	**A2**
Hillsborough Rd.	39	D3
SE22		
Hillside Clo. NW8	16	C1
Hillsleigh Rd. W8	23	A2
Hilltop Rd. NW6	9	B4
Hillworth Rd. SW2	38	G5
Hilly Flds. Cres. SE4	40	E1
Hillyard St. SW9	31	G4
Hilsea St. E5	12	A1
Hinckley Rd. SE15	39	F2
Hind Ct. EC4	**44**	**A2**
Hind Gro. E14	19	E5
Hinde St. W1	17	A4
Hindmans Rd. SE22	39	F3
Hindrey Rd. E5	11	G2
Hinstock Rd. SE18	35	E2
Hinton Rd. SE24	39	A1
Hippodrome Pl. W11	22	G1
Hiroshima Wk. SE7	27	E4
Hitchin Sq. E3	19	A1
Hither Grn. La. SE13	40	G3
Hobart Pl. SW1	24	B4
Hobbes Wk. SW15	36	B3
Hobday St. E14	19	F4
Hobury St. SW10	30	D2
Hockett Clo. SE8	26	C5
Hockley Ave. E6	21	A1
Hocroft Rd. NW2	9	A3
Hofland Rd. W14	22	F4
Hogarth Clo. E16	20	G4
Hogarth Ct. EC3	**44**	**J3**
Hogarth La. W4	29	A2
Hogarth Rd. SW5	23	C5
Hogarth Roundabout	29	A2
W4		
Holbeach Gdns., Sid.	42	G4
Holbeach Rd. SE6	40	F5
Holbeck Row SE15	32	F3
Holbein Ms. SW1	31	A1
Holbein Pl. SW1	24	A5
Holberton Gdns.	15	D2
NW10		
Holborn EC1	17	G4
Holborn Rd. E13	20	E3
Holborn Viaduct EC1	17	G4
Holbrook Rd. E15	20	E1
Holburne Clo. SE3	34	F4
Holburne Gdns. SE3	34	G4
Holburne Rd. SE3	34	F4
Holcombe St. W6	29	D1
Holcroft Rd. E9	12	A4
Holden St. SW11	31	A5
Holdenby Rd. SE4	40	C3
Holford St. WC1	17	G2
Holgate Ave. SW11	37	E1
Holland Gdns. W14	22	G4
Holland Gro. SW9	31	G3

Holland Pk. W8	23	A3
Holland Pk. W11	22	G2
Holland Pk. Ave. W11	22	G2
Holland Pk. Gdns.	22	G3
W14		
Holland Pk. Ms. W11	23	A2
Holland Pk. Rd. W14	23	A4
Holland Rd. E6	14	B5
Holland Rd. E15	20	B2
Holland Rd. NW10	8	C5
Holland Rd. W14	22	F3
Holland St. SE1	**44**	**C5**
Holland St. W8	23	B3
Holland Vill. Rd. W14	22	G3
Holland Wk. W8	23	A3
Hollen St. W1	**43**	**B1**
Holles St. W1	17	B5
Holley Rd. W3	22	A3
Hollingbourne Rd.	39	B3
SE24		
Hollington Rd. E6	21	B2
Holloway Rd. E6	21	B2
Holly Bush Hill NW3	9	D1
Holly Clo. NW10	8	A4
Holly Gro. SE15	32	E5
Holly Hedge Ter.	41	A3
SE13		
Holly Hill NW3	9	D1
Holly St. E8	11	E3
Holly Wk. NW3	9	D1
Hollybush Gdns. E2	18	G2
Hollybush St. E13	20	E2
Hollybush Wk. SW9	39	A2
Hollydale Rd. SE15	33	A4
Hollydene SE15	32	G4
Hollymount Clo. SE10	33	G4
Hollywood Rd. SW10	30	D2
Holman Rd. SW11	30	E5
Holmbush Rd. SW15	36	F4
Holmcote Gdns. N5	11	B2
Holmdale Rd. NW6	9	B2
Holmdene Ave. SE24	39	B3
Holme Lacey Rd.	41	C4
SE12		
Holme Rd. E6	14	A5
Holmead Rd. SW6	30	C3
Holmefield Ct. NW3	9	F3
Holmes Rd. NW5	10	B3
Holmes Ter. SE1	24	G3
Holmesley Rd. SE23	40	C4
Holmewood Gdns.	38	F5
SW2		
Holmewood Rd. SW2	38	E5
Holmewood Rd. SW12	38	A4
Holmwood Vill. SE7	34	D1
Holroyd Rd. SW15	36	E2
Holt Rd. E16	28	A2
Holton St. E1	19	B3
Holwood Pl. SW4	38	D1
Holybourne Ave.	36	C5
SW15		
Holyhead Clo. E3	19	E2
Holyport Rd. SW6	29	E3
Holyrood St. SE1	**44**	**H6**
Holywell Clo. SE3	34	D2
Holywell La. EC2	18	D3
Holywell Row EC2	18	C3
Home Rd. SW11	30	F5
Homefield Rd. W4	29	B1
Homeleigh Rd. SE15	40	B1
Homer Dr. E14	26	E5
Homer Rd. E9	12	C3
Homer Row W1	16	F4
Homer St. W1	16	F4
Homerton Gro. E9	12	B2
Homerton High St. E9	12	A2
Homerton Rd. E9	12	C2
Homerton Row E9	12	A2
Homestall Rd. SE22	40	A4

Homestead Rd. SW6	30	A3
Honey La. EC2	**44**	**E2**
Honeybourne Rd.	9	C2
NW6		
Honeybrook Rd.	38	C5
SW12		
Honeyman Clo. NW6	8	F4
Honeywell Rd. SW11	37	F4
Honeywood Rd.	15	B1
NW10		
Honiton Rd. NW6	16	A1
Honley Rd. SE6	40	F5
Honor Oak Pk. SE23	40	B4
Honor Oak Rd. SE23	40	A4
Hood Ct. EC4	**44**	**A2**
Hooper Rd. E16	20	D5
Hooper St. E1	25	F1
Hope St. SW11	37	E1
Hopedale Rd. SE7	34	E2
Hopefield Ave. NW6	15	G1
Hopewell St. SE5	32	C3
Hopkins St. W1	**43**	**B2**
Hopton Gdns. SE1	**44**	**C5**
Hopton St. SE1	**44**	**C5**
Hopwood Rd. SE17	32	C2
Horace Rd. E7	13	E1
Horatio St. E2	18	F1
Horbury Cres. W11	23	B1
Horder Rd. SW6	29	G4
Horizon Way SE7	27	E5
Hormead Rd. W9	16	A3
Horn La. SE10	27	D5
Horn Pk. Clo. SE12	41	E3
Horn Pk. La. SE12	41	E3
Hornby Clo. NW3	9	E4
Horncastle Clo. SE12	41	D5
Horncastle Rd. SE12	41	D5
Horne Way SW15	29	E5
Hornfair Rd. SE7	34	F2
Hornsey St. N7	10	F2
Hornshay St. SE15	33	A2
Hornton St. W8	23	B3
Horsa Rd. SE12	41	F5
Horse and Dolphin	**43**	**D3**
Yd. W1		
Horse Guards Ave.	**43**	**E6**
SW1		
Horse Guards Rd.	**43**	**D6**
SW1		
Horse Leaze E6	21	C5
Horse Ride SW1	**43**	**C6**
Horseferry Pl. SE10	33	G2
Horseferry Rd. E14	26	B1
Horseferry Rd. SW1	24	D5
Horsell Rd. N5	10	G2
Horselydown La. SE1	25	E3
Horsfeld Gdns. SE9	42	A3
Horsfield Rd. SE9	41	G3
Horsford Rd. SW2	38	F3
Horsley St. SE17	32	C2
Horsmonden Rd. SE4	40	D3
Hortensia Rd. SW10	30	D3
Horton Ave. NW2	8	G1
Horton Rd. E8	11	G3
Horton St. SE13	40	F1
Hosier La. EC1	18	A4
Hoskins Clo. E16	20	F5
Hoskins St. SE10	34	A1
Hotham Rd. SW15	36	E1
Hotham St. E15	13	B5
Hotspur St. SE11	31	G1
Houghton St. WC2	**43**	**H2**
Houndsditch EC3	**44**	**J1**
Hoveden Rd. NW2	8	G2
Howard Clo. NW2	9	G1
Howard Rd. E6	21	B1
Howard Rd. N16	11	C1
Howard Rd. NW2	8	F1
Howard Rd., Bark.	14	F5
Howard Rd., Ilf.	14	D1

Howards La.	36 D3	Hyde Pk. Sq. W2	16 F5
Howards Rd. E13	20 D2	Hyde Pk. St. W2	16 F5
Howbury Rd. SE15	40 A1	Hyde Rd. N1	11 D5
Howden St. SE15	39 F1	Hyde Vale SE10	34 A4
Howick Pl. SW1	24 C4	Hyderabad Way E15	13 B4
Howie St. SW11	30 F3	Hyndman St. SE15	32 G2
Howitt Rd. NW3	9 F3	Hythe Rd. NW10	15 C3
Howland St. W1	17 C4		
Howland Way SE16	26 C3	**I**	
Howletts Rd. SE24	39 B4	Ibbotson Ave. E16	20 C5
Howley Pl. W2	16 D4	Iceland Rd. E3	12 E5
Hows St. E2	18 E1	Ida St. E14	19 G5
Howsman Rd. SW13	29 C2	Idmiston Rd. E15	13 C2
Howson Rd. SE4	40 C2	**Idol La. EC3**	**44 H4**
Hoxton Sq. N1	18 D1	Idonia St. SE8	33 E3
Hoxton St. N1	11 D5	Iffley Rd. W6	22 D4
Hoy St. E16	20 C5	Ifield Rd. SW10	30 C2
Hoylake Rd. W3	15 A5	Ilbert St. W10	15 F2
Hubbard St. E15	13 B5	Ilchester Gdns. W2	23 C1
Hubert Gro. SW9	38 E1	Ilchester Pl. W14	23 A4
Hubert Rd. E6	20 G2	Ilderton Rd. SE15	33 A3
Huddart St. E3	19 D4	Ilderton Rd. SE16	32 G1
Huddleston Clo. E2	19 A1	Ilex Rd. NW10	8 B3
Huddlestone Rd. E7	13 C1	Iliffe St. SE17	32 A1
Huddlestone Rd. NW2	8 D3	Ilkley Rd. E16	20 F4
Hudson Pl. SE18	35 E2	Ilminster Gdns. SW11	37 F2
Huggin Ct. EC4	**44 E3**	Imber St. N1	11 C5
Huggin Hill EC4	**44 E3**	Imperial College Rd. SW7	23 E4
Hugh St. SW1	24 B5	Imperial Rd. SW6	30 C4
Hughan Rd. E15	13 A2	Imperial Sq. SW6	30 C4
Hugo Rd. N19	10 C1	Imperial St. E3	19 G2
Hugon Rd. SW6	37 C1	Inca Dr. SE9	42 D5
Huguenot Pl. E1	18 E4	Indescon Ct. E14	26 E3
Huguenot Pl. SW18	37 D3	**India Pl. WC2**	**44 G3**
Hull Clo. SE16	26 B3	India Way W12	22 D1
Hulse Ave., Bark.	14 F3	Indus Rd. SE7	34 D3
Humber Dr. W10	15 F3	Ingal Rd. E13	20 D3
Humber Rd. SE3	34 C2	Ingate Pl. SW8	31 B4
Humberstone Rd. E13	20 F2	Ingelow Rd. SW8	31 B5
Humbolt Rd. W6	29 G2	Ingersoll Rd. W12	22 D2
Humphrey St. SE1	32 E1	**Ingestre Pl. W1**	**43 B2**
Hungerford Bri. SE1	**43 G6**	Ingestre Rd. E7	13 D1
Hungerford Bri. WC2	**43 G6**	Ingestre Rd. NW5	10 B1
Hungerford La. WC2	**43 F5**	Ingham Rd. NW6	9 B1
Hungerford Rd. N7	10 D3	Ingleborough St. SW9	31 G5
Hunsdon Rd. SE14	33 B3	Ingledew Rd. SE18	35 F1
Hunt St. W11	22 F2	Ingleside Gro. SE3	34 C2
Hunter Rd., Ilf.	14 D2	Inglethorpe St. SW6	29 F4
Hunter St. WC1	17 E3	Ingleton St. SW9	31 G5
Huntingdon St. E16	20 C5	Inglewood Clo. E14	26 E5
Huntingdon St. N1	10 F4	Inglewood Rd. NW6	9 B2
Huntingfield Rd. SW15	36 C2	Inglis St. SE5	32 A4
Huntley St. WC1	17 C3	Ingrave St. SW11	37 E1
Hunton St. E1	18 F4	Inigo Jones Rd. SE7	35 A3
Hunt's Clo. SE3	34 D5	**Inigo Pl. WC2**	**43 E3**
Hunt's Ct. WC2	**43 D4**	Inkerman Rd. NW5	10 B3
Hunts La. E15	19 G1	Inman Rd. NW10	15 A1
Huntsman St. SE17	19 D5	Inman Rd. SW18	37 D5
Hurlingham Ct. SW6	37 A1	Inner Circle NW1	17 A2
Hurlingham Gdns. SW6	37 A1	**Inner Temple La. EC4**	**43 J2**
Hurlingham Rd. SW6	30 A5	Innes Gdns. SW15	36 D4
Hurren Clo. SE3	41 B1	Inniskilling Rd. E13	20 F1
Hurry Clo. E15	13 B4	Inverine Rd. SE7	34 E1
Hurst St. SE24	39 A4	Invermore Pl. SE18	28 E5
Hurstbourne Gdns., Bark.	14 G3	Inverness Pl. W2	23 C1
Huson Clo. NW3	9 F4	Inverness Ter. W2	16 C5
Hutchings St. E14	26 E4	Inverness St. NW1	10 B5
Hutton St. EC4	**44 A2**	Inverton Rd. SE15	40 B2
Huxbear St. SE4	40 D3	Invicta Rd. SE3	34 D3
Huxley St. W10	15 G2	Inville Rd. SE17	32 C1
Hyde Pk. SW7	23 F2	Inwen Ct. SE8	33 C5
Hyde Pk. W1	23 F2	Inworth St. SW11	30 F5
Hyde Pk. W2	23 F2	Iona Clo. SE6	41 A5
Hyde Pk. Cor. W1	24 A3	**Ireland Yd. EC4**	**44 C2**
Hyde Pk. Cres. W2	16 F5	Irene Rd. SW6	30 B4
Hyde Pk. Gdns. W2	23 E1	Iris Clo. E6	21 A4
Hyde Pk. Gate SW7	23 D3	Iron Bri. Clo. NW10	8 A2
		Iron Mill Rd. SW18	37 C4
		Ironmonger La. EC2	**44 F2**

Ironmonger Row EC1	18 B2	Jelf Rd. SW2	38
Irving Gro. SW9	31 F5	Jenkins La. E6	21
Irving Rd. W14	22 F4	Jenkins La., Bark.	21
Irving St. WC2	**43 D4**	Jenkins Rd. E13	20
Irwin Ave. SE18	35 G3	Jenner Ho. SE3	34
Irwin Gdns. NW10	8 D5	Jenner Pl. SW13	29
Isabel St. SW9	31 F4	Jennings Rd. SE22	39
Isabella Rd. E9	12 A2	Jephson Rd. E7	13
Isabella St. SE1	**44 B6**	Jephtha Rd. SW18	37
Isambard Ms. E14	26 G4	Jeremiah St. E14	19
Isis Clo. SW15	36 E2	**Jermyn St. SW1**	**43**
Isla Rd. SE18	35 E2	Jerningham Rd. SE14	33
Islington Grn. N1	11 A5	Jerome Cres. NW8	16
Islington High St. N1	17 G1	Jerrard St. SE13	40
Islington Pk. St. N1	10 G4	Jersey Rd., Ilf.	14
Islip St. NW5	10 C2	Jessica Rd. SW18	37
Ismailia Rd. E7	13 E4	Jessup Clo. SE18	28
Ivanhoe Rd. SE5	39 E1	Jewry St. EC3	18
Ivatt Pl. W14	30 A1	Jew's Row SW18	37
Iveagh Clo. E9	12 B3	Jeymer Ave. NW2	8
Iveley Rd. SW4	31 C5	Jeypore Rd. SW18	37
Iverna Ct. W8	23 B4	Joan Cres. SE9	41
Iverna Gdns. W8	23 B4	**Joan St. SE1**	**44**
Iverson Rd. NW6	9 A3	Jocelyn St. SE15	32
Ives Rd. E16	20 B4	Jockey's Flds. WC1	17
Ives St. SW3	23 F5	Jodane St. SE8	26
Ivestor Ter. SE23	40 A5	Jodrell Rd. E3	12
Ivimey St. E2	18 F2	**John Adam St. WC2**	**43**
Ivor Pl. NW1	16 G3	John Ashby Clo. SW2	38
Ivor St. NW1	10 C4	John Burns Dr., Bark.	14
Ivy Rd. NW2	8 E1	John Campbell Rd. N16	11
Ivy Rd. SE4	40 D2	**John Carpenter St. EC4**	**44**
Ivy St. N1	11 D1	John Cornwall VC Ho. E12	14
Ivybridge La. WC2	**43 F4**	John Felton Rd. SE16	25
Ivydale Rd. SE15	40 B1	John Fisher St. E1	25
Ixworth Pl. SW3	30 F1	John Islip St. SW1	31
		John Maurice Clo. SE17	
J		John Penn St. SE13	33
Jack Clow Rd. E15	20 B1	John Princes St. W1	17
Jack Cornwell St. E12	14 C1	John Roll Way SE16	25
Jack Dash Way E6	21 A3	John Ruskin St. SE5	32
Jack Walker Ct. N5	11 A1	John Silkin La. SE8	33
Jackman St. E8	11 G5	John Smith Ave. SW6	30
Jackson Rd. N7	10 F1	John Spencer Sq. N1	11
Jackson Rd., Bark.	14 F5	John St. E15	13
Jackson St. SE18	35 C2	John St. WC1	17
Jacob St. SE1	25 E3	John Williams Clo. SE14	33
Jacobs Ho. E13	20 F2	John Wilson St. SE18	28
Jade Clo. E16	20 G5	John Woolley Clo. SE13	41
Jaggard Way SW12	37 G5	John's Ms. WC1	17
Jago Clo. SE18	35 E2	Johnson Clo. E8	11
Jamaica Rd. SE1	25 E3	Johnson's Pl. SW1	31
Jamaica Rd. SE16	25 F4	Johnstone Rd. E6	21
Jamaica St. E1	19 A4	**Joiner St. SE1**	**44**
James Ave. NW2	8 E2	Jonathan St. SE11	31
James Sinclair Pl. E13	13 F1	Joseph St. E3	19
James St. W1	17 A5	Josephine Ave. SW2	38
James St. WC2	**43 F3**	Joubert St. SW11	30
James St., Bark.	14 E4	Jowett St. SE15	32
Jameson St. W8	23 B2	Jubilee Cres. E14	26
Jamestown Rd. NW1	10 B5	Jubilee Pl. SW3	30
Janet St. E14	26 E4	Jubilee St. E1	19
Janeway St. SE16	25 F3	Judd St. WC1	17
Janson Rd. E15	13 B2	Jude St. E16	20
Jardine Rd. E1	26 B1	Juer St. SW11	30
Jarrow Rd. SE16	26 A5	Julian Pl. E14	33
Jarrow Way E9	12 D2	Juliette Rd. E13	20
Jasmine Clo., Ilf.	14 E2	Junction App. SW11	37
Jasper Rd. E16	20 G5	Junction Rd. E13	20
Jasper Rd. SE19	39 D3	Junction Rd. N19	10
Jay Ms. SW7	23 D3	Junction Wf. N1	18
Jebb Ave. SW2	38 E4	Juniper Cres. NW1	10
Jebb St. E3	19 E1	Juniper La. E6	21
Jedburgh Rd. E13	20 F2		
Jedburgh St. SW11	38 A2		
Jeddo Rd. W12	22 B3		
Jeffreys Rd. SW4	31 F4		
Jeffreys St. NW1	10 C4		
Jeffreys Wk. SW4	31 F4		
Jeger Ave. E2	11 F5		
Jeken Rd. SE9	41 F2		

r Rd., Ilf. 14 D1
r St. E1 26 A1
Vay SE14 33 B2
Way N7 10 F3
d. E15 13 A4
d. W. E15 12 G5
l Rd. E13 20 D3
l Rd. SE6 40 G5
St. SE11 24 F5

K

la Rd. SW11 37 E1
ir Rd. SE7 34 G3
a Rd. SW11 30 G4
Trd. Est., 21 G2
k.
ine Gdns. SE9 41 G2
ine Rd. E6 13 G4
ine Rd. E7 13 F3
en Rd. SW11 37 G1
l. SW9 31 E5
. E2 18 F1
. E15 13 A4
St. WC2 43 G2
Gro. NW3 9 F1
Rd., Well. 35 G4
o. SE16 26 B2
St. WC2 43 G2
g Rd. SE9 41 G3
The SE3 34 D5
St. SE17 32 C2
s Rd. SE16 25 G4
Dr. SW19 36 F5
n Rd. SW11 37 G2
Gro. W12 22 C3
Rd., Bark. 21 F1
ok Rd. SE3 35 A5
d Gdns. W10 15 E5
d Rd. E13 20 D3
ay Rd. SE3 34 F5
Cres. E12 13 G1
on Rd. SE13 41 B3
Rd. SW2 38 G2
St. NW1 10 B3
n Clo. SW4 31 D5
re Gro. SE22 39 F2
cott Gdns. W12 22 C4
cott Rd. SW11 37 F3
s Rd. N5 11 B1
Clo. SE3 34 E5
St. E2 18 F3
Pl. W8 23 C4
Ho. E14 26 G4
don Rd. SW6 30 A3
Rd. N5 11 A1
gton Rd. SE15 40 B3
e St. WC2 43 G2
ton Rd. SE5 39 B1
s St. E9 12 C2
Rd. NW6 15 F1
ay Rd. NW3 9 E1
s Ct. W1 43 B2
sford Gdns. 30 B1
5
sford Rd. SE11 24 G5
son Rd. SW6 30 B4
St. SE18 35 C2
horne Rd. SE8 26 C5
on Rd. E6 14 B5
ng Rd. SE10 34 D1
ry St. SE5 32 B5
ester Clo. SW8 31 E3
l Ave., Bark. 14 G4
l Clo. SW9 32 A3
l Rd. NW10 8 C1
l St. W2 16 F5
r St. SE14 33 A4
a Rd. SW4 38 D2
ck Pl. SW7 23 E5
rd Rd. SW12 38 B5

Kenilworth Ct. SW15 36 F1
Kenilworth Gdns. SE18 35 D5
Kenilworth Rd. E3 19 C1
Kenilworth Rd. NW6 9 A5
Kenmont Gdns. NW10 15 D2
Kenmure Rd. E8 11 G2
Kennard Rd. E15 13 A4
Kennard St. E16 28 B2
Kennard St. SW11 31 A4
Kennedy Clo. E13 20 D1
Kennedy Rd., Bark. 14 G5
Kennel Hill SE22 39 D1
Kennet Rd. W9 16 A3
Kennet St. E1 25 F2
Kennet Wf. La. EC4 44 E3
Kenneth Ave., Ilf. 14 D1
Kenneth Cres. NW2 8 D2
Kenning Ter. N1 11 D5
Kennings Way SE11 31 G1
Kennington La. SE11 31 E1
Kennington Oval SE11 31 F2
Kennington Pk. Pl. SE11 31 G2
Kennington Pk. Rd. SE11 31 G2
Kennington Rd. SE1 24 G4
Kennington Rd. SE11 24 G4
Kensal Rd. W10 15 F3
Kensington Ave. E12 14 A3
Kensington Ch. Ct. W8 23 C3
Kensington Ch. St. W8 23 B2
Kensington Ch. Wk. W8 23 C3
Kensington Ct. W8 23 C3
Kensington Ct. Pl. W8 23 C4
Kensington Gdns. W2 23 C2
Kensington Gdns. Sq. W2 16 C5
Kensington Gate W8 23 D4
Kensington Gore SW7 23 D3
Kensington High St. W8 23 B4
Kensington High St. W14 23 A4
Kensington Mall W8 23 B2
Kensington Palace Gdns. W8 23 C2
Kensington Pk. Gdns. W11 23 A1
Kensington Pk. Rd. W11 16 A5
Kensington Pl. W8 23 B2
Kensington Rd. SW7 23 D3
Kensington Rd. W8 23 C3
Kensington Sq. W8 23 C3
Kent St. E2 18 E1
Kent St. E13 20 E2
Kent Ter. NW1 16 F2
Kentish Town Rd. NW1 10 B4
Kentish Town Rd. NW5 10 B3
Kentmere Rd. SE18 28 G5
Kenton Rd. E9 12 B3
Kenton St. WC1 17 E3
Kentwode Grn. SW13 29 C3
Kenward Rd. SE9 41 F3
Kenway Rd. SW5 23 C5
Kenworthy Rd. E9 12 C2
Kenwyn Rd. SW4 38 D2
Kenya Rd. SE7 34 G3
Kenyon St. SW6 29 F4
Keogh Rd. E15 13 B3
Kepler Rd. SW4 38 E2
Keppel Rd. E6 14 B4
Keppel Row SE1 44 D6

Keppel St. WC1 17 D4
Kerbey St. E14 19 F5
Kerfield Pl. SE5 32 C4
Kerrison Rd. E15 13 A5
Kerrison Rd. SW11 37 F1
Kerry Clo. E16 20 E5
Kerry Rd. SE14 33 D2
Kersfield Rd. SW15 36 F4
Kersley Ms. SW11 30 G5
Kersley St. SW11 30 G5
Keslake Rd. NW6 15 F1
Keston Rd. SE15 39 F1
Kestrel Ave. SE24 39 A3
Keswick Rd. SW15 36 G3
Kett Gdns. SW2 38 F3
Key Clo. E1 18 G3
Keybridge Ho. SW8 31 E2
Keyes Rd. NW2 8 F2
Keynsham Gdns. SE9 42 A3
Keynsham Rd. SE9 41 G3
Keyworth Clo. E5 12 C1
Keyworth St. SE1 25 A4
Khartoum Rd. E13 20 E2
Khartoum Rd., Ilf. 14 D2
Khyber Rd. SW11 30 F5
Kibworth St. SW8 31 F3
Kidbrooke Gdns. SE3 34 D5
Kidbrooke Gro. SE3 34 D4
Kidbrooke La. SE9 42 A2
Kidbrooke Pk. Clo. SE3 34 E4
Kidbrooke Pk. Rd. SE3 34 E4
Kidbrooke Way SE3 34 E5
Kidd Pl. SE7 35 A1
Kidderpore Ave. NW3 9 B1
Kidderpore Gdns. NW3 9 B1
Kilburn High Rd. NW6 9 A4
Kilburn La. W9 15 F2
Kilburn La. W10 15 F2
Kilburn Pk. Rd. NW6 16 B2
Kilburn Pl. NW6 9 B5
Kilburn Priory NW6 9 C5
Kildare Gdns. W2 16 B5
Kildare Rd. E16 20 D4
Kildare Ter. W2 16 B5
Kildoran Rd. SW2 38 E3
Kilgour Rd. SE23 40 C4
Kilkie St. SW6 30 D5
Killarney Rd. SW18 37 D4
Killick St. N1 17 F1
Killip Clo. E16 20 C5
Killowen Rd. E9 12 B3
Killyon Rd. SW8 31 C5
Kilmaine Rd. SW6 29 G3
Kilmarsh Rd. W6 22 E5
Kilmington Rd. SW13 29 C2
Kiln Pl. NW5 10 A1
Kilner St. E14 19 E4
Kilravock St. W10 15 G2
Kimbell Gdns. SW6 29 G4
Kimber Rd. SW18 37 B5
Kimberley Ave. E6 21 A1
Kimberley Ave. SE15 32 G5
Kimberley Rd. E16 20 C3
Kimberley Rd. NW6 8 G5
Kimberley Rd. SW9 31 E5
Kimbolton Clo. SE12 41 C4
Kimpton Rd. SE5 32 C4
Kinburn St. SE16 26 B3
Kincaid Rd. SE15 32 G3
King & Queen St. SE17 32 B1
King Arthur Clo. SE15 33 A3
King Charles St. SW1 24 D3
King David La. E1 26 A1
King Edward Ms. SW13 29 C4
King Edward St. EC1 44 D1
King Edward Wk. SE1 24 G4

King Edwards Rd. E9 11 G5
King Edwards Rd., Bark. 14 F5
King George Ave. E16 20 G5
King George St. SE10 33 G3
King Henry St. N16 11 D2
King Henry's Rd. NW3 9 F4
King Henry's Wk. N1 11 D3
King James St. SE1 25 A3
King John St. E1 19 B4
King St. E13 20 D3
King St. EC2 44 E2
King St. SW1 43 B6
King St. W6 22 C5
King St. WC2 43 E3
King William St. EC4 44 G4
King William Wk. SE10 33 G2
Kingdon Rd. NW6 9 B3
Kingfield St. E14 26 G5
Kingfisher St. E6 21 A4
Kingham Clo. SW18 37 D5
Kingham Clo. W11 22 G3
Kinglake St. SE17 32 D1
Kingly Ct. W1 43 B3
Kingly St. W1 43 A3
Kings Arms Yd. EC2 44 F1
King's Ave. SW4 38 E3
Kings Bench Wk. EC4 44 A2
Kings College Rd. NW3 9 F4
Kings Ct. E13 13 E5
King's Cross Rd. WC1 17 F2
Kings Gro. SE15 32 G4
Kings Head Yd. SE1 44 F6
Kings Highway SE18 35 G2
King's Ms. WC1 17 F3
King's Orchard SE9 42 A4
King's Reach Twr. SE1 44 A5
Kings Rd. E6 13 F5
Kings Rd. NW10 8 D4
King's Rd. SW1 30 E2
King's Rd. SW3 30 E2
King's Rd. SW6 30 C3
King's Rd. SW10 30 D3
Kingsbridge Rd. W10 15 E5
Kingsbridge Rd., Bark. 21 F1
Kingsbury Rd. N1 11 D3
Kingsbury Ter. N1 11 D3
Kingsclere Clo. SW15 36 C5
Kingscote St. EC4 44 B3
Kingscroft Rd. NW2 9 A3
Kingsdale Gdns. W11 22 F2
Kingsdown Ave. W3 22 A1
Kingsdown Clo. W10 15 F5
Kingsford St. NW5 9 G2
Kingsford Way E6 21 B4
Kingsgate Pl. NW6 9 B4
Kingsgate Rd. NW6 9 B4
Kingsground SE9 42 A5
Kingshold Rd. E9 12 A4
Kingsholm Gdns. SE9 41 G2
Kingshurst Rd. SE12 41 D5
Kingsland Grn. E8 11 D3
Kingsland High St. E8 11 E3
Kingsland Rd. E2 18 D2
Kingsland Rd. E8 11 D5
Kingsland Rd. E13 20 F2
Kingsley Rd. E7 13 D4
Kingsley Rd. NW6 9 A5
Kingsley St. SW11 37 G1
Kingsman St. SE18 28 B4
Kingsmead Way E9 12 C1
Kingsmill Ter. NW8 16 E1
Kingston Rd., Ilf. 14 D1
Kingstown St. NW1 10 A5
Kingsway WC2 43 G1
Kingswood Ave. NW6 8 G5

Kingswood Pl. SE13 41 B2
Kingswood Rd. SW2 38 E4
Kingwood Rd. SW6 29 G3
Kinlet Rd. SE18 35 E4
Kinnear Rd. W12 22 B3
Kinnerton St. SW1 24 A3
Kinnoul Rd. W6 29 G2
Kinsale Rd. SE15 39 F1
Kinveachy Gdns. SE7 35 A1
Kipling Est. SE1 25 C3
Kipling St. SE1 25 C3
Kirby Est. SE16 25 G4
Kirby Gro. SE1 25 D3
Kirk La. SE18 35 E2
Kirkham Rd. E6 21 A5
Kirkham St. SE18 35 G2
Kirkland Clo., Sid. 42 G4
Kirkside Rd. SE3 34 D2
Kirkwall Pl. E2 19 A2
Kirkwood Rd. SE15 32 G5
Kirtling St. SW8 31 C3
Kirton Rd. E13 20 F1
Kirwyn Way SE5 32 A3
Kitcat Ter. E3 19 E2
Kitchener Rd. E7 13 E3
Kitson Rd. SE5 32 C3
Kitson Rd. SW13 29 C4
Kitto Rd. SE14 33 B5
Klea Ave. SW4 38 C4
Knapp Clo. NW10 8 A3
Knapp Rd. E3 19 E3
Knaresborough Pl. SW5 23 C5
Knatchbull Rd. SE5 32 A5
Kneller Rd. SE4 40 C2
Knighten St. E1 25 F2
Knighton St. E1 25 F2
Knights Rd. E16 27 D3
Knightsbridge SW1 23 G3
Knightsbridge SW7 23 F3
Knightsbridge Grn. SW1 23 G3
Knivet Rd. SW6 30 B2
Knobs Hill Rd. E15 12 F5
Knockholt Rd. SE9 41 G3
Knoll Rd. SW18 37 D3
Knottisford St. E2 19 A2
Knowle Clo. SW9 38 G1
Knowles Hill Cres. SE13 41 A3
Knowles Wk. SW4 38 C1
Knowsley Rd. SW11 30 G5
Knox Rd. E7 13 C3
Knox St. W1 16 G4
Kossuth St. SE10 34 B1
Kreedman Wk. E8 11 F2
Kylemore Rd. NW6 9 B4
Kynance Ms. SW7 23 D4
Kynance Pl. SW7 23 D4
Kyrle Rd. SW11 37 G4

L

Laburnum St. E2 11 E5
Lacey Wk. E3 19 E1
Lackington St. EC2 18 C4
Lacon Rd. SE22 39 F2
Lacy Rd. SW15 36 F2
Ladbroke Gdns. W11 23 A1
Ladbroke Gro. W10 15 F3
Ladbroke Gro. W11 15 G5
Ladbroke Rd. W11 23 A2
Ladbroke Sq. W11 23 A1
Ladbroke Ter. W11 23 A1
Ladbroke Wk. W11 23 A2
Lady Margaret Rd. N19 10 C1
Lady Margaret Rd. NW5 10 C2
Lady Somerset Rd. NW5 10 B1
Ladycroft Rd. SE13 40 F1
Ladysmith Ave. E6 21 A1
Ladysmith Rd. E16 20 C2
Ladysmith Rd. SE9 42 C4
Ladywell Rd. SE13 40 F3
Lafone St. SE1 25 E3
Lagado Ms. SE16 26 B2
Lainson St. SW18 37 B5
Lakedale Rd. SE18 35 G1
Laker Pl. SW15 36 G4
Lakeside Rd. W14 22 F4
Laleham Rd. SE6 40 G5
Lalor St. SW6 29 G5
Lamb La. E8 11 G4
Lamb St. E1 18 E4
Lambert Rd. E16 20 E5
Lambert Rd. SW2 38 E3
Lambert St. N1 10 G4
Lambeth Bri. SE1 24 E5
Lambeth Bri. SW1 24 E5
Lambeth High St. SE1 24 F5
Lambeth Hill EC4 44 D3
Lambeth Palace Rd. SE1 24 F4
Lambeth Rd. SE1 24 F4
Lambeth Rd. SE11 24 F4
Lambeth Wk. SE11 24 F5
Lamble St. NW5 10 A2
Lambolle Pl. NW3 9 F3
Lambolle Rd. NW3 9 F3
Lambourn Rd. SW4 38 B1
Lambourne Rd., Bark. 14 G4
Lambrook Ter. SW6 29 G4
Lamb's Conduit St. WC1 17 F3
Lamb's Pas. EC1 18 C4
Lamerton St. SE8 33 E2
Lamington St. W6 22 D5
Lammas Rd. E9 12 B4
Lammermoor Rd. SW12 38 B5
Lamont Rd. SW10 30 D2
Lampmead Rd. SE12 41 C3
Lamport Clo. SE18 28 B5
Lanark Pl. W9 16 D3
Lanark Rd. W9 16 C1
Lanark Sq. E14 26 F4
Lanbury Rd. SE15 40 B2
Lancaster Ave., Bark. 14 G4
Lancaster Ct. SW6 30 A3
Lancaster Dr. NW3 9 F3
Lancaster Gate W2 23 D1
Lancaster Gro. NW3 9 E3
Lancaster Ms. W2 23 D1
Lancaster Pl. WC2 43 G3
Lancaster Rd. E7 13 D4
Lancaster Rd. NW10 8 C2
Lancaster Rd. W11 15 G5
Lancaster St. SE1 25 A3
Lancaster Ter. W2 23 E1
Lancaster Wk. W2 23 E2
Lancefield St. W10 16 A2
Lancelot Pl. SW7 23 G3
Lancresse Ct. N1 11 D5
Landcroft Rd. SE22 39 E3
Landells Rd. SE22 39 E4
Landford Rd. SW15 36 E1
Landmann Way SE14 33 B2
Landon Pl. SW1 23 G4
Landons Clo. E14 26 G2
Landor Rd. SW9 38 E1
Landor Wk. W12 22 C3
Landridge Rd. SW6 30 A5
Landseer Ave. E12 14 C2
Landstead Rd. SE18 35 F3
Lane, The SE3 41 D1
Lanfranc Rd. E3 19 C1
Lang St. E1 19 A3
Langbrook Rd. SE3 41 G1
Langdale Clo. SE17 32 B2
Langdale Rd. SE10 33 G3
Langdon Ct. NW10 8 A5
Langdon Cres. E6 21 C1
Langdon Rd. E6 14 C5
Langford Clo. E8 11 F2
Langford Grn. SE5 39 D1
Langford Pl. NW8 16 D1
Langham Pl. W1 17 B4
Langham St. W1 17 B4
Langland Gdns. NW3 9 C2
Langler Rd. NW10 15 E1
Langley Ct. SE9 42 C4
Langley Ct. WC2 43 E3
Langley La. SW8 31 E2
Langley St. WC2 43 E2
Langside Ave. SW15 36 C2
Langthorn Ct. EC2 44 G1
Langthorne St. SW6 29 F4
Langton Ave. E6 21 C2
Langton Ri. SE23 39 G5
Langton Rd. SW9 32 A3
Langton St. SW10 30 D2
Langton Way SE3 34 C4
Langtry Rd. NW8 9 C5
Lanhill Rd. W9 16 B3
Lanier Rd. SE13 40 G4
Lanrick Rd. E14 20 A5
Lansbury Est. E14 19 F5
Lansbury Gdns. E14 19 G5
Lansdown Rd. E7 13 F4
Lansdowne Cres. W11 23 A1
Lansdowne Dr. E8 11 F3
Lansdowne Gdns. SW8 31 E4
Lansdowne Gro. NW10 8 A1
Lansdowne La. SE7 34 G1
Lansdowne Ms. SE7 34 G1
Lansdowne Ri. W11 22 G1
Lansdowne Rd. W11 22 G1
Lansdowne Ter. WC1 17 E3
Lansdowne Wk. W11 23 A2
Lansdowne Way SW8 31 D4
Lant St. SE1 25 B3
Lantern Clo. SW15 36 C2
Lanterns Ct. E14 26 E3
Lanvanor Rd. SE15 33 A5
Lapford Clo. W9 16 A3
Lara Clo. SE13 40 G4
Larch Ave. W3 22 A2
Larch Clo. E13 20 E3
Larch Rd. NW2 8 E1
Larcom St. SE17 25 B5
Larden Rd. W3 22 A2
Lark Row E2 12 A5
Larkhall La. SW4 31 D5
Larkhall Ri. SW4 38 C1
Larkhill Ter. SE18 35 C3
Larks Gro., Bark. 14 G4
Larkspur Clo. E6 21 A4
Larnach Rd. W6 29 F2
Larpent Ave. SW15 36 E3
Lassa Rd. SE9 42 A3
Lassell St. SE10 34 A1
Latchmere Rd. SW11 30 G5
Latchmere St. SW11 30 G5
Latham Ho. E1 19 B5
Lathom Rd. E6 14 A4
Latimer Ave. E6 14 B5
Latimer Pl. W10 15 E5
Latimer Rd. E7 13 E1
Latimer Rd. W10 15 E4
Latona Rd. SE15 32 F2
Lattimer Pl. W4 29 B3
Latymer Ct. W6 22 F5
Lauderdale Rd. W9 16 C2
Launceston Pl. W8 23 D4
Launch St. E14 26 G4
Laundry Rd. W6 29 G2
Laura Pl. E5 12 A1
Laurel Rd. SW13
Laurel St. E8
Laurence Pountney Hill EC4
Laurence Pountney La. EC4
Laurie Gro. SE14
Lauriston Rd. E9
Lausanne Rd. SE15
Lavell St. N16
Lavender Gdns. SW11
Lavender Gro. E8
Lavender Hill SW11
Lavender Pl., Ilf.
Lavender Rd. SE16
Lavender Rd. SW11
Lavender Sweep SW11
Lavender Wk. SW11
Laverstoke Gdns. SW15
Laverton Pl. SW5
Lavington St. SE1
Law St. SE1
Lawford Rd. N1
Lawford Rd. NW5
Lawless St. E14
Lawley St. E5
Lawn Ho. Clo. E14
Lawn La. SW8
Lawn Rd. NW3
Lawn Ter. SE3
Lawnside SE3
Lawrence Ave. E12
Lawrence Clo. E3
Lawrence La. EC2
Lawrence Rd. E6
Lawrence Rd. E13
Lawrence St. E16
Lawrence St. SW3
Lawson Clo. E16
Lawton Rd. E3
Laxley Clo. SE5
Layard Rd. SE16
Layard Sq. SE16
Laycock St. N1
Laystall St. EC1
Leabank Sq. E9
Leacroft Ave. SW12
Leadenhall Mkt. EC3
Leadenhall Pl. EC3
Leadenhall St. EC3
Leader Ave. E12
Leahurst Rd. SE13
Leake St. SE1
Leamington Clo. E12
Leamington Rd. Vill. W11
Leamore St. W6
Leamouth Rd. E6
Leamouth Rd. E14
Leander Ct. SE8
Leander Rd. SW2
Learoyd Gdns. E6
Leather La. EC1
Leathermarket Ct. SE1
Leathermarket St. SE1
Leathwaite Rd. SW11
Leathwell Rd. SE8
Lebanon Gdns. SW18
Lebanon Rd. SW18
Lebrun Sq. SE3
Lechmere Rd. NW2
Lecky St. SW7
Leconfield Ave. SW13
Leconfield Rd. N5
Leda Rd. SE18
Ledbury Est. SE15

ury Rd. W11 16 A5
ury St. SE15 32 F3
ri. SE13 40 G1
ch. St. SE13 41 B2
Conservancy Rd. 12 D2
rn. SE12 41 C3
igh Rd. SE12 41 C2
igh Rd. SE13 41 A2
k. SE3 41 A2
d. SE3 11 E5
t. E8 11 E5
er. SE3 41 B1
er. SE13 41 B1
orn Rd. W12 22 C3
ate SE12 41 C3
t. WC1 17 F2
nd Way NW10 8 B1
am Dr. E14 26 G4
Pl. W1 24 A1
on Rd. SE24 38 G2
ay SE8 33 D1
vay Rd. W12 22 B3
att Rd. SE9 19 G1
att Rd. E15 19 G1
ct. SE13 40 G3
orn Rd. NW10 15 B1
ton Rd. E18 35 F1
n Clo. N1 10 G4
Gdns. NW10 15 E1
a Rd. E8 14 C3
a Rd. N5 11 A1
St. E13 17 E3
nton Ave. E12 14 C2
nton Gdns. NW10 15 D1
nton Gro. NW5 10 C2
nton Pl. NW5 10 C2
nton Rd. NW5 10 C2
Parnell Pl. SE7 34 F2
ster Gdns. W2 16 D5
ster Ms. W2 23 D1
ster Pl. W2 16 D5
ster Sq. W2 16 B5
ster Ter. W2 23 D1
an St. E1 18 E5
mon Rd. SE10 34 B2
onwell Ct. SE9 42 E3
Gdns. W6 22 D4
tal Ter. SW4 38 D1
am Rd. SE12 41 C2
on Rd. NW2 8 E3
ox Gdns. NW10 8 B1
ox Gdns. SW1 23 G4
ox Conservs. Ms. 23 G4
W1
Rd. E7 13 F4
hall Rd. E8 11 F4
horp Rd. SE10 27 C5
on St. SE18 28 F5
St. SE15 32 G3
ard Rd. E7 13 D1
ard St. E16 28 A2
ard St. EC2 18 C3
tine Clo. SE15 32 F3
old Rd. NW10 8 A4
old St. E3 19 D4
oc Rd. SW4 38 D3
y St. E11 12 G1
e Rd. E11 12 G1
e Rd. E16 20 E5
ar Way. SW4 38 B3
ing St. SE23 40 C5
er Ave. E15 20 B3
nford Gdns. 15 C2
W10
bridge Clo. SE13 33 G3

Lett Rd. E15 13 A4
Lettice St. SW6 30 A4
Lettsom St. SE5 32 D5
Levehurst Way SW9 31 E5
Leven Rd. E14 19 G4
Lever St. EC1 18 A2
Leverton St. NW5 10 C2
Levett Rd., Bark 14 G3
Lewey Ho. E3 19 D3
Lewis Gro. SE13 40 G1
Lewis St. NW1 10 B3
Lewisham High St. 40 F4
SE13
Lewisham Hill SE13 33 G5
Lewisham Pk. SE13 40 G3
Lewisham Rd. SE13 33 F4
Lewisham Way SE4 33 E5
Lewisham Way SE14 33 D4
Lexham Gdns. W8 23 B5
Lexham Ms. W8 23 B5
Lexington St. W1 43 B3
Leybourne Rd. NW1 10 B4
Leybridge Ct. SE12 41 D3
Leyes Rd. E16 20 F5
Leyland Rd. SE12 41 C3
Leylang Rd. SE14 33 B3
Leysfield Rd. W12 22 C4
Leyton Rd. E15 13 A2
Leytonstone Rd. E15 13 A4
Leywick St. E15 20 B1
Liardet St. SE14 33 C2
Liberia Rd. N5 11 A3
Liberty Ms. SW12 38 B4
Liberty St. SW9 31 F4
Libra Rd. E3 12 D5
Libra Rd. E13 20 D1
Library St. SE1 25 A3
Lichfield Rd. E3 19 C2
Lichfield Rd. E6 20 G2
Lichfield Rd. NW2 8 G1
Lidcote Gdns. SW9 31 G5
Liddell Gdns. NW10 15 E1
Liddell Rd. NW6 9 B3
Liddington Rd. E15 13 C5
Liddon Rd. E13 20 E2
Lidfield Rd. N16 11 C1
Lidlington Pl. NW1 17 C1
Liffler Rd. SE18 35 G1
Lifford St. SW15 37 F2
Liffords Pl. SW13 29 B5
Lighter Clo. SE16 26 E3
Lightermans Rd. E14 26 E3
Lightermans Wk. 37 B2
SW18
Lilac St. W12 22 C1
Lilburne Gdns. SE9 42 A3
Lilburne Rd. SE9 42 A3
Lilestone St. NW8 16 F3
Lilford Rd. SE5 32 A5
Lilian Barker Clo. 41 D3
SE12
Lilian Rd. SW13 29 C2
Lillie Rd. SW6 29 F2
Lillie Yd. SW6 30 B2
Lillieshall Rd. SW4 38 B1
Lily Pl. EC1 17 G4
Lilyville Rd. SW6 30 A4
Limburg Rd. SW11 37 G2
Lime Clo. E1 25 F2
Lime Gro. W12 22 E3
Lime St. EC3 44 H3
Lime St. Pas. EC3 44 H3
Limeburner La. EC4 44 B2
Limeharbour E14 26 F4
Limehouse 26 D1
Causeway E14
Limehouse Flds. Est. 19 C5
E14
Limekiln Dr. SE7 34 E2

Limerick Clo. SW12 38 C5
Limerston St. SW10 30 D2
Limes Ave. SW13 29 B5
Limes Gdns. SW18 37 B4
Limes Gro. SE13 40 G2
Limes Wk. SE15 39 G2
Limesford Rd. SE15 40 B2
Linacre Ct. W6 29 F1
Linacre Rd. NW2 8 C3
Linchmere Rd. SE12 41 C5
Lincoln Rd. E7 13 G3
Lincoln Rd. E13 20 E3
Lincoln St. SW3 23 G5
Lincoln's Inn Flds. 43 G1
WC2
Lind St. SE8 33 E5
Lindal Rd. SE4 40 D3
Linden Ave. NW10 15 F1
Linden Ct. W12 22 E2
Linden Gdns. W2 23 B1
Linden Gdns. W4 29 A1
Linden Gro. SE15 39 G1
Linden Ms. W2 23 B1
Lindfield Gdns. NW3 9 C2
Lindfield St. E14 19 E5
Lindisfarne Way E9 12 C1
Lindley Rd. E1 19 A4
Lindore Rd. SW11 37 G2
Lindrop St. SW6 30 D5
Lindsay Sq. SW1 31 D1
Lindsell St. SE10 33 G4
Lindsey Ms. N1 11 B4
Lindsey St. EC1 18 A4
Linford St. SW8 31 C4
Ling Rd. E16 20 D4
Lingards Rd. SE13 40 G2
Lingfield Cres. SE9 42 F2
Lingham St. SW9 31 E5
Linhope St. NW1 16 G3
Link St. E9 12 A2
Linnell Rd. SE5 32 D5
Linnet Ms. SW12 38 A5
Linom Rd. SW4 38 E2
Linscott Rd. E5 12 A1
Linsdell Rd., Bark 14 E5
Linsey St. SE16 25 F5
Linstead St. NW6 9 B4
Linstead Way SW18 36 G5
Linton Gdns. E6 21 A5
Linton Rd., Bark 14 E4
Linton St. N1 11 B5
Lintons, The, Bark 14 E4
Linver Rd. SW6 30 A5
Linwood Clo. SE5 32 E5
Lion Clo. SE4 40 E4
Lion Rd. E6 21 B4
Lionel Gdns. SE9 41 G3
Lionel Rd. SE9 41 G3
Liphook Cres. SE23 40 A5
Lisburne Rd. NW3 9 G1
Lisford St. SE15 32 E4
Lisgar Ter. W14 23 A5
Liskeard Gdns. SE3 34 D4
Lisle St. WC2 43 D3
Lissenden Gdns. NW5 10 A1
Lisson Grn. Est. NW8 16 F2
Lisson Gro. NW1 16 E3
Lisson Gro. NW8 16 E3
Lisson St. NW1 16 F4
Lister Ho. SE3 34 B2
Liston Rd. SW4 38 C1
Litchfield Ave. E15 13 B3
Litchfield Gdns. 8 C3
NW10
Litchfield St. WC2 43 D3
Lithos Rd. NW3 9 C3
Little Argyll St. W1 43 A2
Little Boltons, The 30 C1
SW5

Little Boltons, The 30 C1
SW10
Little Britain EC1 18 A4
Little Chester St. SW1 24 B4
Little Dorrit Ct. SE1 25 B3
Little Essex St. WC2 43 J3
Little Heath SE7 35 A1
Little Ilford La. E12 14 B1
Little Marlborough 43 A2
St. W1
Little New St. EC4 44 B1
Little Newport St. 43 D3
WC2
Little Portland St. W1 17 C5
Little Russell St. WC1 17 E4
Little St. James's St. 43 A6
SW1
Little Trinity La. EC4 44 E3
Littlebury Rd. SW4 38 D1
Littlecombe SE7 34 E2
Littlecombe Clo. 36 F4
SW15
Littlecote Clo. SW19 36 F5
Littlecroft SE9 42 C1
Littlewood SE13 40 G3
Livermere Rd. E8 11 E5
Liverpool Gro. SE17 32 C1
Liverpool Rd. E16 20 B4
Liverpool Rd. N1 10 G4
Liverpool Rd. N7 10 G2
Liverpool St. EC2 18 D4
Livingstone Rd. E15 12 G5
Livingstone Wk. 37 E1
SW11
Livonia St. W1 43 B2
Lizard St. EC1 18 B2
Lizban St. SE3 34 E3
Llanover Rd. SE18 35 C2
Lloyd Baker St. WC1 17 F2
Lloyd Rd. E6 14 B5
Lloyd Sq. WC1 17 G2
Lloyd St. WC1 17 G2
Lloyd's Ave. EC3 44 J2
Lloyds St. SE3 34 B5
Loampit Hill SE13 33 E5
Loampit Vale SE13 40 F1
Loats Rd. SW2 38 E4
Lochaber Rd. SE13 41 B2
Lochaline St. W6 29 F2
Lochinvar St. SW12 38 B5
Lochnagar St. E14 19 G4
Lock Chase SE3 41 B1
Lockesfield Pl. E14 33 F1
Lockhart Clo. N7 10 F3
Lockhart St. E3 19 D3
Lockhurst St. E5 12 B1
Lockington Rd. SW8 31 B4
Lockmead Rd. SE13 40 G1
Locksley Est. E14 19 D5
Locksley St. E14 19 D4
Lockwood Sq. SE16 25 G4
Loddiges Rd. E9 12 A4
Loder St. SE15 33 A3
Lodge Ave. SW14 36 A1
Lodge Rd. NW8 16 E2
Lodore St. E14 19 G5
Loftie St. SE16 25 F3
Lofting Rd. N1 10 F4
Loftus Rd. W12 22 D2
Logan Ms. W8 23 B5
Logan Pl. W8 23 B5
Lollard St. SE11 24 G5
Loman St. SE1 25 A3
Lomas St. E8 11 E4
Lomas St. E1 18 F4
Lombard Ct. EC3 44 G3
Lombard La. EC4 44 A2
Lombard Rd. SW11 30 E5
Lombard St. EC3 44 G2
Lombard Wall SE7 27 E4

Lomond Gro. SE5 32 C3
Loncroft Rd. SE5 32 D2
Londesborough Rd. N16 11 D1
London Bri. EC4 44 G5
London Bri. SE1 44 G5
London Bri. St. SE1 44 G6
London Bri. Wk. SE1 44 G5
London City Airport E16 28 A2
London Flds. E8 11 G4
London Flds. E. Side E8 11 G4
London Flds. W. Side E8 11 F4
London Ind. Pk. E6 21 D4
London La. E8 11 G4
London Rd. E13 20 D1
London Rd. SE1 25 A4
London Rd., Bark. 14 D4
London St. EC3 44 J3
London St. W2 16 E5
London Wall EC2 18 B4
Long Acre WC2 43 E3
Long Ct. WC2 43 D4
Long Dr. W3 15 A5
Long La. EC1 18 A4
Long La. SE1 25 C3
Long Pond Rd. SE3 34 B4
Long Reach Ct., Bark. 21 F1
Long Rd. SW4 38 B2
Long St. E2 18 E2
Long Wk. SE18 35 D2
Long Yd. WC1 17 F3
Longbeach Rd. SW11 37 G1
Longbridge Rd., Bark. 14 F3
Longbridge Way SE13 40 G3
Longfield Est. SE1 25 E5
Longfield St. SW18 37 B5
Longford St. NW1 17 B3
Longhedge St. SW11 31 A5
Longhope Clo. SE15 32 D2
Longhurst Rd. SE13 41 A3
Longley St. SE1 25 F5
Longmoore St. SW1 24 C5
Longnor Rd. E1 19 B2
Longridge Rd. SW5 23 B5
Longshore SE8 26 D5
Longstaff Cres. SW18 37 B4
Longstaff Rd. SW18 37 B4
Longstone Ave. NW10 8 B4
Longwood Dr. SW15 36 C4
Lonsdale Ave. E6 20 G2
Lonsdale Rd. NW6 9 A5
Lonsdale Rd. SW13 29 B4
Lonsdale Rd. W4 22 B5
Lonsdale Rd. W11 16 A5
Lonsdale Sq. N1 10 G5
Loraine Rd. N7 10 F1
Lord Hills Rd. W2 16 C4
Lord N. St. SW1 24 E4
Lord Roberts Ter. SE18 35 C1
Lord St. E16 28 A2
Lord Warwick St. SE18 28 B4
Lordship La. SE22 39 E4
Lorenzo St. WC1 17 F2
Loris Rd. W6 22 E4
Lorn Rd. SW9 31 F5
Lorne Gdns. W11 22 F3
Lorne Rd. E7 13 E1
Lorrimore Rd. SE17 32 A2
Lorrimore Sq. SE17 32 A2
Lothbury EC2 44 F1
Lothian Rd. SW9 32 A4
Lothrop St. W10 15 G2
Lots Rd. SW10 30 D3
Loudoun Rd. NW8 9 D4
Lough Rd. N7 10 F2
Loughborough Pk. SW9 39 A2
Loughborough Rd. SW9 31 G5
Loughborough St. SE11 31 F1
Louisa St. E1 19 B3
Louise Rd. E15 13 B3
Louvaine Rd. SW11 37 E2
Lovage App. E6 21 A4
Lovat La. EC3 44 H4
Love La. EC2 44 E1
Love La. SE18 28 D5
Love Wk. SE5 32 C5
Lovegrove St. SE1 32 F1
Lovegrove Wk. E14 26 G2
Lovelace Grn. SE9 42 B1
Lovelinch Clo. SE15 33 A2
Lovell Ho. E8 11 F5
Loveridge Rd. NW6 9 A3
Lovers Wk. SE10 34 B3
Lover's Wk. W1 24 A2
Lowbrook Rd., Ilf. 14 D1
Lowden Rd. SE24 39 B2
Lowell St. E14 19 C5
Lower Addison Gdns. W14 22 G3
Lower Belgrave St. SW1 24 B4
Lower Clapton Rd. E5 12 A2
Lower Common S. SW15 36 D1
Lower Grosvenor Pl. SW1 24 B4
Lower James St. W1 43 B3
Lower John St. W1 43 B3
Lower Lea Crossing E14 27 B1
Lower Mall W6 29 D1
Lower Marsh SE1 24 F3
Lower Merton Ri. NW3 9 F4
Lower Richmond Rd. SW15 36 D1
Lower Rd. SE8 26 B5
Lower Rd. SE16 26 A4
Lower Robert St. WC2 43 F4
Lower Sloane St. SW1 24 A5
Lower Thames St. EC3 44 G4
Lowfield Rd. NW6 9 B4
Lowman Rd. N7 10 F1
Lowndes Clo. SW1 24 A4
Lowndes Pl. SW1 24 A4
Lowndes Sq. SW1 23 G3
Lowndes St. SW1 23 G4
Lowth Rd. SE5 32 B5
Lowther Hill SE23 40 C5
Lowther Rd. SW13 29 B4
Loxford Ave. E6 20 G1
Loxford La., Ilf. 14 E2
Loxford Rd., Bark. 14 D3
Lubbock St. SE14 33 A3
Lucan Pl. SW3 23 F5
Lucas Ave. E13 13 E5
Lucas St. SE8 33 E4
Lucerne Rd. N5 11 A1
Lucey Rd. SE16 25 F4
Lucknow St. SE18 35 G3
Lucorn Clo. SE12 41 C4
Ludgate Bdy. EC4 44 B2
Ludgate Circ. EC4 44 B2
Ludgate Hill EC4 44 B2
Ludgate Sq. EC4 44 C2
Ludovick Wk. SW15 36 A2
Ludwick Ms. SE14 33 C3
Lugard Rd. SE15 32 G5
Luke Ho. E1 18 G5
Luke St. EC2 18 D3
Lukin St. E1 19 A5
Lulworth Rd. SE15 32 G5
Lumley Ct. WC2 43 F4
Lumley St. W1 17 A5
Lupton St. NW5 10 C1
Lupus St. SW1 31 B1
Lurgan Ave. W6 29 F2
Lurline Gdns. SW11 31 A4
Luscombe Way SW8 31 E3
Lushington Rd. NW10 15 D1
Luton Pl. SE10 33 G3
Luton St. NW8 16 E3
Luttrell Ave. SW15 36 D3
Luxborough St. W1 17 A4
Luxemburg Gdns. W6 22 F5
Luxford St. SE16 26 B5
Luxmore St. SE4 33 D4
Luxor St. SE5 39 B1
Lyal Rd. E3 19 C1
Lyall Ms. SW1 24 A4
Lyall St. SW1 24 A4
Lydden Ct. SE9 42 G4
Lydden Gro. SW18 37 C5
Lydden Rd. SW18 37 C5
Lydeard Rd. E6 14 B4
Lydford Rd. NW2 8 E3
Lydford Rd. W9 16 A3
Lydon Rd. SW4 38 C1
Lyford Rd. SW18 37 E5
Lyham Clo. SW2 38 E4
Lyham Rd. SW2 38 E3
Lyme Fm. Rd. SE12 41 D2
Lyme St. NW1 10 C4
Lymington Rd. NW6 9 C3
Lympstone Gdns. SE15 32 F3
Lyncott Cres. SW4 38 B2
Lyncroft Gdns. NW6 9 B2
Lyndale NW2 9 A1
Lyndale Clo. SE3 34 C2
Lyndhurst Gdns. NW3 9 E2
Lyndhurst Gdns., Bark. 14 G3
Lyndhurst Gro. SE15 32 D5
Lyndhurst Rd. NW3 9 E2
Lyndhurst Sq. SE15 32 E4
Lyndhurst Ter. NW3 9 E2
Lyndhurst Way SE15 32 E4
Lynette Ave. SW4 38 B4
Lynn Rd. SW12 38 B5
Lynne Way NW10 8 A3
Lynsted Gdns. SE9 41 G1
Lynton Clo. NW10 8 A2
Lynton Rd. NW6 9 A5
Lynton Rd. SE1 25 E5
Lyon Business Pk., Bark. 21 G1
Lyons Pl. NW8 16 E3
Lyons Wk. W14 22 G5
Lyric Rd. SW13 29 B4
Lysia St. SW6 29 F3
Lysias Rd. SW12 38 B4
Lytcott Gro. SE22 39 E3
Lytham St. SE17 32 C1
Lytton Gro. SW15 36 F3
Lyveden Rd. SE3 34 E3

M

Mabledon Pl. WC1 17 D2
Mablethorpe Rd. SW6 29 G3
Mabley St. E9 12 C2
MacArthur Clo. E7 13 D3
Macarthur Ter. SE7 34 G2
Macaulay Ct. SW4 38 B1
Macaulay Rd. E6 20 G1
Macaulay Rd. SW4 38 B1
Macaulay Sq. SW4 38 B2
Macauley Ms. SE13 33 G4
Macbean St. SE18 28
Macbeth St. W6 29
Macclesfield Bri. NW1 16
Macclesfield Rd. EC1 18
Macclesfield St. W1 43
Macdonald Rd. E7 13
Macduff Rd. SW11 31
Mace St. E2 19
Macfarlane Rd. W12 22
Macgregor Rd. E16 20
Machell Rd. SE15 40
Mackay Rd. SW4 38
Mackennal St. NW8 16
Mackenzie Rd. N7 10
Mackeson Rd. NW3 9
Mackie Rd. SW2 38
Macklin St. WC2 43
Macks Rd. SE16 25
Mackworth St. NW1 17
Maclean Rd. SE23 40
Macleod St. SE17 32
Maclise Rd. W14 22
Macoma Rd. SE18 35
Macoma Ter. SE18 35
Maconochies Rd. E14 33
Macquarie Way E14 26
Macroom Rd. W9 16
Maddams St. E3 19
Maddox St. W1 24
Madeline Gro., Ilf. 14
Madinah Rd. E8 11
Madras Pl. N7 10
Madras Rd., Ilf. 14
Madrid Rd. SW13 29
Madrigal La. SE5 32
Madron St. SE17 32
Mafeking Ave. E6 21
Mafeking Rd. E16 20
Magdalen St. SE1 44
Magdalene Gdns. E6 21
Magee St. SE11 31
Magnolia Pl. SW4 38
Magpie All. EC4 44
Magpie Clo. E7 13
Maguire St. SE1 25
Mahogany Clo. SE16 26
Maida Ave. W2 16
Maida Vale W9 16
Maiden La. NW1 10
Maiden La. SE1 44
Maiden La. WC2 43
Maiden Rd. E15 13
Maidenstone Hill SE10 33
Maidstone Bldgs. SE1 44
Maitland Clo. SE10 33
Maitland Pk. Est. NW3 9
Maitland Pk. Rd. NW3 9
Maitland Pk. Vill. NW3 9
Maitland Rd. E15 13
Majendie Rd. SE18 35
Major Rd. E15 13
Makins St. SW3 23
Malabar St. E14 26
Malbrook Rd. SW15 36
Malcolm Pl. E2 19
Malcolm Rd. E1 19
Malden Cres. NW1 10
Malden Rd. NW5 9
Maldon Clo. N1 11
Maldon Clo. SE5 39
Malet Pl. WC1 17
Malet St. WC1 17
Malfort Rd. SE5 39
Mall, The SW1 24
Mall Rd. W6 29
Mallard Clo. E9 12
Mallet Rd. SE13 41
Mallinson Rd. SW11 37
Mallord St. SW3 30

ory Clo. SE4 40 C2
ory St. NW8 16 F3
nesbury Rd. E3 19 D2
nesbury Rd. E16 20 B4
nesbury Ter. E16 20 C4
as Rd. E8 11 G3
as Rd. SE4 33 D5
St. SE1 32 F2
by St. SE1 25 E4
house Dr. W4 29 A2
ngs Pl. SW6 30 C4
on St. SE18 35 G2
ravers St. WC2 43 H3
ern Clo. W10 16 A4
ern Ct. SW7 23 E5
ern Gdns. NW6 16 A1
ern Pl. NW6 16 A2
ern Rd. E6 14 A5
ern Rd. E8 11 F4
ern Rd. NW6 16 B2
ern Ter. N1 10 G5
wood Rd. SW12 38 B4
ons Rd. SE13 40 F4
ons Ter. SE13 40 F3
aton Clo. SE15 39 G1
bey Gro. E15 13 B3
bey Pk. Rd. E15 13 B3
bey Rd. E15 13 B3
bey St. E15 13 B3
borough Ave. E6 21 B2
ore Rd. W6 29 E2
chester Dr. W10 15 G3
chester Gro. E14 33 G1
chester Rd. E14 33 G1
chester Sq. W1 17 A5
chester St. W1 17 A4
churia Rd. SW11 38 A4
ciple St. SE1 25 C3
dalay Rd. SW4 38 C3
dela Rd. E16 20 D5
dela St. NW1 10 C5
dela St. SW9 31 G3
dela Way SE1 25 D5
deville Pl. W1 17 A5
drell Rd. SW2 38 E3
ette St. W1 43 D2
fred Rd. SW15 37 A3
ger Rd. N7 10 E3
hattan Wf. E16 27 D3
illa St. E14 26 E3
ley St. NW1 10 A5
or Ave. SE4 33 D5
or Est. SE16 25 G5
or Flds. SW15 36 F4
or Gro. SE15 33 A2
or Ho. Dr. NW6 8 F4
or La. SE12 41 B4
or La. SE13 41 B3
or La. Ter. SE13 41 B2
or Ms. SE4 33 D5
or Pk. SE13 41 A3
or Pk. Rd. E12 13 G1
or Pk. Rd. NW10 8 B5
or Pl. SE17 32 A1
or Rd. E15 20 B1
or Rd. E16 20 B3
or Way SE3 41 C2
orbrook SE3 41 D2
resa Rd. SW3 30 F1
sell St. E1 18 E5
sergh Clo. SE18 35 A3
sfield Rd. NW3 9 G2
sfield St. W1 17 B4
sford St. E2 18 F1
sion Ho. EC4 44 F2
sion Ho. Pl. EC4 44 F2
son Ms. SW7 23 D5
son Pl. SW7 23 E5
stone Rd. NW2 8 G2
thorp Rd. SE18 35 E1
Mantle Rd. SE4 40 C1
Mantua St. SW11 37 E1
Mantus Rd. E1 19 A3
Manwood Rd. SE4 40 D3
Manwood St. E16 28 B2
Mape St. E2 18 G3
Mapesbury Rd. NW2 8 G4
Mapeshill Pl. NW2 8 E3
Maple Ave. W3 22 A2
Maple Clo. SW4 38 D4
Maple St. W1 17 C4
Mapledene Rd. E8 11 F4
Maplestead Rd. SW2 38 F5
Mapleton Cres. SW18 37 C4
Mapleton Rd. SW18 37 B4
Maplin Rd. E16 20 D5
Maplin St. E3 19 D2
Marban Rd. W9 16 A2
Marble Arch W1 23 G1
Marble Quay E1 25 F2
Marchbank Rd. W14 30 A2
Marchmont St. WC1 17 E3
Marchwood Clo. SE5 32 D3
Marcia Rd. SE1 25 D5
Marcilly Rd. SW18 37 E3
Marco Rd. W6 22 D4
Marcon Pl. E8 11 G2
Marcus Ct. E15 13 B5
Marcus Garvey Way SE24 38 G2
Marcus St. E15 13 B5
Marcus St. SW18 37 C4
Marcus Ter. SW18 37 C4
Marden Sq. SE16 25 G4
Mardon St. E14 19 C4
Mare St. E8 11 G5
Maresfield Gdns.NW3 9 D2
Margaret Ct. W1 43 A1
Margaret St. W1 17 B5
Margaretta Ter. SW3 30 F2
Margate Rd. SW2 38 E3
Margery Pk. Rd. E7 13 D3
Margery St. WC1 17 G2
Margravine Gdns. W6 29 F1
Margravine Rd. W6 29 F1
Maria Ter. E1 19 B3
Marian Pl. E2 18 G1
Marian Way NW10 8 B4
Marigold All. SE1 44 B4
Marigold St. SE16 25 G3
Marina Dr., Well. 35 G5
Marine Dr. SE18 28 B5
Marinefield Rd. SW6 30 C5
Mariners Ms. E14 27 A5
Marischal Rd. SE13 41 A1
Maritime St. E3 19 D3
Marjorie Gro. SW11 37 G2
Mark La. EC3 44 J3
Market Ct. W1 43 A1
Market Hill SE18 28 C4
Market Pl. W1 43 A1
Market Rd. N7 10 E3
Market St. E6 21 B1
Market St. SE18 28 C5
Markham Pl. SW3 30 G1
Markham Sq. SW3 30 G1
Markham St. SW3 30 F1
Marl Rd. SW18 37 C2
Marlborough Ave. E8 11 F5
Marlborough Bldgs. SW3 23 F5
Marlborough Ct. W8 23 B5
Marlborough Gro. SE1 32 F1
Marlborough Hill NW8 9 D5
Marlborough La. SE7 34 F2
Marlborough Pl. NW8 16 D1
Marlborough Rd. E7 13 F4
Marlborough Rd. SW1 43 B6
Marlborough St. SW3 23 F5
Marloes Rd. W8 23 C4
Marlow Ct. NW6 8 F4
Marlow Rd. E6 21 B2
Marlow Way SE16 26 B3
Marlowe Gdns. SE9 42 C4
Marlowes, The NW8 9 E5
Marmion Rd. SW11 38 A2
Marmont Rd. SE15 32 F4
Marmora Rd. SE22 40 A4
Marne St. W10 15 G2
Marney Rd. SW11 38 A2
Marnham Ave. NW2 8 G1
Marnock Rd. SE4 40 D3
Maroon St. E14 19 C4
Marquess Rd. N1 11 C3
Marquis Rd. NW1 10 D3
Marrick Clo. SW15 36 C2
Marriott Rd. E15 13 B5
Marryat Sq. SW6 29 G4
Marsala Rd. SE13 40 F2
Marsden Rd. SE15 39 E1
Marsden St. NW5 10 A3
Marsh Hill E9 12 C2
Marsh Wall E14 26 E2
Marshall St. W1 43 B2
Marshall's Gro. SE18 28 A5
Marshalsea Rd. SE1 25 B3
Marsham St. SW1 24 D4
Marshbrook Clo. SE3 41 G1
Marshfield St. E14 26 G4
Marshgate La. E15 12 F4
Marsland Clo. SE17 32 A1
Mart St. WC2 43 F3
Martello St. E8 11 G4
Martello Ter. E8 11 G4
Martha Rd. E15 13 B3
Martha St. E1 18 G5
Martin Bowes Rd. SE9 42 B1
Martin La. EC4 44 G3
Martindale Ave. E16 27 D1
Martindale Rd. SW12 38 B5
Martineau Est. E1 26 A1
Martineau Rd. N5 11 A1
Martlett Ct. WC2 43 F2
Marville Rd. SW6 30 A3
Mary Ann Gdns. SE8 33 E2
Mary Datchelor Clo. SE5 32 C4
Mary Grn. NW8 9 C5
Mary Pl. W11 22 G1
Mary St. N1 11 B5
Marybank SE18 28 B5
Maryland Pk. E15 13 B2
Maryland Rd. E15 13 A2
Maryland Sq. E15 13 B2
Maryland St. E15 13 A2
Marylands Rd. W9 16 B3
Marylebone High St. W1 17 A4
Marylebone La. W1 17 A5
Marylebone Ms. W1 17 B4
Marylebone Pas. W1 43 B1
Marylebone Rd. NW1 16 F4
Marylebone St. W1 17 A4
Marylee Way SE11 24 F5
Maryon Gro. SE7 28 A5
Maryon Rd. SE7 28 A5
Maryon Rd. SE18 28 A5
Masbro Rd. W14 22 F4
Mascalls Rd. SE7 34 F2
Mascotte Rd. SW15 36 F2
Masefield Gdns. E6 21 C3
Mashie Rd. W3 15 A5
Maskelyne Clo. SW11 30 F4
Mason Clo. E16 27 D1
Mason St. SE17 25 C5
Masons Ave. EC2 44 F1
Masons Hill SE18 28 D5
Mason's Pl. EC1 18 B2
Mason's Yd. SW1 43 B5
Massingham St. E1 19 B3
Mast Ho. Ter. E14 26 E5
Master Gunner Pl. SE18 35 A3
Masterman Rd. E6 21 A2
Masters St. E1 19 B4
Mastmaker Rd. E14 26 E3
Matchless Dr. SE18 35 C3
Matham Gro. SE22 39 E2
Matheson Rd. W14 23 A5
Mathews Pk. Ave. E15 13 C3
Matilda St. N1 10 F5
Matlock Clo. SE24 39 B2
Matlock St. E14 19 C5
Matthew Clo. W10 15 F3
Matthew Parker St. SW1 24 D3
Matthews Ave. E6 21 C1
Matthews St. SW11 30 G5
Matthews Yd. WC2 43 E2
Matthias Rd. N16 11 C2
Maud Cashmore Way SE18 28 B4
Maud Gdns. E13 13 C5
Maud Rd. E13 20 C1
Maud St. E16 20 C4
Maude Rd. SE5 32 D4
Maudslay Rd. SE9 42 B1
Mauleverer Rd. SW2 38 E3
Maunsel St. SW1 24 D5
Maurice St. W12 15 D5
Mauritius Rd. SE10 27 B5
Maverton Rd. E3 12 E5
Mawbey Est. SE1 32 E1
Mawbey Pl. SE1 32 E1
Mawbey St. SW8 31 E3
Maxey Rd. SE18 28 E5
Maxted Rd. SE15 39 E1
Maxwell Rd. SW6 30 C3
May Rd. E13 20 D1
Mayall Rd. SE24 39 A3
Maybury Gdns. NW10 8 D3
Maybury Rd. E13 20 F3
Mayday Gdns. SE3 35 A5
Mayerne Rd. SE9 41 G3
Mayfair Pl. W1 24 B2
Mayfield Ave. W4 22 A5
Mayfield Clo. SW4 38 D3
Mayfield Rd. E8 11 E4
Mayfield Rd. E13 20 C3
Mayfield Rd. W12 22 A3
Mayflower Rd. SW9 38 E1
Mayflower St. SE16 26 A3
Mayford Clo. SW12 37 G5
Mayford Rd. SW12 37 G5
Maygood St. N1 17 F1
Maygrove Rd. NW6 9 A3
Mayhill Rd. SE7 34 E2
Mayo Rd. NW10 8 A3
Mayola Rd. E5 12 A1
Mayplace La. SE18 35 D3
Mays Ct. WC2 43 E4
Maysoule Rd. SW11 37 E2
Mayville Rd., Ilf. 14 D2
Maze Hill SE3 34 B3
Maze Hill SE10 34 B2
Mazenod Ave. NW6 9 B4
McAuley Clo. SE1 24 G4
McAuley Clo. SE9 42 D3
McCall Cres. SE7 35 A1
McCullum Rd. E3 12 D5
McDermott Clo. SW11 37 F1
McDermott Rd. SE15 39 F1
McDowall Rd. SE5 32 B4
McDowell Clo. E16 20 C4
McEwan Way E15 13 A5
McGrath Rd. E15 13 C2
McGregor Rd. W11 16 A4

McKerrell Rd. SE15 32 F4
McLeod's Ms. SW7 23 C5
McMillan St. SE8 33 E2
McNeil Rd. SE5 32 D5
Mead Pl. E9 12 A3
Meadcroft Rd. SE11 32 A2
Meadow Clo. E9 12 D2
Meadow Ms. SW8 31 F2
Meadow Pl. SW8 31 E3
Meadow Rd. SW8 31 F3
Meadow Row SE1 25 B4
Meadowbank NW3 9 G4
Meadowbank SE3 41 C1
Meadowbank Clo. SW6 29 E3
Meadowcourt Rd. SE3 41 C2
Meadowside SE9 41 F2
Meadway, Ilf. 14 G1
Meakin Est. SE1 25 D4
Meanley Rd. E12 14 A1
Meard St. W1 43 C2
Meath Rd. E15 20 C1
Meath St. SW11 31 B4
Mecklenburgh Pl. WC1 17 F3
Mecklenburgh Sq. WC1 17 F3
Mecklenburgh St. WC1 17 F2
Medburn St. NW1 17 D1
Medebourne Clo. SE3 41 D1
Medfield St. SW15 36 C5
Median Rd. E5 12 A2
Medlar St. SE5 32 B4
Medley Rd. NW6 9 B3
Medora Rd. SW2 38 F5
Medusa Rd. SE6 40 F4
Medway Rd. E3 19 C1
Medway St. SW1 24 D4
Medwin St. SW4 38 F2
Meerbrook Rd. SE3 41 F1
Meeson Rd. E15 13 C5
Meeson St. E5 12 C1
Meeting Ho. La. SE15 32 G4
Mehetabel Rd. E9 12 A3
Melba Way SE13 33 F4
Melbourne Gro. SE22 39 D2
Melbourne Ms. SE6 40 G5
Melbourne Ms. SW9 31 G4
Melbourne Pl. WC2 43 H2
Melbourne Rd. E6 14 B5
Melbury Ct. W8 23 A4
Melbury Rd. W14 23 A4
Melbury Ter. NW1 16 F3
Melcombe Pl. NW1 16 G4
Melcombe St. NW1 16 G3
Melford Ave., Bark. 14 G3
Melford Rd. E6 21 B3
Melford Rd. SE22 39 F5
Melgund Rd. N5 10 G2
Melina Pl. NW8 16 E2
Melina Rd. W12 22 D3
Melior St. SE1 25 C3
Melling St. SE18 35 G2
Mellish St. E14 26 E4
Mellitus St. W12 15 B5
Melody Rd. SW18 37 D3
Melon Rd. SE15 32 F4
Melrose Ave. NW2 8 D2
Melrose Gdns. W6 22 E4
Melrose Rd. SW13 29 B5
Melrose Rd. SW18 37 A4
Melrose Ter. W6 22 E3
Melthorpe Gdns. SE3 34 G4
Melton Ct. SW7 23 E5
Melton St. NW1 17 C2
Melville Rd. SW13 29 C4
Memorial Ave. E15 20 B2
Mendip Rd. SW11 37 D1
Mendora Rd. SW6 29 G3
Menelik Rd. NW2 8 G1
Mentmore Ter. E8 11 G4
Mepham St. SE1 43 J6
Merbury Clo. SE13 41 A3
Merbury Rd. SE28 28 G3
Mercator Rd. SE13 41 A2
Mercer St. WC2 43 E2
Merceron St. E1 18 G3
Mercers Clo. SE10 27 C5
Mercers Pl. W6 22 E5
Merchant St. E3 19 D2
Mercia Gro. SE13 40 G2
Mercier Rd. SW15 36 G3
Mercury Way SE14 33 B2
Mercy Ter. SE13 40 F2
Mere Clo. SW15 36 F5
Meredith Ave. NW2 8 E2
Meredith St. E13 20 D2
Meredyth Rd. SW13 29 C5
Meretone Clo. SE4 40 C2
Mereworth Dr. SE18 35 D3
Meridian Gate E14 26 G3
Meridian Rd. SE7 34 G3
Meridian Trd. Est. SE7 27 E5
Merifield Rd. SE9 41 F2
Merivale Rd. SW15 36 G2
Mermaid Ct. SE1 25 C3
Mermaid Ct. SE16 26 D2
Merredene St. SW2 38 F4
Merrick Sq. SE1 25 B4
Merriman Rd. SE3 34 F4
Merrington Rd. SW6 30 B2
Merritt Rd. SE4 40 D3
Merrow St. SE17 32 B2
Merryfield SE3 34 C5
Merryfields Way SE6 40 F5
Mersea Ho., Bark. 14 D3
Merthyr Ter. SW13 29 D2
Merton Ave. W4 22 B5
Merton Ri. NW3 9 F4
Merton Rd. SW18 37 B3
Merttins Rd. SE15 40 B3
Mervan Rd. SW2 38 G2
Messent Rd. SE9 41 F3
Messeter Pl. SE9 42 C4
Messina Ave. NW6 9 B4
Meteor St. SW11 38 A2
Methley St. SE11 31 G1
Methwold Rd. W10 15 F4
Mews St. E1 25 F2
Mexfield Rd. SW15 37 A3
Meymott St. SE1 44 B6
Meynell Cres. E9 12 B4
Meynell Gdns. E9 12 B4
Meynell Rd. E9 12 B4
Meyrick Rd. NW10 8 C3
Meyrick Rd. SW11 37 E1
Micawber St. N1 18 B2
Michael Rd. SW6 30 C4
Michaels Clo. SE13 41 B2
Micheldever Rd. SE12 41 B4
Michigan Ave. E12 14 B1
Micklethwaite Rd. SW6 30 B2
Middle Fld. NW8 9 E5
Middle Pk. Ave. SE9 41 G4
Middle Row W10 15 G3
Middle Temple EC4 43 J3
Middle Temple La. EC4 43 J2
Middle Yd. SE1 44 H5
Middlesex St. E1 18 D4
Middleton Dr. SE16 26 B3
Middleton Gro. N7 10 E2
Middleton Rd. E8 11 E4
Middleton St. E2 18 G2
Middleton Way SE13 41 A2
Midland Rd. NW1 17 D1
Midlothian Rd. E3 19 C4
Midstrath Rd. NW10 8 A1
Miers Clo. E6 14 C5
Milborne Gro. SW10 30 D1
Milborne St. E9 12 A3
Milborough Cres. SE12 41 B4
Milcote St. SE1 25 A3
Mildenhall Rd. E5 12 A1
Mildmay Ave. N1 11 C3
Mildmay Gro. N. N1 11 C2
Mildmay Gro. S. N1 11 C2
Mildmay Pk. N1 11 C2
Mildmay Rd. N1 11 C2
Mildmay St. N1 11 C3
Mile End Pl. E1 19 B3
Mile End Rd. E1 19 A4
Mile End Rd. E3 19 C3
Miles St. SW8 31 E2
Milfoil St. W12 22 C1
Milford La. WC2 43 J3
Milk St. E16 28 D2
Milk St. EC2 44 E1
Milk Yd. E1 26 A1
Milkwell Yd. SE5 32 B4
Milkwood Rd. SE24 39 A3
Mill Hill Rd. SW13 29 C5
Mill La. NW6 8 G2
Mill La. SE18 35 C1
Mill Rd. E16 27 E2
Mill Row N1 11 D5
Mill Shot Clo. SW6 29 E4
Mill St. SE1 25 E3
Mill St. W1 43 A3
Millais Ave. E12 14 C2
Millais Rd. E11 12 G1
Millbank SW1 24 E5
Millbank Twr. SW1 24 E5
Millbank Way SE12 41 D3
Millbrook Ave., Well. 42 F2
Millbrook Rd. SW9 39 A1
Millender Wk. SE16 26 A5
Miller St. NW1 17 C1
Miller's Ave. E8 11 E2
Miller's Ter. E8 11 E2
Millers Way W6 22 E3
Millfields Rd. E5 12 A1
Millgrove St. SW11 31 A4
Millharbour E14 26 F4
Milligan St. E14 26 D1
Millman Ms. WC1 17 F3
Millman St. WC1 17 F3
Millmark Gro. SE14 33 C5
Millstream Rd. SE1 25 E3
Millwall Dock Rd. E14 26 E4
Milman Rd. NW6 15 F1
Milman's St. SW10 30 E2
Milne Gdns. SE9 42 A3
Milner Pl. N1 10 G5
Milner Rd. E15 20 B2
Milner Sq. N1 11 A4
Milner St. SW3 23 G5
Milo Rd. SE22 39 E4
Milroy Wk. SE1 44 B5
Milson Rd. W14 22 F4
Milton Ave. E6 13 G4
Milton Clo. SE1 25 E5
Milton Ct. Rd. SE14 33 C2
Milton Gro. N16 11 C1
Milton Rd. SE24 39 A4
Milton St. EC2 18 C4
Milverton Rd. NW6 8 E4
Milverton St. SE11 31 G1
Mimosa St. SW6 30 A4
Mina Rd. SE17 32 D1
Minard Rd. SE6 41 B5
Mincing La. EC3 44 H3
Minera Ms. SW1 24 A5
Mineral St. SE18 28 G5
Minerva Clo. SW9 31 G3
Minerva St. E2 18 G1
Minet Ave. NW10 15 A1
Minet Gdns. NW10 1
Minet Rd. SW9 3
Minford Gdns. W14 2
Ming St. E14 2
Minories EC3 1
Minson Rd. E9 1
Minstead Gdns. SW15 3
Minster Rd. NW2
Mintern St. N1 1
Mirabel Rd. SW6 3
Mirfield St. SE7 2
Miriam Rd. SE18 3
Mission Pl. SE15 3
Mitcham Rd. E6 2
Mitchell St. EC1 1
Mitchison Rd. N1 1
Mitre Ct. EC2 4
Mitre Ct. EC4 4
Mitre Rd. E15 2
Mitre Rd. SE1 2
Mitre Sq. EC3 4
Mitre St. EC3 4
Mitre Way NW10 1
Moat Pl. SW9 3
Moberley Rd. SW4 3
Moiety Rd. E14 2
Moira Rd. SE9 4
Molesford Rd. SW6 3
Molesworth St. SE13 4
Molly Huggins Clo. SW12 3
Molyneux St. W1 1
Mona Rd. SE15 3
Mona St. E16 2
Monarch Dr. E16 2
Monck St. SW1 2
Monclar Rd. SE5 3
Moncrieff St. SE15 3
Monega Rd. E7 1
Monega Rd. E12 1
Monier Rd. E3 1
Monk Dr. E16 2
Monk St. SE18 2
Monkton St. SE11 2
Monmouth Rd. E6 2
Monmouth Rd. W2 1
Monmouth St. WC2 4
Monnow Rd. SE1 3
Monson Rd. NW10 1
Monson Rd. SE14 3
Montacute Rd. SE6 4
Montagu Ms. N. W1 1
Montagu Pl. W1 1
Montagu Sq. W1 1
Montagu St. W1 1
Montague Ave. SE4 4
Montague Clo. SE1 4
Montague Pl. WC1 1
Montague Rd. E8 1
Montague St. EC1 1
Montague St. WC1 1
Montcalm Rd. SE7 3
Monteagle Ave., Bark. 1
Monteagle Way SE15 3
Montefiore St. SW8 3
Monteith Rd. E3 1
Montem Rd. SE23 4
Montford Pl. SE11 3
Montholme Rd. SW11 3
Montolieu Gdns. SW15 3
Montpelier Gdns. E6 2
Montpelier Gro. NW5 1
Montpelier Pl. SW7 2
Montpelier Rd. SE15 3
Montpelier Row SE3 3
Montpelier Sq. SW7 2
Montpelier St. SW7 2

pelier Vale SE3 34 C5
pelier Wk. SW7 23 F4
'eal Pl. WC2 43 G3
'ose Ave. NW6 15 G1
'ose Ave., Well. 42 F1
'ose Ct. SW7 23 E3
rose Pl. SW1 24 A3
serrat Rd. 36 G2
/15
ment Gdns. 40 G3
13
ment St. EC3 44 G3
a St. E1 26 A1
kee St. SE16 26 A4
y St. E1 19 B2
St. N1 11 A5
La. EC2 18 C4
St. W1 43 D2
down SE18 35 C4
e Pk. Rd. SW6 30 C3
e St. SW3 23 G5
ields EC2 18 C4
gate EC2 18 C4
gate Pl. EC2 44 F1
head Way SE3 41 E1
house Rd. W2 16 B5
and Rd. SW9 39 A2
ands Est. SW9 38 G2
Rd. NW2 8 E1
St. EC1 18 B2
nt St. E14 26 E1
St. SW9 31 F4
ian St. E2 19 A2
unt St. SW9 38 F1
en Clo. SE13 33 G5
en Hill SE13 33 G5
en La. SE13 33 G4
en Rd. SE3 34 D5
en Rd. Ms. SE3 34 D5
en St. SE13 33 F4
en Wf. Rd. SE10 27 B4
Clo. E16 20 C5
Clo. W14 22 F5
ambe Clo. E1 19 B4
ambe St. SE17 25 B5
and St. EC1 18 A2
la Rd. SW12 37 G5
a St. SE6 40 F5
by Wk. SW8 31 B5
on Pl. SW1 31 C1
on St. SW1 31 C1
on Ter. SW1 31 C1
n Rd. N7 10 G2
n Rd. W10 16 A4
n St. E3 19 C2
n St. E16 20 C4
ns La. SE1 44 H6
ry Clo. N7 10 E1
St. SW18 37 C2
Rd. E15 20 C1
Rd. SE13 40 G2
Rd., Bark. 14 F5
St. SE1 24 G4
Rd. SE5 32 B5
ng La. E9 12 A3
ngton Ave. 23 A5
4
ngton Cres. 17 C1
1
ngton Gro. E3 19 E2
ngton Ms. SE5 32 B4
ngton Rd. SE8 33 D3
ngton St. NW1 17 B1
ngton Ter. NW1 17 B1
co St. SE1 25 D3
th Gro. E9 12 B5
th Rd. E9 12 A5
th St. E2 19 B2
th Ter. SW1 24 C4
Ave. E12 14 B2

Morris Gdns. SW18 37 B5
Morris Rd. E14 19 F4
Morris Rd. E15 13 A1
Morris St. E1 18 G5
Morrish Rd. SW2 38 E5
Morrison St. SW11 38 A1
Morse Clo. E13 20 D2
Morshead Rd. W9 16 B2
Morten Clo. SW4 38 D4
Mortham St. E15 13 B5
Mortimer Cres. NW6 9 C5
Mortimer Est. NW6 9 C5
Mortimer Pl. NW6 9 C5
Mortimer Rd. E6 21 B2
Mortimer Rd. N1 11 D4
Mortimer Rd. NW10 15 E2
Mortimer St. W1 43 A1
Mortlake Rd. E16 20 E5
Mortlake Rd., Ilf. 14 E1
Morton Rd. E15 13 C4
Morton Rd. N1 11 B4
Morval Rd. SW2 38 G3
Morville St. E3 19 E1
Moscow Rd. W2 23 C1
Mossbury Rd. SW11 37 F1
Mossford St. E3 19 D3
Mossop St. SW3 23 F5
Mostyn Gdns. NW10 15 F2
Mostyn Gro. E3 19 E1
Mostyn Rd. SW9 31 G4
Motcomb St. SW1 24 A4
Mothers Sq., The E5 11 G1
Moulins Rd. E9 12 A4
Mount Adon Pk. SE22 39 F5
Mount Pleasant WC1 17 G3
Mount Pleasant Rd. NW10 8 E4
Mount Pleasant Rd. SE13 40 G4
Mount Rd., Ilf. 14 D2
Mount Row W1 24 B1
Mount St. W1 24 A1
Mount Vernon NW3 9 D1
Mountague Pl. E14 26 G1
Mountbatten Clo. SE18 35 G2
Mountfield Clo. SE6 41 A5
Mountfield Rd. E6 21 C1
Mounts Pond Rd. SE3 34 A5
Mountsfield Ct. SE13 41 A4
Movers La., Bark. 14 F5
Mowbray Rd. NW6 8 G4
Mowlem St. E2 18 G1
Mowll St. SW9 31 G3
Moxon St. W1 17 A4
Moylan Rd. W6 29 G2
Mozart St. W10 16 A2
Mudlarks Way SE7 27 E4
Mudlarks Way SE10 27 C4
Muir Rd. E5 11 F1
Muirfield W3 15 A5
Mulberry Clo. SE7 34 G2
Mulberry Clo. SE22 39 F4
Mulberry Rd. E8 11 E4
Mulberry Wk. SW3 30 E2
Mulgrave Rd. NW10 8 B1
Mulgrave Rd. SW6 30 A2
Muller Rd. SW4 38 D4
Multon Rd. SW18 37 E5
Mulvaney Way SE1 25 C3
Mumford Ct. EC2 44 E1
Muncaster Rd. SW11 37 G3
Mund St. W14 30 A1
Mundania Rd. SE22 39 G4
Munday Rd. E16 20 D5
Munden St. W14 22 G5
Mundy St. N1 18 D2
Munro Ms. W10 15 G4

Munro Ter. SW10 30 E2
Munster Rd. SW6 29 G3
Munster Sq. NW1 17 B2
Munton Rd. SE17 25 B5
Murdock St. SE15 32 G2
Muriel St. N1 10 F5
Murillo Rd. SE13 41 A2
Murphy St. SE1 24 G3
Murray Gro. N1 18 B1
Murray Ms. NW1 10 D4
Murray Sq. E16 20 D5
Murray St. NW1 10 D4
Mursell Est. SW8 31 F4
Musard Rd. W6 29 G2
Musbury St. E1 19 A5
Muscal W6 29 G2
Muschamp Rd. SE15 39 E1
Muscovy St. EC3 44 J4
Museum St. WC1 17 E4
Musgrave Cres. SW6 30 B3
Musgrove Rd. SE14 33 B4
Mutrix Rd. NW6 9 B5
Myatt Rd. SW9 32 A4
Myatt's Flds. S. SW9 31 G5
Mycenae Rd. SE3 34 D3
Myddelton Sq. EC1 17 G2
Myddelton St. EC1 17 G2
Myers La. SE14 33 B2
Mylne St. EC1 17 G1
Myrdle St. E1 18 F4
Myron Pl. SE13 40 G1
Myrtle Rd. E6 14 A5
Myrtle Wk. N1 18 D1
Mysore Rd. SW11 37 G1

N

Nadine St. SE7 34 F1
Nagasaki Wk. SE7 27 F4
Nairn St. E14 19 G4
Nairne Gro. SE24 39 C3
Naish Ct. N1 10 E5
Nankin St. E14 19 E5
Nansen Rd. SW11 38 A2
Nantes Clo. SW18 37 D2
Napier Ave. E14 33 E1
Napier Ave. SW6 37 A1
Napier Gro. N1 18 B1
Napier Pl. W14 23 A4
Napier Rd. E6 14 C5
Napier Rd. E11 13 B1
Napier Rd. E15 20 B1
Napier Rd. NW10 15 D2
Napier Rd. W14 22 G4
Napier Ter. N1 11 A3
Narbonne Ave. SW4 38 C3
Narborough St. SW6 30 C5
Narcissus Rd. NW6 9 B2
Narrow St. E14 26 C1
Nascot St. W12 15 E5
Nash Rd. SE4 40 C2
Nasmyth St. W6 22 D4
Nassau Rd. SW13 29 B4
Nassau St. W1 17 C4
Nassington Rd. NW3 9 F1
Natal Rd., Ilf. 14 D1
Nathan Way SE28 28 G4
Naval Row E14 26 G1
Navarino Gro. E8 11 F3
Navarino Rd. E8 11 F3
Navarre Rd. E6 21 A1
Navarre St. E2 18 E3
Navy St. SW4 38 D1
Naylor Rd. SE15 32 G3
Nazareth Gdns. SE15 32 G5
Nazrul St. E2 18 E2
Neal St. WC2 43 E2
Nealden St. SW9 38 F1
Neal's Yd. WC2 43 E2
Neasden Clo. NW10 8 A2
Neate St. SE5 32 D2

Neatscourt Rd. E6 20 G4
Neckinger SE16 25 E4
Neckinger Est. SE16 25 E4
Neckinger St. SE1 25 E3
Nectarine Way SE13 33 F5
Needleman St. SE16 26 B3
Nelgarde Rd. SE6 40 E5
Nella Rd. W6 29 F2
Nelldale Rd. SE16 26 A5
Nelson Gdns. E2 18 F2
Nelson Mandela Rd. SE3 41 F1
Nelson Pas. EC1 18 B2
Nelson Pl. N1 18 A1
Nelson Rd. SE10 33 G2
Nelson Sq. SE1 25 A3
Nelson St. E1 18 G5
Nelson St. E6 21 B1
Nelson Ter. N1 18 A1
Nelson's Row SW4 38 D2
Nepean St. SW15 36 C4
Neptune St. SE16 26 A4
Nesbit Rd. SE9 41 G2
Nesham St. E1 25 F2
Netheravon Rd. N. W4 22 B5
Netheravon Rd. S. W4 29 B1
Netherby Rd. SE23 40 A5
Netherfield Gdns., Bark. 14 F3
Netherford Rd. SW4 31 C5
Netherhall Gdns. NW3 9 D3
Netherton Gro. SW10 30 D2
Netherwood Rd. W14 22 F4
Netherwood St. NW6 9 A4
Nettleton Rd. SE14 33 B4
Nevada St. SE10 33 G2
Nevern Pl. SW5 23 B5
Nevern Rd. SW5 23 B5
Nevern Sq. SW5 23 B5
Nevill Rd. N16 11 D1
Neville Clo. NW6 16 A1
Neville Clo. SE15 32 F3
Neville Gill Clo. SW18 37 C4
Neville Rd. E7 13 D4
Neville Rd. NW6 16 A1
Neville St. SW7 30 E1
Neville Ter. SW7 30 E1
New Barn St. E13 20 D3
New Bond St. W1 17 B5
New Bri. St. EC4 44 B2
New Burlington Ms. W1 43 A3
New Burlington Pl. W1 43 A3
New Burlington St. W1 43 A3
New Butt La. SE8 33 E3
New Cavendish St. W1 17 A4
New Change EC4 44 D2
New Ch. Rd. SE5 32 C3
New City Rd. E13 20 F2
New Compton St. WC2 43 D2
New Ct. EC4 43 J3
New Covent Gdn. Mkt. SW8 31 D3
New Coventry St. W1 43 D4
New Cross Rd. SE14 33 A3
New End NW3 9 D1
New End Sq. NW3 9 E1
New Ferry App. SE18 28 C4
New Fetter La. EC4 44 A1
New Globe Wk. SE1 44 D5
New Inn Pas. WC2 43 H2
New Inn Yd. EC2 18 D3
New Kent Rd. SE1 25 B4
New King St. SE8 33 E2

New Kings Rd. SW6 30 A5
New London St. EC3 44 J3
New Lydenburgh St. SE7 27 F4
New Mt. St. E15 13 A4
New N. Rd. N1 11 B4
New N. St. WC1 17 F4
New Oxford St. WC1 43 D1
New Pk. Ct. SW2 38 E5
New Pl. Sq. SE16 25 G4
New Plaistow Rd. E15 13 B5
New Quebec St. W1 16 G5
New Rd. E1 18 G4
New Row WC2 43 E3
New Sq. WC2 43 H1
New St. EC2 18 D4
New St. Sq. EC4 44 A1
New Union Clo. E14 26 G4
New Union St. EC2 18 C4
New Wf. Rd. N1 17 E1
Newark Knok E6 21 C5
Newark St. E1 18 G4
Newburgh St. W1 43 A2
Newburn St. SE11 31 F1
Newby Pl. E14 26 G1
Newby St. SW8 38 B1
Newcastle Clo. EC4 44 B1
Newcastle Pl. W2 16 E4
Newcomen Rd. SW11 37 E1
Newcomen St. SE1 25 C3
Newcourt St. NW8 16 F1
Newell St. E14 19 'D5
Newent Clo. SE15 32 D3
Newgate St. EC1 44 C1
Newham Way E6 21 C3
Newham Way E16 20 C4
Newhaven Gdns. SE9 41 G2
Newhaven La. E16 20 C3
Newington Butts SE1 25 A5
Newington Butts SE11 25 A5
Newington Causeway SE1 25 A4
Newington Grn. N1 11 C2
Newington Grn. N16 11 C2
Newington Grn. Rd. N1 11 C3
Newland St. E16 28 A2
Newlands Ct. SE9 42 C4
Newlands Quay E1 26 A1
Newman Rd. E13 20 E2
Newman St. W1 17 C4
Newman Yd. W1 43 B1
Newman's Ct. EC3 44 G2
Newport Ct. WC2 43 D3
Newport Pl. WC2 43 D3
Newport Rd. SW13 29 C4
Newport St. SE11 24 F5
Newstead Rd. SE12 41 C5
Newton Gro. W4 22 A5
Newton Rd. E15 13 A2
Newton Rd. W2 16 C5
Newton St. WC2 43 F1
Nicholas La. EC4 44 G3
Nicholas Rd. E1 19 A3
Nicholl St. E2 11 F5
Nicholson St. SE1 44 B6
Nicoll Rd. NW10 8 A5
Nicosia Rd. SW18 37 F5
Nigel Ms., Ilf. 14 D1
Nigel Rd. E7 13 F2
Nigel Rd. SE15 39 F1
Nigeria Rd. SE7 34 F3
Nightingale Gro. SE13 41 A3
Nightingale La. SW4 38 B4
Nightingale La. SW12 37 G5
Nightingale Pl. SE18 35 C2
Nightingale Rd. NW10 15 B1
Nightingale Sq. SW12 38 A5
Nightingale Vale SE18 35 C2
Nightingale Wk. SW4 38 B4
Nightingale Way E6 21 A4
Nile Rd. E13 20 F1
Nile St. N1 18 C2
Nile Ter. SE15 32 E1
Nine Acres Clo. E12 14 A2
Nine Elms La. SW8 31 C3
Nithdale Rd. SE18 35 D3
Niton St. SW6 29 F3
Noble St. EC2 44 D1
Noel Rd. E6 21 A3
Noel Rd. N1 18 A1
Noel St. W1 43 B2
Nolan Way E5 11 F1
Norbiton Rd. E14 19 D5
Norbroke St. W12 22 B1
Norcroft Gdns. SE22 39 F5
Norfolk Cres. W2 16 F5
Norfolk Cres., Sid. 42 G5
Norfolk Ho. SE3 34 B2
Norfolk Pl. W2 16 E5
Norfolk Rd. E6 14 B5
Norfolk Rd. NW8 9 E5
Norfolk Rd. NW10 8 A4
Norfolk Rd., Bark. 14 G4
Norfolk Row SE1 24 F4
Norfolk Sq. W2 16 E5
Norfolk St. E7 13 D2
Norland Pl. W11 22 G2
Norland Rd. W11 22 F2
Norland Sq. W11 22 G2
Norman Gro. E3 19 C1
Norman Rd. E6 21 B3
Norman Rd. SE10 33 F3
Norman Rd., Ilf. 14 D2
Normanby Rd. NW10 8 B1
Normand Rd. W14 30 A2
Normandy Rd. SW9 31 G4
Normandy Ter. E16 20 E5
Norris St. SW1 43 C4
Norroy Rd. SW15 36 F2
North Audley St. W1 24 A1
North Bank NW8 16 F2
North Carriage Dr. W2 23 F1
North Circular Rd. NW10 8 A1
North Colonnade E14 26 E2
North Cres. E16 20 A3
North Cross Rd. SE22 39 E3
North End Cres. W14 23 A5
North End Ho. W14 22 G5
North End Rd. SW6 30 A2
North End Rd. W14 22 G5
North Gower St. NW1 17 C2
North Ms. WC1 17 F3
North Pk. SE9 42 C4
North Pas. SW18 37 B3
North Peckham Est. SE15 32 D3
North Pole Rd. W10 15 E4
North Ride W2 23 F2
North Rd. N7 10 E3
North Rd. SE18 28 G5
North Row W1 23 G1
North St. E13 20 E1
North St. SW4 38 C1
North St., Bark. 14 D3
North Tenter St. E1 18 E5
North Vw. Cres. NW10 8 B1
North Vill. NW1 10 D3
North Wf. Rd. W2 16 E4
North Woolwich Rd. E16 27 D2
Northampton Pk. N1 11 B3
Northampton Rd. EC1 17 G3
Northampton Sq. EC1 18 A2
Northampton St. N1 11 B4
Northbourne Rd. SW4 38 D2
Northbrook Rd. SE13 41 A3
Northburgh St. EC1 18 A3
Northchurch Rd. N1 11 C4
Northchurch Ter. N1 11 D4
Northcote Rd. NW10 8 A4
Northcote Rd. SW11 37 F3
Northdown St. N1 17 E1
Northern Relief Rd., Bark. 14 D4
Northern Rd. E13 20 E1
Northey St. E14 26 C1
Northfield Rd. E6 14 B4
Northfields SW18 37 B2
Northiam St. E9 11 G5
Northington St. WC1 17 F3
Northlands St. SE5 32 B5
Northolme Rd. N5 11 B1
Northport St. N1 11 C5
Northumberland All. EC3 44 J2
Northumberland Ave. WC2 43 E5
Northumberland Ave., Well. 42 F2
Northumberland Pl. W2 16 B5
Northumberland Rd. E6 21 A5
Northumberland St. WC2 43 E5
Northumbria St. E14 19 E5
Northway Rd. SE5 39 B1
Northwick Ter. NW8 16 E3
Norton Folgate E1 18 D4
Norway Gate SE16 26 C4
Norway St. SE10 33 F2
Norwich Rd. E7 13 D2
Norwich St. EC4 43 J1
Notley St. SE5 32 C3
Notre Dame Est. SW4 38 C2
Notting Barn Rd. W10 15 F3
Notting Hill Gate W11 23 B2
Nottingham Ave. E16 20 F4
Nottingham Ct. WC2 43 E2
Nottingham Pl. W1 17 A4
Nottingham St. W1 17 A4
Novello St. SW6 30 B4
Nowell Rd. SW13 29 C2
Nuding Clo. SE13 40 E1
Nugent Ter. NW8 16 D1
Nun Ct. EC2 44 F1
Nunhead Cres. SE15 39 G1
Nunhead Est. SE15 39 G2
Nunhead Grn. SE15 39 G1
Nunhead Gro. SE15 39 G1
Nunhead La. SE15 39 G1
Nursery Clo. SE4 33 D5
Nursery Clo. SW15 36 F2
Nursery La. E2 11 E5
Nursery La. E7 13 D3
Nursery La. W10 15 E4
Nursery Rd. SW9 38 F2
Nutbourne St. W10 15 G2
Nutbrook St. SE15 39 F1
Nutcroft Rd. SE15 32 G3
Nutfield Rd. E15 12 G1
Nutfield Rd. SE22 39 E3
Nutford Pl. W1 16 F5
Nuthatch Gdns. SE28 28 F3
Nutley Ter. NW3 9 D3
Nutmeg La. E14 20 A5
Nutt St. SE15 32 E3
Nuttall St. N1 18 D1
Nyanza St. SE18 35 F2
Nynehead St. SE14 33 C3

O

Oak Cres. E16 20 B4
Oak Gro. NW2 8 F1
Oak Hill Pk. NW3 9 C1
Oak Hill Pk. Ms. NW3 9 D1
Oak Hill Way NW3
Oak La. E14
Oak Pk. Gdns. SW19
Oak Tree Rd. NW8
Oak Village NW5
Oak Way W3
Oakbank Gro. SE24
Oakbury Rd. SW6
Oakcroft Rd. SE13
Oakdale Rd. E7
Oakdale Rd. SE15
Oakden St. SE11
Oake Ct. SW15
Oakfield Rd. E6
Oakfield St. SW10
Oakford Rd. NW5
Oakhill Ave. NW3
Oakhill Rd. SW15
Oakhurst Gro. SE22
Oakington Rd. W9
Oaklands Est. SW4
Oaklands Gro. W12
Oaklands Rd. NW2
Oakley Gdns. SW3
Oakley Pl. SE1
Oakley Rd. N1
Oakley Sq. NW1
Oakley St. SW3
Oaks, The SE18
Oakshaw Rd. SW18
Oaktree Gro., Ilf.
Oakways SE9
Oakwood Ct. W14
Oakwood La. W14
Oakworth Rd. W10
Oat La. EC2
Oban Clo. E13
Oban Rd. E13
Oban St. E14
Oberstein Rd. SW11
Oborne Clo. SE24
Observatory Gdns. W8
Occupation La. SE18
Occupation Rd. SE17
Ocean Est. E1
Ocean St. E1
Ockendon Rd. N1
Octavia St. SW11
Octavius St. SE8
Odessa Rd. E7
Odessa Rd. NW10
Odessa St. SE16
Odger St. SW11
Odhams Wk. WC2
Offerton Rd. SW4
Offley Rd. SW9
Offord Rd. N1
Offord St. N1
Ogilby St. SE18
Oglander Rd. SE15
Ogle St. W1
Ohio Rd. E13
Oil Mill La. W6
Okehampton Rd. NW10
Olaf St. W11
Old Bailey EC4
Old Bethnal Grn. Rd. E2
Old Bond St. W1
Old Brewers Yd. WC2
Old Broad St. EC2
Old Brompton Rd. SW5
Old Brompton Rd. SW7
Old Bldgs. WC2
Old Burlington St. W1

astle St. E1 18 E5
avendish St. W1 17 B5
h. Rd. E1 19 B5
h. St. SW3 30 E1
ompton St. W1 43 C3
t. Pl. W8 23 C3
evonshire Rd. 38 B5
/12
over Rd. SE3 34 D3
ish St. Hill EC4 44 D3
leet La. EC4 44 B1
ord Rd. E2 19 A1
ord Rd. E3 19 B1
loucester St. 17 E4
C1
amaica Rd. SE16 25 F4
ames St. SE15 39 G1
ewry EC2 44 F2
ent Rd. SE1 25 D5
ent Rd. SE15 32 G2
larylebone Rd. 16 F4
V1
lill La. W6 29 C1
Aill Rd. SE18 35 F2
Aontague St. E1 18 F4
lichol St. E2 18 E3
ak Common 15 A3
NW10
ak Common 15 A4
W3
ak La. NW10 15 B2
ak Rd. W3 22 B1
alace Yd. SW1 24 E4
aradise St. SE11 24 F5
k. Ave. SW12 38 A4
k. La. W1 24 A2
ye St. SW1 24 D4
uebec St. W1 16 G5
ueen St. SW1 24 D3
d. SE13 41 B2
oyal Free Sq. N1 10 G5
eacoal La. EC4 44 B2
. Lambeth Rd. 31 E3
/8
q. WC2 43 H1
t. E13 20 E1
t. EC1 18 B3
own SW4 38 C1
Voolwich Rd. 34 A1
10
ork Rd. SW18 37 C3
ury Pl. W1 17 A4
eld Gro. SE16 26 B5
eld Rd. NW10 8 B4
dge Rd. SW12 38 A5
ary Sq. E1 19 A4
ant St. W10 15 F2
Rd. E13 20 F2
Rd. NW2 8 E1
Gdns. E6 21 A5
on Grn. E3 12 D5
r Clo. W12 22 B2
e St. E14 26 G4
r St. SE1 32 F2
y Rd. SE17 32 A2
Rd. SE18 35 E2
pia Way W14 22 G4
n Ave. NW2 8 D1
ara St. SE1 44 E6
ga St. SE14 33 E4
aney Rd. SE14 33 B4
ne Rd. SE15 39 E2
Tree Clo. SE23 40 A4
a Gate SE16 26 C4
r Rd. SW6 30 B2
ow Gdns. SW7 30 E1
ow Sq. SW7 23 E5
io Way E14 26 E1
Clo. E16 20 G5
St. SE11 25 A5

Ophir Ter. SE15 32 F4
Oppenheim Rd. SE13 33 G5
Oppidans Rd. NW3 9 G4
Orange St. WC2 43 D4
Orange Yd. W1 43 D2
Orangery La. SE9 42 B3
Orb St. SE17 25 C5
Orbain Rd. SW6 29 G3
Orbel St. SW11 30 F4
Orchard, The SE3 34 A5
Orchard Clo. W10 15 G4
Orchard Dr. SE3 34 B5
Orchard Pl. E14 27 B1
Orchard Ri. E., Sid. 42 G3
Orchard Ri. W., Sid. 42 G3
Orchard Rd. SE18 28 F5
Orchard St. W1 17 A5
Orchardson St. NW8 16 E3
Orchid Clo. E6 21 A4
Orchid St. W12 22 C1
Orde Hall St. WC1 17 F4
Ordell Rd. E3 19 D1
Ordnance Cres. SE10 27 B3
Ordnance Hill NW8 9 E5
Ordnance Rd. E16 20 C4
Ordnance Rd. SE18 35 C2
Oregano Dr. E14 20 A5
Oregon Ave. E12 14 B1
Oriel Rd. E9 12 B3
Oriental Rd. E16 27 G2
Orissa Rd. SE18 35 G1
Orkney St. SW11 31 A5
Orlando Rd. SW4 38 C1
Orleston Ms. N7 10 G3
Orleston Rd. N7 10 G3
Orlop St. SE10 34 B1
Orme Ct. W2 23 C1
Orme La. W2 23 C1
Ormeley Rd. SW12 38 B5
Ormiston Gro. W12 22 D2
Ormiston Rd. SE10 34 D1
Ormond Yd. SW1 43 B5
Ormonde Gate SW3 30 G1
Ormonde Ter. NW8 9 G5
Ormsby St. E2 18 E1
Ormside St. SE15 33 A2
Ornan Rd. NW3 9 F2
Orpheus St. SE5 32 C4
Orsett St. SE11 31 F1
Orsett Ter. W2 16 C5
Orsman Rd. N1 11 D5
Orville Rd. SW11 30 E5
Orwell Ct. N5 11 B1
Orwell Rd. E13 13 F5
Osberton Rd. SE12 41 D3
Osborn Clo. E8 11 F5
Osborn La. SE23 40 C5
Osborn St. E1 18 E4
Osborne Rd. E7 13 E2
Osborne Rd. E9 12 D3
Osborne Rd. NW2 8 D3
Oscar St. SE8 33 E4
Oseney Cres. NW5 10 C3
O'Shea Gro. E3 12 D5
Osier Ms. W4 29 B2
Osier St. E1 19 A3
Osiers Rd. SW18 37 B2
Osnaburgh St. NW1 17 B3
Ospringe Ct. SE9 42 F4
Ospringe Rd. NW5 10 C1
Ossington St. W2 23 C1
Ossory Rd. SE1 32 F2
Ossulston St. NW1 17 D1
Ostade Rd. SW2 38 F5
Osterley Rd. N16 11 D1
Oswin St. SE11 25 A5
Oswyth Rd. SE5 32 D5
Otford Cres. SE4 40 D4
Otis St. E3 19 G2
Otley Rd. E16 20 F5

Otto St. SE17 32 A2
Outer Circle NW1 17 A3
Outgate Rd. NW10 8 B4
Outram Pl. N1 10 E5
Outram Rd. E6 14 A5
Outwich St. EC3 44 J1
Oval, The E2 18 G1
Oval Pl. SW8 31 F3
Oval Rd. NW1 10 B5
Oval Way SE11 31 F1
Overbury St. E5 12 B1
Overcliff Rd. SE13 40 E1
Overhill Rd. SE22 39 F5
Overmead, Sid. 42 F5
Oversley Ho. W2 16 B4
Overstone Rd. W6 22 E4
Overton Rd. SW9 31 G5
Ovex Clo. E14 26 G3
Ovington Gdns. SW3 23 F4
Ovington Ms. SW3 23 F4
Ovington Sq. SW3 23 F4
Ovington St. SW3 23 F5
Owens Way SE23 40 C5
Oxberry Ave. SW6 29 G5
Oxendon St. SW1 43 C4
Oxenford St. SE15 39 E1
Oxenholme NW1 17 C1
Oxestalls Rd. SE8 33 C1
Oxford Circ. Ave. W1 43 A2
Oxford Ct. EC4 44 F3
Oxford Gdns. W10 15 F5
Oxford Gate W6 22 F5
Oxford Rd. E15 13 A3
Oxford Rd. NW6 16 B1
Oxford Rd. SW15 36 G2
Oxford Rd., Ilf. 14 E2
Oxford Sq. W2 16 F5
Oxford St. W1 17 A5
Oxleas E6 21 D5
Oxleas Clo., Well. 35 F5
Oxley Clo. SE1 32 E1
Oxonian St. SE22 39 E2
Ozolins Way E16 20 D5

P

Pacific Rd. E16 20 D5
Packington Sq. N1 11 B5
Packington St. N1 11 A5
Packmores Rd. SE9 42 F3
Padbury Ct. E2 18 E2
Paddenswick Rd. W6 22 C4
Paddington Grn. W2 16 E4
Paddington St. W1 17 A4
Paddock Clo. SE3 41 D1
Padfield Rd. SE5 39 B1
Pagden St. SW8 31 B4
Page St. SW1 24 D5
Pageantmaster Ct. 44 B2
EC4
Pages Wk. SE1 25 D5
Paget Ri. SE18 35 C2
Paget Rd., Ilf. 14 D1
Paget Ter. SE18 35 C2
Pagnell St. SE14 33 D3
Pagoda Gdns. SE3 34 A5
Pakenham St. WC1 17 F2
Palace Ave. W8 23 C2
Palace Ct. NW3 9 C2
Palace Ct. W2 23 C1
Palace Gdn. Ms. W8 23 B2
Palace Gdns. Ter. W8 23 B2
Palace Gate W8 23 D3
Palace Grn. W8 23 C3
Palace St. SW1 24 C4
Palatine Rd. N16 11 D1
Palermo Rd. NW10 15 C1
Palfrey Pl. SW8 31 F3
Palgrave Rd. W12 22 B4
Pall Mall SW1 43 B6
Pall Mall E. SW1 43 D5

Pall Mall Pl. SW1 43 B6
Pallet Way SE18 35 A4
Palliser Rd. W14 29 G1
Palmer Pl. N7 10 G2
Palmer Rd. E13 20 E3
Palmer St. SW1 24 D4
Palmers Rd. E2 19 B1
Palmerston Cres. 35 E2
SE18
Palmerston Rd. E7 13 E2
Palmerston Rd. NW6 9 A4
Pancras La. EC4 44 E2
Pancras Rd. NW1 17 D1
Pandora Rd. NW6 9 B3
Pangbourne Ave. W10 15 E4
Panmure Clo. N5 11 A1
Pansy Gdns. W12 22 C1
Panton St. SW1 43 C4
Panyer All. EC4 44 D1
Papillons Wk. SE3 41 D1
Papworth Way SW2 38 G5
Parade, The SW11 30 G3
Paradise Rd. SW4 31 E5
Paradise St. SE16 25 G3
Paradise Wk. SW3 30 G2
Paragon, The SE3 34 C5
Paragon Clo. E16 20 D5
Paragon Pl. SE3 34 C5
Paragon Rd. E9 12 A3
Parbury Rd. SE23 40 C4
Pardoner St. SE1 25 C4
Parfett St. E1 18 F4
Parfrey St. W6 29 E2
Paris Gdns. SE1 44 B5
Parish Gate Dr., Sid. 42 G4
Park Ave. E6 14 C5
Park Ave. E15 13 B3
Park Ave. NW2 8 D3
Park Ave., Bark. 14 E3
Park Ave. N. NW10 8 D2
Park Clo. W14 23 A4
Park Cres. W1 17 B3
Park Dr. SE7 35 A2
Park Dr. Clo. SE7 35 A1
Park Gro. E15 13 D5
Park Hill SW4 38 D3
Park La. W1 23 G1
Park Par. NW10 15 B1
Park Pl. E14 26 E2
Park Pl. SW1 43 A6
Park Pl. Vill. W2 16 D4
Park Rd. E6 13 F5
Park Rd. E15 13 D5
Park Rd. NW1 16 G3
Park Rd. NW8 16 F2
Park Rd. NW10 8 A5
Park Row SE10 34 A2
Park Sq. E. NW1 17 B3
Park Sq. Ms. NW1 17 B3
Park Sq. W. NW1 17 B3
Park St. SE1 44 D5
Park St. W1 24 A1
Park Vw. Rd. NW10 8 B1
Park Village E. NW1 17 B1
Park Village W. NW1 17 B1
Park Vista SE10 34 A2
Park Wk. SW10 30 D2
Parkcroft Rd. SE12 41 C5
Parkdale Rd. SE18 35 G1
Parke Rd. SW13 29 C4
Parker Clo. E16 28 A2
Parker Ms. WC2 43 F1
Parker St. E16 28 A2
Parker St. WC2 43 F1
Parkfield Ave. SW14 36 A2
Parkfield Rd. NW10 8 C4
Parkfield Rd. SE14 33 D4
Parkfield St. N1 17 G1
Parkfields SW15 36 E2
Parkgate SE3 41 C1

Parkgate Rd. SW11 30 F3
Parkham St. SW11 30 E4
Parkhill Rd. NW3 9 G2
Parkhill Wk. NW3 9 G2
Parkholme Rd. E8 11 F3
Parkhouse St. SE5 32 C3
Parkhurst Rd. E12 14 C1
Parkhurst Rd. N7 10 E1
Parkmead SW15 36 D4
Parkside SE3 34 C3
Parkside Rd. SW11 31 A4
Parkstead Rd. SW15 36 C3
Parkthorne Rd. SW12 38 D5
Parkville Rd. SW6 30 A3
Parkway NW1 10 B5
Parliament Hill NW3 9 F1
Parliament Sq. SW1 24 E3
Parliament St. SW1 24 E3
Parma Cres. SW11 37 G2
Parmiter St. E2 18 G1
Parnell Rd. E3 12 D5
Parr Rd. E6 13 G5
Parr St. N1 18 C1
Parry Ave. E6 21 B5
Parry Pl. SE18 28 D5
Parry Rd. W10 15 G2
Parry St. SW8 31 E2
Parsifal Rd. NW6 9 B2
Parsonage St. E14 26 G5
Parsons Grn. SW6 30 B5
Parsons Grn. La. SW6 30 B4
Parthenia Rd. SW6 30 B4
Parvin St. SW8 31 D4
Pascal St. SW8 31 D3
Pascoe Rd. SE13 41 A3
Passey Pl. SE9 42 B4
Passmore St. SW1 31 A1
Paston Cres. SE12 41 E5
Pastor St. SE11 25 A5
Patcham Ter. SW8 31 B4
Pater St. W8 23 B4
Paternoster Row EC4 44 D2
Paternoster Sq. EC4 44 C1
Patience Rd. SW11 30 F5
Patio Clo. SW4 38 D4
Patmore Est. SW8 31 C4
Patmore St. SW8 31 C4
Patmos Rd. SW9 32 A3
Paton Clo. E3 19 E2
Patrick Pas. SW11 30 F5
Patrick Rd. E13 20 F2
Patriot Sq. E2 18 G1
Patrol Pl. SE6 40 F4
Patshull Rd. NW5 10 C3
Patten Rd. SW18 37 F5
Patterdale Rd. SE15 33 A3
Paul St. E15 13 B5
Paul St. EC2 18 C3
Paulet Rd. SE5 32 A5
Paultons Sq. SW3 30 E2
Paultons St. SW3 30 E2
Paveley Dr. SW11 30 F3
Paveley St. NW8 16 F3
Pavement, The SW4 38 C2
Pavilion Rd. SW1 23 G4
Paxton Rd. W4 29 A2
Paxton Ter. SW1 31 B2
Payne Rd. E3 19 F1
Payne St. SE8 33 D2
Peabody Est. SE1 44 A6
Peabody Est. SE24 39 B5
Peabody Est. W6 29 E1
Peabody Est. W10 15 E3
Peabody Sq. SE1 25 A3
Peabody Trust SE1 44 D6
Peach Rd. W10 15 F2
Peachum Rd. SE3 34 C2
Pear Tree Clo. E2 11 E5
Pear Tree Ct. EC1 17 G3
Peardon St. SW8 31 B5
Pearl Clo. E6 21 C5
Pearman St. SE1 24 G4
Pearscroft Ct. SW6 30 C4
Pearscroft Rd. SW6 30 C4
Pearson St. E2 18 E1
Peartree St. EC1 18 A3
Peckford Pl. SW9 31 G5
Peckham Gro. SE15 32 D3
Peckham High St. SE15 32 F4
Peckham Hill St. SE15 32 F3
Peckham Pk. Rd. SE15 32 F3
Peckham Rd. SE5 32 D4
Peckham Rd. SE15 32 E4
Peckham Rye SE15 39 F1
Peckham Rye SE22 39 F2
Peckwater St. NW5 10 C2
Pedlars Wk. N7 10 E3
Pedley St. E1 18 F3
Peel Gro. E2 19 A1
Peel Prec. NW6 16 B1
Peel Rd. NW6 16 A2
Peel St. W8 23 B2
Peerless St. EC1 18 C2
Pegwell St. SE18 35 G3
Pekin St. E14 19 E5
Pelham Clo. SE5 39 D1
Pelham Cres. SW7 23 F5
Pelham Pl. SW7 23 F5
Pelham St. SW7 23 E5
Pelican Est. SE15 32 E4
Pellant Rd. SW6 29 G3
Pellatt Rd. SE22 39 E3
Pellerin Rd. N16 11 D2
Pelling St. E14 19 E5
Pellipar Gdns. SE18 35 B1
Pelly Rd. E13 13 D5
Pelter St. E2 18 E2
Pelton Rd. SE10 34 B1
Pember Rd. NW10 15 F2
Pemberton Row EC4 44 A1
Pembridge Cres. W11 23 B1
Pembridge Gdns. W2 23 B1
Pembridge Ms. W11 23 B1
Pembridge Pl. W2 23 B1
Pembridge Rd. W11 23 B1
Pembridge Sq. W2 23 B1
Pembridge Vill. W11 23 B1
Pembroke Clo. SW1 24 A3
Pembroke Gdns. W8 23 A5
Pembroke Gdns. Clo. W8 23 A4
Pembroke Pl. W8 23 B4
Pembroke Rd. E6 21 B4
Pembroke Rd. W8 23 B5
Pembroke Sq. W8 23 B4
Pembroke St. N1 10 E4
Pembroke Studios W8 23 A4
Pembroke Vill. W8 23 B5
Pembroke Wk. W8 23 B5
Pembury Pl. E5 11 G2
Pembury Rd. E5 11 G2
Penang St. E1 25 G2
Penarth St. SE15 33 A2
Pencraig Way SE15 32 G2
Penderyn Way N7 10 D1
Pendrell Rd. SE4 33 C5
Pendrell St. SE18 35 F2
Penfold Pl. NW1 16 F4
Penfold St. NW1 16 E3
Penfold St. NW8 16 E3
Penford Gdns. SE9 41 G1
Penford St. SE5 32 A5
Penge Rd. E13 13 F5
Penhall Rd. SE7 27 G5
Penn Rd. N7 10 E2
Penn St. N1 11 C5
Pennack Rd. SE15 32 E2
Pennant Ms. W8 23 C5
Pennard Rd. W12 22 E3
Pennethorne Rd. SE15 32 G3
Pennington St. E1 25 F1
Pennyfields E14 26 E1
Pennyroyal Ave. E6 21 C5
Penpoll Rd. E8 11 G3
Penrith Clo. SW15 36 G3
Penrose Gro. SE17 32 B1
Penrose St. SE17 32 B1
Penryn St. NW1 17 D1
Pensbury Pl. SW8 31 C5
Pensbury St. SW8 31 C5
Penshurst Rd. E9 12 B4
Pentland St. SW18 37 D4
Pentlow St. SW15 36 E1
Penton Pl. SE17 32 A1
Penton Ri. WC1 17 F2
Penton St. N1 17 G1
Pentonville Rd. N1 17 F1
Pentridge St. SE15 32 E3
Penywern Rd. SW5 30 B1
Penzance Pl. W11 22 G2
Penzance St. W11 22 G2
Peony Gdns. W12 22 C1
Peploe Rd. NW6 15 F1
Pepper Clo. E6 21 B4
Pepper St. E14 26 F4
Peppermead Sq. SE13 40 E3
Pepys Rd. SE14 33 B4
Pepys St. EC3 44 J3
Perceval Ave. NW3 9 F2
Perch St. E8 11 E1
Percival St. EC1 18 A3
Percy Circ. WC1 17 F2
Percy Rd. E16 20 B4
Percy Rd. W12 22 C3
Percy St. W1 17 D4
Peregrine Ho. EC1 18 A2
Perham Rd. W14 29 G1
Peridot St. E6 21 A4
Periton Rd. SE9 41 G2
Perkin's Rents SW1 24 D4
Perkins Sq. SE1 44 E5
Perpins Rd. SE9 42 F4
Perrers Rd. W6 22 D5
Perrins La. NW3 9 D1
Perrin's Wk. NW3 9 D1
Perrott St. SE18 28 E5
Perryman Ho., Bark. 14 E5
Perrymead St. SW6 30 B4
Perrys Pl. W1 43 C1
Perseverance Pl. SW9 31 G3
Perth Rd. E13 20 E1
Perth Rd., Bark. 14 F5
Peter Ave. NW10 8 D4
Peter St. W1 43 C3
Peterborough Ms. SW6 30 B5
Peterborough Rd. SW6 30 B5
Peterborough Vill. SW6 30 C4
Petergate SW11 37 D2
Peters Clo., Well. 35 G5
Peters Hill EC4 44 D2
Petersham La. SW7 23 D4
Petersham Ms. SW7 23 D4
Petersham Pl. SW7 23 D4
Petherton Rd. N5 11 B2
Petley Rd. W6 29 E2
Peto Pl. NW1 17 B3
Petrie Clo. NW2 8 G3
Pett St. SE18 28 A5
Pettiward Clo. SW15 36 E2
Pettman Cres. SE28 28 F4
Petty France SW1 24 C4
Petworth St. SW11 30 F4
Petyward SW3 23 F5
Pevensey Rd. E7 13 C1
Peyton Pl. SE10 33 G3
Phelp St. SE17
Phene St. SW3
Philbeach Gdns. SW5
Philip St. E13
Philip Wk. SE15
Philippa Gdns. SE9
Phillimore Gdns. NW10
Phillimore Gdns. W8
Phillimore Pl. W8
Phillimore Wk. W8
Phillipp St. N1
Philpot La. EC3
Philpot St. E1
Phineas Pett Rd. SE9
Phipp St. EC2
Phoebeth Rd. SE4
Phoenix Pl. WC1
Phoenix St. WC2
Phoenix Wf. SE10
Piccadilly W1
Piccadilly Arc. SW1
Piccadilly Circ. W1
Piccadilly Pl. W1
Pickering Ave. E6
Pickering Pl. SW1
Pickets St. SW12
Pickford Wf. N1
Pickwick Rd. SE21
Picton St. SE5
Piedmont Rd. SE18
Pier Rd. E16
Pier St. E14
Pier Way SE28
Piermont Grn. SE22
Piermont Rd. SE22
Pigott St. E14
Pilgrim St. EC4
Pilgrimage St. SE1
Pilgrims Ct. SE3
Pilgrim's La. NW3
Pilkington Rd. SE15
Pimlico Rd. SW1
Pinchin St. E1
Pindar St. EC2
Pine Ave. E15
Pine Rd. NW2
Pine St. EC1
Pinefield Clo. E14
Pinnell Pl. SE9
Pinnell Rd. SE9
Pinto Way SE3
Pioneer St. SE15
Piper Clo. N7
Pirie St. E16
Pitchford St. E15
Pitfield St. N1
Pitfold Clo. SE12
Pitfold Rd. SE12
Pitman St. SE5
Pitsea St. E1
Pitt St. SE15
Pitt St. W8
Pittman Gdns., Ilf.
Pitt's Head Ms. W1
Pixley St. E14
Plaistow Gro. E15
Plaistow Pk. Rd. E13
Plaistow Rd. E13
Plaistow Rd. E15
Plantation, The SE3
Plantation Wf. SW11
Plashet Gro. E6
Plashet Rd. E13
Plassy Rd. SE6
Plato Rd. SW2
Platt, The SW15
Platt St. NW1
Platt's La. NW3
Playfield Cres. SE22

'house Yd. EC4 44 B2
sance, The SW15 36 D2
sance Rd. SW15 36 D3
sant Pl. N1 11 A4
der St. NW1 10 C5
ney Rd. N7 10 D1
na St. E14 26 G4
dell Ave. W6 22 B5
dell St. EC4 44 A2
gh Ct. EC3 44 G3
gh La. SE22 39 E4
gh Pl. EC4 44 A1
gh Rd. SW11 37 E1
gh Ter. SW11 37 E2
gh Way SE16 26 B5
gh Yd. EC2 18 D3
er Way SE16 26 C4
n La. SE18 35 D3
nbers Row E1 18 F4
nmer Rd. SW4 38 D5
nstead Common Rd. SE18 35 D2
nstead High St. SE18 28 F5
nstead Rd. SE18 28 D5
ntree Ct. EC4 44 B1
nouth Rd. E16 20 D4
nouth Wf. E14 27 A5
npton Ave. NW6 9 A4
npton Rd. NW6 9 A4
npton St. NW8 16 F3
ck St. SE1 25 A3
more Rd. SW18 37 D2
s Rd. N5 11 C2
t Hill SE10 33 G3
t Pleasant SW18 37 B2
ters Clo. E14 33 F1
nd St. W1 43 B1
brook Rd. SE3 41 F1
sworth Ho. W2 16 B4
ard Clo. E16 27 D1
ard Clo. N7 10 F1
ard Row E2 18 F2
ard St. E2 18 F2
n St. W1 43 A2
ted Rd. SE6 40 D5
horne Gro. SE18 28 E5
gon Rd. NW1 17 D1
technic St. SE18 28 C5
eroy St. SE14 33 A4
d Clo. SE3 34 C5
d Mead SE21 39 C4
d Pl. SW3 23 F5
d Rd. E15 20 B1
d Rd. SE3 34 C5
d St. NW3 9 F2
der St. N7 10 F4
er St. E1 18 G5
sard Rd. NW10 15 D2
sford St. E9 12 A2
onby Pl. SW1 31 D1
onby Rd. SW15 36 D5
sonby Ter. SW1 31 D1
St. SW1 23 G4
St. Ms. SW1 23 G4
on Rd. SW8 31 D2
e Rd. E9 12 B3
e St. N1 11 C5
mans St. SE16 26 B3
e St. SE1 25 D3
es Rd. SW9 38 G1
ham Rd. N1 11 B5
ham St. N1 11 B5
ar Gro. W6 22 E3
ar High St. E14 26 F1
ar Pl. W2 23 C1
ar Rd. SE24 39 B2
ar Wk. SE24 39 B2
ars Ave. NW10 8 E3
pins Ct. EC4 44 B2
Porchester Gdns. W2 23 C1
Porchester Pl. W2 16 F5
Porchester Rd. W2 16 C4
Porchester Sq. W2 16 C5
Porchester Ter. W2 23 D1
Porchester Ter. N. W2 16 C5
Porden Rd. SW2 38 F2
Porlock St. SE1 25 C3
Portchester Clo. SE5 39 C2
Portelet Rd. E1 19 B2
Porten Rd. W14 22 G4
Porter Rd. E6 21 B5
Porter St. SE1 44 E5
Porteus Rd. W2 16 D4
Portgate Clo. W9 16 A3
Portia Way E3 19 D3
Portinscale Rd. SW15 36 G3
Portland Gro. SW8 31 F4
Portland Ms. W1 43 B2
Portland Pl. W1 17 B4
Portland Rd. W11 22 G1
Portland St. SE17 32 C1
Portman Clo. W1 16 G5
Portman Ms. S. W1 17 A5
Portman Pl. E2 19 A2
Portman Sq. W1 17 A5
Portman St. W1 17 A5
Portnall Rd. W9 16 A1
Portobello Rd. W10 15 G4
Portobello Rd. W11 16 A5
Portpool La. EC1 17 G4
Portree St. E14 20 A5
Portslade Rd. SW8 31 C5
Portsmouth Rd. SW15 36 D5
Portsmouth St. WC2 43 G2
Portsoken St. E1 25 E1
Portugal St. WC2 43 G2
Portway E15 13 C5
Post Office App. E7 13 E2
Post Office Ct. EC3 44 G2
Post Office Way SW8 31 D3
Potier St. SE1 25 C4
Pott St. E2 18 G2
Potters Rd. SW6 30 D5
Pottery St. SE16 25 G3
Poulett Rd. E6 21 B1
Poultry EC2 44 F2
Pound La. NW10 8 C3
Pound Pk. Rd. SE7 27 G5
Pound Pl. SE9 42 C4
Pountney Rd. SW11 38 A1
Powell's Wk. W4 29 A2
Powerscroft Rd. E5 12 A1
Powis Gdns. W11 16 A5
Powis Pl. WC1 17 E3
Powis Rd. E3 19 F2
Powis Sq. W11 16 A5
Powis St. SE18 28 C4
Powis Ter. W11 16 A5
Pownall Rd. E8 11 F5
Pownsett Ter., Ilf. 14 E2
Poynders Gdns. SW4 38 C5
Poynders Rd. SW4 38 C4
Poyntz Rd. SW11 30 G5
Poyser St. E2 18 G1
Praed St. W2 16 E5
Pragel St. E13 20 E1
Prague Pl. SW2 38 E3
Prairie St. SW8 31 A5
Pratt St. NW1 10 C5
Pratt Wk. SE11 24 F5
Prebend Gdns. W4 22 B5
Prebend Gdns. W6 22 B5
Prebend St. N1 11 B5
Prendergast Rd. SE3 41 B1
Prentiss Ct. SE7 27 G5
Prescot St. E1 25 E1
Prescott Pl. SW4 38 D1
Prestage Way E14 26 G1
Prestbury Rd. E7 13 F4
Preston Pl. NW2 8 C3
Prestons Rd. E14 26 G3
Pretoria Rd. E16 20 C3
Pretoria Rd., Ilf. 14 D2
Price's Yd. N1 10 F5
Prideaux Pl. WC1 17 F2
Prideaux Rd. SW9 38 E1
Priest Ct. EC2 44 D1
Priests Bri. SW14 36 A1
Priests Bri. SW15 36 A1
Prima Rd. SW9 31 G3
Primrose Gdns. NW3 9 F3
Primrose Hill EC4 44 A2
Primrose Hill Ct. NW3 9 G4
Primrose Hill Rd. NW3 9 G4
Primrose Ms. SE3 34 E3
Primrose St. EC2 18 D4
Primula St. W12 15 C5
Prince Albert Rd. NW1 16 G1
Prince Albert Rd. NW8 16 F2
Prince Arthur Rd. NW3 9 D2
Prince Charles Rd. SE3 34 C5
Prince Consort Rd. SW7 23 D4
Prince Edward Rd. E9 12 D3
Prince George Rd. N16 11 D1
Prince Henry Rd. SE7 34 G3
Prince Imperial Rd. SE18 35 B4
Prince John Rd. SE9 42 A3
Prince of Wales Dr. SW8 31 B3
Prince of Wales Dr. SW11 30 F4
Prince of Wales Gate SW7 23 F3
Prince of Wales Rd. E16 20 F5
Prince of Wales Rd. NW5 10 A3
Prince of Wales Rd. SE3 34 C4
Prince of Wales Ter. W4 29 A1
Prince Regent La. E13 20 E2
Prince Regent La. E16 20 F4
Prince Rupert Rd. SE9 42 B2
Prince St. SE8 33 D2
Princedale Rd. W11 22 G2
Princelet St. E1 18 E4
Prince's Arc. SW1 43 B5
Princes Ct. E1 25 G1
Princes Gdns. SW7 23 E4
Princes Gate SW7 23 F3
Princes Gate Ms. SW7 23 E4
Princes Pl. SW1 43 B5
Princes Pl. W11 22 G2
Princes Ri. SE13 33 G5
Princes Riverside Rd. SE16 26 B2
Princes Sq. W2 23 C1
Princes St. EC2 44 F2
Princes St. W1 17 B5
Princes Ter. E13 13 E5
Princes Way SW19 36 F5
Princess Ct. SE16 26 D4
Princess May Rd. N16 11 D1
Princess Rd. NW1 10 A5
Princess Rd. NW6 16 B1
Princess St. SE1 25 A4
Princethorpe Ho. W2 16 C4
Princeton St. WC1 17 F4
Printer St. EC4 44 A1
Priolo Rd. SE7 34 F1
Prior Bolton St. N1 11 A3
Prior St. SE10 33 G3
Prioress St. SE1 25 C4
Priory, The SE3 41 C2
Priory Ave. W4 22 A5
Priory Ct. SW8 31 D4
Priory Gdns. SW13 36 B1
Priory Gdns. W4 22 A5
Priory Grn. Est. N1 17 F1
Priory Gro. SW8 31 E4
Priory La. SW15 36 A4
Priory Ms. SW8 31 E4
Priory Pk. SE3 41 C1
Priory Pk. Rd. NW6 9 A5
Priory Rd. E6 13 G5
Priory Rd. NW6 9 C5
Priory Rd., Bark. 14 F4
Priory Ter. NW6 9 C5
Priory Wk. SW10 30 D1
Pritchard's Rd. E2 18 F1
Priter Rd. SE16 25 F4
Probert Rd. SW2 38 G3
Procter St. WC1 17 F4
Promenade, The W4 29 A4
Promenade App. Rd. W4 29 A3
Prospect Pl. E1 26 A2
Prospect Vale SE18 28 A5
Prothero Rd. SW6 29 G3
Prout Gro. NW10 8 A1
Providence Ct. W1 24 A1
Provost Est. N1 18 C1
Provost Rd. NW3 9 G4
Provost St. N1 18 C1
Prudent Pas. EC2 44 F1
Prusom St. E1 25 G2
Pudding La. EC3 44 G4
Pudding Mill La. E15 12 F5
Puddle Dock EC4 44 C3
Pulborough Rd. SW18 37 A5
Pulleyns Ave. E6 21 A2
Pullman Gdns. SW15 36 E4
Pullman Pl. SE9 42 A3
Pulross Rd. SW9 38 F1
Pulteney Clo. E3 12 D5
Pulteney Ter. N1 10 F5
Pulton Pl. SW6 30 B3
Pump Ct. EC4 43 J2
Pump La. SE14 33 A3
Pumping Sta. Rd. W4 29 A3
Pundersons Gdns. E2 18 G2
Purcell Cres. SW6 29 F3
Purcell St. N1 18 D1
Purchese St. NW1 17 D1
Purdy St. E3 19 F3
Purelake Ms. SE13 41 A1
Purneys Rd. SE9 41 G2
Purser's Cross Rd. SW6 30 A4
Purves Rd. NW10 15 D1
Putney Bri. SW6 36 G1
Putney Bri. SW15 36 G1
Putney Bri. App. SW6 36 G1
Putney Bri. Rd. SW15 36 G2
Putney Bri. Rd. SW18 37 B3
Putney Common SW15 36 E1
Putney Heath SW15 36 D5
Putney Heath La. SW15 36 F4
Putney High St. SW15 36 F2
Putney Hill SW15 36 F4
Putney Pk. Ave. SW15 36 C2
Putney Pk. La. SW15 36 D2
Pyrland Rd. N5 11 C2
Pytchley Rd. SE22 39 D1

Q

Quadrant Arc. W1 43 B4
Quadrant Gro. NW5 9 G2
Quaggy Wk. SE3 41 D2
Quaker St. E1 18 E3
Quality Ct. WC2 43 J1

Quarrendon St. SW6 30 B5
Quarry Rd. SW18 37 D4
Quarter Mile La. E12 12 F1
Quarterdeck, The E14 26 E3
Quebec Way SE16 26 E3
Queen Anne St. E9 12 B3
Queen Anne St. W1 17 B4
Queen Anne's Gdns. 22 A4
W4
Queen Anne's Gate 24 D3
SW1
Queen Anne's Gro. 22 A4
W4
Queen Caroline Est. 29 E1
W6
Queen Caroline St. 29 E1
W6
Queen Elizabeth St. 25 E3
SE1
Queen Elizabeth Wk. 29 C4
SW13
Queen Margaret's 11 D2
Gro. N1
Queen of Denmark 26 D4
Ct. SE16
Queen Sq. WC1 17 E3
Queen St. EC4 **44 E3**
Queen St. W1 24 B2
Queen St. Pl. EC4 **44 E4**
Queen Victoria St. 44 C3
EC4
Queenhithe EC4 **44 E3**
Queens Club Gdns. 29 G2
W14
Queens Cres. NW5 10 A3
Queens Gdns. W2 16 D5
Queen's Gate SW7 23 D4
Queen's Gate Gdns. 23 D4
SW7
Queen's Gate Ms. 23 D4
SW7
Queen's Gate Pl. SW7 23 D4
Queen's Gate Pl. Ms. 23 D4
SW7
Queen's Gate Ter. 23 D4
SW7
Queen's Gro. NW8 9 E5
Queens Head St. N1 11 A5
Queens Head Yd. SE1 44 F6
Queens Pk. Ct. W10 15 F2
Queens Ride SW13 36 C1
Queens Ride SW15 36 E1
Queens Rd. E13 13 E5
Queens Rd. SE14 32 G4
Queens Rd. SE15 32 G4
Queens Rd. Bark. 14 E3
Queens Rd., Ilf. 14 E3
Queens Rd. W. E13 13 D5
Queen's Row SE17 32 C2
Queens Ter. E13 13 E5
Queen's Ter. NW8 9 E5
Queen's Wk. SW1 43 A6
Queensberry Pl. SW7 23 E5
Queensborough Ter. 23 C1
W2
Queensbridge Rd. E2 11 E5
Queensbridge Rd. E8 11 E4
Queensbury St. N1 11 B4
Queenscroft Rd. SE9 41 G4
Queensdale Cres. 29 E1
W11
Queensdale Pl. W11 22 G2
Queensdale Rd. W11 22 F2
Queensdale Wk. W11 22 G2
Queensdown Rd. E5 12 G1
Queensgate Pl. NW6 9 B4
Queensland Rd. N7 10 G1
Queensmead NW8 9 E5
Queensmill Rd. SW6 29 F3
Queenstown Rd. SW8 31 B2

Queensville Rd. SW12 38 D5
Queensway W2 16 C5
Quemerford Rd. N7 10 F2
Quentin Pl. SE13 41 B1
Quentin Rd. SE13 41 B1
Querrin St. SW6 30 D5
Quex Rd. NW6 9 B5
Quick Pl. N1 11 A5
Quick Rd. W4 29 A1
Quick St. N1 18 A1
Quill La. SW15 36 F2
Quilter St. E2 18 F2
Quixley St. E14 27 A1
Quorn Rd. SE22 39 D2

R

Rabbits Rd. E12 14 A1
Racton Rd. SW6 30 B2
Radbourne Rd. SW12 38 C5
Radcliffe Ave. NW10 15 C1
Radcliffe Sq. SW15 36 F4
Raddington Rd. W10 15 G4
Radfield Way, Sid. 42 F5
Radford Rd. SE13 40 G3
Radipole Rd. SW6 30 A4
Radland Rd. E16 20 C5
Radlett Clo. E7 13 C3
Radlett Pl. NW8 9 F5
Radley Ms. W8 23 B4
Radnor Pl. W2 16 F5
Radnor Rd. NW6 8 G5
Radnor Rd. SE15 32 F3
Radnor Rd. SE15 32 F3
Radnor Ter. W14 23 A5
Radnor Wk. SW3 30 F1
Radstock St. SW11 30 F3
Raeburn Rd., Sid. 42 G4
Raeburn St. SW2 38 E2
Raglan Ct. SE12 41 D3
Raglan Rd. SE18 35 E1
Raglan St. NW5 10 B3
Railey Ms. NW5 10 C2
Railton Rd. SE24 38 G2
Railway App. SE1 44 G6
Railway Ave. SE16 26 A3
Railway Side SW13 36 A1
Railway St. N1 17 E1
Rainbow Ave. E14 33 F1
Rainbow St. SE5 32 D3
Raine St. E1 25 G2
Rainham Clo. SE9 42 A4
Rainham Clo. SW11 37 F4
Rainham Rd. NW10 15 F2
Rainhill Way E3 19 E2
Rainsborough Ave. 26 C5
SE8
Rainton Rd. SE7 34 D1
Rainville Rd. W6 29 E2
Raleana Rd. E14 26 G2
Raleigh St. N1 11 A5
Ram St. SW18 37 C3
Ramac Ind. Est. SE7 27 D5
Ramac Way SE7 34 E1
Ramilles Clo. SW2 38 E4
Ramillies Pl. W1 43 A2
Ramillies St. W1 43 A2
Rampayne St. SW1 31 D1
Ramsay Rd. E7 13 B1
Ramsden Rd. SW12 38 A4
Ramsey St. E2 18 F2
Rancliffe Gdns. SE9 42 A2
Rancliffe Rd. E6 21 A1
Randall Clo. SW11 30 F4
Randall Pl. SE10 33 G3
Randall Rd. SE11 31 F1
Randell's Rd. N1 10 E5
Randolph Ave. W9 16 D3
Randolph Cres. W9 16 D3
Randolph Gdns. NW6 16 C1
Randolph Ms. W9 16 D3

Randolph Rd. W9 16 D3
Randolph St. NW1 10 C4
Ranelagh Ave. SW6 37 A1
Ranelagh Ave. SW13 29 C5
Ranelagh Gdns. SW6 37 A1
Ranelagh Gdns. W6 22 B4
Ranelagh Gro. SW1 31 A1
Ranelagh Rd. E6 14 C5
Ranelagh Rd. E11 13 B1
Ranelagh Rd. E15 13 B5
Ranelagh Rd. NW10 15 B1
Rangers Sq. SE10 34 A4
Rannoch Rd. W6 29 E2
Ranulf Rd. NW2 9 A1
Ranwell St. E3 12 D5
Raphael St. SW7 23 G3
Ratcliff Rd. E7 13 F2
Ratcliffe Clo. SE12 41 D5
Ratcliffe Cross St. E1 19 B5
Ratcliffe La. E14 19 C5
Ratcliffe Orchard E1 26 B1
Rathbone Pl. W1 17 D4
Rathbone St. E16 20 D4
Rathbone St. W1 17 C4
Rathmell Dr. SW4 38 D4
Rathmore Rd. SE7 34 E1
Rattray Rd. SW2 38 G2
Raul Rd. SE15 32 F4
Raveley St. NW5 10 C1
Raven Row E1 18 G4
Ravenhill Rd. E13 20 F1
Ravenna Rd. SW15 36 F3
Ravens Way SE12 41 D3
Ravensbourne Pk. 40 C5
SE6
Ravensbourne Pk. 40 D5
Cres. SE6
Ravensbourne Pl. 33 F5
SE13
Ravenscourt Ave. W6 22 C5
Ravenscourt Gdns. 22 C5
W6
Ravenscourt Pk. W6 22 C4
Ravenscourt Pl. W6 22 D5
Ravenscourt Rd. W6 22 D5
Ravenscourt Sq. W6 22 C4
Ravenscroft Clo. E16 20 D4
Ravenscroft Rd. E16 20 D4
Ravenscroft St. E2 18 E1
Ravensdon St. SE11 31 G1
Ravenshaw St. NW6 9 A2
Ravenslea Rd. SW12 37 G5
Ravensmede Way W4 22 B1
Ravenswood Rd. 38 B5
SW12
Ravensworth Rd. 15 D2
NW10
Ravent Rd. SE11 24 F5
Ravine Gro. SE18 35 G2
Rawlings St. SW3 23 G5
Rawstorne St. EC1 18 A2
Ray St. EC1 18 A3
Rayford Ave. SE12 41 C5
Rayleas Clo. SE18 35 D4
Raymere Gdns. SE18 35 F3
Raymond Rd. E13 13 F4
Raymouth Rd. SE16 25 G5
Rayners Rd. SW15 36 G3
Raynham Rd. W6 22 D5
Reading La. E8 11 G3
Reardon Path E1 25 G2
Reardon St. E1 25 G2
Reaston St. SE14 33 B3
Record St. SE15 33 A2
Rector St. N1 11 B5
Rectory Fld. Cres. SE7 34 F3
Rectory Gdns. SW4 38 C1
Rectory Gro. SW4 38 C1
Rectory Pl. SE18 35 C1

Rectory Rd. E12 14 [cut]
Rectory Rd. SW13 29 [cut]
Rectory Sq. E1 19 A[cut]
Reculver Rd. SE16 33 [cut]
Red Barracks Rd. 28 [cut]
SE18
Red Lion Ct. EC4 44 [cut]
Red Lion La. SE18 35 [cut]
Red Lion Row SE17 32 [cut]
Red Lion Sq. WC1 17 [cut]
Red Lion St. WC1 17 [cut]
Red Post Hill SE21 39 [cut]
Red Post Hill SE24 39 [cut]
Redan Pl. W2 16 [cut]
Redan St. W14 22 [cut]
Redbridge Gdns. SE5 32 [cut]
Redburn St. SW3 30 [cut]
Redcar St. SE5 32 [cut]
Redcastle Clo. E1 26 [cut]
Redchurch St. E2 18 [cut]
Redcliffe Gdns. SW5 30 [cut]
Redcliffe Gdns. SW10 30 [cut]
Redcliffe Ms. SW10 30 [cut]
Redcliffe Pl. SW10 30 [cut]
Redcliffe Rd. SW10 30 [cut]
Redcliffe Sq. SW10 30 [cut]
Redcliffe St. SW10 30 [cut]
Redclyffe Rd. E6 13 [cut]
Redcross Way SE1 25 [cut]
Reddins Rd. SE15 32 [cut]
Redesdale St. SW3 30 [cut]
Redfern Rd. NW10 15 [cut]
Redfern Rd. SE6 40 [cut]
Redfield La. SW5 23 [cut]
Redgrave Rd. SW15 36 [cut]
Redhill St. NW1 17 [cut]
Redington Gdns. NW3 9 [cut]
Redington Rd. NW3 9 [cut]
Redlands Way SW2 38 [cut]
Redman's Rd. E1 19 [cut]
Redmore Rd. W6 22 [cut]
Redriff Est. SE16 26 [cut]
Redriff Rd. SE16 26 [cut]
Redriffe Rd. E13 13 [cut]
Redruth Rd. E9 12 [cut]
Redwald Rd. E5 12 [cut]
Redwood Clo. SE16 26 [cut]
Reece Ms. SW7 23 [cut]
Reed Clo. E16 20 [cut]
Reed Clo. SE12 41 [cut]
Reedham St. SE15 32 [cut]
Reedworth St. SE11 24 [cut]
Rees St. N1 11 [cut]
Reesland Clo. E12 14 [cut]
Reeves Ms. W1 24 [cut]
Reeves Rd. E3 19 [cut]
Reeves Rd. SE18 35 [cut]
Reform St. SW11 30 [cut]
Regan Way N1 11 [cut]
Regency St. SW1 24 [cut]
Regent Pl. W1 43 [cut]
Regent Rd. SE24 38 [cut]
Regent Sq. E3 19 [cut]
Regent Sq. WC1 17 [cut]
Regent St. SW1 43 [cut]
Regent St. W1 17 [cut]
Regents Bri. Gdns. 3[cut]
SW8
Regent's Pk. NW1 16 [cut]
Regent's Pk. Rd. NW1 9 [cut]
Regent's Pl. SE3 3[cut]
Regents Row E8 1[cut]
Reginald Rd. E7 1[cut]
Reginald Rd. SE8 3[cut]
Reginald Sq. SE8 3[cut]
Regis Rd. NW5 1[cut]
Reidhaven Rd. SE18 3[cut]
Relay Rd. W12 2[cut]
Relf Rd. SE15 3[cut]
Rembrandt Clo. E14 2[cut]

brandt Rd. SE13 41 B2
ington Rd. E6 21 A5
ington St. N1 18 A1
nant St. WC2 43 G1
dlesham Rd. E5 11 F1
orth St. SE16 26 A3
rew Clo. E6 28 C1
rew Rd. SE11 25 A5
nets Clo. SE9 42 G3
nets Wd. Rd. SE9 42 F3
nie Est. SE16 25 G5
nie St. SE1 44 B5
orton Rd. SW6 29 G4
ository Rd. SE18 35 B2
ton St. E14 19 C5
ervoir Rd. SE4 33 C5
ell Clo. SE3 34 B2
tons Cres. SE9 42 F4
eat Pl. E9 12 A3
elon Rd. SE4 40 C1
erdy Rd. SE1 25 F5
vell St. SW6 30 D3
nolds Ave. E12 14 C2
nolds Pl. SE3 34 E3
nolds Rd. SE15 40 A3
idol Ter. N1 11 B5
desia Rd. SW9 31 E5
deswell Rd. E14 19 C4
ndda Gro. E3 19 C2
l St. NW5 10 A3
ardo St. E14 19 F5
St. E14 26 D1
hard Clo. SE18 28 A5
hardson Rd. E15 20 B1
hborne Ter. SW8 31 F3
hborough Rd. NW2 8 G1
hford Rd. E15 13 C5
hford St. W6 22 E3
hmond Ave. N1 10 F5
hmond Ave. NW10 8 E3
hmond Bldgs. W1 43 C2
hmond Cres. N1 10 F5
hmond Gro. N1 11 A4
hmond Ms. W1 43 C2
hmond Pl. SE18 28 E5
hmond Rd. E7 13 E2
hmond Rd. E8 11 E4
hmond St. E13 20 D1
hmond Ter. SW1 24 E3
hmond Way W12 22 F3
hmond Way W14 22 F3
hmount Gdns. SE3 41 D1
k Roberts Way E15 12 G5
kett St. SW6 30 B2
kyard Path SE9 42 A2
eout St. SE18 28 B5
er Clo., Sid. 42 G4
gdale St. E3 19 E1
gebrook Rd. SE3 41 F1
geway Rd. SW9 39 A1
geway W., Sid. 42 G3
gmount Rd. SW18 37 C3
gwell Rd. E16 20 F4
ing Ho. St. W1 17 C4
ley Rd. E7 13 F1
ley Rd. E8 11 E2
ley Rd. NW10 15 C1
field Rd. SE9 42 E2
fel Rd. NW2 8 E2
le Pl. W11 22 F2
le St. E14 19 F4
gault Rd. SW6 29 G5
gden St. E14 19 F5
geley Rd. NW10 15 C2
gge Pl. SW4 38 D2
ey Rd. SE1 25 E4
ey St. SW10 30 E3
haldo Rd. SW12 38 B5
ng, The W2 23 E1
ng Rd. W12 22 E1

Ringcroft St. N7 10 G2
Ringford Rd. SW18 37 A3
Ringmer Ave. SW6 29 G4
Ringmore Ri. SE23 39 G5
Ringstead Rd. SE6 40 F5
Ringwood Gdns. E14 26 E5
Ripley Rd. E16 20 F5
Ripon Rd. SE18 35 D2
Ripple Rd., Bark. 14 F5
Ripplevale Gro. N1 10 F4
Riseldine Rd. SE23 40 C4
Risinghill St. N1 17 F1
Rita Rd. SW8 31 E2
Ritchie St. N1 17 G1
Ritson Rd. E8 11 F3
Ritter St. SE18 35 C2
Rivaz Pl. E9 12 A3
River Pl. N1 11 B4
River Rd., Bark. 21 G1
River St. EC1 17 G2
River Way SE10 27 C4
Rivercourt Rd. W6 22 D5
Rivermead Ct. SW6 37 A1
Riverside Ct. SW8 31 D2
Riverside Gdns. W6 29 D1
Riverside Ind. Est. SE10 27 C4
Riverside Rd. E15 19 G1
Riverside Wk. SE1 43 H5
Riverton Clo. W9 16 A2
Riverview Gdns. SW13 29 D2
Rivington Ct. NW10 8 C5
Rivington St. EC2 18 D2
Rixsen Rd. E12 14 A2
Roach Rd. E3 12 E4
Roan St. SE10 33 F3
Robert Adam St. W1 17 A5
Robert Dashwood Way SE17 25 B5
Robert Lowe Clo. SE14 33 B3
Robert Owen Ho. SW6 29 F4
Robert St. E16 28 D2
Robert St. NW1 17 B2
Robert St. SE18 35 F1
Robert St. WC2 43 F4
Roberta St. E2 18 F2
Robertson Rd. E15 12 G5
Robertson St. SW8 38 B1
Robin Ct. SE16 25 F5
Robin Cres. E6 21 A4
Robin Hood La. E14 19 G5
Robinson Rd. E2 19 A1
Robsart St. SW9 31 F5
Robson Ave. NW10 8 C5
Rochelle Clo. SW11 37 E2
Rochester Ave. E13 13 F5
Rochester Ms. NW1 10 C4
Rochester Pl. NW1 10 C3
Rochester Rd. NW1 10 C3
Rochester Row SW1 24 C5
Rochester Sq. NW1 10 C4
Rochester St. SW1 24 D4
Rochester Ter. NW1 10 C3
Rochester Wk. SE1 44 F5
Rochester Way SE3 34 F5
Rochester Way SE9 42 B1
Rochester Way Relief Rd. SE3 34 E4
Rochester Way Relief Rd. SE9 41 F2
Rochford St. NW5 9 G2
Rockells Pl. SE22 39 G4
Rockhall Rd. NW2 8 F1
Rockingham Clo. SW15 36 B2
Rockingham Est. SE1 25 B4
Rockingham St. SE1 25 B4

Rockland Rd. SW15 36 G2
Rockley Rd. W14 22 F3
Rocks La. SW13 36 C1
Rocombe Cres. SE23 40 A5
Rocque La. SE3 41 C1
Rodenhurst Rd. SW4 38 C4
Roderick Rd. NW3 9 G1
Roding Rd. E5 12 C1
Roding Rd. E6 21 D4
Roding Trd. Est., Bark. 14 D4
Rodmarton St. W1 16 G4
Rodmill La. SW2 38 E5
Rodney Pl. SE17 25 B5
Rodney Rd. SE17 25 B5
Rodney St. N1 17 F1
Rodway Rd. SW15 36 C5
Rodwell Rd. SE22 39 E4
Roebourne Way E16 28 C3
Roedean Cres. SW15 36 A4
Roehampton Clo. SW15 36 C2
Roehampton Gate SW15 36 A4
Roehampton High St. SW15 36 C5
Roehampton La. SW15 36 C2
Roffey St. E14 26 G3
Roger St. WC1 17 F3
Rogers Rd. E16 20 C5
Rokeby Rd. SE4 33 D5
Rokeby St. E15 13 A5
Rokesby Clo., Well. 35 F5
Roland Gdns. SW7 30 D1
Roland Way SE17 32 C1
Rollins St. SE15 33 A2
Rolls Bldgs. EC4 43 J1
Rolls Pas. EC4 43 J1
Rolls Rd. SE1 32 E1
Rollscourt Ave. SE24 39 B3
Rolt St. SE8 33 C2
Roman Rd. E2 19 A2
Roman Rd. E3 19 C1
Roman Rd. E6 20 G3
Roman Rd. W4 22 B5
Roman Rd., Ilf. 14 D3
Roman Way N7 10 F3
Romborough Gdns. SE13 40 G3
Romborough Way SE13 40 G3
Romero Sq. SE3 41 F2
Romford Rd. E7 13 E2
Romford Rd. E12 14 A1
Romford Rd. E15 13 B3
Romford St. E1 18 F4
Romilly St. W1 43 C3
Romney Rd. SE10 33 G2
Romney St. SW1 24 E4
Ron Leighton Way E6 14 A5
Rona Rd. NW3 10 A1
Ronald Ave. E15 20 B2
Ronalds Rd. N5 10 G2
Ronaldstone Rd., Sid. 42 G4
Rondu Rd. NW2 8 G2
Rood La. EC3 44 H3
Rooke Way SE10 34 C1
Rookery Rd. SW4 38 C2
Rootes Dr. W10 15 F3
Rope St. SE16 26 C4
Rope Yd. Rails SE18 28 D4
Ropemaker Rd. SE16 26 C3
Ropemaker St. EC2 18 C4
Roper St. SE9 42 B4
Ropery St. E3 19 D3
Ropley St. E2 18 F1
Rosaline Rd. SW6 29 G3
Rosary Gdns. SW7 23 D5
Rosaville Rd. SW6 30 A3

Rose All. SE1 44 E5
Rose & Crown Ct. EC2 44 D1
Rose & Crown Yd. SW1 43 B5
Rose St. WC2 43 E3
Rose Way SE12 41 D3
Rosebank Gdns. E3 19 D1
Roseberry Pl. E8 11 E3
Roseberry St. SE16 25 G5
Rosebery Ave. E12 14 A3
Rosebery Ave. EC1 17 G3
Rosebery Ave., Sid. 42 G5
Rosebery Rd. SW2 38 E4
Rosebury Rd. SW6 30 C5
Rosedale Rd. E7 13 F2
Rosedene NW6 8 F5
Rosedew Rd. W6 29 F2
Rosefield Gdns. E14 26 E1
Rosehill Rd. SW18 37 D4
Roseleigh Ave. N5 11 A1
Rosemary Dr. E14 20 A5
Rosemary Rd. SE15 32 E3
Rosemont Rd. NW3 9 D3
Rosemoor St. SW3 23 G5
Rosenau Cres. SW11 30 F4
Rosenau Rd. SW11 30 F4
Rosendale Rd. SE21 39 B5
Rosendale Rd. SE24 39 B5
Roseneath Rd. SW11 38 A4
Rosenthal Rd. SE6 40 F4
Rosenthorpe Rd. SE15 40 B3
Roserton St. E14 26 G3
Rosethorn Clo. SW12 38 D5
Roseway SE21 39 C4
Rosher Clo. E15 13 A4
Rosina St. E9 12 B2
Roskell Rd. SW15 36 F1
Rosmead Rd. W11 22 G1
Rosoman St. EC1 17 G2
Ross Ct. SW15 36 F5
Ross Way SE9 42 A1
Rossdale Rd. SW15 36 E2
Rosse Ms. SE3 34 E4
Rossendale Way NW1 10 C5
Rossetti Rd. SE16 32 G1
Rosslyn Ave. SW13 36 A1
Rosslyn Hill NW3 9 E1
Rosslyn Rd., Bark. 14 F4
Rossmore Rd. NW1 16 F3
Rostrevor Rd. SW6 30 A4
Rothbury Rd. E9 12 D4
Rotherfield St. N1 11 B4
Rotherham Wk. SE1 44 B6
Rotherhithe New Rd. SE16 32 G1
Rotherhithe Old Rd. SE16 26 B5
Rotherhithe St. SE16 26 A3
Rotherhithe Tunnel E1 26 B2
Rotherhithe Tunnel App. E14 26 C1
Rotherhithe Tunnel App. SE16 26 A3
Rotherwood Rd. SW15 36 F1
Rothsay Rd. E7 13 F4
Rothsay St. SE1 25 D4
Rothwell St. NW1 9 G5
Rotten Row SW7 23 F3
Rotterdam Dr. E14 26 G4
Rouel Rd. SE16 25 F4
Roundwood Rd. NW10 8 B3
Rounton Rd. E3 19 E3
Roupell St. SE1 44 A6
Rousden St. NW1 10 C4
Routemaster Clo. E13 20 E2

Routh Rd. SW18 37 F5
Routh St. E6 21 B4
Rowallan Rd. SW6 29 G3
Rowan Rd. W6 22 F5
Rowberry Clo. SW6 29 E3
Rowcross St. SE1 32 E1
Rowditch La. SW11 31 A5
Rowdon Ave. NW10 8 D4
Rowe La. E9 12 A2
Rowena Cres. SW11 30 F5
Rowhill Rd. E5 11 G1
Rowington Clo. W2 16 C4
Rowland Ct. E16 20 C3
Rowland Hill St. NW3 9 F2
Rowley Way NW8 9 C5
Rowse Clo. E15 12 G5
Rowstock Gdns. N7 10 D2
Rowton Rd. SE18 35 E3
Roxby Pl. SW6 30 B2
Roxley Rd. SE13 40 F4
Roxwell Rd. W12 22 C3
Royal Albert Dock E16 28 A1
Royal Albert Way E16 27 F1
Royal Arc. W1 43 A4
Royal Ave. SW3 30 G1
Royal College St. NW1 10 C4
Royal Cres. W11 22 F2
Royal Docks Rd. E6 21 D5
Royal Docks Rd., Bark. 21 D5
Royal Ex. EC3 44 G2
Royal Ex. Ave. EC3 44 G2
Royal Ex. Bldgs. EC3 44 G2
Royal Hill SE10 33 G3
Royal Hospital Rd. SW3 30 G2
Royal Mint Ct. EC3 25 E1
Royal Mint St. E1 25 E1
Royal Naval Pl. SE14 33 D3
Royal Oak Pl. SE22 39 G4
Royal Oak Rd. E8 11 G3
Royal Opera Arc. SW1 43 C5
Royal Orchard Clo. SW18 36 G5
Royal Par. SE3 34 C5
Royal Pl. SE10 33 G3
Royal Rd. E16 20 F5
Royal Rd. SE17 32 A2
Royal St. SE1 24 F4
Royal Victor Pl. E3 19 B1
Royal Victoria Dock E16 27 D1
Royalty Ms. W1 43 C2
Roydene Rd. SE18 35 G2
Royston St. E2 19 A1
Rozel Ct. N1 11 D5
Rozel Rd. SW4 38 C1
Ruby St. SE15 32 G2
Ruckholt Rd. E10 12 F1
Rucklidge Ave. NW10 15 B1
Ruddington Clo. E5 12 C1
Ruddstreet Clo. SE18 28 D5
Rudloe Rd. SW12 38 C5
Rudolph Ct. SE22 39 F5
Rudolph Rd. E13 20 C1
Rudolph Rd. NW6 16 B1
Rufford St. N1 10 E5
Rugby Rd. W4 22 A3
Rugby St. WC1 17 F3
Rugg St. E14 26 E1
Rum Clo. E1 26 A1
Rumbold Rd. SW6 30 C3
Rumsey Rd. SW9 38 F1
Runcorn Pl. W11 22 G1
Rupert Ct. W1 43 C3
Rupert Gdns. SW9 32 A5
Rupert Rd. NW6 16 A1
Rupert Rd. W4 22 A4
Rupert St. W1 43 C3
Ruscoe Rd. E16 20 C5
Rush Gro. St. SE18 28 B5
Rush Hill Rd. SW11 38 A1
Rusham Rd. SW12 37 G4
Rushcroft Rd. SW2 38 G2
Rushey Grn. SE6 40 F5
Rushey Mead SE4 40 E3
Rushford Rd. SE4 40 D4
Rushmore Rd. E5 12 A1
Rusholme Rd. SW15 36 F4
Rushton St. N1 18 C1
Rushworth St. SE1 25 A3
Ruskin Ave. E12 14 A3
Ruskin Pk. Ho. SE5 39 C1
Ruskin Wk. SE24 39 B3
Russell Clo. SE7 34 F3
Russell Clo. W4 29 B2
Russell Ct. SW1 43 B6
Russell Gdns. W14 22 G4
Russell Gdns. Ms. W14 22 G3
Russell Gro. SW9 31 G4
Russell Rd. E16 20 D5
Russell Rd. W14 22 G4
Russell Sq. WC1 17 E3
Russell St. WC2 43 F3
Russia Ct. EC2 44 E2
Russia Dock Rd. SE16 26 C2
Russia La. E2 19 A1
Russia Row EC2 44 E2
Rust Sq. SE5 32 C3
Ruston St. E3 12 D5
Rutherford St. SW1 24 D5
Ruthin Rd. SE3 34 D2
Rutland Gdns. SW7 23 F3
Rutland Gate SW7 23 F3
Rutland Gro. W6 29 D1
Rutland Pk. NW2 8 E3
Rutland Rd. E7 13 G4
Rutland Rd. E9 12 A5
Rutland Rd., Ilf. 14 D1
Rutland St. SW7 23 F4
Rutts Ter. SE14 33 B4
Ruvigny Gdns. SW15 36 F1
Ryan Clo. SE3 41 F2
Rycuff Sq. SE3 34 C5
Ryder Ct. SW1 43 B5
Ryder Dr. SE16 32 G1
Ryder St. SW1 43 B5
Ryder Yd. SW1 43 B5
Rydons Clo. SE9 42 A1
Rye Hill Est. SE15 40 A2
Rye Hill Pk. SE15 40 A2
Rye La. SE15 32 F5
Rye Pas. SE15 39 F1
Rye Rd. SE15 40 B2
Ryecroft Rd. SE13 40 G3
Ryecroft St. SW6 30 C4
Ryedale SE22 39 G4
Ryelands Cres. SE12 41 F4
Ryland Rd. NW5 10 B3
Rylett Cres. W12 22 B3
Rylett Rd. W12 22 B4
Rylston Rd. SW6 30 A2
Rymer St. SE24 39 A4
Rymill St. E16 28 C2
Rysbrack St. SW3 23 G4

S

Sabine Rd. SW11 37 G1
Sackville St. W1 43 B4
Saffron Ave. E14 27 A1
Saffron Hill EC1 17 G3
Sail St. SE11 24 F5
St. Agnes Pl. SE11 32 A2
St. Aidan's Rd. SE22 39 G4
St. Albans Ave. E6 21 B2
St. Albans Gro. W8 23 C4
St. Alban's Pl. N1 11 A5
St. Albans Rd. NW10 8 A5
St. Albans St. SW1 43 C4
St. Alfege Pas. SE10 33 G2
St. Alfege Rd. SE7 34 G2
St. Alphonsus Rd. SW4 38 D2
St. Andrew St. EC4 17 G4
St. Andrew's Hill EC4 44 C3
St. Andrews Rd. E13 20 E2
St. Andrews Rd. NW10 8 D3
St. Andrews Rd. W3 15 A5
St. Andrews Rd. W14 29 G2
St. Andrews Way E3 19 F3
St. Anne's Ct. W1 43 C2
St. Anne's Row E14 19 D5
St. Ann's, Bark. 14 E5
St. Ann's Cres. SW18 37 C4
St. Ann's Hill SW18 37 C3
St. Ann's Pk. Rd. SW18 37 D4
St. Ann's Rd. SW13 29 B5
St. Anns Rd. W11 22 F1
St. Ann's St. SW1 24 D4
St. Ann's Ter. NW8 16 E1
St. Anns Vill. W11 22 F2
St. Anthonys Clo. E1 25 F2
St. Antony's Rd. E7 13 E4
St. Asaph Rd. SE4 40 B1
St. Augustine's Path N5 11 A2
St. Augustines Rd. NW1 10 D4
St. Austell Rd. SE13 33 G5
St. Awdry's Rd., Bark. 14 F4
St. Barnabas St. SW1 31 A1
St. Barnabas Ter. E9 12 B2
St. Barnabas Vill. SW8 31 E4
St. Bartholomew's Rd. E6 21 B1
St. Benet's Pl. EC3 44 G3
St. Bernard's Rd. E6 13 G5
St. Botolph St. EC3 18 E5
St. Bride St. EC4 44 B1
St. Bride's Pas. EC4 44 B2
St. Chad's Pl. WC1 17 E2
St. Chad's St. WC1 17 E2
St. Charles Sq. W10 15 G4
St. Clair Rd. E13 20 E1
St. Clement's La. WC2 43 H2
St. Clements St. N1 10 G3
St. Clements St. N7 10 G3
St. Crispins Clo. NW3 9 F1
St. Cross St. EC1 17 G4
St. Cuthberts Rd. NW2 9 A3
St. Dionis Rd. SW6 30 A5
St. Donatts Rd. SE14 33 D4
St. Dunstan's All. EC3 44 H4
St. Dunstan's Hill EC3 44 H4
St. Dunstan's La. EC3 44 H4
St. Dunstan's Rd. E7 13 F3
St. Dunstans Rd. W6 29 F1
St. Edmunds Ter. NW8 16 F1
St. Elmo Rd. W12 22 B2
St. Elmos Rd. SE16 26 B3
St. Erkenwald Rd., Bark. 14 F5
St. Ervans Rd. W10 16 A4
St. Francis Rd. SE22 39 D2
St. Gabriels Rd. NW2 8 F2
St. George St. W1 24 B1
St. Georges Ave. E7 13 E4
St. Georges Ave. N7 10 D1
St. Georges Circ. SE1 25 A4
St. Georges Ct. E6 21 B3
St. Georges Ct. EC4 44 B1
St. George's Dr. SW1 24 B5
St. Georges Flds. W2 16 F5
St. Georges La. EC3 44
St. Georges Rd. E7 13
St. Georges Rd. SE1 24
St. Georges Sq. E7 13
St. Georges Sq. E14 26
St. Georges Sq. SE8 26
St. George's Sq. SW1 31
St. George's Sq. Ms. SW1 31
St. Georges Way SE15 32
St. Gerards Clo. SW4 38
St. German's Pl. SE3 34
St. Giles High St. WC2 43
St. Giles Pas. WC2 43
St. Giles Rd. SE5 32
St. Helena Rd. SE16 26
St. Helens Gdns. W10 15
St. Helens Pl. EC3 44
St. Hildas Clo. NW6 8
St. Hilda's Rd. SW13 29
St. James Ave. E2 19
St. James Gdns. W11 22
St. James Ms. E14 26
St. James Rd. E15 13
St. James St. W6 29
St. James's SE14 33
St. James's Ct. SW1 24
St. James's Cres. SW9 38
St. James's Mkt. SW1 43
St. James's Palace SW1 43
St. James's Pk. SW1 24
St. James's Pas. EC3 44
St. James's Pl. SW1 43
St. James's Rd. SE1 32
St. James's Rd. SE16 25
St. James's Sq. SW1 43
St. James's St. SW1 43
St. James's Ter. Ms. NW8 9
St. John St. EC1 17
St. John's Ave. NW10 8
St. John's Ave. SW15 36
St. John's Ch. Rd. E9 12
St. John's Cres. SW9 38
St. John's Est. N1 18
St. John's Gdns. W11 22
St. John's Hill SW11 37
St. John's Hill Gro. SW11 37
St. John's La. EC1 18
St. John's Pk. SE3 34
St. Johns Rd. E16 20
St. John's Rd. SW11 37
St. John's Rd., Bark. 14
St. Johns Ter. E7 13
St. Johns Ter. SE18 35
St. Johns Vale SE8 33
St. John's Wd. High St. NW8 16
St. John's Wd. Pk. NW8 9
St. John's Wd. Rd. NW8 16
St. John's Wd. Ter. NW8 16
St. Joseph's Ct. SE7 34
St. Joseph's Vale SE3 41
St. Jude St. N16 11
St. Jude's Rd. E2 18
St. Julian's Rd. NW6 9
St. Katharine's Way E1 25
St. Katherine's Row EC3 44
St. Laurence Clo. NW6 8

awrence St. E14 26 G2
awrence Ter. /10 15 G4
awrence Way W9 31 G5
eonards Gdns., f. 14 E2
eonards Rd. E14 19 F4
.eonards Sq. NW5 10 A3
.eonards St. E3 19 F2
.eonard's Ter. W3 30 G1
.oo Ave. SW3 30 F2
.uke's Ave. SW4 38 D2
.uke's Ave., Ilf. 14 D2
.uke's Est. EC1 18 C2
.ukes Rd. W11 16 A4
.ukes Sq. E16 20 C5
.uke's St. SW3 30 F1
.uke's Yd. W9 16 A2
Margarets, Bark. 14 E5
Margaret's Ct. E1 44 F6
Margarets Cres. SW15 36 D3
Margaret's Gro. SE18 35 E2
Margarets La. W8 23 C4
Margaret's Rd. NW10 15 E2
Margarets Rd. SE4 40 D2
Margaret's St. SW1 24 E3
Margaret's Ter. SE18 35 E1
Mark St. E1 18 E5
Marks Cres. NW1 10 A5
Mark's Gro. SW10 30 C2
Marks Pl. W11 15 G5
Marks Ri. E8 11 E2
Marks Rd. W10 15 F4
Marks Rd. W11 15 G5
Martins Ave. E6 20 G1
Martin's Clo. NW1 10 C5
Martin's Ct. WC2 43 E3
Martin's La. WC2 43 E3
Martin's Pl. WC2 43 E4
Martin's Rd. SW9 31 F5
Martin's St. WC2 43 D4
Martin's-le-Grand EC1 44 D1
Mary Abbots Pl. W8 23 A4
Mary Abbots Ter. W14 23 A4
Mary at Hill EC3 44 H4
Mary Axe EC3 44 H2
Mary St. SE18 28 C5
Marychurch St. SE16 26 A3
Marys, Bark. 14 F5
Marys App. E12 14 B2
Marys Ct. E6 21 B3
Mary's Ct. SE7 34 G3
Mary's Gdns. SE11 24 G5
Mary's Gate W8 23 C4
Mary's Gro. N1 11 A3
Mary's Gro. SW13 36 D1
Marys Mans. W2 16 E4
Marys Path N1 11 A5
Mary's Pl. W8 23 C4
Marys Rd. E13 20 E1
Mary's Rd. NW10 8 A5
Mary's Rd. SE15 33 A4
Marys Sq. W2 16 E4
Marys Ter. W2 16 E4
Mary's Wk. SE11 24 G5
Matthew's Rd. SW2 38 F2
St. Matthew's Row E2 18 F2
St. Maur Rd. SW6 30 A4
St. Merryn Clo. SE18 35 F3
St. Michael's All. EC3 44 G2
St. Michaels Rd. NW2 8 E1
St. Michael's Rd. SW9 31 F5
St. Michaels St. W2 16 E5
St. Mildred's Ct. EC2 44 F2
St. Mildreds Rd. SE12 41 C5
St. Norbert Grn. SE4 40 C2
St. Norbert Rd. SE4 40 B3
St. Olaf's Rd. SW6 29 G3
St. Olaves Ct. EC2 44 F2
St. Olaves Rd. E6 14 C5
St. Oswald's Pl. SE11 31 F1
St. Pancras Way NW1 10 C4
St. Paul St. N1 11 B5
St. Paul's Ave. NW2 8 E3
St. Paul's Ave. SE16 26 B2
St. Paul's Chyd. EC4 44 C2
St. Paul's Clo. SE7 34 G1
St. Paul's Cres. NW1 10 D4
St. Pauls Dr. E15 13 A2
St. Paul's Pl. N1 11 C3
St. Paul's Rd. N1 11 A3
St. Paul's Rd., Bark. 14 E5
St. Paul's Shrubbery N1 11 C3
St. Paul's Way E3 19 D4
St. Paul's Way E14 19 D4
St. Peter's All. EC3 44 G2
St. Peter's Clo. E2 18 F1
St. Peter's Gro. W6 22 C5
St. Peter's Rd. W6 29 C1
St. Peter's Sq. W6 29 C1
St. Peters St. N1 11 A5
St. Peters Ter. SW6 30 A3
St. Peter's Vill. W6 22 C5
St. Peter's Way N1 11 D4
St. Petersburgh Ms. W2 23 C1
St. Petersburgh Pl. W2 23 C1
St. Philip Sq. SW8 31 B5
St. Philip St. SW8 31 B5
St. Philip's Rd. E8 11 F3
St. Quintin Ave. W10 15 E4
St. Quintin Gdns. W10 15 E4
St. Quintin Rd. E13 20 E1
St. Rule St. SW8 31 C5
St. Saviour's Est. SE1 25 E4
St. Saviour's Rd. SW2 38 F3
St. Silas Pl. NW5 10 A3
St. Silas St. Est. NW5 10 A3
St. Simon's Ave. SW15 36 E3
St. Stephens Ave. W12 22 D3
St. Stephens Clo. NW8 9 F5
St. Stephens Gdns. W2 16 B5
St. Stephens Gro. SE13 40 G1
St. Stephen's Rd. E3 12 C5
St. Stephens Rd. E6 13 F4
St. Stephens Row EC4 44 F3
St. Stephens Ter. SW8 31 F3
St. Swithin's La. EC4 44 F3
St. Swithun's Rd. SE13 41 A3
St. Thomas Gdns., Ilf. 14 E3
St. Thomas Rd. E16 20 D5
St. Thomas St. SE1 44 G6
St. Thomas's Pl. E9 12 A4
St. Thomas's Rd. NW10 8 A5
St. Thomas's Sq. E9 12 A4
St. Thomas's Way SW6 30 A3
St. Winefride's Ave. E12 14 B2
Saints Dr. E7 13 G2
Salamanca St. SE1 24 F5
Salcombe Rd. N16 11 D2
Salcott Rd. SW11 37 F3
Sale Pl. W2 16 F5
Sale St. E2 18 F3
Salehurst Rd. SE4 40 D4
Salem Rd. W2 23 C1
Salisbury Ave., Bark. 14 F4
Salisbury Ct. EC4 44 A2
Salisbury Pl. SW9 32 A3
Salisbury Pl. W1 16 G4
Salisbury Rd. E7 13 D3
Salisbury Rd. E12 13 G2
Salisbury Sq. EC4 44 A2
Salisbury St. NW8 16 F3
Salisbury Ter. SE15 40 A1
Salmen Rd. E13 20 C1
Salmon La. E14 19 C5
Saltcoats Rd. W4 22 A3
Salter Rd. SE16 26 B2
Salter St. E14 26 E1
Salter St. NW10 15 C2
Salters Hall Ct. EC4 44 F3
Salters Rd. W10 15 F3
Saltoun Rd. SW2 38 G2
Saltram Cres. W9 16 A2
Saltwell St. E14 26 E1
Salusbury Rd. NW6 8 G5
Salvin Rd. SW15 36 F1
Salway Rd. E15 13 A3
Sam Bartram Clo. SE7 34 F1
Samford St. NW8 16 F3
Sampson St. E1 25 F2
Samson St. E13 20 F1
Samuel Clo. SE14 33 B2
Samuel Clo. SE18 28 A5
Samuel Lewis Trust Dws. SW6 30 B3
Samuel St. SE18 28 B5
Sancroft St. SE11 31 F1
Sandal St. E15 13 B5
Sandall Rd. NW5 10 C3
Sandbach Pl. SE18 35 E1
Sandbourne Rd. SE4 33 C5
Sandby Grn. SE9 42 A1
Sanderson Clo. NW5 10 B1
Sandford Clo. E6 21 B3
Sandford Rd. E6 21 A2
Sandgate St. SE15 32 G2
Sandilands Rd. SW6 30 C4
Sandison St. SE15 39 E1
Sandland St. WC1 17 F4
Sandmere Rd. SW4 38 E2
Sandpiper Clo. SE16 26 D3
Sandpit Pl. SE7 35 A1
Sandringham Dr., Well. 35 G5
Sandringham Rd. E7 13 F2
Sandringham Rd. E8 11 E2
Sandringham Rd. NW2 8 D3
Sandrock Rd. SE13 40 E1
Sand's End La. SW6 30 C4
Sandtoft Rd. SE7 34 E2
Sandwell Cres. NW6 9 B3
Sandwich St. WC1 17 E2
Sandy Hill Ave. SE18 35 D1
Sandy Hill Rd. SE18 35 D1
Sandyhill Rd., Ilf. 14 D1
Sandy's Row E1 18 D4
Sanford St. SE14 33 C2
Sangley Rd. SE6 40 F5
Sangora Rd. SW11 37 E2
Sans Wk. EC1 17 G3
Sansom St. SE5 32 C3
Santley St. SW4 38 E2
Santos Rd. SW18 37 B3
Sapphire Clo. E6 21 C5
Sapphire Rd. SE8 33 C1
Saracen St. E14 19 E5
Saratoga Rd. E5 12 A1
Sardinia St. WC2 43 G2
Sark Wk. E16 20 E5
Sarre Rd. NW2 9 A2
Sartor Rd. SE15 40 B2
Satchwell Rd. E2 18 F2
Saunders Ness Rd. E14 33 G1
Savage Gdns. E6 21 B5
Savage Gdns. EC3 44 J3
Savernake Rd. NW3 9 G1
Savile Row W1 43 A3
Saville Rd. E16 28 A2
Savona Est. SW8 31 C3
Savona St. SW8 31 C3
Savoy Bldgs. WC2 43 G4
Savoy Ct. WC2 43 F4
Savoy Hill WC2 43 G4
Savoy Pl. WC2 43 F4
Savoy Row WC2 43 G4
Savoy Steps WC2 43 G4
Savoy St. WC2 43 G4
Savoy Way WC2 43 G4
Sawley Rd. W12 22 B2
Sawyer St. SE1 25 B3
Saxby Rd. SW2 38 E5
Saxon Rd. E3 19 D1
Saxon Rd. E6 21 B3
Saxon Rd., Ilf. 14 D3
Saxton Clo. SE13 41 A1
Sayes Ct. St. SE8 33 D2
Scala St. W1 17 C4
Scampston Ms. W10 15 F5
Scandrett St. E1 25 G2
Scarsbrook Rd. SE3 41 G1
Scarsdale Vill. W8 23 B4
Scarth Rd. SW13 36 B1
Scawen Rd. SE8 33 C1
Scawfell St. E2 18 E1
Sceaux Est. SE5 32 D4
Sceaux Gdns. SE5 32 E4
Sceptre Rd. E2 19 A2
School Rd. E12 14 B1
Schoolhouse La. E1 26 B1
Schubert Rd. SW15 37 A3
Sclater St. E1 18 E3
Scoresby St. SE1 44 B6
Scotland Pl. SW1 43 E6
Scotsdale Rd. SE12 41 E3
Scott Ellis Gdns. NW8 16 E2
Scott Lidgett Cres. SE16 25 F3
Scott St. E1 18 G3
Scotts Rd. W12 22 D3
Scott's Yd. EC4 44 F3
Scoulding Rd. E16 20 D5
Scout App. NW10 8 A1
Scriven St. E8 11 E5
Scrooby St. SE6 40 F4
Scrubs La. NW10 15 C2
Scrubs La. W10 15 C2
Scrutton Clo. SW12 38 D5
Scrutton St. EC2 18 D3
Scutari Rd. SE22 40 A3
Scylla Rd. SE15 39 G1
Seaford St. WC1 17 F2
Seaforth Cres. N5 11 B2
Seagrave Rd. SW6 30 B2
Seal St. E8 11 E1
Searles Clo. SW11 30 F3
Searles Rd. SE1 25 C5
Sears St. SE5 32 C3
Seaton Ave., Ilf. 14 G2
Sebastian St. EC1 18 A2

Sebbon St. N1 11 A4
Sebert Rd. E7 13 E2
Secker St. SE1 43 J6
Second Ave. E12 14 A1
Second Ave. E13 20 D2
Second Ave. SW14 36 A1
Second Ave. W3 22 B2
Second Ave. W10 15 G3
Sedding St. SW1 24 A5
Sedgebrook Rd. SE3 34 G5
Sedgeford Rd. W12 22 B2
Sedgmoor Pl. SE5 32 D3
Sedgwick St. E9 12 B2
Sedleigh Rd. SW18 37 A4
Sedlescombe Rd. SW6 30 A2
Seething La. EC3 44 J3
Sefton St. SW15 36 E1
Segal Clo. SE23 40 C5
Sekforde St. EC1 18 A3
Selbie Ave. NW10 8 B2
Selby Rd. E13 20 E4
Selby St. E1 18 F3
Selden Rd. SE15 33 A5
Sellons Ave. NW10 8 B5
Selsdon Rd. E13 13 F5
Selsdon Way E14 26 F4
Selsey St. E14 19 E4
Selwood Pl. SW7 30 E1
Selwyn Ct. SE3 41 C1
Selwyn Rd. E3 19 D1
Selwyn Rd. E13 13 E5
Semley Pl. SW1 24 A5
Senate St. SE15 33 A5
Senior St. W2 16 C4
Senrab St. E1 19 B5
Serjeants Inn EC4 44 A2
Serle St. WC2 43 H1
Serpentine Rd. W2 23 G2
Settles St. E1 18 F4
Settrington Rd. SW6 30 C5
Sevenoaks Rd. SE4 40 C4
Seventh Ave. E12 14 B1
Severn Way NW10 8 B2
Severnake Clo. E14 26 E5
Severus Rd. SW11 37 F2
Seville Ms. N1 11 D4
Seville St. SW1 23 G3
Sevington St. W9 16 C3
Seward St. EC1 18 A3
Sewardstone Rd. E2 19 A1
Sewdley St. E5 12 B1
Sewell St. E13 20 D2
Sextant Ave. E14 27 A5
Seymour Gdns. SE4 40 C1
Seymour Ms. W1 17 A5
Seymour Pl. W1 16 F4
Seymour Rd. E6 20 G1
Seymour Rd. SW18 37 A5
Seymour St. W1 16 G5
Seymour St. W2 16 G5
Seymour Wk. SW10 30 D2
Seyssel St. E14 26 G5
Shacklewell La. E8 11 E2
Shacklewell Rd. N16 11 E1
Shacklewell Row E8 11 E1
Shacklewell St. E2 18 E2
Shad Thames SE1 25 E3
Shaftesbury Ave. W1 43 C3
Shaftesbury Ave. WC2 43 C4
Shaftesbury Gdns. NW10 15 A3
Shaftesbury Rd. E7 13 F4
Shaftesbury St. N1 18 B1
Shaftesburys, The, Bark. 21 E1
Shafton Rd. E9 12 B5
Shakespeare Cres. E12 14 B3
Shakespeare Rd. SE24 39 A3
Shakspeare Wk. N16 11 D1
Shalcomb St. SW10 30 D2
Shalfleet Dr. W10 22 F1
Shamrock St. SW4 38 D1
Shand St. SE1 25 D3
Shandon Rd. SW4 38 C4
Shandy St. E1 19 B4
Shannon Gro. SW9 38 F2
Shardcroft Ave. SE24 39 A3
Shardeloes Rd. SE14 33 D5
Sharon Gdns. E9 12 A5
Sharpleshall St. NW1 9 G4
Sharratt St. SE15 33 A2
Sharsted St. SE17 32 A1
Shavers Pl. SW1 43 C4
Shaw Rd. SE22 39 D2
Shawbrooke Rd. SE9 41 F3
Shawbury Rd. SE22 39 E3
Shawfield St. SW3 30 F1
Shawford Ct. SW15 36 C5
Shearling Way N7 10 E3
Shearman Rd. SE3 41 C2
Sheep La. E8 11 G5
Sheepcote La. SW11 30 G5
Sheerwater Rd. E16 20 G4
Sheffield St. WC2 43 G2
Sheffield Ter. W8 23 B2
Shelburne Rd. N7 10 F1
Shelbury Rd. SE22 39 G3
Sheldon Clo. SE12 41 E3
Sheldon Rd. NW2 8 F1
Sheldrake Pl. W8 23 B3
Shelduck Clo. E15 13 C2
Shelgate Rd. SW11 37 F3
Shell Rd. SE13 40 F1
Shelley Ave. E12 14 A3
Shelley Dr., Well. 35 G4
Shellgrove Est. N16 11 D2
Shellness Rd. E5 11 G2
Shellwood Rd. SW11 30 G5
Shelmerdine Clo. E3 19 E4
Shelton St. WC2 43 E2
Shenfield St. N1 18 D1
Shenley Rd. SE5 32 D4
Shepherdess Wk. N1 18 B1
Shepherds Bush Grn. W12 22 E3
Shepherds Bush Pl. W12 22 F3
Shepherds Bush Rd. W6 22 E5
Shepherds La. E9 12 B3
Shepherds Wk. NW3 9 E1
Sheppard Dr. SE16 32 G1
Sheppard St. E16 20 C3
Shepperton Rd. N1 11 B5
Sherard Rd. SE9 42 A3
Sheraton St. W1 43 C2
Sherborne La. EC4 44 F3
Sherborne St. N1 11 C5
Sherbrooke Rd. SW6 29 G3
Sherfield Gdns. SW15 36 B4
Sheridan Rd. E12 14 A2
Sheringham Ave. E12 14 B1
Sheringham Rd. N7 10 F3
Sherington Rd. SE7 34 E2
Sherrard Rd. E7 13 F3
Sherrard Rd. E12 13 G3
Sherrick Grn. Rd. NW10 8 D2
Sherriff Rd. NW6 9 B3
Sherrin Rd. E10 12 E1
Sherwin Rd. SE14 33 B4
Sherwood Gdns. E14 26 E5
Sherwood Gdns. SE16 32 F1
Sherwood Gdns., Bark. 14 F4
Sherwood Rd., Well. 35 G5
Sherwood St. W1 43 B3
Shetland Rd. E3 19 D1
Shinfield St. W12 15 E5
Ship St. SE8 33 E4
Ship Tavern Pas. EC3 44 H3
Shipman Rd. E16 20 E5
Shipton St. E2 18 E1
Shipwright Rd. SE16 26 C3
Shirbutt St. E14 26 F1
Shirebrook Rd. SE3 41 G1
Shirland Ms. W9 16 A2
Shirland Rd. W9 16 A2
Shirley Gdns., Bark. 14 G3
Shirley Gro. SW11 38 A1
Shirley Ho. Dr. SE7 34 F3
Shirley Rd. E15 13 B4
Shirley St. E16 20 C5
Shirlock Rd. NW3 9 G1
Shoe La. EC4 44 A1
Shoebury Rd. E6 14 B4
Shoot Up Hill NW2 8 G2
Shooter's Hill SE18 35 C4
Shooter's Hill, Well. 35 E5
Shooter's Hill Rd. SE3 34 C4
Shooter's Hill Rd. SE10 34 A4
Shooter's Hill Rd. SE18 34 G4
Shore Pl. E9 12 A4
Shore Rd. E9 12 A4
Shoreditch High St. E1 18 D3
Shorncliffe Rd. SE1 32 E1
Shorrolds Rd. SW6 30 A3
Short Rd. E15 13 A5
Short Rd. W4 29 A2
Short Way SE9 42 A1
Shorter St. E1 25 E1
Shortlands W6 22 F5
Shorts Gdns. WC2 43 E2
Shottendane Rd. SW6 30 B4
Shottfield Ave. SW14 36 A2
Shouldham St. W1 16 F4
Shrapnel Clo. SE18 35 A3
Shrapnel Rd. SE9 42 B1
Shrewsbury La. SE18 35 D4
Shrewsbury Rd. E7 13 G2
Shrewsbury Rd. W2 16 B5
Shrewsbury St. W10 15 E3
Shroton St. NW1 16 F4
Shrubland Rd. E8 11 E5
Shuttleworth Rd. SW11 30 E5
Sibella Rd. SW4 31 D5
Sibley Gro. E12 14 A4
Sibthorpe Rd. SE12 41 E4
Sidbury St. SW6 29 G4
Sidcup Rd. SE9 41 F4
Sidcup Rd. SE12 41 E3
Sidmouth Rd. NW2 8 E4
Sidmouth Rd. SE15 32 E4
Sidmouth St. WC1 17 F2
Sidney Est. E1 19 A5
Sidney Rd. SW9 31 F5
Sidney Sq. E1 19 A4
Sidney St. E1 19 A4
Sidworth St. E8 11 G4
Siebert Rd. SE3 34 D2
Siemens Rd. SE18 27 G4
Sigdon Rd. E8 11 F2
Silchester Rd. W10 15 F5
Silex St. SE1 25 A3
Silk Clo. SE12 41 D3
Silk Mills Path SE13 33 G5
Silk St. EC2 18 B4
Silkmills Sq. E9 12 D3
Silver Birch Gdns. E6 21 B3
Silver Pl. W1 43 B3
Silver Rd. W12 22 F1
Silver Wk. SE16 26 D2
Silverland St. E16 28
Silvermere Rd. SE6 40
Silverthorne Rd. SW8 31
Silverton Rd. W6 29
Silvertown Way E16 20
Silvester Rd. SE22 39
Silwood St. SE16 26
Simmons Rd. SE18 35
Simms Rd. SE1 25
Simnel Rd. SE12 41
Simpson St. SW11 30
Simpsons Rd. E14 26
Sinclair Gdns. W14 22
Sinclair Rd. W14 22
Sir Alexander Clo. W3 22
Sir Alexander Rd. W3 22
Sirdar Rd. W11 22
Sirinham Pt. SW8 31
Sise La. EC4 44
Sisley Rd., Bark. 14
Sispara Gdns. SW18 37
Sisters Ave. SW11 37
Sisulu Pl. SW9 38
Sivill Ho. E2 18
Sixth Ave. E12 14
Sixth Ave. W10 15
Skardu Rd. NW2 8
Skeena Hill SW18 36
Skeffington Rd. E6 14
Skelgill Rd. SW15 37
Skelley Rd. E15 13
Skelton Rd. E7 13
Skelwith Rd. W6 29
Sketchley Gdns. SE16 33
Skiers St. E15 13
Skinner St. EC1 17
Skinners La. EC4 44
Skipsey Ave. E6 21
Skipworth Rd. E9 12
Slade, The SE18 35
Sladebrook Rd. SE3 41
Sladedale Rd. SE18 35
Slaidburn St. SW10 30
Slaithwaite Rd. SE13 40
Sleaford St. SW8 31
Slingsby Pl. WC2 43
Slippers Pl. SE16 25
Sloane Ave. SW3 23
Sloane Ct. W. SW3 31
Sloane Gdns. SW1 24
Sloane Sq. SW1 23
Sloane St. SW1 23
Sloane Ter. SW1 23
Smart St. E2 19
Smart's Pl. WC2 43
Smeaton Rd. SW18 37
Smeaton St. E1 25
Smedley St. SW4 31
Smedley St. SW8 31
Smeed Rd. E3 12
Smiles Pl. SE13 33
Smith Clo. SE16 26
Smith Sq. SW1 24
Smith St. SW3 30
Smith Ter. SW3 30
Smith's Ct. W1 43
Smithy St. E1 19
Smokehouse Yd. EC1 18
Smugglers Way SW18 37
Smyrks Rd. SE17 32
Smyrna Rd. NW6 9
Smythe St. E14 26
Snarsgate St. W10 15
Sneyd Rd. NW2 8
Snow Hill EC1 18
Snow Hill Ct. EC1 44
Snowbury Rd. SW6 30
Snowden St. EC2 18

wman Ho. NW6 9 C4
wsfields SE1 25 C3
wshill Rd. E12 14 A2
mes St. SE15 39 E1
o Sq. W1 43 C1
o St. W1 43 C1
bay St. E1 19 C3
ent Ri. E13 20 D2
ent Rd. NW6 9 B2
na Ave. SW15 36 E3
omon's Pas. SE15 39 G2
on New Rd. SW4 38 E2
on Rd. SW2 38 E2
way Rd. SE22 39 F2
nali Rd. NW2 9 A2
nerby Rd., Bark. 14 F4
nerford Gro. N16 11 E1
nerford St. E1 18 G3
nerford Way SE16 26 C3
nerleyton Pas. W9 39 A2
nerleyton Rd. W9 38 G2
ners Cres. W2 16 F5
ners Pl. SW2 38 F5
ners Rd. SW2 38 F4
nerset Est. SW11 30 E4
nerset Gdns. SE13 33 F5
nerset Sq. W14 22 G3
nerton Rd. SE15 39 G2
des St. SE17 32 C2
ia Gdns. NW10 8 B1
hia Rd. E16 20 E5
with Way SW8 31 B3
rel Gdns. E6 21 A4
rel La. E14 20 A5
neran Clo. E8 11 F5
neron Rd. SW6 30 C3
dan Rd. SW11 30 G4
ldern Rd. W14 22 F4
th Africa Rd. W12 22 D2
th Audley St. W1 24 A1
th Black Lion La. V6 29 C1
th Bolton Gdns. W5 30 C1
th Carriage Dr. W1 23 F3
th Carriage Dr. W7 23 F3
th Colonnade E14 26 E2
th Cres. E16 20 A3
th Cres. WC1 17 D4
th Eaton Pl. SW1 24 A5
th Edwardes Sq. V8 23 A4
th End Clo. NW3 9 F1
th End Rd. NW3 9 F1
th End Row W8 23 C4
th Esk Rd. E7 13 F3
th Hill Pk. NW3 9 F1
th Hill Pk. Gdns. IW3 9 F1
th Island Pl. SW9 31 F3
th Lambeth Pl. W8 31 E2
th Lambeth Rd. W8 31 E2
th Molton La. W1 17 B5
th Molton Rd. E16 20 D5
th Molton St. W1 17 B5
th Par. SW3 30 E1
th Pk. SW6 30 B5
th Pk. Ms. SW6 37 C1
th Pl. EC2 18 C4
th Ri. Way SE18 35 F1
th Row SE3 34 C5
th Sea St. SE16 26 D4
th Side W6 22 B4
th St. W1 24 A2

South Tenter St. E1 25 E1
South Ter. SW7 23 F5
South Vill. NW1 10 D3
South W. India Dock Entrance E14 26 G3
South Wf. Rd. W2 16 E5
South Woodford to Barking Relief Rd. E12 14 C1
South Woodford to Barking Relief Rd., Bark. 14 C1
Southall Pl. SE1 25 C3
Southam St. W10 15 G3
Southampton Pl. WC1 17 E4
Southampton Rd. NW5 9 G2
Southampton Row WC1 17 E4
Southampton St. WC2 43 F3
Southampton Way SE5 32 C3
Southborough Rd. E9 12 B4
Southbourne Gdns. SE12 41 E3
Southbourne Gdns., Ilf. 14 E2
Southbrook Ms. SE12 41 C4
Southbrook Rd. SE12 41 C4
Southchurch Rd. E6 21 B1
Southcombe St. W14 22 G5
Southcote Rd. N19 10 C1
Southcroft Ave., Well. 42 G1
Southend Clo. SE9 42 D4
Southend Cres. SE9 42 D4
Southend Rd. E6 14 B4
Southern Gro. E3 19 D2
Southern Rd. E13 20 E1
Southern Row W10 15 G3
Southern St. N1 17 F1
Southerngate Way SE14 33 C3
Southerton Rd. W6 22 E4
Southey Rd. SW9 31 G4
Southfields Rd. SW18 37 B4
Southgate Gro. N1 11 C4
Southgate Rd. N1 11 C5
Southmoor Way E9 12 D3
Southolm St. SW11 31 B4
Southport Rd. SE18 28 F5
Southspring, Sid. 42 F5
Southvale Rd. SE3 34 B5
Southview Ave. NW10 8 B2
Southville SW8 31 D4
Southwark Bri. EC4 44 E4
Southwark Bri. SE1 44 E4
Southwark Bri. Rd. SE1 25 A4
Southwark Gro. SE1 44 D6
Southwark Pk. Est. SE16 25 G5
Southwark Pk. Rd. SE16 25 E5
Southwark St. SE1 44 C5
Southwater Clo. E14 19 D5
Southwell Gdns. SW7 23 D5
Southwell Rd. SE5 39 B1
Southwick Pl. W2 16 F5
Southwick St. W2 16 F5
Sovereign Clo. E1 25 G1
Sowerby Clo. SE9 42 A3
Spa Rd. SE16 25 E4
Spanby Rd. E3 19 E3
Spanish Pl. W1 17 A5
Spanish Rd. SW18 37 D3
Sparrows La. SE9 42 E5
Sparsholt Rd., Bark. 14 G5
Sparta St. SE10 33 G4

Spear Ms. SW5 23 B5
Spearman St. SE18 35 C2
Speke Ho. SE5 32 B3
Speldhurst Rd. E9 12 B4
Spelman St. E1 18 F4
Spencer Gdns. SE9 42 B3
Spencer Pk. SW18 37 E3
Spencer Ri. NW5 10 B1
Spencer Rd. E6 13 G5
Spencer Rd. SW18 37 E2
Spencer St. EC1 18 A2
Spencer Wk. SW15 36 F2
Spenser Gro. N16 11 D1
Spenser Rd. SE24 38 G3
Spenser St. SW1 24 C4
Spert St. E14 26 C1
Spey St. E14 19 G4
Spezia Rd. NW10 15 C1
Spicer Clo. SW9 32 A5
Spindrift Ave. E14 26 E5
Spital Sq. E1 18 D4
Spital St. E1 18 F4
Spitalfields Mkt. E1 18 E4
Sportsbank St. SE6 40 G5
Spray St. SE18 28 D5
Sprimont Pl. SW3 23 G5
Spring Gdns. SW1 43 D5
Spring Path NW3 9 E2
Spring Pl. NW5 10 B2
Spring St. W2 16 E5
Springall St. SE15 32 G3
Springbank Rd. SE13 41 A4
Springdale Rd. N16 11 C1
Springfield Gro. SE7 34 F2
Springfield La. NW6 9 C5
Springfield Rd. E6 14 B4
Springfield Rd. E15 20 B2
Springfield Rd. NW8 9 D5
Springfield Wk. NW6 9 C5
Springhill Clo. SE5 39 C1
Springrice Rd. SE13 41 A4
Springvale Ter. W14 22 F4
Springwater Clo. SE18 35 C4
Springwell Ave. NW10 8 B5
Sprowston Ms. E7 13 D3
Sprowston Rd. E7 13 D2
Sprules Rd. SE4 33 C5
Spur Rd. SW1 24 C3
Spur Rd., Bark. 21 E2
Spurgeon St. SE1 25 C4
Spurling Rd. SE22 39 E2
Spurstowe Ter. E8 11 G2
Square, The W6 29 E1
Squirries St. E2 18 F2
Stable Yd. Rd. SW1 24 C3
Stables Way SE11 31 G1
Stacey St. WC2 43 D2
Stadium Rd. SE18 35 B3
Stadium St. SW10 30 D3
Stafford Clo. NW6 16 B2
Stafford Pl. SW1 24 C4
Stafford Rd. E3 19 D1
Stafford Rd. E7 13 F4
Stafford Rd. NW6 16 B2
Stafford St. W1 43 A5
Stafford Ter. W8 23 B3
Staffordshire St. SE15 32 F4
Stag Pl. SW1 24 C4
Stainer St. SE1 44 G6
Staines Rd., Ilf. 14 F1
Staining La. EC2 44 E1
Stainsby Pl. E14 19 E5
Stainsby Rd. E14 19 E5
Stainton Rd. SE6 41 A4
Stalham St. SE16 25 G4
Stamford Brook Ave. W6 22 B4

Stamford Brook Rd. W6 22 B4
Stamford Rd. E6 14 A5
Stamford Rd. N1 11 D4
Stamford St. SE1 43 J6
Stamp Pl. E2 18 E2
Stanbridge Rd. SW15 36 E1
Stanbury Rd. SE15 32 G4
Standard Ind. Est. E16 28 B3
Standen Rd. SW18 37 A5
Standish Rd. W6 22 C5
Stane Way SE18 35 A3
Stanfield Rd. E3 19 C1
Stanford Rd. W8 23 C4
Stanhope Gdns. SW7 23 D5
Stanhope Gate W1 24 A2
Stanhope Ms. E. SW7 23 D5
Stanhope Ms. W. SW7 23 D5
Stanhope Pl. W2 23 G1
Stanhope St. NW1 17 C2
Stanhope Ter. W2 23 E1
Stanlake Ms. W12 22 E2
Stanlake Rd. W12 22 E2
Stanlake Vill. W12 22 E2
Stanley Clo. SW8 31 F2
Stanley Cres. W11 23 A1
Stanley Gdns. NW2 8 E2
Stanley Gdns. W3 22 A3
Stanley Gdns. W11 23 A1
Stanley Gro. SW8 31 A5
Stanley Rd. E12 14 A2
Stanley Rd. E15 13 A5
Stanley St. SE8 33 D3
Stanmer St. SW11 30 F4
Stannard Rd. E8 11 F3
Stannary St. SE11 31 G2
Stansfeld Rd. E6 20 G4
Stansfield Rd. SW9 38 F1
Stanton Rd. SW13 29 B5
Stanton St. SE15 32 F4
Stanway St. N1 18 D1
Stanwick Rd. W14 23 A5
Stanworth St. SE1 25 E3
Staple St. SE1 25 C3
Staplehurst Rd. SE13 41 B3
Staples Clo. SE16 26 C2
Star La. E16 20 B3
Star Rd. W14 30 A2
Star St. E16 20 C4
Star St. W2 16 F5
Star Yd. WC2 43 J1
Starboard Way E14 26 E4
Starcross St. NW1 17 C2
Starfield Rd. W12 22 C3
Station App. SW6 36 G1
Station Cres. SE3 34 D1
Station Par. NW2 8 E3
Station Par., Bark. 14 E4
Station Rd. E7 13 D1
Station Rd. E12 13 G1
Station Rd. NW10 15 B1
Station Rd. SW13 29 B5
Station St. E15 13 A4
Station St. E16 28 D2
Station Ter. NW10 15 F1
Station Ter. SE5 32 B4
Staunton St. SE8 33 D2
Stave Yd. Rd. SE16 26 C2
Staverton Rd. NW2 8 E4
Stavordale Rd. N5 11 A1
Stayner's Rd. E1 19 B3
Stead St. SE17 25 C5
Stean St. E8 11 E5
Stebondale St. E14 33 G1
Stedham Pl. WC1 43 E1
Steele Rd. E11 13 B1
Steeles Rd. NW3 9 G3
Steeple Clo. SW6 29 G5
Steers Way SE16 26 C3

Stephan Clo. E8 11 F5
Stephen St. W1 17 D4
Stephendale Rd. SW6 37 C1
Stephen's Rd. E15 13 B5
Stephenson St. E16 20 B3
Stephenson St. NW10 15 A2
Stephenson Way NW1 17 C3
Stepney Causeway E1 19 B5
Stepney Grn. E1 19 A4
Stepney High St. E1 19 B4
Stepney Way E1 18 G4
Sterling Gdns. SE14 33 C2
Sterndale Rd. W14 22 F4
Sterne St. W12 22 F3
Sternhall La. SE15 39 F1
Sterry St. SE1 25 C3
Stevenage Rd. E6 14 C3
Stevenage Rd. SW6 29 F3
Stevens Ave. E9 12 A3
Stevenson Cres. SE16 32 F1
Steventon Rd. W12 22 B1
Steward St. E1 18 D4
Stewart Rainbird Ho. E12 14 C2
Stewart Rd. E15 12 G1
Stewart St. E14 26 G3
Stewart's Gro. SW3 30 F1
Stewart's Rd. SW8 31 C3
Stillingfleet Rd. SW13 29 C2
Stillington St. SW1 24 C5
Stillness Rd. SE23 40 C4
Stirling Rd. E13 20 E1
Stirling Rd. SW9 31 E5
Stock Orchard Cres. N7 10 F2
Stock Orchard St. N7 10 F2
Stock St. E13 20 D1
Stockholm Rd. SE16 33 A1
Stockhurst Clo. SW15 29 E5
Stockwell Ave. SW9 38 F1
Stockwell Gdns. SW9 31 F4
Stockwell Gdns. Est. SW9 31 E5
Stockwell Grn. SW9 31 F5
Stockwell La. SW9 31 F5
Stockwell Pk. Cres. SW9 31 F5
Stockwell Pk. Est. SW9 31 F5
Stockwell Pk. Rd. SW9 31 F4
Stockwell Pk. Wk. SW9 38 F1
Stockwell Rd. SW9 31 F5
Stockwell St. SE10 33 G2
Stockwell Ter. SW9 31 F4
Stoford Clo. SW19 36 G5
Stoke Newington Rd. N16 11 E2
Stoke Pl. NW10 15 B2
Stokenchurch St. SW6 30 C4
Stokes Rd. E6 21 A3
Stokesley St. W12 15 B5
Stondon Pk. SE23 40 C4
Stone Bldgs. WC2 17 F5
Stone Ho. Ct. EC3 44 J1
Stonecutter St. EC4 44 B1
Stonefield St. N1 10 G5
Stoneleigh Pl. W11 22 F1
Stoneleigh St. W11 22 F1
Stones End St. SE1 25 B3
Stonewall E6 21 C4
Stoney All. SE18 35 C5
Stoney St. SE1 44 F5
Stoneycroft Clo. SE12 41 C5
Stonhouse St. SW4 38 D1
Stonor Rd. W14 23 A5
Stopford Rd. E13 13 D5
Stopford Rd. SE17 32 A1
Store Rd. E16 28 C3
Store St. E15 13 A2
Store St. WC1 17 D4
Storers Quay E14 27 A5
Storey St. E16 28 C2
Storey's Gate SW1 24 D3
Stories Ms. SE5 32 D5
Stories Rd. SE5 39 D1
Stork Rd. E7 13 C3
Storks Rd. SE16 25 F4
Stormont Rd. SW11 38 A1
Stour Rd. E3 12 E4
Stourcliffe St. W1 16 G5
Stowage SE8 33 E2
Stowe Rd. W12 22 D3
Stracey Rd. E7 13 D1
Stradbroke Rd. N5 11 B1
Stradella Rd. SE24 39 B4
Strafford St. E14 26 E3
Strahan Rd. E3 19 C2
Straightsmouth SE10 33 G3
Strait Rd. E6 28 A1
Straker's Rd. SE15 39 G2
Strand WC2 43 E4
Strand La. WC2 43 H3
Strandfield Clo. SE18 35 G1
Stranraer Way N1 10 E4
Strasburg Rd. SW11 31 B4
Stratford Gro. SW15 36 F2
Stratford Pl. W1 17 B5
Stratford Rd. E13 13 C5
Stratford Rd. W8 23 B4
Stratford Vill. NW1 10 C4
Strath Ter. SW11 37 F2
Strathan Clo. SW18 36 G4
Strathaven Rd. SE12 41 E4
Strathblaine Rd. SW11 37 E3
Strathearn Pl. W2 23 F1
Stratheden Rd. SE3 34 D4
Strathfield Gdns., Bark. 14 F3
Strathleven Rd. SW2 38 E2
Strathnairn St. SE1 25 F5
Strathray Gdns. NW3 9 F3
Stratton St. W1 24 B2
Strattondale St. E14 26 G4
Streatfield Ave. E6 14 B5
Streatham Pl. SW2 38 E5
Streatham St. WC1 43 E1
Streatley Rd. NW6 9 A4
Streetfield Ms. SE3 41 D1
Streimer Rd. E15 19 G1
Strelley Way W3 22 A1
Strickland Row SW18 37 E5
Strickland St. SE8 33 E4
Stride Rd. E13 20 C1
Strode Rd. E7 13 D1
Strode Rd. NW10 8 C3
Strode Rd. SW6 29 G3
Strone Rd. E7 13 F3
Strone Rd. E12 13 G3
Strongbow Cres. SE9 42 B3
Strongbow Rd. SE9 42 B3
Stronsa Rd. W12 22 B3
Stroudley Wk. E3 19 F2
Strutton Grd. SW1 24 D4
Stuart Rd. NW6 16 B2
Stuart Rd. SE15 40 A2
Stuart Twr. W9 16 D2
Stubbs Dr. SE16 32 G1
Stubbs Pt. E13 20 D3
Studd St. N1 11 A5
Studdridge St. SW6 30 B5
Studholme Ct. NW3 9 B1
Studholme St. SE15 32 G3
Studland St. W6 22 D5
Studley Clo. E5 12 C2
Studley Est. SW4 31 E4
Studley Rd. E7 13 E3
Studley Rd. SW4 31 E4
Stukeley Rd. E7 13 E4
Stukeley St. WC2 43 F1
Sturdy Rd. SE15 32 G5
Sturgeon Rd. SE17 32 A1
Sturry St. E14 19 F5
Sturt St. N1 18 B1
Stutfield St. E1 18 F5
Styles Gdns. SW9 39 A1
Sudbourne Rd. SW2 38 E3
Sudbrooke Rd. SW12 37 G4
Sudbury Ct. E5 12 C1
Sudeley St. N1 18 A1
Sudlow Rd. SW18 37 B3
Suffolk La. EC4 44 F3
Suffolk Pl. SW1 43 D5
Suffolk Rd. E13 20 D2
Suffolk Rd. NW10 8 A4
Suffolk Rd. SW13 29 B3
Suffolk Rd., Bark. 14 F4
Suffolk St. E7 13 D2
Suffolk St. SW1 43 D4
Sugar Bakers Ct. EC3 44 J2
Sugar Ho. La. E15 19 G1
Sugden Rd. SW11 38 A1
Sulgrave Rd. W6 22 E4
Sulina Rd. SW2 38 E5
Sulivan Ct. SW6 30 B5
Sulivan Rd. SW6 37 B1
Sullivan Ave. E16 20 G4
Sullivan Clo. SW11 37 F1
Sullivan Rd. SE11 24 G5
Sultan St. SE5 32 B3
Sumatra Rd. NW6 9 B2
Sumburgh Rd. SW12 38 A4
Summercourt Rd. E1 19 A5
Summerfield Ave. NW6 15 G1
Summerfield St. SE12 41 C5
Summit Ct. NW2 8 G2
Sumner Est. SE15 32 E3
Sumner Pl. SW7 23 E5
Sumner Rd. SE15 32 E3
Sumner St. SE1 44 C5
Sumpter Clo. NW3 9 D3
Sun Ct. EC3 44 G2
Sun La. SE3 34 E3
Sun Rd. W14 30 A1
Sun St. EC2 18 C4
Sunbeam Cres. W10 15 E3
Sunbury La. SW11 30 E4
Sunbury St. SE18 28 B4
Sunderland Ct. SE22 39 F5
Sunderland Ter. W2 16 C5
Sundew Ave. W12 22 C1
Sundorne Rd. SE7 34 E1
Sundridge Ave., Well. 35 F5
Sunfields Pl. SE3 34 E3
Sunningdale Ave. W3 22 A1
Sunningdale Ave., Bark. 14 F5
Sunninghill Rd. SE13 33 F5
Sunnydale Rd. SE12 41 E3
Sunnyhill Clo. E5 12 C1
Sunnymead Rd. SW15 36 D3
Sunray Ave. SE24 39 C2
Sunset Rd. SE5 39 B2
Surma Clo. E1 18 F3
Surr St. N7 10 E2
Surrendale Pl. W9 16 B3
Surrey Canal Rd. SE14 33 B2
Surrey Canal Rd. SE15 33 A2
Surrey La. SW11 30 F4
Surrey La. Est. SW11 30 F4
Surrey Quays Rd. SE16 26 A4
Surrey Rd. SE15 40
Surrey Rd., Bark. 14
Surrey Row SE1 25
Surrey Sq. SE17 32
Surrey St. E13 20
Surrey St. WC2 43
Surrey Ter. SE17 25
Surrey Water Rd. SE16 26
Susan Rd. SE3 34
Susannah St. E14 19
Sussex Gdns. W2 16
Sussex Pl. NW1 16
Sussex Pl. W2 16
Sussex Pl. W6 29
Sussex Rd. E6 14
Sussex Sq. W2 23
Sussex St. E13 20
Sussex St. SW1 31
Sussex Wk. SW9 39
Sutcliffe Rd. SE18 35
Sutherland Ave. W9 16
Sutherland Ave., Well. 42
Sutherland Gdns. SW14 36
Sutherland Gro. SW18 36
Sutherland Pl. W2 16
Sutherland Rd. W4 29
Sutherland Row SW1 31
Sutherland Sq. SE17 32
Sutherland St. SW1 31
Sutherland Wk. SE17 32
Sutlej Rd. SE7 34
Sutterton St. N7 10
Sutton Ct. Rd. E13 20
Sutton Est. SW3 30
Sutton Est. W10 15
Sutton Est., The N1 11
Sutton Pl. E9 12
Sutton Rd. E13 20
Sutton Rd., Bark. 21
Sutton Row W1 43
Sutton St. E1 26
Sutton Way W10 15
Swaffield Rd. SW18 37
Swainson Rd. W3 22
Swallow Clo. SE14 33
Swallow St. E6 21
Swallow St. W1 43
Swallowfield Rd. SE7 34
Swan App. E6 21
Swan La. EC4 44
Swan Mead SE1 25
Swan Pl. SW13 29
Swan Rd. SE16 26
Swan Rd. SE18 27
Swan St. SE1 25
Swan Wk. SW3 30
Swanage Rd. SW18 37
Swandon Way SW18 37
Swanfield St. E2 18
Swanscombe Rd. W4 29
Swanscombe Rd. W11 22
Swanwick Clo. SW15 36
Swaton Rd. E3 19
Sweden Gate SE16 26
Swedenborg Gdns. E1 25
Sweeney Cres. SE1 25
Swete St. E13 20
Sweyn Pl. SE3 34
Swift St. SW6 30
Swinbrook Rd. W10 15
Swinburne Rd. SW15 36
Swindon St. W12 22
Swinford Gdns. SW9 39
Swingate La. SE18 35

Toland Sq. SW15 36 C3
Tollet St. E1 19 B3
Tollgate Gdns. NW6 16 C1
Tollgate Rd. E6 20 G4
Tollgate Rd. E16 20 F4
Tollington Rd. N7 10 F1
Tolpuddle St. N1 17 G1
Tolsford Rd. E5 11 G2
Tom Cribb Rd. SE28 28 E4
Tom Mann Clo., Bark. 14 G5
Tom Nolan Clo. E15 20 B1
Tomlins Gro. E3 19 E2
Tomlins Orchard, Bark. 14 E5
Tomlinson Clo. E2 18 E2
Tonbridge St. WC1 17 E2
Tonsley Hill SW18 37 C3
Tonsley Pl. SW18 37 C3
Tonsley Rd. SW18 37 C3
Tonsley St. SW18 37 C3
Took's Ct. EC4 43 J1
Tooley St. SE1 44 G5
Topley St. SE9 41 G2
Tor Gdns. W8 23 B3
Torbay Rd. NW6 9 A4
Tormount Rd. SE18 35 G2
Toronto Ave. E12 14 B1
Toronto Rd. E11 13 A1
Torrens Rd. E15 13 C3
Torrens Rd. SW2 38 F3
Torrens Sq. E15 13 C3
Torrens St. EC1 17 G1
Torriano Ave. NW5 10 D2
Torridge Gdns. SE15 40 A2
Torridon Rd. SE6 41 A5
Torridon Rd. SE13 41 B5
Torrington Pl. E1 25 F2
Torrington Pl. WC1 17 D4
Torrington Sq. WC1 17 D3
Torwood Rd. SW15 36 C3
Tothill St. SW1 24 D3
Tottenham Ct. Rd. W1 17 C3
Tottenham Rd. N1 11 D3
Tottenham St. W1 17 C4
Toulmin St. SE1 25 B3
Toulon St. SE5 32 B3
Tournay Rd. SW6 30 A3
Towcester Rd. E3 19 F3
Tower Bri. E1 25 E2
Tower Bri. SE1 25 E2
Tower Bri. App. E1 25 E2
Tower Bri. Rd. SE1 25 D4
Tower Ct. WC2 43 E2
Tower Hamlets Rd. E7 13 C1
Tower Hill EC3 44 J4
Tower Pier EC3 44 J5
Tower Pl. EC3 44 J4
Tower Rd. NW10 8 C4
Tower Royal EC4 44 E3
Tower St. WC2 43 D2
Town Hall Rd. SW11 37 G1
Town Quay, Bark. 14 D5
Townley Ct. E15 13 C3
Townley Rd. SE22 39 D3
Townmead Rd. SW6 37 C1
Townsend St. SE17 25 C5
Townshend Est. NW8 16 F1
Townshend Rd. NW8 9 F5
Toynbee St. E1 18 E4
Tracey Ave. NW2 8 E2
Trader Rd. E6 21 D5
Tradescant Rd. SW8 31 E3
Trafalgar Ave. SE15 32 E1
Trafalgar Gdns. E1 19 B4
Trafalgar Gro. SE10 34 A2
Trafalgar Rd. SE10 34 A2
Trafalgar Sq. SW1 43 D5
Trafalgar Sq. WC2 43 D5
Trafalgar St. SE17 32 C1
Trafalgar Way E14 26 G2
Trafford Clo. E15 12 F2
Tramway Ave. E15 13 B4
Tranquil Vale SE3 34 B5
Transept St. NW1 16 F4
Transom Sq. E14 26 F5
Tranton Rd. SE16 25 F4
Treadgold St. W11 22 F1
Treadway St. E2 18 G1
Treaty St. N1 10 F5
Trebovir Rd. SW5 30 B1
Treby St. E3 19 D3
Tredegar Rd. E3 19 D1
Tredegar Sq. E3 19 D2
Tredegar Ter. E3 19 D2
Trederwen Rd. E8 11 F5
Tree Rd. E16 20 F5
Treen Ave. SW13 36 A1
Trefil Wk. N7 10 E1
Trefoil Rd. SW18 37 D3
Tregarvon Rd. SW11 38 A2
Trego Rd. E9 12 E4
Tregothnan Rd. SW9 38 E1
Tregunter Rd. SW10 30 D2
Trehurst St. E5 12 C2
Trelawn Rd. SW2 38 G3
Trelawney Est. E9 12 A3
Trellick Twr. W10 16 A3
Tremadoc Rd. SW4 38 D2
Tremaine Clo. SE4 33 E5
Trenchard St. SE10 34 A1
Trenchold St. SW8 31 E2
Trenmar Gdns. NW10 15 D2
Trent Rd. SW2 38 F3
Treport St. SW18 37 C5
Tresco Rd. SE15 39 G2
Tresham Cres. NW8 16 F3
Tressillian Cres. SE4 40 E1
Tressillian Rd. SE4 40 D2
Trevanion Rd. W14 22 G5
Trevelyan Ave. E12 14 B1
Trevelyan Gdns. NW10 8 E5
Trevelyan Rd. E15 13 C1
Treveris St. SE1 44 C6
Treverton St. W10 15 G3
Treville St. SW15 36 D5
Trevithick St. SE8 33 E2
Trevor Pl. SW7 23 F3
Trevor Sq. SW7 23 F4
Trevor St. SW7 23 F3
Triangle Pl. SW4 38 D2
Triangle Rd. E8 11 G5
Trident St. SE16 26 B5
Trig La. EC4 44 D3
Trigon Rd. SW8 31 F3
Trim St. SE14 33 D2
Trinidad St. E14 26 D1
Trinity Ch. Pas. SW13 29 D2
Trinity Ch. Rd. SW13 29 D2
Trinity Ch. Sq. SE1 25 B4
Trinity Clo. E8 11 E3
Trinity Gdns. SW9 38 F2
Trinity Gro. SE10 33 G4
Trinity Rd. SW18 37 E3
Trinity Sq. EC3 44 J4
Trinity St. SE1 25 B3
Trinity Wk. NW3 9 D3
Trinity Way W3 22 A1
Tristan Sq. SE3 41 B1
Triton Sq. NW1 17 C3
Triumph Rd. E6 21 B5
Trossachs Rd. SE22 39 D3
Trott St. SW11 30 E4
Troughton Rd. SE7 34 E1
Troutbeck Rd. SE14 33 C4
Trouville Rd. SW4 38 C4
Trowbridge Rd. E9 12 D3
Troy Ct. SE18 28 D5
Troy Town SE15 39 F1
Truesdale Rd. E6 21 B5
Truman's Rd. N16 11 D2
Trump St. EC2 44 E2
Trumpington Rd. E7 13 C1
Trundleys Rd. SE8 33 B1
Trundleys Ter. SE8 26 B5
Truro St. NW5 10 A3
Trussley Rd. W6 22 E4
Tryon St. SW3 30 G1
Tuam Rd. SE18 35 F2
Tubbs Rd. NW10 15 B1
Tudor Clo. NW3 9 F2
Tudor Gro. E9 12 A4
Tudor Pl. W1 43 C1
Tudor Rd. E6 13 F5
Tudor Rd. E9 11 G5
Tudor St. EC4 44 A3
Tudway Rd. SE3 41 E1
Tufnell Pk. Rd. N7 10 D1
Tufnell Pk. Rd. N19 10 C1
Tufton St. SW1 24 D4
Tugboat St. SE28 28 G3
Tulip Dr., Ilf. 14 D2
Tulip Gdns., Ilf. 14 D3
Tulse Hill SW2 38 G4
Tulse Hill Est. SW2 38 G4
Tunis Rd. W12 22 D2
Tunley Rd. NW10 8 A5
Tunmarsh La. E13 20 E2
Tunnan Leys E6 21 C5
Tunnel Ave. SE10 27 A3
Tunstall Rd. SW9 38 F2
Tunworth Cres. SW15 36 B4
Turenne Clo. SW18 37 D2
Turin St. E2 18 F2
Turks Row SW3 30 G1
Turley Clo. E15 13 B5
Turnagain La. EC4 44 B1
Turner St. E1 18 G4
Turner St. E16 20 C5
Turners Rd. E3 19 D4
Turneville Rd. W14 30 A2
Turney Rd. SE21 39 B5
Turnham Grn. Ter. W4 22 A5
Turnham Rd. SE4 40 C3
Turnmill St. EC1 17 G3
Turnpin La. SE10 33 G2
Turnstone Clo. E13 20 D2
Turret Gro. SW4 38 C1
Tuscan Rd. SE18 35 F1
Tuskar St. SE10 34 B1
Tustin Est. SE15 33 A2
Tweedale Ct. E15 12 G2
Tweedmouth Rd. E13 20 E1
Tweezer's All. WC2 43 J3
Twelvetrees Cres. E3 19 G3
Twilley St. SW18 37 C5
Twine Ct. E1 26 A1
Twisden Rd. NW5 10 B1
Twyford Pl. WC2 43 G1
Twyford Rd., Ilf. 14 E2
Twyford St. N1 10 F5
Tyas Rd. E16 20 C3
Tyers Est. SE1 25 D3
Tyers St. SE11 31 F1
Tyers Ter. SE11 31 F1
Tylehurst Gdns., Ilf. 14 E2
Tyler Clo. E2 18 E1
Tyler St. SE10 34 B1
Tyler's Ct. W1 43 C2
Tylney Rd. E7 13 F1
Tyndale Ct. E14 33 F1
Tyneham Rd. SW11 31 A5
Tynemouth St. SW6 30 D5
Type St. E2 19 B1
Tyrawley Rd. SW6 30 C4
Tyrone Rd. E6 21 B1
Tyrrell Rd. SE22 39 F2
Tyrwhitt Rd. SE4 40 E1
Tyson Rd. SE23 40 A5
Tyssen St. E8 1

U

Uamvar St. E14 19
Uffington Rd. NW10 8
Ufford St. SE1 24
Ufton Gro. N1 11
Ufton Rd. N1 11
Ullswater Rd. SW13 29
Ulundi Rd. SE3 34
Ulverscroft Rd. SE22 39
Ulysses Rd. NW6 9
Umbria St. SW15 36
Undercliff Rd. SE13 40
Underhill Rd. SE22 39
Undershaft EC3 44
Underwood Rd. E1 18
Underwood Row N1 18
Underwood St. N1 18
Undine Rd. E14 26
Union Ct. EC2 44
Union Gro. SW8 31
Union Rd. SW4 31
Union Rd. SW8 31
Union Sq. N1 11
Union St. E15 12
Union St. SE1 44
Unity Clo. NW10 8
Unity Way SE18 27
University St. WC1 17
Unwin Clo. SE15 32
Upcerne Rd. SW10 30
Uphall Rd., Ilf. 14
Upham Pk. Rd. W4 22
Upland Rd. SE22 39
Upney La., Bark. 14
Upper Addison Gdns. W14 22
Upper Belgrave St. SW1 24
Upper Berkeley St. W1 16
Upper Brockley Rd. SE4 33
Upper Brook St. W1 24
Upper Cheyne Row SW3 30
Upper Grosvenor St. W1 24
Upper Grd. SE1 43
Upper Harley St. NW1 17
Upper James St. W1 43
Upper John St. W1 43
Upper Mall W6 29
Upper Marsh SE1 24
Upper Montagu St. W1 16
Upper N. St. E14 19
Upper Pk. Rd. NW3 9
Upper Phillimore Gdns. W8 23
Upper Richmond Rd. SW15 36
Upper Rd. E13 20
Upper St. Martin's La. WC2 43
Upper St. N1 11
Upper Tachbrook St. SW1 24
Upper Thames St. EC4 44
Upper Tulse Hill SW2 38
Upper Wimpole St. W1 17
Upper Woburn Pl. WC1 17
Upperton Rd. W. E13 20
Upstall St. SE5 32
Upton Ave. E7 13
Upton La. E7 13

n Pk. Rd. E7 13 E4
n Rd. SE18 35 E2
ood Rd. SE12 41 D4
in St. SE5 32 B2
in Wk. SW9 31 G4
la St. SW11 30 F4
vick Rd. E9 12 A2
orne Ms. SW8 31 F3
er Rd. E3 19 D1
Rd. SW11 37 D2
St. E2 19 B2
dale Rd. SW10 30 D3
ridge Rd. W12 22 C2
ridge St. W8 23 B2

V

, The SW3 30 E2
Rd. E7 13 E3
Royal N7 10 E4
ntine Pl. SE1 25 A3
ntine Rd. E9 12 B3
rian Way E15 20 B2
tta Gro. E13 20 D1
tta Rd. W3 22 A3
tte St. E9 11 G3
ant Ho. SE7 34 F1
ant Way E6 21 B4
ance Rd. E1 18 F3
ance Rd. E2 18 F2
ey Gro. SE7 34 F1
iere Rd. NW10 15 C2
nar Rd. SE5 32 B4
nia Gdns. SW18 37 A4
bery Rd. SE18 35 E2
brugh Flds. SE3 34 C2
brugh Hill SE3 34 C2
brugh Hill SE10 34 C2
brugh Pk. SE3 34 C3
brugh Pk. Rd. SE3 34 C3
brugh Pk. Rd. W. 34 C3
E3
brugh Ter. SE3 34 C4
dome Clo. E16 20 E5
don St. SW1 24 C4
dyke Clo. SW15 36 F4
dyke Cross SE9 42 A3
e Clo. NW3 9 E1
guard St. SE8 33 E4
sittart Rd. E7 13 C1
sittart St. SE14 33 C3
ston Pl. SW6 30 B3
coe Rd. SE16 32 G1
den St. E1 18 G5
dens Rd. SW11 37 E2
ey Rd. E16 20 E5
na Rd. SW6 29 G3
ndell St. NW1 17 C2
sall Rd. SW9 31 G3
ban Est. SE16 25 E4
ban St. SE16 25 E4
ghan Ave. W6 22 B5
ghan Rd. E15 13 C3
ghan Rd. SE5 39 B1
ghan St. SE16 26 D3
ghan Way E1 25 F1
xhall Bri. SE1 31 E1
xhall Bri. SW1 31 E1
xhall Bri. Rd. SW1 24 C4
xhall Gdns. Est. 31 F1
SE11
xhall Gro. SW8 31 F2
xhall St. SE11 31 F1
xhall Wk. SE11 31 F1
wdrey Clo. E1 19 A3
da Rd. SE13 40 E2
nables St. NW8 16 E3
ncourt Pl. W6 22 C5
netian Rd. SE5 32 B5
nn St. SW4 38 C2
ntnor Gdns., Bark. 14 G3

Ventnor Rd. SE14 33 B3
Venue St. E14 19 G4
Venus Rd. SE18 28 B4
Vera Rd. SW6 29 G4
Verbena Gdns. W6 29 C1
Verdun Rd. SW13 29 C2
Vere St. W1 17 B5
Vereker Rd. W14 29 G1
Verity Clo. W11 15 G5
Vermont Rd. SW18 37 C4
Verney Rd. SE16 32 F2
Verney Way SE16 32 G1
Vernham Rd. SE18 35 E2
Vernon Ave. E12 14 B1
Vernon Pl. WC1 17 E4
Vernon Ri. WC1 17 F2
Vernon Rd. E3 19 D1
Vernon Rd. E15 13 B4
Vernon St. W14 22 G5
Vespan Rd. W12 22 C3
Vesta Rd. SE4 33 C5
Vestry Ms. SE5 32 D4
Vestry Rd. SE5 32 D4
Vestry St. N1 18 C2
Viaduct St. E2 18 G2
Vian St. SE13 40 F1
Vibart Gdns. SW2 38 F5
Vicarage Ave. SE3 34 D3
Vicarage Cres. SW11 30 E4
Vicarage Dr., Bark. 14 E4
Vicarage Gate W8 23 C2
Vicarage Gro. SE5 32 C4
Vicarage La. E6 21 B2
Vicarage La. E15 13 B4
Vicarage Pk. SE18 35 E1
Vicarage Rd. E15 13 C4
Vicarage Rd. SE18 35 E1
Vicars Clo. E15 13 D5
Vicars Hill SE13 40 F2
Vicars Rd. NW5 10 A2
Viceroy Rd. SW8 31 E4
Victor Rd. NW10 15 D1
Victoria Ave. E6 13 G5
Victoria Dock Rd. E16 27 D1
Victoria Dr. SW19 36 F5
Victoria Embk. EC4 43 H4
Victoria Embk. SW1 24 E3
Victoria Embk. WC2 43 H4
Victoria Gdns. W11 23 B2
Victoria Gro. W8 23 D4
Victoria Ind. Est. 15 A2
NW10
Victoria Ms. NW6 9 B5
Victoria Pk. E9 12 C5
Victoria Pk. Rd. E9 12 A5
Victoria Pk. Sq. E2 19 A2
Victoria Ri. SW4 38 B1
Victoria Rd. E11 13 B1
Victoria Rd. E13 20 D1
Victoria Rd. NW6 16 A1
Victoria Rd. NW10 15 A3
Victoria Rd. W8 23 D3
Victoria Rd., Bark. 14 D3
Victoria Sta. SW1 24 B5
Victoria St. E15 13 B4
Victoria St. SW1 24 C4
Victoria Way SE7 34 E1
Victorian Gro. N16 11 D1
Victory Pl. SE17 25 B5
Victory Way SE16 26 C3
Viewfield Rd. SW18 37 A4
Vigo St. W1 43 A4
Viking Ct. SW6 30 B2
Villa Rd. SW9 38 G1
Villa St. SE17 32 C1
Village, The SE7 34 F2
Village Way SE21 39 C4
Villas Rd. SE18 28 E5
Villiers Rd. NW2 8 C3
Villiers St. WC2 43 F5

Vince St. EC1 18 C2
Vincent Clo. SE16 26 C3
Vincent Rd. SE18 28 D5
Vincent Sq. SW1 24 C5
Vincent St. E16 20 C4
Vincent St. SW1 24 D5
Vincent Ter. N1 18 A1
Vine Gdns., Ilf. 14 E2
Vine La. SE1 44 J6
Vine Rd. E15 13 C4
Vine Rd. SW13 36 B1
Vine Sq. W14 30 A1
Vine St. W1 43 B4
Vine St. Bri. EC1 17 G3
Viney Rd. SE13 40 F1
Vining St. SW9 38 G2
Viola Sq. W12 22 B1
Violet Hill NW8 16 D1
Violet Rd. E3 19 F3
Virgil St. SE1 24 F4
Virginia Rd. E2 18 E2
Virginia St. E1 25 F1
Viscount Dr. E6 21 B4
Vista, The SE9 41 G4
Vivian Rd. E3 19 C1
Voce Rd. SE18 35 F3
Voltaire Rd. SW4 38 D1
Voss St. E2 18 F2
Vulcan Rd. SE4 33 D5
Vulcan Ter. SE4 33 D5
Vulcan Way N7 10 F3
Vyner St. E2 11 G5

W

Wadding St. SE17 25 C5
Waddington Rd. E15 13 A2
Waddington St. E15 13 A3
Wades Pl. E14 26 F1
Wadeson St. E2 18 G1
Wadham Gdns. NW3 9 F4
Wadham Rd. SW15 36 G2
Wadhurst Rd. SW8 31 C4
Wager St. E3 19 D3
Waghorn Rd. E13 13 F5
Waghorn St. SE15 39 F1
Wagner St. SE15 33 A3
Waite Davies Rd. 41 C5
SE12
Waite St. SE15 32 E2
Waithman St. EC4 44 B2
Wakefield St. E6 13 G5
Wakefield St. WC1 17 E2
Wakeham St. N1 11 C3
Wakehurst Rd. SW11 37 F3
Wakelin Rd. E15 20 B1
Wakeling St. E14 19 C5
Wakeman Rd. NW10 15 E2
Wakering Rd., Bark. 14 E3
Wakley St. EC1 18 A2
Walberswick St. SW8 31 E3
Walbrook EC4 44 F3
Walcot Sq. SE11 24 G5
Waldair Wf. E16 28 D3
Waldemar Ave. SW6 29 G4
Walden St. E1 18 G5
Waldo Clo. SW4 38 C3
Waldo Rd. NW10 15 C2
Walerand Rd. SE13 33 G5
Waley St. E1 19 C4
Walford Rd. N16 11 D1
Walham Gro. SW6 30 B3
Walker Clo. SE18 28 E5
Walkers Ct. W1 43 C3
Wall End Rd. E6 14 C4
Wall St. N1 11 C3
Wallace Rd. N1 11 B3
Wallbutton Rd. SE4 33 C5
Waller Rd. SE14 33 B4
Wallflower St. W12 22 B1
Wallgrave Rd. SW5 23 C5

Wallingford Ave. W10 15 F4
Wallis Clo. SW11 37 E1
Wallis Rd. E9 12 D3
Walliss Cotts. SW2 38 E5
Wallwood St. E14 19 D4
Walm La. NW2 8 E3
Walmer Rd. W11 22 G1
Walmer Ter. SE18 28 E5
Walnut Tree Clo. 29 B4
SW13
Walnut Tree Rd. SE10 34 B1
Walnut Tree Wk. 24 G5
SE11
Walpole Rd. E6 13 F4
Walpole St. SW3 30 G1
Walsham Rd. SE14 33 B5
Walter St. E2 19 B2
Walter Ter. E1 19 B5
Walters Way SE23 40 B4
Walterton Rd. W9 16 A3
Walton Clo. SW8 31 E3
Walton Pl. SW3 23 G4
Walton Rd. E12 14 C1
Walton Rd. E13 20 F1
Walton St. SW3 23 F5
Walworth Pl. SE17 32 B1
Walworth Rd. SE1 25 B5
Walworth Rd. SE17 25 B5
Wandon Rd. SW6 30 C3
Wandsworth Bri. 37 C1
SW6
Wandsworth Bri. 37 C1
SW18
Wandsworth Bri. Rd. 30 C4
SW6
Wandsworth 37 G5
Common SW12
Wandsworth 37 D3
Common N. Side
SW18
Wandsworth 37 D3
Common W. Side
SW18
Wandsworth High St. 37 B3
SW18
Wandsworth Plain 37 B3
SW18
Wandsworth Rd. 38 B1
SW8
Wanless Rd. SE24 39 B1
Wanley Rd. SE5 39 C2
Wanlip Rd. E13 20 E3
Wansbeck Rd. E9 12 D4
Wansey St. SE17 25 B5
Wantage Rd. SE12 41 C3
Wapping High St. E1 25 F2
Wapping La. E1 25 G1
Wapping Wall E1 26 A2
Warbeck Rd. W12 22 D3
Warburton Rd. E8 11 G5
Ward Rd. E15 13 A5
Wardalls Gro. SE14 33 A3
Warden Rd. NW5 10 A3
Wardens Gro. SE1 44 D6
Wardle St. E9 12 B2
Wardo Ave. SW6 29 G4
Wardour Ms. W1 43 B2
Wardour St. W1 43 B1
Wardrobe Pl. EC4 44 C2
Wardrobe Ter. EC4 44 C3
Warepoint Dr. SE28 28 F3
Warfield Rd. NW10 15 F2
Warham St. SE5 32 A3
Warland Rd. SE18 35 F3
Warley St. E2 19 B2
Warlock Rd. W9 16 A3
Warlters Rd. N7 10 E1
Warmington Rd. 39 B4
SE24
Warndon St. SE16 26 A5

Warneford St. E9 11 G5
Warner Clo. E15 13 B2
Warner Pl. E2 18 F1
Warner Rd. SE5 32 B4
Warner St. EC1 17 G3
Warple Way W3 22 A3
Warren, The E12 14 A1
Warren La. SE18 28 D4
Warren St. W1 17 C3
Warren Wk. SE7 34 F2
Warriner Gdns. SW11 30 G4
Warrington Cres. W9 16 D3
Warrior Sq. E12 14 C1
Warspite Rd. SE18 27 G4
Warton Rd. E15 12 G4
Warwall E6 21 D5
Warwick Ave. W2 16 D4
Warwick Ave. W9 16 C3
Warwick Ct. SE15 32 F5
Warwick Cres. W2 16 D4
Warwick Dr. SW15 36 D1
Warwick Est. W2 16 C4
Warwick Gdns. W14 23 A4
Warwick Ho. St. SW1 43 D5
Warwick La. EC4 44 C2
Warwick Pl. W9 16 D4
Warwick Pl. N. SW1 24 C5
Warwick Rd. E12 14 A2
Warwick Rd. E15 13 C3
Warwick Rd. SW5 23 A5
Warwick Rd. W14 23 A5
Warwick Row SW1 24 B4
Warwick Sq. EC4 44 C1
Warwick Sq. SW1 31 C1
Warwick St. W1 43 B3
Warwick Ter. SE18 35 F2
Warwick Way SW1 31 B1
Warwickshire Path SE8 33 D3
Washington Ave. E12 14 A1
Washington Rd. SW13 29 C3
Wat Tyler Rd. SE3 33 G5
Wat Tyler Rd. SE10 33 G5
Water La. E15 13 B3
Water La. SE14 33 A3
Water St. WC2 43 H3
Waterden Rd. E15 12 E2
Waterford Rd. SW6 30 C3
Watergate EC4 44 B3
Watergate St. SE8 33 E2
Watergate Wk. WC2 43 F4
Waterhouse Clo. E16 20 G4
Waterhouse Sq. EC1 17 G4
Waterloo Bri. SE1 43 G4
Waterloo Bri. WC2 43 G4
Waterloo Est. E2 19 A1
Waterloo Gdns. E2 19 A1
Waterloo Pas. NW6 9 A4
Waterloo Pl. SW1 43 C5
Waterloo Rd. E6 13 F4
Waterloo Rd. SE1 24 G2
Waterloo Ter. N1 11 A4
Waterman St. SW15 36 F1
Waterman Way E1 25 G2
Watermeadow La. SW6 30 D5
Waterside Pt. SW11 30 F3
Waterson St. E2 18 D2
Waterworks Rd. SW2 38 F4
Watford Rd. E16 20 D4
Watkinson Rd. N7 10 F3
Watling Ct. EC4 44 E2
Watling Gdns. NW2 8 G3
Watling St. EC4 44 D2
Watney St. E1 18 G5
Watson Ave. E6 14 C4
Watson St. E13 20 E1
Watson's St. SE8 33 E3
Watts Gro. E3 19 F4
Watts St. E1 25 G2
Wavell Dr., Sid. 42 G4
Waveney Ave. SE15 39 G2
Waverley Cres. SE18 35 F2
Waverley Gdns., Bark. 21 G1
Waverley Pl. NW8 16 E1
Waverley Rd. SE18 35 E1
Waverley Wk. W2 16 B4
Waverton Ho. E3 12 D5
Waverton Rd. SW18 37 D5
Waverton St. W1 24 A2
Wayfield Link SE9 42 F4
Wayford St. SW11 30 F5
Wayland Ave. E8 11 F2
Wayman Ct. E8 11 G3
Waynflete Sq. W10 15 F5
Wear Pl. E2 18 G2
Weardale Rd. SE13 41 A2
Wearside Rd. SE13 40 F3
Weatherley Clo. E3 19 D4
Weaver St. E1 18 F3
Weavers Way NW1 10 D4
Webb Rd. SE3 34 C2
Webb St. SE1 25 D4
Webber Row SE1 24 G3
Webber St. SE1 24 G3
Webbs Rd. SW11 37 G2
Webster Rd. SE16 25 F4
Wedderburn Rd. NW3 9 E2
Wedderburn Rd., Bark. 14 F5
Wedgwood Ms. W1 43 D2
Weech Rd. NW6 9 B1
Weedington Rd. NW5 10 A2
Weigall Rd. SE12 41 D2
Weighouse St. W1 17 A5
Weimar St. SW15 36 G1
Weir Est. SW12 38 C5
Weir Rd. SW12 38 C5
Weir's Pas. NW1 17 D2
Weiss Rd. SW15 36 F1
Welbeck Rd. E6 20 G2
Welbeck St. W1 17 A4
Welbeck Way W1 17 B5
Welby St. SE5 32 A4
Welfare Rd. E15 13 B4
Well Ct. EC4 44 E2
Well Hall Rd. SE9 42 A1
Well St. E9 12 A4
Well St. E15 13 B3
Well Wk. NW3 9 E1
Welland St. SE10 33 G2
Wellclose Sq. E1 25 F1
Wellesley Ave. W6 22 D4
Wellesley Rd. NW5 10 A2
Wellesley St. E1 19 B4
Wellesley Ter. N1 18 B2
Welling Way SE9 42 F1
Welling Way, Well. 42 G1
Wellington Gdns. SE7 34 F1
Wellington Ms. SE7 34 F2
Wellington Pl. NW8 16 E2
Wellington Rd. E6 14 B5
Wellington Rd. E7 13 C1
Wellington Rd. NW8 16 E1
Wellington Rd. NW10 15 F2
Wellington Row E2 18 E2
Wellington Sq. SW3 30 G1
Wellington St. SE18 28 C5
Wellington St. WC2 43 F3
Wellington Way E3 19 E2
Wellmeadow Rd. SE6 41 B5
Wellmeadow Rd. SE13 41 B4
Wells Ho. Rd. NW10 15 A4
Wells Ri. NW8 9 G5
Wells Rd. W12 22 E3
Wells St. W1 17 C4
Wells Way SE5 32 D2
Wells Way SW7 23 E4
Wellstead Rd. E6 21 C1
Welsford St. SE1 32 F1
Welsh Clo. E13 20 D2
Weltje Rd. W6 22 C5
Welton Rd. SE18 35 G3
Wemyss Rd. SE3 34 C5
Wendell Rd. W12 22 B4
Wendle Ct. SW8 31 E2
Wendon St. E3 12 D5
Wendover Rd. NW10 15 B1
Wendover Rd. SE9 41 G1
Wenlock Rd. N1 18 B1
Wenlock St. N1 18 B1
Wennington Rd. E3 19 B1
Wensley Clo. SE9 42 B4
Wentworth Cres. SE15 32 F3
Wentworth Rd. E12 13 G1
Wentworth St. E1 18 E5
Wernbrook St. SE18 35 E2
Werrington St. NW1 17 C1
Werter Rd. SW15 36 G2
Wessex St. E2 19 A2
West Arbour St. E1 19 A5
West Carriage Dr. W2 23 E1
West Cen. St. WC1 43 E1
West Cotts. NW6 9 B2
West Cromwell Rd. SW5 23 A5
West Cromwell Rd. W14 30 A1
West Cross Route W10 22 F1
West Cross Route W11 22 F2
West Eaton Pl. SW1 24 A5
West Ella Rd. NW10 8 A4
West End La. NW6 9 B2
West Gdns. E1 25 G1
West Gro. SE10 33 G4
West Halkin St. SW1 24 A4
West Ham La. E15 13 A4
West Ham Pk. E7 13 C4
West Hampstead Ms. NW6 9 C3
West Harding St. EC4 44 A1
West Hill SW15 36 F5
West Hill SW18 36 F5
West Hill Rd. SW18 37 A4
West India Ave. E14 26 E2
West India Dock Rd. E14 19 D5
West La. SE16 25 G3
West Rd. E15 13 C5
West Rd. SW3 30 G1
West Rd. SW4 38 D3
West Row W10 15 G3
West Smithfield EC1 18 A4
West Sq. SE11 25 A4
West St. E2 18 G1
West St. WC2 43 D2
West Tenter St. E1 18 E5
West Warwick Pl. SW1 24 C5
Westbere Rd. NW2 8 G1
Westbourne Bri. W2 16 D4
Westbourne Cres. W2 23 E1
Westbourne Gdns. W2 16 C5
Westbourne Gro. W2 16 B5
Westbourne Gro. W11 23 A1
Westbourne Gro. Ter. W2 16 C5
Westbourne Pk. Pas. W2 16 B4
Westbourne Pk. Rd. W2 16 B4
Westbourne Pk. Rd. W11 15 G5
Westbourne Pk. Vill. W2 16
Westbourne Rd. N7 10
Westbourne St. W2 23
Westbourne Ter. W2 16
Westbourne Ter. Ms. W2 16
Westbourne Ter. Rd. W2 16
Westbridge Rd. SW11 30
Westbrook Rd. SE3 34
Westbury Rd. E7 13
Westbury Rd., Bark. 14
Westbury St. SW8 31
Westbury Ter. E7 13
Westcombe Hill SE3 34
Westcombe Hill SE10 34
Westcombe Pk. Rd. SE3 34
Westcott Rd. SE17 32
Westcroft Clo. NW2 8
Westcroft Sq. W6 22
Westcroft Way NW2 8
Westdale Rd. SE18 35
Westdean Clo. SW18 37
Westdown Rd. E15 12
Westdown Rd. SE6 40
Westerdale Rd. SE10 34
Western Gateway E16 27
Western La. SW12 38
Western Rd. E13 13
Western Rd. SW9 38
Western Way SE28 28
Westferry Circ. E14 26
Westferry Rd. E14 26
Westfield Clo. SW10 30
Westfield St. SE18 27
Westfield Way E1 19
Westfields SW13 36
Westfields Ave. SW13 36
Westgate St. E8 11
Westgate Ter. SW10 30
Westgrove La. SE10 33
Westhorne Ave. SE9 41
Westhorne Ave. SE12 41
Westhorpe Rd. SW15 36
Westleigh Ave. SW15 36
Westmead SW15 36
Westminster Bri. SE1 24
Westminster Bri. SW1 24
Westminster Bri. Rd. SE1 24
Westminster Gdns., Bark. 21
Westmoor St. SE7 27
Westmoreland Ave., Well. 42
Westmoreland Pl. SW1 31
Westmoreland Rd. SE17 32
Westmoreland Rd. SW13 29
Westmoreland St. W1 17
Westmoreland Ter. SW1 31
Westmount Rd. SE9 35
Weston Ri. WC1 17
Weston St. SE1 25
Westover Rd. SW18 37
Westport Rd. E13 20
Westport St. E1 19
Westrow SW15 36
Westvale Ms. W3 22
Westview Clo. NW10 8
Westview Clo. W10 15
Westville Rd. W12 22
Westway W2 16
Westway W9 16
Westway W10 15

tway W12 22 B1
twick Gdns. W14 22 F3
twood Gdns. W13 36 B1
twood Pk. SE23 39 G5
twood Rd. E16 27 E2
twood Rd. SW13 36 B1
nerby Gdns. SW5 23 D5
herby Pl. SW7 23 D5
nerell Rd. E9 12 B5
ford Rd. SW12 37 G5
bridge Pt. SW11 30 G5
man Rd. SE3 34 F4
mouth Ms. W1 17 B4
mouth St. W1 17 A4
mouth Ter. E2 18 E1
lebone Ct. EC2 44 G1
rf Pl. E2 11 F5
rf Rd. E15 13 A5
rf Rd. N1 18 B1
rf St. E16 20 B4
rfdale Rd. N1 17 E1
rfside Rd. E16 20 B4
rton Clo. NW10 8 A3
rton St. WC1 17 F2
teley Rd. SE22 39 E3
tman Rd. SE23 40 B5
eatsheaf La. SW6 29 E3
eatsheaf La. SW8 31 E3
eatstone Rd. W10 15 G4
eelers Cross, ark. 21 F1
eelwright St. N7 10 F4
eler St. E1 18 E3
ellock Rd. W4 22 A4
etstone Pk. WC2 43 G1
etstone Rd. SE3 34 F5
chcote St. SE1 43 G6
dborne St. WC1 17 E2
nchat Rd. SE28 28 F4
nyates Rd. SE9 42 A1
skin St. EC1 18 A2
stler St. N5 11 A2
stlers Ave. SW11 30 E3
ston Rd. E2 18 E1
tbread Rd. SE4 40 C2
tburn Rd. SE13 40 F2
tby Rd. SE18 28 B5
tchurch Rd. W11 22 F1
tcomb St. WC2 43 D4
te Ch. La. E1 18 F5
ite City Clo. W12 22 E1
te City Est. W12 22 D1
te City Rd. W12 22 D1
te Hart La. SW13 29 A5
te Hart Rd. SE18 28 G5
te Hart St. SE11 31 G1
te Hart Yd. SE1 44 F6
te Horse La. E1 19 B3
te Horse Rd. E1 19 C5
te Horse Rd. E6 21 B2
te Horse St. W1 24 B2
te Kennet St. E1 44 J1
te Lion Ct. EC3 44 H2
te Lion Hill EC4 44 C3
te Lion St. N1 17 G1
te Post La. E9 12 D4
te Post La. SE13 40 E1
te Post St. SE15 33 A3
te Rd. E15 13 B4
tear Wk. E15 13 A3
itechapel High St. E1 18 E5
itechapel Rd. E1 18 F4
itecross St. EC1 18 B3
itecross St. EC2 18 B4
itefield Clo. SW15 36 G4
itefriars St. EC4 44 A2
itehall SW1 43 E5
itehall Ct. SW1 43 F6
Whitehall Gdns. SW1 43 E6
Whitehall Pl. SW1 43 E6
Whitehead Clo. SW18 37 D5
Whitehead's Gro. SW3 30 F1
Whitelegg Rd. E13 20 C1
Whiteleys Cotts. W14 23 A5
Whites Grds. SE1 25 D3
White's Row E1 18 E4
Whitethorn St. E3 19 E3
Whitfield Rd. E6 13 F4
Whitfield Rd. SE3 34 A4
Whitfield St. W1 17 C3
Whitgift St. SE11 24 F5
Whiting Ave., Bark. 14 D4
Whitings Way E6 21 C4
Whitlock Dr. SW19 36 G5
Whitman Rd. E3 19 C3
Whitmore Gdns. NW10 15 E1
Whitmore Rd. N1 11 D5
Whitnell Way SW15 36 E3
Whitta Rd. E12 13 G1
Whittaker Rd. E6 13 G4
Whittaker St. SW1 24 A5
Whittingstall Rd. SW6 30 A4
Whittington Ave. EC3 44 H2
Whittlesey St. SE1 44 A6
Whitton Wk. E3 19 E2
Whitwell Rd. E13 20 D2
Whitworth Pl. SE18 28 D5
Whitworth Rd. SE18 35 C2
Whitworth St. SE10 34 B1
Whorlton Rd. SE15 39 G1
Whyteville Rd. E7 13 E3
Wick La. E3 12 D4
Wick Rd. E9 12 B3
Wickersley Rd. SW11 31 A5
Wickford St. E1 19 A3
Wickham Gdns. SE4 40 D1
Wickham Ms. SE4 33 D5
Wickham Rd. SE4 40 D1
Wickham St. SE11 31 F1
Wickham St., Well. 35 G5
Wicklow St. WC1 17 F2
Wickwood St. SE5 32 A5
Widdenham Rd. N7 10 F1
Widdin St. E15 13 A4
Widley Rd. W9 16 B2
Wigeon Path SE28 28 F4
Wigham Ho., Bark. 14 E4
Wigmore Pl. W1 17 B5
Wigmore St. W1 17 A5
Wigston Rd. E13 20 E3
Wilbraham Pl. SW1 23 G5
Wilby Ms. W11 23 A1
Wilcox Clo. SW8 31 E3
Wilcox Rd. SW8 31 E3
Wild Ct. WC2 43 G1
Wild Goose Dr. SE14 33 A4
Wild St. WC2 43 F2
Wildcroft Rd. SW15 36 E5
Wilde Clo. E8 11 F5
Wildfell Rd. SE6 40 F5
Wild's Rents SE1 25 D4
Wildwood Clo. SE12 41 C5
Wilfred St. SW1 24 C4
Wilkes St. E1 18 E4
Wilkin St. NW5 10 B3
Wilkinson Rd. E16 20 F5
Wilkinson St. SW8 31 F3
Will Crooks Gdns. SE9 41 F2
Willard St. SW8 38 B1
Willenhall Rd. SE18 35 D1
Willes Rd. NW5 10 B3
Willesden La. NW2 8 E3
Willesden La. NW6 9 A5
William Bonney Est. SW4 38 D2
William Dunbar Ho. NW6 16 A1
William IV St. WC2 43 E4
William Gdns. SW15 36 D3
William Morley Clo. E6 13 G5
William Morris Way SW6 37 D1
William Rd. NW1 17 C2
William Saville Ho. NW6 16 A1
William St. SW1 23 G3
William St., Bark. 14 E4
Williams Bldgs. E2 19 A3
Williamson St. N7 10 E1
Willington Rd. SW9 38 E1
Willis Rd. E15 20 C1
Willis St. E14 19 F5
Willoughby Rd. NW3 9 E1
Willoughby Way SE7 27 E5
Willow Ave. SW13 29 B5
Willow Bank SW6 36 G1
Willow Bri. Rd. N1 11 B3
Willow Pl. SW1 24 C5
Willow Rd. NW3 9 E1
Willow St. EC2 18 D3
Willow Vale W12 22 C2
Willow Wk. SE1 25 D5
Willowbrook Rd. SE15 32 E2
Wilman Gro. E8 11 F4
Wilmcote Ho. W2 16 B4
Wilmer Gdns. N1 11 D5
Wilmer Lea Clo. E15 12 G4
Wilmington Gdns., Bark. 14 F3
Wilmington Sq. WC1 17 G2
Wilmot Clo. SE15 32 F3
Wilmot Pl. NW1 10 C4
Wilmot St. E2 18 G3
Wilmount St. SE18 28 D5
Wilna Rd. SW18 37 D5
Wilsham St. W11 22 F2
Wilshaw St. SE14 33 E4
Wilson Gro. SE16 25 G3
Wilson Rd. E6 20 G2
Wilson Rd. SE5 32 D4
Wilson St. EC2 18 C4
Wilsons Rd. W6 29 F1
Wilton Ave. W4 29 A1
Wilton Cres. SW1 24 A3
Wilton Ms. SW1 24 A4
Wilton Pl. SW1 24 A3
Wilton Rd. SW1 24 C5
Wilton Row SW1 24 A3
Wilton Sq. N1 11 C5
Wilton St. SW1 24 B4
Wilton Ter. SW1 24 A4
Wilton Vill. N1 11 C5
Wilton Way E8 11 F3
Wiltshire Rd. SW9 38 G1
Wiltshire Row N1 11 C5
Wimbart Rd. SW2 38 F5
Wimbolt St. E2 18 F2
Wimborne Clo. SE12 41 C3
Wimbourne St. N1 18 C1
Wimpole Ms. W1 17 B4
Wimpole St. W1 17 B5
Winans Wk. SW9 31 G5
Wincanton Rd. SW18 37 A5
Winchcomb Gdns. SE9 41 G1
Winchelsea Clo. SW15 36 F3
Winchelsea Rd. E7 13 D1
Winchendon Rd. SW6 30 A3
Winchester Ave. NW6 8 G5
Winchester Clo. SE17 25 A5
Winchester Rd. NW3 9 E4
Winchester Sq. SE1 44 F5
Winchester St. SW1 31 B1
Winchester Wk. SE1 44 F5
Wincott St. SE11 24 G5
Wincrofts Dr. SE9 42 F2
Windermere Ave. NW6 8 G5
Windermere Ct. SW13 29 B2
Winders Rd. SW11 30 F5
Windlass Pl. SE8 26 C5
Windmill Clo. SE13 33 G5
Windmill Ct. NW2 8 G3
Windmill Dr. SW4 38 B3
Windmill La. E15 13 A3
Windmill Rd. SW18 37 E4
Windmill Rd. W4 22 A5
Windmill Row SE11 31 G1
Windmill St. W1 17 D4
Windmill Wk. SE1 44 A6
Windrose Clo. SE16 26 B3
Windsock Clo. SE16 26 D4
Windsor Gdns. W9 16 B4
Windsor Rd. E7 13 E2
Windsor Rd. NW2 8 D3
Windsor Rd., Ilf. 14 D1
Windsor St. N1 11 A5
Windsor Ter. N1 18 B2
Windsor Wk. SE5 32 C5
Windsor Way W14 22 F5
Windsor Wf. E9 12 D2
Wine Clo. E1 26 A1
Wine Office Ct. EC4 44 A2
Winforton St. SE10 33 G4
Winfrith Rd. SW18 37 D5
Wingate Rd. W6 22 D4
Wingate Rd., Ilf. 14 D2
Wingfield Rd. E15 13 B1
Wingfield St. SE15 39 F1
Wingford Rd. SW2 38 E4
Wingmore Rd. SE24 39 B1
Wingrave Rd. W6 29 E2
Winifred Gro. SW11 37 G2
Winifred St. E16 28 B2
Winkfield Rd. E13 20 E1
Winkley St. E2 18 G1
Winn Common Rd. SE18 35 G2
Winnett St. W1 43 C3
Winsham Gro. SW11 38 A3
Winslade Rd. SW2 38 E3
Winsland St. W2 16 E5
Winsley St. W1 43 A1
Winslow Rd. W6 29 E2
Winsor Ter. E6 21 C4
Winstanley Est. SW11 37 E1
Winstanley Rd. SW11 37 E1
Winston Rd. N16 11 C1
Winter Ave. E6 14 A5
Winterbrook Rd. SE24 39 B4
Winterton Ho. E1 18 G5
Winterwell Rd. SW2 38 E3
Winthorpe Rd. SW15 36 G2
Wise Rd. E15 13 A5
Wishart Rd. SE3 34 G5
Wisley Rd. SW11 38 A3
Wisteria Clo., Ilf. 14 D2
Wisteria Rd. SE13 41 A2
Witan St. E2 18 G2
Witherington Rd. N5 10 G2
Withycombe Rd. SW19 36 F5
Wivenhoe Clo. SE15 39 G1
Wixs La. SW4 38 B1
Woburn Pl. WC1 17 D3
Woburn Sq. WC1 17 D3
Woking Clo. SW15 36 B2
Wolfe Cres. SE7 34 G1
Wolfe Cres. SE16 26 B3
Wolferton Rd. E12 14 B1
Wolffe Gdns. E15 13 C3

Wolffram Clo. SE13	41	B3
Wolftencroft Clo. SW11	37	E1
Wolseley Rd. E7	13	E4
Wolseley St. SE1	25	F3
Wolsey Ave. E6	21	C2
Wolsey Ms. NW5	10	C3
Wolsey Rd. N1	11	F3
Wolverton Gdns. W6	22	F5
Wood Clo. E2	18	F3
Wood La. W12	15	E5
Wood St. EC2	**44**	**E2**
Wood St. W4	29	A1
Wood Vale Est. SE23	40	A4
Woodborough Rd. SW15	36	D2
Woodbridge St. EC1	18	A3
Woodchester Sq. W2	16	F3
Woodchurch Rd. NW6	9	B4
Woodcocks E16	20	F4
Wooder Gdns. E7	13	D1
Woodfall St. SW3	30	G1
Woodfarrs SE5	39	C2
Woodfield Pl. W9	16	A3
Woodfield Rd. W9	16	A4
Woodford Rd. E7	13	E1
Woodgrange Rd. E7	13	E2
Woodhill SE18	28	A5
Woodhouse Gro. E12	14	A3
Woodington Clo. SE9	42	C4
Woodison St. E3	19	C3
Woodland Cres. SE10	34	B2
Woodland Gro. SE10	34	B1
Woodland Ter. SE7	28	A5
Woodland Ter. SE18	28	A5
Woodlands, The SE13	41	A5
Woodlands Pk. Rd. SE10	34	B2
Woodlands Rd. SW13	36	B1
Woodlands St. SE13	41	A5
Woodlawn Clo. SW15	37	A3
Woodlawn Rd. SW6	29	F3
Woodman St. E16	28	C2
Woodmans Gro. NW10	8	B2
Woodmere SE9	42	B5
Woodpecker Rd. SE14	33	C2
Woodquest Ave. SE24	39	B3
Woodrow SE18	28	B5
Woods Ms. W1	24	A1
Woods Rd. SE15	32	G4
Woodseer St. E1	18	E1
Woodsford Sq. W14	22	G3
Woodside Rd. E13	20	F3
Woodstock Ct. SE12	41	D4
Woodstock Gro. W12	22	F3
Woodstock Rd. E7	13	F4
Woodstock Rd. W4	22	A4
Woodstock Ter. E14	26	F1
Woodthorpe Rd. SW15	36	C1
Woodville SE3	34	E4
Woodville Clo. SE12	41	D3
Woodville Rd. N16	11	D2
Woodville Rd. NW6	16	A1
Woodwarde Rd. SE22	39	D5
Woodyard La. SE21	39	D5
Woodyates Rd. SE12	41	D4
Woolacombe Rd. SE3	34	F4

Wooler St. SE17	32	C1
Woolmore St. E14	26	G1
Woolneigh St. SW6	37	C1
Woolwich Ch. St. SE18	28	A4
Woolwich Common SE18	35	C2
Woolwich Dockyard Ind. Est. SE18	28	A4
Woolwich Ferry Pier E16	28	C3
Woolwich High St. SE18	28	C4
Woolwich Manor Way E6	21	B3
Woolwich Manor Way E16	28	D1
Woolwich New Rd. SE18	28	D5
Woolwich Rd. SE7	34	C1
Woolwich Rd. SE10	34	C1
Wooster Gdns. E14	20	A5
Wootton St. SE1	**44**	**A6**
Worcester Rd. E12	14	B1
Wordsworth Ave. E12	14	A4
Wordsworth Rd. N16	11	D2
Wordsworth Rd., Well.	35	G4
Worfield St. SW11	30	F3
Worgan St. SE11	31	F1
Worgan St. SE16	26	B4
Worland Rd. E15	13	B4
World Trade Cen. E1	25	E1
World's End Est. SW10	30	D3
Worlidge St. W6	29	E1
Worlingham Rd. SE22	39	E2
Wormholt Rd. W12	22	C2
Wormwood St. EC2	**44**	**H1**
Wornington Rd. W10	15	G3
Woronzow Rd. NW8	9	E5
Worship St. EC2	18	C3
Worsley Rd. E11	13	B1
Worsopp Dr. SW4	38	C3
Wortley Rd. E6	13	G4
Wotton Rd. SE8	33	D2
Wouldham Rd. E16	20	C5
Wrekin Rd. SE18	35	E3
Wren Ave. NW2	8	E2
Wren Path SE28	28	F4
Wren Rd. SE5	32	C4
Wren St. WC1	17	F3
Wrentham Ave. NW10	15	F1
Wrexham Rd. E3	19	E1
Wricklemarsh Rd. SE3	34	F4
Wrigglesworth St. SE14	33	B3
Wrights La. W8	23	C4
Wrights Rd. E3	19	D1
Wrottesley Rd. NW10	15	C1
Wrottesley Rd. SE18	35	E2
Wroughton Rd. SW11	37	G3
Wroxton St. SE15	32	G5
Wulfstan St. W12	15	B4
Wyatt Clo. SE16	26	D2
Wyatt Dr. SW13	29	D2
Wyatt Rd. E7	13	D3
Wycherley Clo. SE3	34	C3
Wycliffe Rd. SW11	31	A5
Wycombe Pl. SW18	37	D4
Wye St. SW11	30	E5

Wyfold Rd. SW6	29	G4
Wyke Rd. E3	12	E4
Wyleu St. SE23	40	C5
Wyllen Clo. E1	19	A3
Wymering Rd. W9	16	B2
Wymond St. SW15	36	E1
Wynan Rd. E14	33	F1
Wyndcliff Rd. SE7	34	E2
Wyndham Est. SE5	32	B3
Wyndham Pl. W1	16	G4
Wyndham Rd. E6	13	G4
Wyndham Rd. SE5	32	B3
Wyndham St. W1	16	G4
Wyneham Rd. SE24	39	C1
Wynford Rd. N1	17	F1
Wynne Rd. SW9	31	G5
Wynnstay Gdns. W8	23	B4
Wynter St. SW11	37	B2
Wynyard Ter. SE11	31	F1
Wythens Wk. SE9	42	D4
Wythes Rd. E16	28	A2
Wythfield Rd. SE9	42	B4
Wyvil Rd. SW8	31	E2
Wyvis St. E14	19	F4

Y

Yabsley St. E14	26	G2
Yalding Rd. SE16	25	F4
Yardley St. WC1	17	G2
Yarrow Cres. E6	21	A4
Yateley St. SE18	27	G4
Yates Ct. NW2	8	F3
Yeate St. N1	11	C4
Yeats Clo. NW10	8	A3
Yeldham Rd. W6	29	F1
Yelverton Rd. SW11	30	E5
Yeo St. E3	19	F4
Yeoman St. SE8	26	C5
Yeoman's Row SW3	23	F4
Yew Gro. NW2	8	F1
Yew Tree Rd. W12	22	B1
Yewfield Rd. NW10	8	B3
Yolande Gdns. SE9	42	A3
York Bri. NW1	17	A3
York Bldgs. WC2	**43**	**F4**
York Gate NW1	17	A3
York Gro. SE15	33	A4
York Ho. Pl. W8	23	C3
York Pl. SW11	37	D2
York Pl. WC2	**43**	**F4**
York Rd. E7	13	D3
York Rd. SE1	24	F3
York Rd. SW11	37	D2
York Rd. SW18	37	D2
York Sq. E14	19	C5
York St. W1	16	G4
York Ter. E. NW1	17	A3
York Ter. W. NW1	17	A3
York Way N1	10	E5
York Way N7	10	D3
York Way Ct. N1	10	E5
Yorkshire Rd. E14	19	C5
Yorkton St. E2	18	F1
Young Rd. E16	20	F5
Young St. W8	23	C3
Yukon Rd. SW12	38	B5
Yuletide Clo. NW10	8	A4

Z

Zampa Rd. SE16	33	A1
Zangwill Rd. SE3	34	G4
Zealand Rd. E3	19	C1
Zenoria St. SE22	39	E2
Zetland St. E14	19	F4
Zoar St. SE1	**44**	**D5**

Key to lines

Bakerloo
Central — Peak hours only
Circle
District — Restricted service
East London — Peak hours and Sunday mornings
Hammersmith & City — Peak hours only
Jubilee — Under construction
Metropolitan — Peak hours only
Northern
Piccadilly — Peak hours only
Victoria
Waterloo & City†
Docklands Light Railway† — Under construction
≠ British Rail — Restricted service

○ Interchange stations
≠ Connections with British Rail
≠ Connections with British Rail within walking distance
✈ Airport interchange
★ Closed Sundays
★★ Closed Saturdays and Sundays

† For opening times see poster journey planners
Certain stations are closed during public holidays

Travel Information 0171-222-1234
Travelcheck 0171-222-1200

UNDERGROUND

Amersham / Chesham / Uxbridge / Watford
West Ruislip / Ealing Broadway
Richmond
Heathrow / Uxbridge
Ealing Broadway / Richmond
Stanmore
Edgware
High Barnet / Mill Hill East
Cockfosters
Walthamstow Central ≠
North Woolwich
Epping / Hainault
Upminster
Beckton / Island Gardens
Wimbledon
Morden

≠ Harrow & Wealdstone, Kenton, Northwick Park, Harrow-on-the-Hill ≠, South Kenton, North Wembley, Wembley Central, Stonebridge Park, Harlesden, ≠ Willesden Junction, Kensal Green, Queen's Park ≠, Kilburn Park, Maida Vale, Warwick Avenue, Royal Oak, Westbourne Park, Ladbroke Grove, Latimer Road, White City, East Acton, Acton Central, South Acton, Shepherd's Bush, Goldhawk Road, Hammersmith, Ravenscourt Park, Barons Court, West Kensington, Kensington (Olympia), Earl's Court, West Brompton ★★, Holland Park, Queensway, Notting Hill Gate, High Street Kensington, Gloucester Road, South Kensington, Lancaster Gate, Bayswater, Paddington ≠, Edgware Road, Marylebone ≠, Marble Arch, Bond Street, Hyde Park Corner, Knightsbridge, Sloane Square, Victoria ≠, St. James's Park, Pimlico, Vauxhall ≠, Stockwell, Clapham North, ≠ Clapham High Street, Oval, Kennington, Brixton ≠

Preston Road, Wembley Park, Queensbury, Kingsbury, Neasden, Dollis Hill, Willesden Green, Kilburn, Kensal Rise, Brondesbury Park, Brondesbury, West Hampstead ≠, Finchley Road & Frognal, Finchley Road, Swiss Cottage, St. John's Wood, Baker Street, Regent's Park, Oxford Circus, Green Park, Piccadilly Circus, Westminster, Charing Cross ≠, ≠ Charing Cross, Embankment, Waterloo ≠, Lambeth North, Elephant & Castle ≠, Borough, Southwark, London Bridge ≠, Bermondsey, Canada Water, Rotherhithe, Surrey Quays, ≠ New Cross Gate, New Cross ≠, Wapping

Hendon Central, Brent Cross, Golders Green, Hampstead, Hampstead Heath, Gospel Oak, Belsize Park, Chalk Farm, Kentish Town West, Camden Town, Mornington Crescent, Great Portland Street, Euston ≠, Warren Street, Euston Square, ≠ Euston, Goodge Street, Tottenham Court Road, Holborn, Covent Garden, Leicester Square, Chancery Lane ★, ★★ City Thameslink, ★ Temple, Blackfriars, Mansion House, Cannon Street ≠ †, St. Paul's, Bank, Monument, Tower Hill, ≠ Fenchurch Street, Tower Gateway, Aldgate, Aldgate East, Whitechapel, Stepney Green, Mile End, Shadwell, Limehouse ≠, Westferry, Shoreditch †

East Finchley, Highgate, Archway, Tufnell Park, Kentish Town ≠, Camden Road, ≠ North London, King's Cross St. Pancras ≠, Russell Square, Angel, Farringdon, Barbican †, Moorgate, Old Street, Liverpool Street ≠, Bethnal Green, Essex Road † ★★, Caledonian Road & Barnsbury, Caledonian Road, Holloway Road, Arsenal, Drayton Park ★★ †, Highbury & Islington, Canonbury, Dalston Kingsland, Hackney Central, Finsbury Park ≠, Manor House, Turnpike Lane, Wood Green, Seven Sisters ≠, Blackhorse Road ≠

North London
Thameslink
Mondays to Fridays until 2030 hours only
River Thames
Under construction

LRT Registered User No. 97/1496
Diary 1E 4.96

NICHOLSON COMPUTER MAPPING

ISBN 0-7028-3772-5
9 780702 837722
£3.2
R.R.